The Privileged Eye

The Privileged Eye

Essays on Photography

Max Kozloff

UNIVERSITY OF NEW MEXICO PRESS
Albuquerque

To Pedro

Design by Milenda Nan Ok Lee

Library of Congress Cataloging in Publication Data

Kozloff, Max.
The privileged eye.

Includes bibliographical references.
1. Photography. I. Title.
TR185.K69 1987 770 86-16062
ISBN 0-8263-0891-0
ISBN 0-8263-0892-9 (pbk.)

First edition

Contents

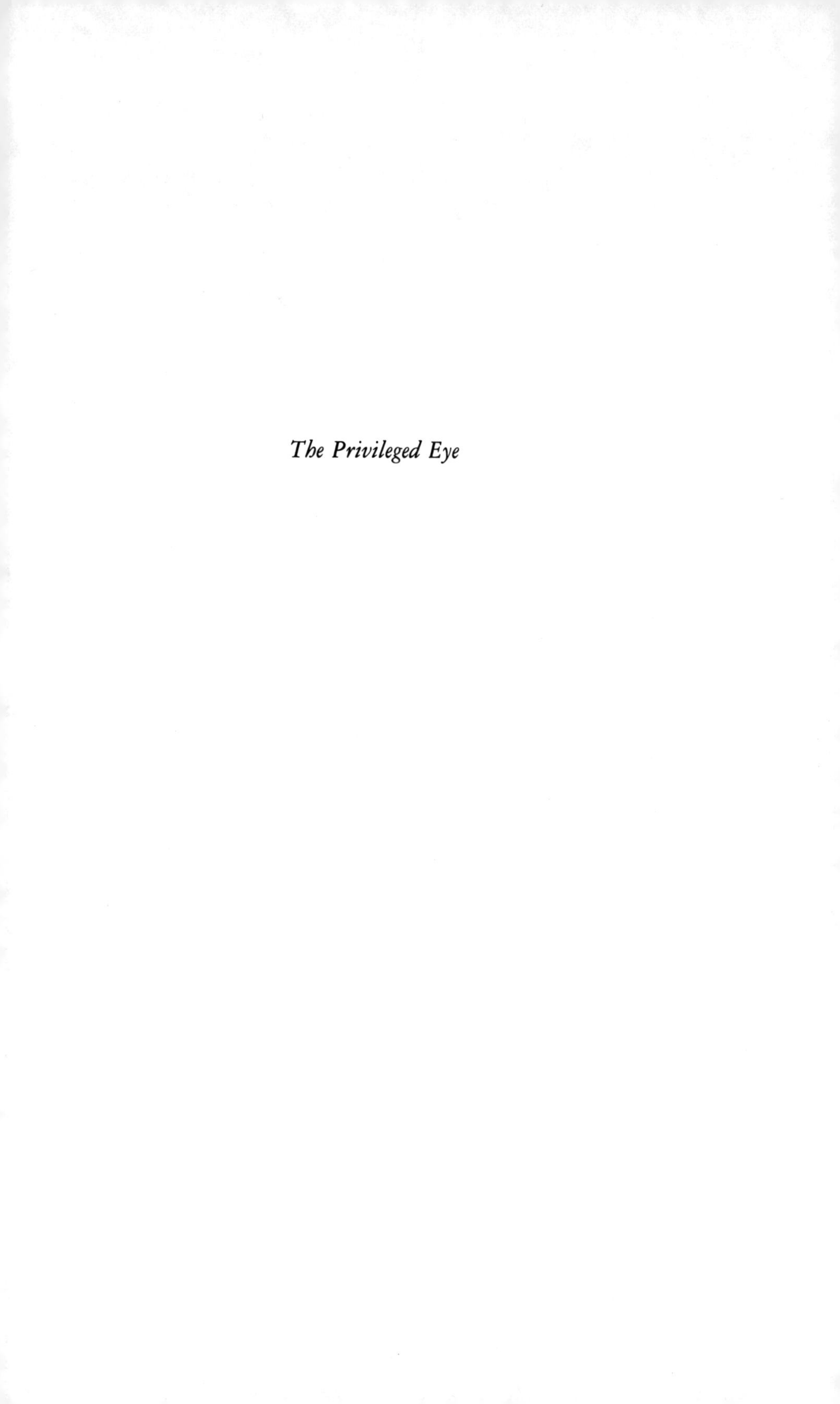

The Privileged Eye

I

Photography and the Street Tradition

The Privileged Eye

Consider an action photograph in which one or a bunch of figures is on the move. No matter how visually explicit, its story content is moot. Because it's unnaturally congealed, the pictorial activity becomes literally equivocal in its drive or purposes. In the next instant the ball which looks about to be triumphantly caught might have been fumbled. The head that turned might have signified denial rather than distraction. Everyone is willing to take that into account, if need be. Show us where we may be hasty in interpreting an event and we shall delay our judgment, admit a different outcome . . . provided there are no stakes in the matter.

Most of the time, we don't have such stakes, so that we make confident determinations about the incident without being aware that they're conjectural. By the shortest common-sense route, we work on a number of cues that invite us to make a provisional settlement of the narrative issue framed by the picture. I may not know what I'm looking at—the actual circumstances—but I scan quickly for the approximate import of the scene. If it doesn't unduly disturb my sense of probability, the situation is *typed* for response. I have to get on with my intercourse with images, which requires that I don't think of them as problematical, even if I can't convince myself of the benign stability of their meaning. My impatience doesn't presume to exhaust the real possibilities of the image, it just fades them in comparison with the preferred scenario. Were I not conventional in this manner, wouldn't I be perpetually staggered and stymied by the overload of inexplicable images around me?

Still, without my having helped it, the photo can return to me more than the little enough I may have put into it. I can very well conceive of people profoundly affected by a photographic subject for natural reasons of ego, and yet being inattentive to the picture which contains and phrases it. What difference does it make to those who have an intense experience that it was easily elicited? The image seeks them out and grips them in their unwarned, passive state. This seemingly direct visual transmission from the outer world finds them credulous in the extreme, so that it isn't an affair of willful attention or inattention, but only of stimulus and hyper-subjective reflex.

The claims of the subjective ego are, in every interpretive sense, privileged, nominally unsharable, a despair to those interested in a consensual approach to photography. My psychic idiosyncracies or yours are our own singular and primary virtues or defects. In either case they cannot be argued with.

Yet it's exactly with such privilege, the leaning of our sensitive and personal organism, that we have to start figuring out the difference which these photo pictures make to us.

John Berger was right in stating (of imagery in capitalist culture):

> There is no space for the social function of subjectivity. All subjectivity is treated as private, and the only (false) form of it which is socially allowed is that of the individual consumer's dream. . . . It seems likely that the denial of the innate ambiguity of the photograph is closely connected with the denial of the social function of subjectivity.

When I *think* of photographs, not just react to them, that phrase of Berger's, "the social function of subjectivity," becomes a suggestive one.

It implies that there is a value in our psychological reception of imagery that is neither economic nor ideological. It hints that we are creatures of our fantasy, but are not locked up in it. If responses were only self-regarding and self-confirming, we could not recognize them in others. We would be alienated from our fellows, therefore, and without society. And if, on the other hand, we could be counted on to react in a predictable and standard fashion to photographic stimuli, how, then, could we be called individuals in the least? We would have become all too socialized, put instantly in range of everyone else but hardly in touch with ourselves.

Photographs make the possibilities of social misapprehension very pointed and critical. If their "truth" quotient weren't so high, they could not deceive as indiscriminately as they often do. But if they were outright fictions, they wouldn't grant me the privilege of feeling that I can hold the world, sporadically, in a set of miniature durations. Because I am informed, though only partially, by this set of images, I am all the more prone to inject my internal states into it. Is there any way into productive talk about this seduction, where facts and feelings are so entangled with each other? That is, can I make my subjectivity social?

Cartier-Bresson has a strange picture, *Alicante, Spain, 1932,* in which the probabilities are so askew that it seems that we're all, when looking at it, very much on our own. It pictures three people, an epicene creature in an undershirt, center, flanked on the left by a fat lady in a Phrygian cap, brandishing a table knife, and a frizzy-haired black woman on the right. The whole frame is aflutter with their arms and kindled by their glaring eyes. Nothing prevents me from imagining that Cartier-Bresson seized unexpectedly upon a lived moment that was, perhaps, nondescript and ordinary. I can entertain the possibility that nothing of any consequence was occurring here. I can discount any significance to the frame whatsoever—in the name of prudence. All this would be a reasonable reaction, to be sure, and an irrelevant one.

For the last thing one would want to say, subjectively, about these people is that their behavior looks humdrum. The action gives priority to another sense altogether—of a human exchange that is vaguely indecent, perverse, a ritual these individuals practice which we were not intended to know. The photograph seems to be making an argument about the kind of life observed, but evasively, and to no clear end. There is no probable rationale here, only a mysterious opportunity, an unpleasant invitation.

How does the idea of "privilege" work in this interim estimate of Cartier-Bresson's photo? To have known, more or less precisely, what was going on—as the photographer could have known—this strikes me first off as *not* an advantage. Lacking an "approximate import," this image throws me into what I must recognize as a fruitful perplexity.

The viewers of photographs fall, structurally, into two groups, one immeasurably larger, and even so, with every moment, gaining over the other. They are the outsiders to the photographic event, with every conceivable disparity in background and understanding, and the insiders . . . who were there. The number of actual witnesses to anything naturally shrinks through attrition, while those whose prepared or imperfect knowledge of it can come only by hearsay is bound to increase. Space and time, in these matters, divide us very unevenly. Most of our knowledge is hearsay, that is, indirect, vicarious, pre-

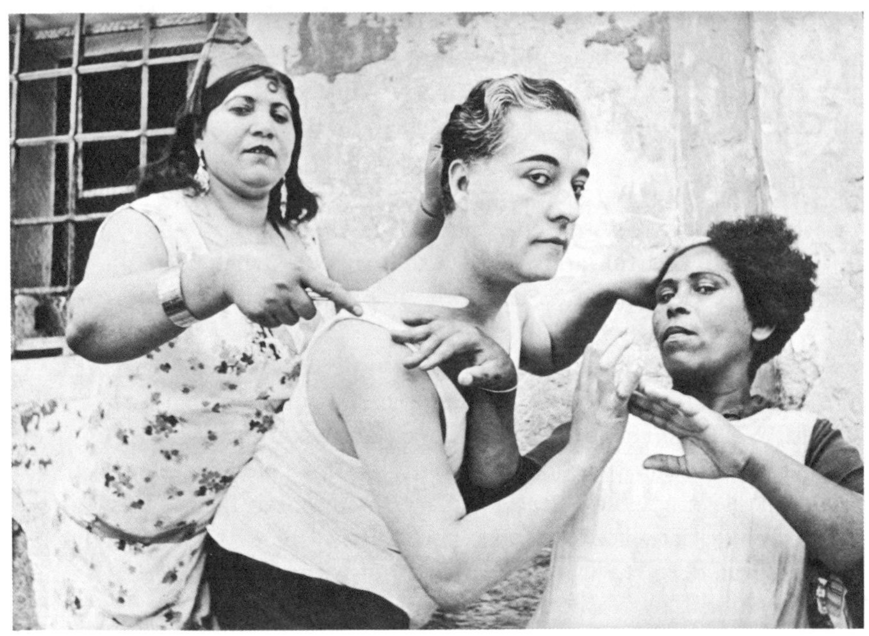

Figure 1. Henri Cartier-Bresson, *Alicante, Spain,* 1933 (Magnum).

filtered, secondary. Photography is one of those modern devices intended to give greater magnitude to hearsay experience. By now, the magnitude has conferred its own level of privilege upon us, so that very few feel any embarrassment or qualification when they claim that a photograph has given them to know something.

But here I am saying of Cartier-Bresson's picture that not knowing, a decided lack of knowledge (except of visual specifics that don't add up), can become a value in itself. In this photo, I believe that I have learned something beyond hearsay, but I don't know what it is. If there is any such thing as a revelation that does not explain its content, this is an example. (Religious faith, which this sounds like, I'll admit, is not the parallel. I would liken the sensation, rather, to a dream.)

A formula comes to mind: With many photos, one is introduced to other people's lives, of which the interruptive frame presents an aspect. These lives may be relatively exotic, but they are still earthly, still obviously social, as ours is. With the dream, one is seduced into thinking that one has been given the semblance of another, perhaps a shadow life. In the rational light of scrutiny, the viewer wants almost to reject the photographic appearances, as in Cartier-Bresson's picture. So much do they seem unconvincing, implausible, strange, incongruous. The fingers that touch—heads, shoulders, palms—in a kind of crazy pavanne; and then, the grasping of scalps, as if they were to be sheared! That soft, flabby flesh and those hard stares. Lacking any evidence that the scene was staged, I have to accept that it was like this, if only momentarily.

The expressive power of the photographic experience does not vanish, nor does its imaginative grip weaken because it has a verifiably material and historical base. I can fancy that someone might have been having an outdoor shave in 1932, or that three prostitutes were hassling each other or horsing around. But that judgment could do nothing but shrivel in the heat of an explosive emotional effect that is as ferocious as it is uncalled for. I would rather have the effect and forget entirely about the question of knowledge, that is, of cause. Yet the dream would not be dreamlike if it were not built out of the peculiar facts at my disposal.

They set my mind to wander and yet, paradoxically, the last thing I want to do is to free associate. The concrete peculiarities in a photo can release fantasies but keep me also on line, with a more or less interesting slack. All that the eye sees are surfaces, but "surface," says Cesare Pavese in his journal "This Business of Living," "is never anything more than a play of reflections of *other* things." Cartier-Bresson could not have done other than to have given me an array of surfaces. But the way they are here wrinkled, that is, animated, expressed, configured, is so out of countenance with historical and social expectations that I am buoyed by an enigma. I am at sea in these matters and cast about; but I know my place.

I seem to be describing a false insecurity or an anxious certainty. On one thing I'm clear: this is a privileged state sometimes given to us by photographs in particular. The privileged ones are those outside the experience, the majority of us. Photography redefines what privilege might be because the medium simultaneously gives a kind of entrée to events or situations and denies it. Photographs provide at best a form of pseudo-intimacy. The picture places us close to something in a once extant guise, but only at a remove. Without many sensuous properties of its own, the photograph either tempts or figuratively insulates the flesh, according to the desire elicited by the subject. Attraction and repulsion are felt but are unconsummated or short-circuited. One has no genuine privilege and no concrete alienation, though the whole gamut of these real possibilities is implied by photographic culture.

No one ever said that photos make anything definitive. But I'm interested here in how they qualify their content, and with that, address our psychic needs. In the sense of benefit, prerogative, and advantage, photographic privilege contributes a great deal. It's customary to speak of how scanty or mendacious the photographic material is, but one of its perennial features, nevertheless, is its gift of allowing us to see more, at any one instant, than its subjects could have seen. "Seen," I say, not necessarily known; and "more," that is, in terms of consultable information, not the knowledge that comes from participating.

In view of the fetching but abortive character of photographic meaning, we have a lot to learn about how these images really satisfy us. I think that they induce a peculiar state of pleasurable ambivalence, unknown before the invention of the medium. In photography, someone is always acting for us and probing ahead, a proxy figure on reconnaissance, so that whatever is sent back has been gained without our effort or risk. The ambivalence consists in being thankful for that but yet also in feeling jealous and deprived (or possibly delighted!) in not having been there, not having literally seen it . . . the event. To be made pleasurably ambivalent is to be teased—the surrogate eye roams appetizingly far, but is still only a surrogate. Couldn't it be that before we are interested, excited, repelled, or moved by a photograph, it's the tease that gets it all going, just as the spark plug ignites the gas that starts the piston?

But this is all, by definition, still preliminary. I go back to the moot, inconclusive Cartier-Bresson. The people it shows are by now probably all extinct, or soon enough will be. There's nothing special about that . . . and so what? But what if I say this *moment* of their lives, which the photograph gives me, this, too, is extinct? Again, this certainly doesn't distinguish it from the moment of every other photo. What it shows in the present has long since evaporated in the past. If it were a question of an epoch that was somehow epitomized in this shot, or a singular instant in the personal lives of three people, or an iconic reinforcement of character, then the expressive value of the image might also have an historical significance. (As in Eisenstaedt's picture of the malign Goebbels.) But this issue isn't raised in the Cartier-Bresson.

Just the same, the moment is amazing, an instantly memorable occasion that has been extracted and recorded out of those countless micro-intervals that, in themselves, one supposes, would hardly raise an eyebrow. The suspicion of these subjects, their apparent fractiousness, of which, all the more excitingly they may not have been conscious, inflames my awareness of them. It may even be that this long past moment has power over me because it appears as a sudden, strange whole much greater than the partial excitement of its subjects. The circuit of energy writhes from left to right and then just as forcefully back again. All is movement, action, yet I don't know who acts and who is acted upon, who is doing what to whom (although there can be no doubt about the purposeful doing). The interplay of arms and hands, particularly the nexus of fingers that touch the shoulder, has all the elaborate nervousness of Botticelli's *Primavera,* but is much more sinister and ridiculous.

Evidently, the scene is one in which an intruder happens upon a self-contained activity and ruffles it, so that a new emotion, perhaps a surprised wariness, is superimposed upon a residue of past behavior. Between the occurrence that is about to vanish and the stance that is beginning to form there is a minuscule balance, a temporal lever, which Cartier-Bresson has divined and visualized. The bodies go towards each other, the eyes look away and outward . . . at our proxy . . . and now at us. At this point, though I'm not curious about Cartier-Bresson himself, I perceive that he has become part of the action, is even responsible for an element of it—the splayed and deflected bearing of the subjects themselves. Insofar as his presence is the cause of their turned heads and embryonic displeasure, he has created an effect that vibrates and becomes its own content.

I have before me an image of three people whose personal territory has been transgressed at what has been called "the killing range." If it were only a matter of someone's having been startled at the trespass of a photographer, or caught off guard (as in Weegee), there would have been no lasting disturbance or enigma. An unforeseen stimulus merely triggers a predictable reflex. Being able to fish out the unseen cause from the obvious effect, though hardly a precise science, is one of the more mechanistic aspects of photographic experience. Generally, when a photographer intervenes, he or she brandishes the product of the intervention, profiled against the trace of the recessive events that preceded it. The relation between the two kinds of temporal episodes might be likened to that between figure and ground, if I wanted to intuit a spatial coefficient for a social reflex.

But here, body language as opposed to facial expression, neither yielding to the instinct of the other, part ways in a manner so odd and intimidating that a psychological space is opened up in the narrative moment. The "ground" wrestles with but hardly overcomes the figures, which are fierce enough in their own right. "An instant photographed can only acquire meaning," says Berger, "insofar as the viewer can read into it a duration extending beyond itself. When we find a photograph meaningful, we are lending it a past and a future. . . ." Contra Berger, this photograph is meaningful to me *because* of its discontinuity. I cannot disarm it by placing it in any larger flux or social order. With its brutal tension, it entirely possesses the moment at hand and wards off all others. If I want to extend the given duration beyond itself, I flounder in an interpretive void. I am not moved by this scene, not touched by pity or tenderness. It is all surface, yet I have the impression that an interior life has erupted and charged into view. It is what I see and it is shocking.

Sightings of this sort do occur in life, but so fleetingly that they can be pondered only after the fact. The cinema provokes and manipulates us with these spectacles, by constructing and then magnifying them. In film, viewers are lavished with total privilege of this kind, closeted as they are with an artful and heightened mimicry of life called acting. Those who consent or allow their persons to be the object of still photography are, of course, already acting, but mostly as directed or improvised by and for themselves. Since it's matrixed in self-imagery, such amateur performance still has an historical value relative to the actor, unlike the professional kind which plays a different role.

Besides, as Barthes remarks, film is "deteriorated photography," in the sense that it is animated. ". . . In the Photograph, something *has posed* {he means happened} in front of the tiny hole and has remained there forever . . . but in cinema, something has *passed* in front of this same tiny hole: the pose is swept away and denied by the continuous series of images." Film transmits nuances of expression, even instructs us as to how and why they might occur, but then dissolves them right away by its fluidity. Only the stilted photograph can precipitate and restore one from the infinity of poses that existed.

When Hinckley shot Reagan, TV kept on replaying the video, asking viewers to look for the hand holding the gun, an image totally obscured until it was finally freeze-framed. As relayed in time, the sequence gave a general, invaluable idea of the scattering of its main lines through space, that is, their short-term duration. I got the most kinetic sense of what happened with the popping of the pistol, an event from which a score of bodies recoiled at as many angles. Contrarily, the stopped-action image, taken out of time, provided the once invisible cause of the scatter, but at the cost of arbitrarily arresting any physical effect.

This is simply to review the obvious. A photo sometimes yields crucial and precise evidence about how things were once disposed. And it does so as no other medium can, but it reveals nothing distinct about their course of action. A film, on the other hand, can be very articulate on that score, but doesn't *pinpoint* anything.

Like life, one's tempted to say, except that life segments are rarely experienced as broken down and spliced together, as they are in film cutting. When something unexpected happens to us in life we may very well perceive it as abrupt, but we don't understand it as a controlled event or as a fragment inserted among others according to some principle of order. Movies and stills are both photographic media built out of discontinuity exemplified by frames that mark off incident. With film, though, the seemingly endless "frames" are invisible, for though they're the boundaries of each "still" shot, extracting material surely enough, they come to us without pause, or without any more pause than the merest blink. With photographs, on the other hand, the single frame not only makes the pause indefinitely "long," but overtly materializes the edges. Range is sacrificed in favor of concentration.

Establishing a total, one-shot discontinuity, the photograph is contacted without warning. It may have the most elaborate contextual prelude but in terms of its *moment* there's no way of easing into it. All appearances there are eternally pointed, in the sense that there can be no narrative transitions that slope toward or away from them, no intervals that can cushion or reinforce the attention we give to them. Everything happens irrevocably at once. We either first deal with the Cartier-Bresson in this discommoded way or we may demur and turn aside. No matter when the shot occurs in time, relative to the significance of an episode, the image is literally dissociated from the business at hand. The relation of the image to the subject depends on how the subject is defined, but the photograph has unquestionably cut away from it, not only as a part is taken from the whole, but as an inert presence differs from an active process. There can be no photographic restitution of that process, and therefore no matching of its thrust. In reading a photograph, we realize that everything we see is "between the lines," temporally, and yet capable of being explicit, spatially.

A photograph can be endowed or gifted with visual form, but that of itself does not rescue it from its only inferential status as a document of time. The way appearances can be said to be visually organized in a photograph does not imply a principle of order, but only an opportune fit of changing variables and static frame. It's tempting to talk about arrangements in photographs because they can be analyzed. One speaks of connecting passages or preparatory planes, of subordinate and dominant masses. But that is to miss the point of the problem that really nags and finally excites us in photography—the problem of time, which levels out all the contents of the image on one historical plane.

I can't distinguish between the instants in a photograph (since there is only one), as I can discriminate between the masses seemingly disposed within that instant. The same applies to expressions and gestures. It's not as if human subjects contribute to the moment in their differing states of awareness, but rather that their being "trapped" in those states defines the moment—such of it as we have. Paradoxically, the explicit space is malleable and divisible—it can be blocked or opened in printing, right out to the resources of the negative. It can also be cropped, which might radically change its character. But I cannot, *a posteriori,* "crop" the time of the shot. From the temporal point of view, everything in the picture has the same fixed historical stratum, urgent or trivial as that may be. Performing physical surgery on the image does nothing whatsoever to alter the temporal identity of its moment. And that moment, whatever else it is, is abrupt.

If I want to look for meaning in the picture, I have to search for it in that abruptness. The image can only come into existence by a severance (actually an almost simultaneous engagement and exit) from those life appearances which it otherwise registers more faithfully than any other visual mode. The quality of that severance, affected by a range of obvious discrepancies with the original, is sudden, as I want to stress, but also has a certain icy hardness. Sontag speaks of the effect of the photograph on its subject as a "soft murder." Couldn't it be turned around and expressed as a "hardened vivacity"? Though there is a current of transformation implied in this metaphor, it doesn't suggest any necessary principle of order. The figure of speech alludes only to that cardinal thing that has happened to phenomena. For all its incipient preciseness, its array of physical detail, the photograph is vague in meaning. "Hardness" may invoke strength, or a concrete state of being, but also bruteness and resistance to accommodation. The picture does so very much on its own but then stops suddenly short of delivering, not its particulars, but their significance. It supplies an enormous amount of what we may need—visual data—but finally denies us what we want—the import of its message.

Now, the fact that the "hard" photograph in itself can't be digested is intolerable. By and large, it needs to be melted and softened by the warmth of spectator usefulness. It has to be given a job, no unemployment allowed, and here even the Cartier-Bresson is seen to labor, if in nothing else than to strengthen the canon of works by a great photographer. What makes it so interesting, though, is that it's a particularly hard case, one of those sullen, bristling, malingering images that refuses to sign up in decorous work. Given these attributes, isn't discussion of it problematical, other than as art; and, anyway, doesn't the category of art beg the whole question of what's psychologically at stake in the photo?

In his *Theory of Film,* Bela Balazs writes: "The fact that the features of the face can be seen in space . . . loses all reference to space when we see, not a figure of flesh and bone, but an expression—when we see emotions, moods, intentions and thoughts, things which . . . are not in space." Balazs insists on the same kind of observation as Pavese, who spoke of surfaces being the reflection of other things. Balazs coins the term *micro-physiognomy,* meaning the minute, fugitive changes in features that signal emotional states. He was thinking of film, where these flickering configurations can be spooled out almost melodically.

> In one of Eisenstein's films there is a priest, a handsome fine figure of a man. . . . He is like the sublime image of a saint. But then the camera gives an isolated big closeup of one eye; and a cunningly watchful furtive glance slinks out from under his beautiful silky eyelashes like an ugly caterpillar out of a delicate flower.

Where the cinematographer has all the time necessary to stage such expressive transition, the still camera has none, and therefore might give us either the saint or the peasant, but not the critical moment when the one uncoils, becomes, the other.

To get from the first impersonation to the second, the actor does not traverse space, he twitches minimally a few muscles. But even this is too coarse and physical an account of character we're made to sense as a deep current, of which there passes over the face, momentarily, an abbreviated ripple. In any event, a photographer like Cartier-Bresson is not out to type or determine character, but to breach social conduct, and to flush from it micro-physiognomies that are a product of his intervention. With his Leica, equipped for only single shot exposures, the chance of missing the mark far outweighs the possibility of hitting it—assuming that the "mark" actually appears.

In the nature of things, performing an act is generally a slower deed than pulling a face. Once limbs have gotten underway, they engage in motions that are coherently sequenced. Our instantaneous expressions have no such visible progression. Without any determined order, they flare up and dissipate in a twinkling—at such speed that nothing but a still camera can be the wiser. I am not talking about the crests in any psychological dynamic, but the multitude of unproductive occasions between them. Having a filmic trajectory in mind, Eisenstein could plot a telltale passage, a showy visual artifice that was supposed to reveal the inner person. The revelations of the psychologically low-budget photograph, on the contrary, are much more ill-determined, vaguely unwanted but instructive, for all that. For they show, over and over again, that there is no visual analogue in time between what we call character or even mood, and outward demeanor. Examined randomly by the camera, it's found that nominal moments of serenity are fairly loaded with grimaces, and that obviously agitated scenes are filled with numbed faces.

We've glimpsed this kind of dissonant spectacle for about a hundred years, but in the main have not known what to do with it. It makes a shambles of the idea that consciousness is *composed* of perceptions assembled in a certain order that is appropriate to their stimulus. Still photographs illuminate the microhistory of sociability, if you will, and disclose that it does not necessarily conform, at any one point, to our memory or our anticipations. For if living expectancy usefully skims the highlights of an exchange and deduces that they were some sort of composite, this synthesis is as much an artifice as Eisenstein's analysis. The still photograph, as often as not, *decomposes* the norms of this artifice, and shows them as behavioristic guidelines for, not accurate observations of, what has happened. Who is wrong, who is right in this equation? I couldn't possibly guess, nor do I even know if the moral terms are relevant. But I do imagine that the photographic artist can seize these useless micro-physiognomies and appraise them differently than we're wont to do. Photography offers us insights into a social and psychological reality so much counter to the one we know that it might not even be reasonable to call it social.

Sociability, we might say, rises up temporarily on tap, and lasts only as long as it's called for. I should go further and state that even here the intelligible social signal is surrounded and adulterated by physiognomic chaff. There is a core of volatile consciousness, out of which we reckon with each other or our enviroment only fitfully. When purposeful in this manner we're no more authentic as individuals than when we're distracted, but the contrast is nevertheless between masked and unmasked states of being. If the photograph tells me that (as my own introspection implies it), I'm also shown that the same thing happens with the individual's perception of time. Even when the moment is socially identified, it is still not clear from people's faces whom or what they think is asserting it. Their desires for the moment, assuming they have any idea about which moment it is, only sporadically correspond with the interval that we, the privileged viewers, see. *In photography, the responses of subjects to their scene are always given simultaneously, but are rarely shown in unison.* It is an advantage that has to be formulated.

Cartier-Bresson hands me a moment that, for all practical purposes, didn't exist, though he didn't make it up, either. Like thousands of its kind, this scene is an intermission, a sort of time-out from the game of life. As I judge it further, though, it turns for me into something more complex, for the principals seem both on and off-stage simultaneously. They exhibit a priceless fusion of distraction and attention, of vulnerable and armored comportment. I can compare, without being able to measure, the different velocities of their expressions and their action. If they have not yet thoroughly confronted their intruder it's because they're still fuddled in their self-involvement which has, just the same, begun to decay, like an after-image. It looks as if what had been privately social will become publicly aggressive, even antisocial (for good reason, considering the camera's unwarranted presence). The condition is literally unsettled and unsettling. At either end of a probable spectrum, I can dimly imagine these people being more focused in their performance. But the photograph forever maroons them in a bitchy indeterminacy, more alive than I could ever have anticipated.

Could it be that part of my excitement is generated by my advantage over these subjects, my privilege in catching them out, without suffering any of the risk that Cartier-Bresson might have suffered? Still, the excitement is compounded also of provocation because if I know more than they could have known—their disarray in one revealing micro-second of sight—I know far less—what they were actually doing. My hard ignorance crashes into my soft knowledge to produce that singular combustion which is the effect of this picture. Had I been able to identify their activity, I would not have searched so anxiously into faces whose owners were unconscious of how they looked. The delicacy of the timing only sets the whole thing to snarl.

Cartier-Bresson's most famous theoretical statement was written as the introduction to his book *The Decisive Moment,* twenty years after he took this picture. In it he says "To me, photography is the simultaneous recognition, in a fraction of a second, of the significance of an event as well as of a precise organization of forms which give that event its proper expression."

He was here well past that surrealizing moment of Alicante, Spain, which can never be understood, acute though it is, as a "precise organization of forms." His own, subsequent development now, however, prompts him to speak of the decisive moment as the one in which the release of the shutter "fixed a geometric pattern without which the photograph would have been formless and lifeless." It would appear that a temporal sensitivity acts only to support a spatial finesse. If this were so, however, then the most satisfying "compositions" would have the most intense animism, which is clearly not the case. A sentence later, nonetheless, Cartier-Bresson writes:

> I believe that, through the act of living, the discovery of oneself is made

concurrently with the discovery of the world around us, which can mold us, but which can also be affected by us. A balance must be established between these two worlds—the one inside us and the one outside us.

The discovery of which he speaks comes to seem like that in the photograph, an interruption of the act of living, as experienced by the subjects, the photographer, and the viewer.

Cartier-Bresson realized all along that he had been an intruder in that outer world, and he had furnished himself with a "velvet hand," "a hawk's eye." In the fifties, though, his intrusions had to be tactful, for a "false relationship, a wrong word, or attitude, can ruin everything." The relationship he instigated with these Spanish subjects was certainly "wrong," but I, for one, would not care to call it "false." In violating decorum, the photographer began to discover what his inner world, and ours, was like. Good composition, like right thinking, like decorum itself, is, perhaps, his mode of retrospective justification. He knew only afterwards what it looked like and sought for it again on the next prowl. He set store by formal opportunities, which must have quickened him. But the dilemma of the itinerant street photographer is that he cannot make an appointment with "geometry." The self-imagery of the artist as a clandestine observer is more to the point. In Alicante, he had come out of "himself," forsaken his disguise, and aroused hostility. In the heat of the ensuing moment there was reflected some of our own contradictory and teased apprehension of life. It is no more real than it is fictive, no more social than it is savage. One has to think of it, finally, as an enigmatic privilege transmitted by the medium of photography, an experience communicated with the speed of light.

Views, *The Journal of Photography in New England, vol. 5, no. 1, Fall 1983.*

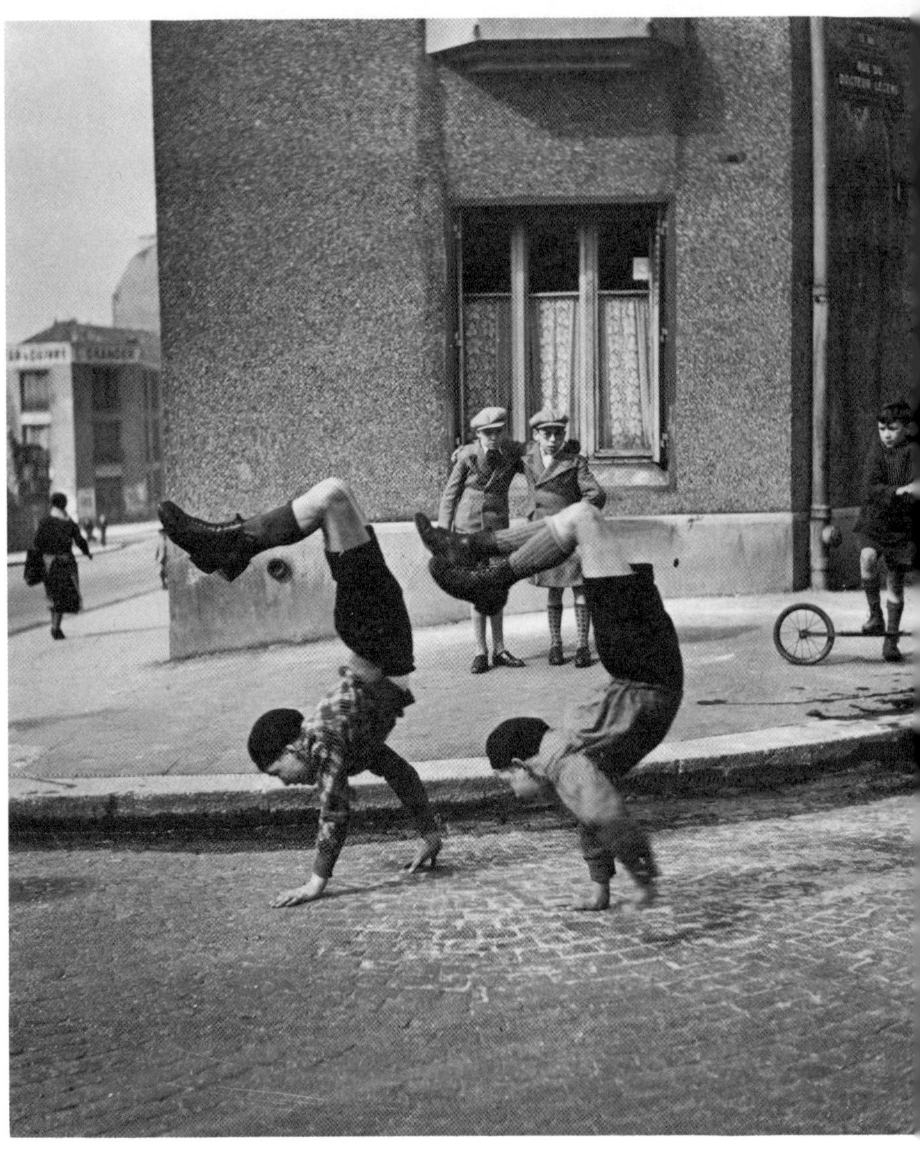

Figure 2. Robert Doisneau, *Les Frères,* 1934 (Doisneau-Rapho).

Robert Doisneau's Oblique Regard

The man who feels," said Horace Walpole in a celebrated *mot,* "will see life as a tragedy; the man who thinks will view it as a comedy." We're discouraged from analyzing comedy because rational words seem always to trail behind and to betray the spirit of the subject. If Walpole was right, though, there may be an element of calculated reason that aids a comic view, a slow process that nourishes a fast humor.

What if it's said: "We think, therefore we must eventually laugh"? Thought can introduce us to the comic because it comprehends how often the vanities of the ego can be tripped up by the realities of the world. It's not as if the comic insight is basically unkind but rather that it's detached from human fate. The critical motion of comedy disengages us from our limitations and frustrations and those of others. Once discovered, however, the actual constraints on our powers and resources are a potentially tragic finding that impels a new compassion for our lot.

One wonders how photography, a spatial art whose images are produced in a split-second, can ever attain any affective depth, comic or tragic. One would seem to need more than a glimpse of a scene, a stimulus through time, to react either way. Yet an instant can be quite enough for an opportune eye to undermine the pretensions of its subjects. Such an event might induce surprise, but a comic possibility is suggested only when surprise appears to exaggerate the silly fate or bad luck or absurd antics of the actors in a play, unknown to themselves. If there's a disaster, in such scenes, comedy insists that it be minor and temporary. For then we don't have to forgive ourselves for enjoying the plight of our fellow beings. Comedy reveals the burlesque of our self-regard, and yet gives us the consciousness, the saving laughter, to defeat it.

Many of the people shown in the work of the French photographer Robert Doisneau act as straight men or women—that is, as mock victims in a comedy. They're the ones to whom unfortunate things happen, but whose dignity is never ruffled. They're never compromised or wounded by the frequent jokes made at their expense, but they're never fully alert to them either. Their obtuseness can be really exquisite. Doisneau makes us laugh at it, but as we do so we also laugh at ourselves.

The mischief at work in his art is that of the humorist rather than of the satirist. A humorist can be touched by human foibles while the satirist tends to exploit them. Instead of deriding his subjects and thereby flattering his viewers, Doisneau reveals how innocently and easily the two roles can be exchanged. His Paris relates to its citizens as a pair of companionable old slippers fits one's feet. People and place are utterly rounded off and habituated to each other, a fact which gives them both a distinctive grace. Yet he superimposes upon this Paris and its suburbs another, treacherous environment which is neither invented nor a reality, but the suggestion of a comic mind.

In one image an old codger casts his fishing line away from the Seine. Seen from behind in another (*Le pigeon indiscret,* 1964), one of eight little boys using a pissoir has been singled out by a dove who perches on his head. What is one to make of the two young brothers walking on their hands (Fig. 2)? Or of the cop whose air of authority gets swallowed whole as he passes a gigantic stone mouth on Boulevard Clichy? Doisneau's subjects are either endearingly oblivious to the illogic of their situation or else they tolerate it very well . . . which is even funnier. They live in a Paris jinxed here or there by an unseasonable change in the force of gravity, all the more suspicious because it is observed with such tact. To walk through Doisneau's city is to be foiled or undone in special ways, at any moment. At the same time, his courtesy is not only disarming, it's positively inviting, a mark of sly wit.

Doisneau is extremely well known, an acknowledged master of twentieth-century photography, and yet his imagery for over forty years has been fondly taken for granted more than it has been studied for its actual depth. Doisneau himself may have been partly accountable for this because the levity of his tone and the modesty of his style have helped to disguise a very reflective temperament. "If my work speaks," he says simply, "it does so by being a little less serious, a little less solemn, and by its lightness it helps people to live."[1]

His own life has been enriched with contrasted interests and experiences that have found their way intimately into his work. Now over seventy years of age but looking more like fifty, he punched a time clock at the Renault factory during the depression, and has labored for *Vogue*. Literary peers such as Jacques Prévert and Blaise Cendrars were his longtime close friends, yet nothing makes him feel more at home than the camaraderie at zinc bars and cafes. Although cosmopolitan in his knowledge, he describes, seemingly from the inside, the lives and gestures of the shopkeepers and artisans, the working classes of the suburbs, whose displacement from the city he keenly regrets, as well as the games of children, who run amok through his art. Their spirit animates much of what he does, as if here, too, he had privileged entrée . . . into an instinctual wonder from which his status as an adult—a very deliberate and patient adult—would remove him.

Nothing, from his point of view, could have been accomplished had he lacked patience, a sense of endless time at his disposal. Time is the resource Doisneau squanders in order to steep himself in a milieu. His work, for that reason, has a totally indigenous character, rare in world-class photography. That does not mean that he is slower or more persistent than others, but that he always plunges in from a definable position in social space. More than simply being on the side of the Parisians, he identifies with them; his patience has earned him the right to speak for a whole community. Paris is his place in a double sense, not only because he was born and raised there but because he has repossessed it in his art.

Loitering but not at loose ends, the photographer imagines himself as an angler in a propitious setting. "They always say that a photographer is 'a hunter of images.' That is . . . flattering . . . it's virile, acquired power. Actually . . . we are really fishermen with hooks and lines!" There may initially be only a locale, a street corner, rue Mouffetard, looked at as if it were a stage indifferently configured by pedestrians. Then, in a poignant moment, all passersby but one are seen turned away from a blind accordionist centered in a drama (Fig. 3). The relationship between these two "actors," one who performs music in his darkness and one who sketches him from the rear, is highlighted by the averted crowd. Not only has Doisneau caught a voyeur in the voyeuristic frame of the photograph, he notes the contrast between two modes of the artistic attention, visual and auditory. Even the sunlight that pours down to illuminate the musician, hooding the hollow sockets of his eyes, cooperates in the stagecraft of the action. The picture pivots on the basis of that which cannot be viewed—whatever attracts the bystanders away toward the edges, and the wheeze of

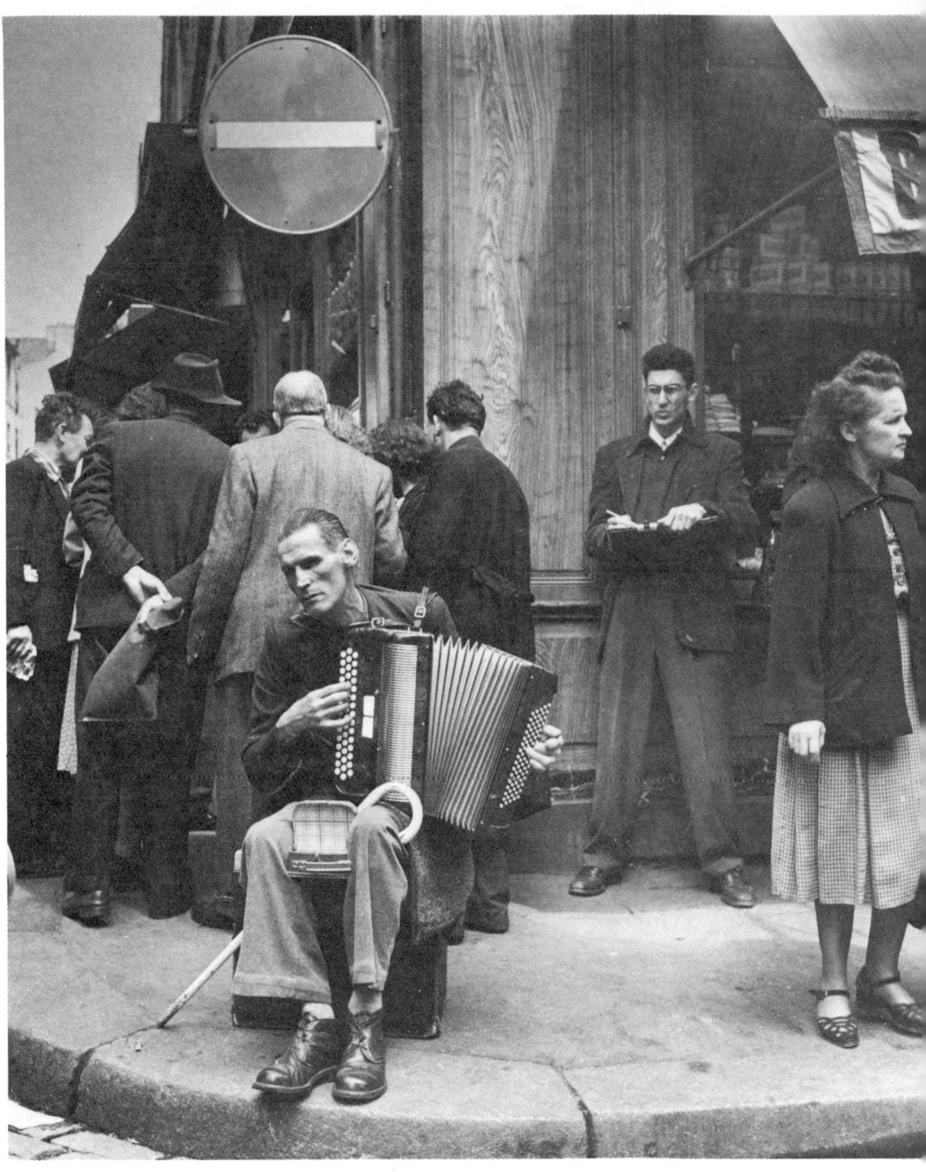

Figure 3. Robert Doisneau, *L'Accordéoniste de la rue Mouffetard,* 1951 (Doisneau-Rapho).

the accordion—though both are sensed as vitally present.

The recurrent figure of the accordionist shares certain attributes with the straight man, but is in the end his opposite because of a genuine vulnerability. Doisneau tenders his respect for the privacy of all those who have to expose themselves in public. In one particularly memorable photograph from 1954, the martyr who endures the most callous and debasing humiliation and rises above it as he meditates on his exposure before the crowd is a monkey. As for those who cause the martyrdom, Doisneau calls them (in the picture's title) *Les animaux supérieurs.*

At the core of his vision is the theme of curiosity. People are forever looking at each other, regarding the photographer, or scrutinizing works of art. In doing so, they only mirror the kindred engagement of Doisneau himself, who is involved with the crisscross of sightlines and with an inspection of the human animal. For him, the mysteries and misadventures of nosiness define the initial terms of sociability. Before they behave as anything else, individuals act as inevitable objects of display to each other. When he is able to show people scandalized by a glimpse of such display—usually they are of the bourgeoisie—Doisneau obtains a comedy of manners. When he projects the shock of display outward, toward his viewers, he ventures into quandaries of social life which can approach the metaphysical.

Take, as an example, the picture of Monsieur Heraut, the art critic, from 1950. In a sense, this is a group portrait of one person, since the debonair but vaguely shabby subject stands in front of nine baby dolls hung on the wall, each with a Doisneau-photographed face of himself. In asking if this is a comment on middle-aged infantilism or a contrast between photography and reality, one is left only with the ridiculous dignity of the display. The same goes for the three guardian funeral workers bemused by Doisneau as they stand behind a casket with such a peculiar shape as to house only a snake. Because they seem genially at home in such very odd circumstances, these people raise questions that are either droll in that they are disconcerting or disconcerting since they are droll.

Out on the street, Doisneau's subjects generally go about their own business yet also seem to be inadvertently acting in a skit prepared for them or improvised by the photographer in the heat of the moment. Master of the ad hoc scenario, he lacks control over events but carries insinuating ideas in his head. No one, seeing an artist painting on a Parisian bridge, would expect to find him working with a nude, as he apparently is in *Fox Terrier au Pont des Arts,* 1953 (Fig. 4). Behind

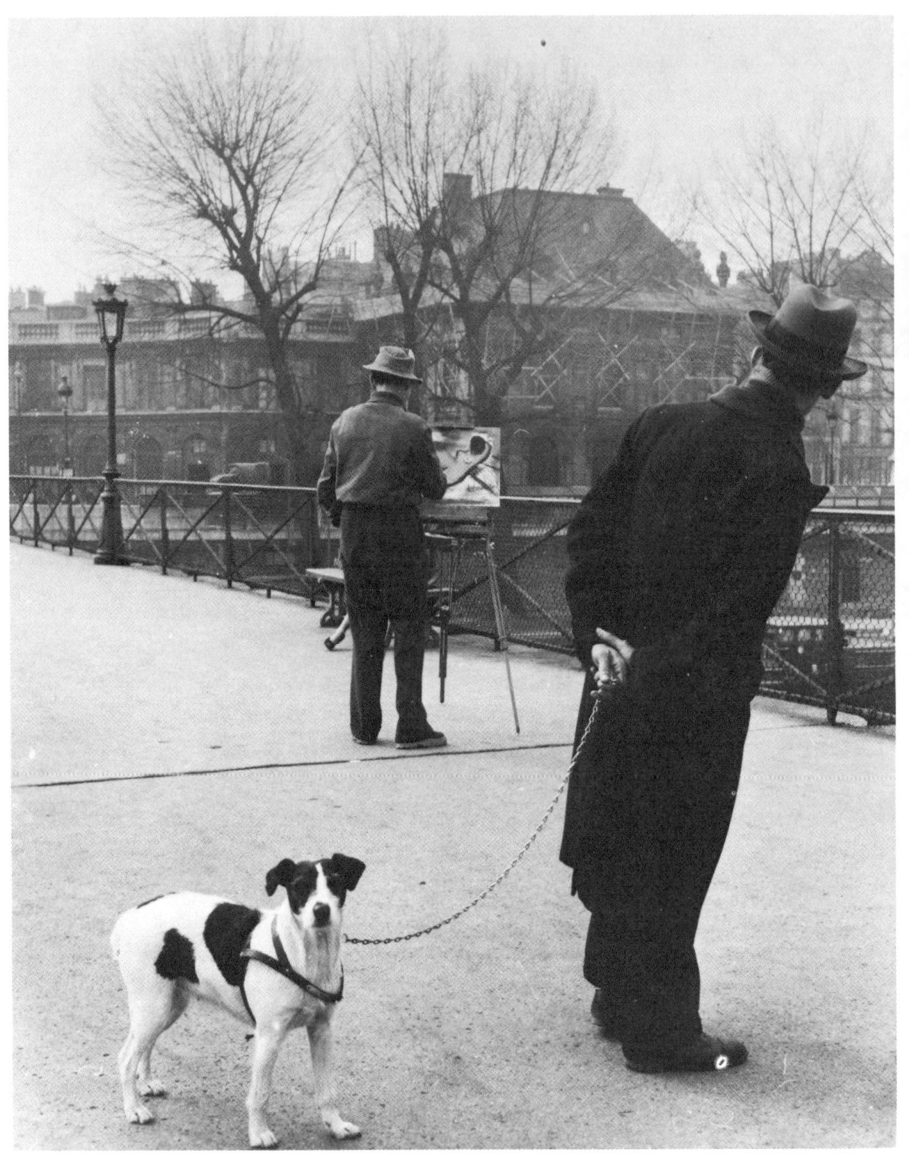

Figure 4. Robert Doisneau, *Fox Terrier au Pont des Arts,* 1953 (Doisneau-Rapho).

him and closer to us, an inquisitive fellow appears to be equally puzzled. Never are people more open to surveillance than when they themselves are gazing at someone else, a fact which lends this picture its conspiratorial charm. There is considerable interest in discovering if the model is indeed unclothed—the artist himself blocks from view all but her foot—but there is greater mirth in not knowing. Then, too, there is the onlooker's dog who, like all canines self-conscious about the photographic act, may be only posing for his picture—or may in this case be truly a superior animal, alert to Doisneau's game.

Such shots grant viewers the privilege of belonging to an expanded audience which gives them a further spectacle than that enjoyed by anyone in the frame. But the original object of desire is teased out of sight, as if one had been listening to music that had all manner of variations but had withheld its theme. A true music lover was once defined as one who, upon hearing a beautiful woman singing in a bathtub, puts his ear to the keyhole. Out of moral scruples *and* artistic delicacy, Doisneau keeps the private presence from becoming a public sensation. By concealing the erotic secrets that he constantly invokes—in a process that is earthy and yet refined—he also assumes a place in a French tradition.

In one of the most famous photographs of the twentieth century, his *Un regard oblique,* 1948, viewers have discerned a typically Gallic anecdote. Looking into an art gallery window, a middle-class wife is intrigued by a canvas front we don't see, while her husband, who wears a porkpie hat, ogles a painted female derrière on the wall. As a joke the scene is recommended only by its naughty ricochet, but it travels further than that, into a puzzle. For the 1890s nude that the husband gazes at, is herself peeking through a crack in the wall at an episode nicely left to our imagination (as is the painting seen by the wife). Doisneau has no trouble recruiting them all into his endless gallery of voyeurs, where he himself is active. More than that, all these players illustrate the infinite regress of the observant eye back into what the photographer has called the "religion of looking."

Doisneau says that he has often been asked the "silly question": what is his "wretched mania for taking photos . . . without a commission?"[2] He answers that it is purely instinct, "an irresistible urge to share with others the delight I've experienced through my eyes." That joy, he could have said, is founded on freedom, a freedom to seek and to act playfully, like a child.

Much of the world he describes is, of course, very grown-up, standardized in its mores, class structure, and conventions. In this zone, he's attracted to characters who slip up when normally guided by rules, or who construct their own rules and styles, like tramps, artists, lovers, and eccentrics. The lure of their behavior for Doisneau is not so much that it is antisocial as presocial, something which allows him to treat the constraints and hypocrisies of the social order as a happy butt of humor. It amuses him to include within that order creatures that are not at all human, but share our traits: his wise dogs, amorous statues, and "shocking scarecrows." Without its realist side, which summons up the toughness of Marcel Carné's films and the bittersweet lyrics of Edith Piaf, Doisneau's art would be incomplete, but it's the enchantment in his work that prevails. Just as his photos assume a likeness between subjects and viewers, they also catch the underlying resemblances between animals and people.

It's a hybrid vision with which we're dealing, an art so knowing that it can only express itself in quips and one-liners which fizz up all over again the moment we realize how cryptic they really are. To bring this off from a seemingly endless stock of epigrams, when everyone knows the artist is permitted only an inexhaustible supply of fragments, is an imaginative feat. With his concise ironies, which are so sophisticated that they look extremely ingenuous, Doisneau joins ranks with the brotherly work of Satie and Tati.

Yet when he actually looks at kids in their world, he has predictably little use for humor or irony. Their freedom from care is too serious to be treated as laughable. With them in mind, even Paris changes in aspect, becoming especially large in contrast to their smallness or particularly drab in relation to their radiance. Doisneau often presents the lives of their elders in terms of a theatrical metaphor, and of a popular theater at that—boulevard farce and vaudeville. Though natural performers, children have not yet learned guile nor given up their native dignity. Perhaps that is why Doisneau views them as existing in a state we once knew but can never re-enter, and therefore with a sense of loss that can only be poetic.

On the whole, children are pictured from further away than are adults, as if to have gotten closer would have been really intrusive. This slight increase in Doisneau's physical distance from the children amplifies an emotional longing which is sweet though it does not cease to be candid. Quite recently, Doisneau said that what he'd like to aim for now is "an isolated image whose contents possess the magic power of remembrance or memorialization. This does not happen just . . . with . . . people. There is light, too. . . . These images . . . stay near like a little tune. . . ." When looking at *L'aéro-*

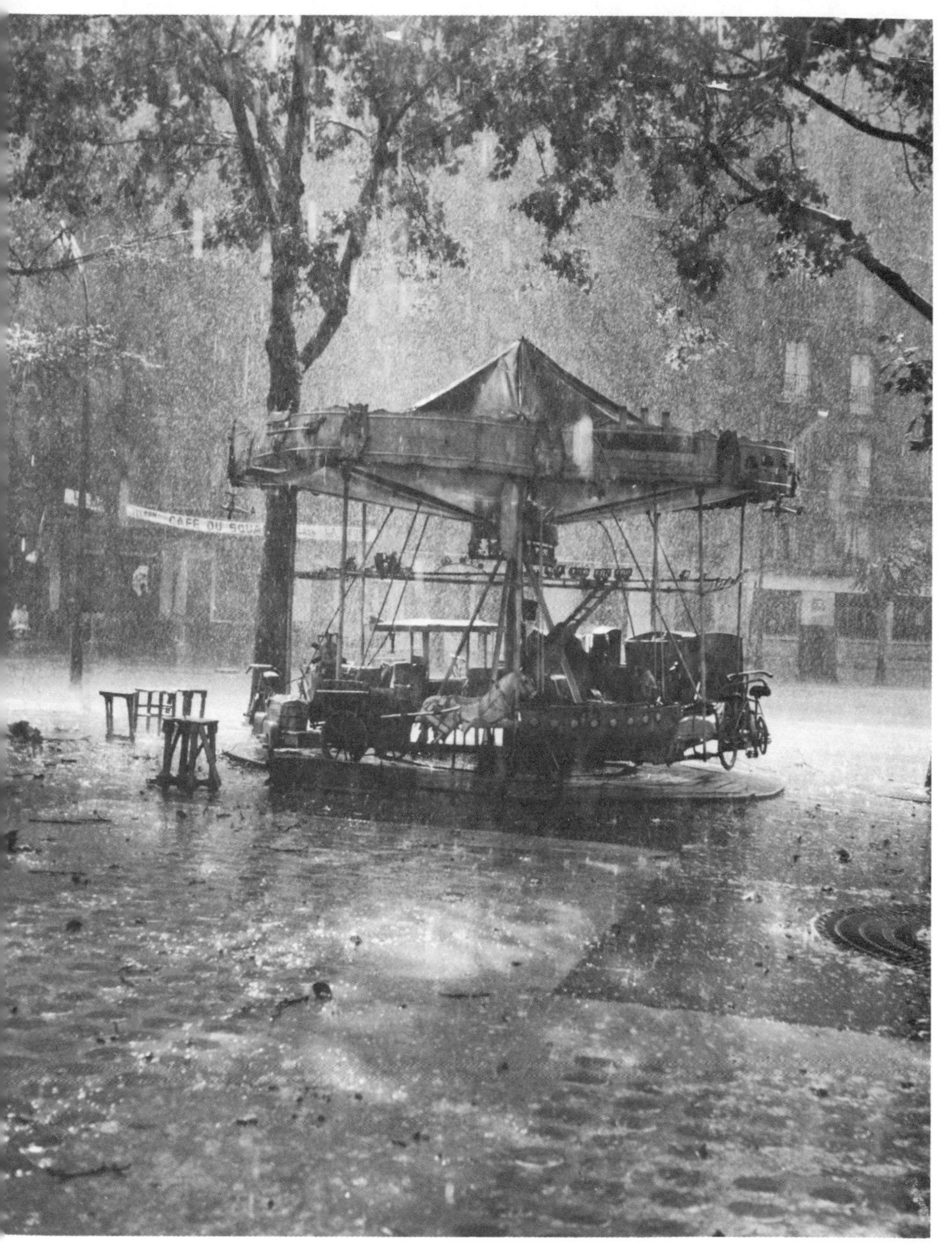

Figure 5. Robert Doisneau, *Le Manège de Monsieur Barré,* 1955 (Doisneau-Rapho).

plane de Papa, 1934, and *Le Manège de M. Barré,* 1955, one realizes that Doisneau has had that "magic power" all along, that, in the simplest way, he has long known how to turn a few shadows on a toy, or a glitter of sun through raindrops, into a music that evokes past time (Fig. 5). A breeze has risen to flutter the hair and flap the collar of *L'enfant papillon,* 1945. One notices the dinginess of the suburban setting, the mud on the cobblestones, and the child's wrinkled leggings. But on his face, with its open mouth and bright eyes, there quickens a luminous joy. Had he wished, Doisneau, in this one instant, could have rested his case for a photography whose "lightness . . . helps people to live." Fortunately for us all, he didn't.

Artforum, *March 1983.*

1. Unless otherwise noted, all quotations from Doisneau in this article are taken from the interview with him in *Dialogue with Photography,* by Paul Hill and Thomas Cooper (New York: Farrar Straus and Giroux, 1979).

2. Robert Doisneau, *Three Seconds from Eternity* (Boston: New York Graphic Society, 1980).

A Way of Seeing and the Act of Touching: Helen Levitt's Photographs of the Forties

Modern street photographers are fluttering, intrusive, yet vaguely stealthy creatures who live on edge in quizzical search of imagery they cannot foresee. They have reason to be nervous, for they work in a chaotic zone of ephemeral "targets" that may be reluctant to appear in the unannounced view, or else are endowed with a speedy, unsettling talent for vanishing from it. But this visual quarry teases not simply because it is disobedient and elusive. The conditions of the field are more bothersome than that, for the motifs presented by the photographer cannot be said to have existed before, and they do not endure after they have been wrought from light in the precise configurations that we later come to know.

To walk the streets is to be confronted with a stupid abundance of confused, jostled, and small incidents. The photograph will fix any instance of it with a drastic particularity, wispy, random, and therefore perhaps trivial. How is the stuff of the image transmuted into a message? How, even more, can its sensations be made to *represent* a view of life, especially since they often pulsed so obscurely and subliminally as to have left little impression in the blur of original contact?

Yet in an archaic sense, photographs predispose us toward what they show, if only by virtue of having uniquely extracted it. I can't help reading a picture as a preferred view, although, without further support, it could only be a gratuitous one. If I am to be *swayed* by a photograph, it must enter culture and be assigned mutually enhancing relationships with its own kind. That desirable state, for all serious photographers, is embodied in the problem of recurrence, of recurrent imagery.

On one hand, recurrence, as a picture-making strategy, works as a form of corroboration of data, themes, or attitudes spread through large arrays of images. On the other hand, recurrence simplifies the stylistic and conceptual demands imposed by a pictorial mode that is basically atomistic in its characteristic results. Raw material is acted upon, approached, and edited to suggest the illusion of an emergent pattern of scattered events. From mysteriously determined points, we catch glimpses of comparable details in disparate scenes and similar manners from separate milieux. There is a psychological link between the phenomena of recurrence and notions of the essential. When it is recurrently embroidered by street photography, the momentary can begin to look momentous. We find ourselves thinking that that is how people really are or what they archetypally do. I need hardly add that most books of photographs are iconically unified through their homogeneous depiction of *classes* of things or scenes. Often, their very topic defines the limits of treatment and typifies a genre, as currently understood.

But the street aesthetic meshes more delicately with these organizational traits because it asserts itself precisely by being on the loose, artistically independent of media directors. The mobility of street photographers, however, does not necessarily lead them to the fictions of the art world, nor do the photographers seek legitimization there. They are in flight, rather, from the stereotypes of photography for hire. The freedom at issue is not so much to allow the photographer to be personal for the ego's sake, but to use the ego to describe intimate and fortuitous realities not otherwise available.

When it breaks out into independent campaigns, street photography acts as a critique of the corporate hypocrisies of photographic culture and opposes its setups, hypes, and unfair samplings—its normal deceits—by hard-won standards of authentic observation.[1] Doubtless, too, its individual criteria of truth-telling, its emphasis on unique or anomalous insights, places street photography in conflict with visual recurrence in its most expedient forms.

For all that, practitioners of street photography ideally treat a specific class of events, though it is an untidy one that permits an extremely wide assortment of subjects. It belongs to a type *least* tainted by the photographer's presence. Underlying street photography is a naturalist argument that goes something like this: The value of the picture resides in its truthful observation. This value is jeopardized to the extent the photographer intervenes in the social circumstances, causing a rupture from what would naturally have happened. The natural is defined as a melange of urban events contingent upon each other, and therefore inherently effervescent and unpredictable. There can be no record of such action unless the photographer is committed to techniques of furtive and opportune surveillance whose goals cannot easily be rationalized. No wonder street photographers are often solitary, and always professional strangers with little to say about their indefinite motives. Still, their overall approach is conceptually articulate, because in practice it integrates the moral goal of credibility, the philosophical notion of contingency, and the professional requirement of freedom and spontaneity, each impossible to realize without engaging with the others.

Although a photography of the streets gradually emerged about a generation after the medium itself was born, the particular variant I have just described dates only from the 1930s. The hectic urbanism of the West could not fail to have been documented by the camera. They were mated with each other as if by industrial contract, and the products of their working union gave innumerable visual records of metropolitan growth, density, and manners. Whether generally accessible or not, such records, particularly those from the nineteenth and twentieth centuries, are thought to contribute to a public archive whose constituent parts are understood to be representative of given themes. But the themes themselves cannot be said to be resolved, apart from the ways in which images have been compiled and their possibilities inventoried. This traditional organizing scheme gives priority to the idea of finite, typical variables that can be classified, as distinct from the infinitude of nonrepeating events that may be placed on several disparate lists, never to be filled in.[2] This newer, more difficult alternative, although sometimes incorporated into archives, presented itself about fifty years ago in the work, for example, of such people as Henri Cartier-Bresson (whose photography had the earliest international influence), André Kertész, and Ben Shahn.

If these street photographers certify that nothing more is seen or even meant than what is shown, they offer concrete findings without any journalistic pretext. More curious about the actual processes of the visual flux than in the debatable causes or outcomes of specific actions, they display a useless respect for their environment. Before there is any judgment in their outlook, it has to have momentum, a powerful drive to the sheer act of looking. Afterward, the providential disorder of the images is structured and encompassed by the conscious sensibility of an individual. Instead of scenes rendered transparently by an impassive camera (for a known social purpose), we have a photographer's actively filtered world, or even an emphasis on how a pronounced *photographic* concern transforms the material of the world. Cartier-Bresson's 1953 *The Decisive Moment* was a summary of well over twenty years of effort on this level. It was the first conclusive book of its type, but could have been preceded by Helen Levitt's mettlesome *A Way of Seeing,* ready in 1946 but not published until 1965![3]

Helen Levitt is a quintessential modern street photographer, and to consider her early work is not only to see how the mode can be animated, but to come close to the moment when it was actually created. Compared to previous titles such as *You Have Seen Their Faces* (Margaret Bourke-White, 1937), or a later one, such as *The Americans* (Robert Frank, 1956), Levitt's *A Way of Seeing* has a flat, nonleading tone, asserting only the relativity of her vision. In contrast to the project-oriented work that surrounded it, the book, which had forty-four uncaptioned photographs in the original edition, promises very little and deliberately refuses to be fit into any category. It could have been called "New York Summers," or "Street Kids," with a dismal explicitness that would have foreclosed its true scope and real poetry. The sense of the book is staked on its "way" . . . the qualities of its regard. At the same time, and this is its particular tension, the matter of the pictures wins out over their manner. One cares about her subjects because the photographer makes us feel they are seen with a caring eye. It is as if they had to be envisioned by her artistry so as, in the end, to become representative, not of any predetermined state of affairs, but of themselves.

Helen Levitt, a predictably circumspect and private person, wary of publicity, says that she does not envy anyone who has the hard task of verbalizing about her images. She clearly was not referring to any imagined complexity, but she could have been thinking about their unassuming directness. We're far more familiar with that stance now than was James Agee, who was startled by it when he wrote a remarkable essay for *A Way of Seeing* in the mid-forties. He had not expected that her off-hand framing could have conducted such volatile and lyric energy.

What attracted that energy at first looks superficially like what once drew Lewis Hine to scrutinize the lives of deprived children. In Hine's output, one is struck by the feeling that too much wisdom, and too much hardship of the kind that instills such wisdom, has been imposed by a harsh environment on those too young to absorb what it means. Their innocence is eerily stunted. Hine's children are at work, or they pose in the workplace, a hellish community in which they've been burdened far too soon by callous bosses and an indifferent society. For their part, Helen Levitt's youngsters, involved in play, are small, explosive parentheses on weary and alien streets. The good cheer, if not the festive savagery, of these juveniles is touchingly out of place. Levitt has in common with Hine a grimy, earthy view of the urban background, but she does not elaborate upon it as material distress. What he reported were "conditions"; what she discovers are nuances.

Instead of building up concrete particulars over and over with each page to give a uniformly dense portrayal, Levitt's book proceeds by way of uninsistent modulation in loose thematic clusters, taking our attentiveness as if on a stroll through a variety of slight urban gestures and expressions. That is why, in talking about her children, I have already speculated too much about the book's meaning and said too little about its actual content. For it depicts not only the sputtering charades of black kids and white ones, but the kibbitzing of their elders, graffiti and the loafing and hugging that goes on among family and friends with time on their hands during the dog days of the New York summer.

From this composite of unlike but naturally related situations, no one emphasis declares itself sufficiently to be read as centrally important. To questions of whether this is an album chiefly about an urban season, about how streets are populated by their communities, the sociology of ghettos, the fantasies of children, or the way parents and their offspring deal with each other, the photographs frequently answer yes and no at the same time. Or rather, the whole range of these topics can be made implicit in individual pictures, lightly, though, and strewn about.

In retrospect, it's clear that by her choice of visual territory and her rapid traverses through it, the photographer foresaw that such interests would ordinarily overlap. And, once again, while we accept overlapping social fluidities in photography today, they were by no means the rule in the late 1930s, when Helen Levitt set out to explore the neighborhoods of her city with a second-hand Leica.

The public life of New York, for a century, had been represented as the dynamic accumulation of innumerable *historic* events, typifying acts and progressive stages, unfurled in collective witness by a chorus of anonymous specialists. Profiled against this simple and heroic version of modernism, there emerged the humble, problematic, and apparently deflating modernity of generalists like Helen Levitt. They took on for themselves the role of individual witnesses whose experience taught them that the city was a jumble of diverse sensations in which they, themselves, had to swim. Nowhere was this reality of the miscellaneous, this field of simultaneous and nonexclusive accents, more available for study than on the street, a setting for the urban mass along whose reaches unsuspecting private conduct mingled with more self-conscious behavior. Their broad but unceremonious concept of the street marked off photographers like Helen Levitt from their corporate brethren. Suddenly it became unclear what such people were looking at.

For good reason. Instead of social hierarchies and history, these photographers took in only phenomena through their eyes—the phenomena of a decomposed present, with all its immediacy and obscurity. Where random glimpses appeared with intermittent frequency before, they now became a constant feature of photographic operations. The result was a far more democratic panorama of multiple happenings, stumbled upon, as it seemed, by pedestrians whose limited vantage and unbiased survey would correspond with our own, in like perspectives. More authenticity of viewpoint was gained at the cost, however, of greater uncertainty of content. It only remained (but what an *only*) for a photographer with depth and insight to make sense of the variables that gushed in the field.

If, as I realize, I've encouraged a view of street photography as a canon of busy forms and diffuse possibilities, I must now state that Helen Levitt's street images are extraordinarily terse. She implies but does not demonstrate that New York is a populous place. She suggests but does not spell out the eruptive power of a crowded underclass. The most talkative element in *A Way of Seeing* is the key fact that most of its pictures were taken when it was hot in New York, often swelteringly hot.

We know this, not only because of the lightness of people's clothes and the oppressive glare of the sun, but through those many frames in which the younger subjects try vainly to cool off at open hydrants or from passing sprinkler trucks. These are the book's most dramatic moments of sport, and they symptomize its expressive drives. Unquestionably, the spewing, graceful water acts as an image of desire, but more important, the memory of it carries over to many other districts to evoke, in the gaming we see there, the idea of primal instinct being released, or liberated, *under pressure.*

This binary process seems reflective of the photographer herself. Always, the purely visual intelligence of her photographs yearns for concision, intimacy, and, as a result, the strong, disjointed isolation of episodes from the indefinite mass, while, with equal force, a social instinct wants to hold in view the affective ties that people have with each other, their expansiveness and their sense of community. In the summer, or at most during the warmer months—the only time when Levitt will work the streets—emotions are proverbially short-fused. It is the season of small but incandescent contacts which rise up in such brief, wired flares that to have caught them at all the photographer must have flown off the handle and held her breath, all in one act.

The steamy compression of their East Harlem apartments had flushed people out into the streets, where they congregated in front of their stoops and doorways, conversed in dialogue between windows and sidewalks or played along the gutters and curbs. Whether among the standing or sitting adults, or the highly active children, the mood was proprietary and familiar. Interior domestic scenes had emptied into a common public arena and a more open space. We viewers are immersed in a spectacle that lacks a proscenium, as if the actors had left the charged cubicle of the stage to join us in the orchestra. Or rather, the difference between audience and actors was confused, and their dramatic parts made up on the spot. In the heady, gabby profusion that resulted, Levitt homed in, plain style, on moments of spontaneous bonding.

A *Way of Seeing* shows people's recurrent need to touch each other, to pair, as it might be, or to act together in groups. It's a reasonable guess that the subjects knew each other well or were related, and though this kind of sociability doesn't accord with the myth of New York as a throng of strangers (an idea, really, of the fifties), it conforms, even now, to the experience of its ethnic neighborhoods. Forty or more years after Hine showed them arriving, the European or Latin-American immigrants (and the southern blacks on a different schedule), had settled in, acculturated to a hugger-mugger existence. This comment about affectionate tribes in seedy circumstances is quite obvious, but should remind us that *A Way of Seeing,* however lyrical, is also an inherently regional study, for it points to and draws visual interest from the physical demonstrativeness of the New Yorkers, whose largely Catholic and Jewish culture stood out in maximum contrast to the Protestant hinterland.

It was during this same period, the 1940s, that Weegee, too, took many of the pictures that were later be gathered in *The Naked City,* a book that sensationalized body contact as a New York specialty. Highlighting hysteria and violence, Weegee carefully described the place as one live-long disaster area, and it was this alarming, yellow press flim-flam that fed so much of the suspicion and enmity toward New

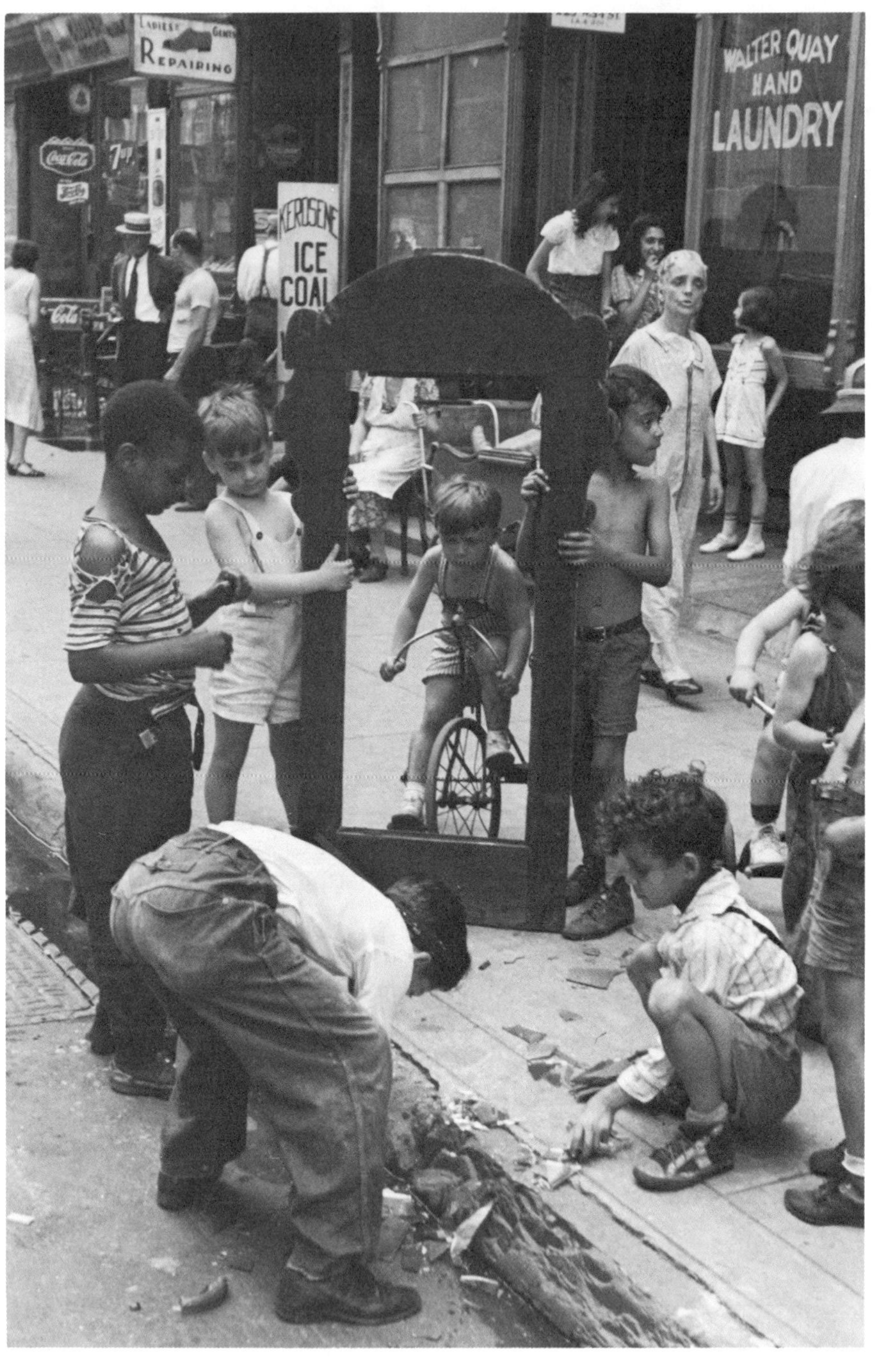

Figure 6. Helen Levitt, *New York, ca. 1942.*

York in the popular culture of the time. Compared to such reportage, Helen Levitt saw New Yorkers not in collision, but as having reached out toward each other—effusively, tenderly, or often in sadness. And there were no anecdotes or myths in this evocation, only a way of seeing.

These inhabitants of the tenements grasp, hold, grip, embrace, and in many ways, support, bridge, or connect themselves with the things and people around them. The searching activity of the hand and the arm is emphatic in these photographs, as if to affirm, beyond any doubt, the existence of nearby presences in the shabby world of Spanish Harlem, the Lower East Side, and what we would now call the East Village. To a photographer, the theme of touching can have a further, critical importance. It intimates the *continuum* of a lived, sentient appetite and response within the necessarily immobile scene. More than that, touching, in the way at least that Helen Levitt's New Yorkers do it, is in collusion with something behind the surface; it's an external gesture that attaches human value to an interior life, or it's the most direct way we're led to infer such attachment.

Cartier-Bresson, whose work Helen Levitt knew in the 1930s, and whom she acknowledges as a prime influence, was a virtuoso in "arranging" graceful visual tangents. No sooner do we comprehend the flow of his configuration than it is seen to unfold through impingements—of shadows, feet, calligraphy, puddles, fingers—that judiciously appear to have just left off or are about to kiss each other. In short, it's the potential energy of the overall field that kindled him, and which he realized through a sequence of chance, kinetic attractions, suspended in time and space. Having digested that lesson, a young American woman, out to explore her New York precincts with a camera, learned that she had a different temper. For her, touch was not an illusion suggested by agile placement of the framing eye, but a real-life event. It was also definitely felt as a compressive, enfolding event, episodic, self-concerned, and indifferent to the picture field.

Too frequent in their appearance to be a trace of passing, unconcerned observation, Helen Levitt's touching figures are persistently estranged in their environment. By *estranged* I do not presume anything about the figures' consciousness, but refer to our own. For we see, as they probably do not, that they're cut off in that space, that it offers a kind of resistance and has to be overcome. Kids can crawl and shinny up to the lintel above their doorways, or the trunk of the only tree in the book (and a blasted one, at that) to fight it out, let's say, with their licorice pistols and wooden swords. Whether they're little Tarzans in the jungle or junior Legionnaires in the desert, the frame nicely contrasts their charade of high adventure with the humdrum reality of the street.

When there's any openness in that space, or any failure of human approach on the part of its actors, or a derelict figure crops up, the effect is especially eloquent and painful. Instead of the buzz that one imagines elsewhere in her work, the effect here is of silence, or retreat to which the city offers no answer. Some of these loners fall back on their imagination. The kids twirl white streamers or waft bubbles in front of these inhospitable, dark stones. The fragile, brief possessiveness of their games and their idle hours is expended against a hard and unresponsive background.

So, the interplay between foreground and rear, or density and vacancy, is not so much an arabesque as a carrier of an empathetic charge. The inhabited street is the site of an on-going theatrical struggle, sometimes momentarily won by the zestful figures and sometimes lost by them to the inanimate slum setting. It makes a difference to see how people are able to invent, or are frustrated in creating their *own* space. Occasionally, and very movingly, it happens that an emotional space is defined (for us now, whatever it was then), as a reflex of some injury that comes from the outside. It is the kind of softened space one sees, in a number of images in the book, where the arms that extend from one figure to another are unmistakably sorrowful and consoling.

I wondered, when I first saw *A Way of Seeing,* how its few pictures, with their simple means, were expressed with such authority. I now think it must be because the photographs realize themselves by making a viewer ask *questions* that are peculiar to Helen Levitt's way of seeing. For example, apart from the book's middle forties chronology, there is some enigma about its *emotional* time zone. The photographs generally suggest an aura that has some intangible, but large and not benign consequence for their subjects. If that aura still holds a viewer in the waning gravitational field of the depression, a number of Levitt's people nevertheless step out of it easily and smile. But they do not ever go so far as to trespass into the middle American area of the *Life* magazine photos of the time, with their depraved wholesomeness.

How, for instance, is one to react to the image of a hugely pregnant woman, arms folded across her bosom, who appears to look down with sniffish hauteur on a girl just then passing lightly in front of her, with two milk bottles and a grin as if she were the cat that had just swallowed the canary (Fig. 7)? The picture has Levitt's significant contrasts in depth and her sensitive account of holding hands, even if their function here, as in several of the book's photographs, is *self-*

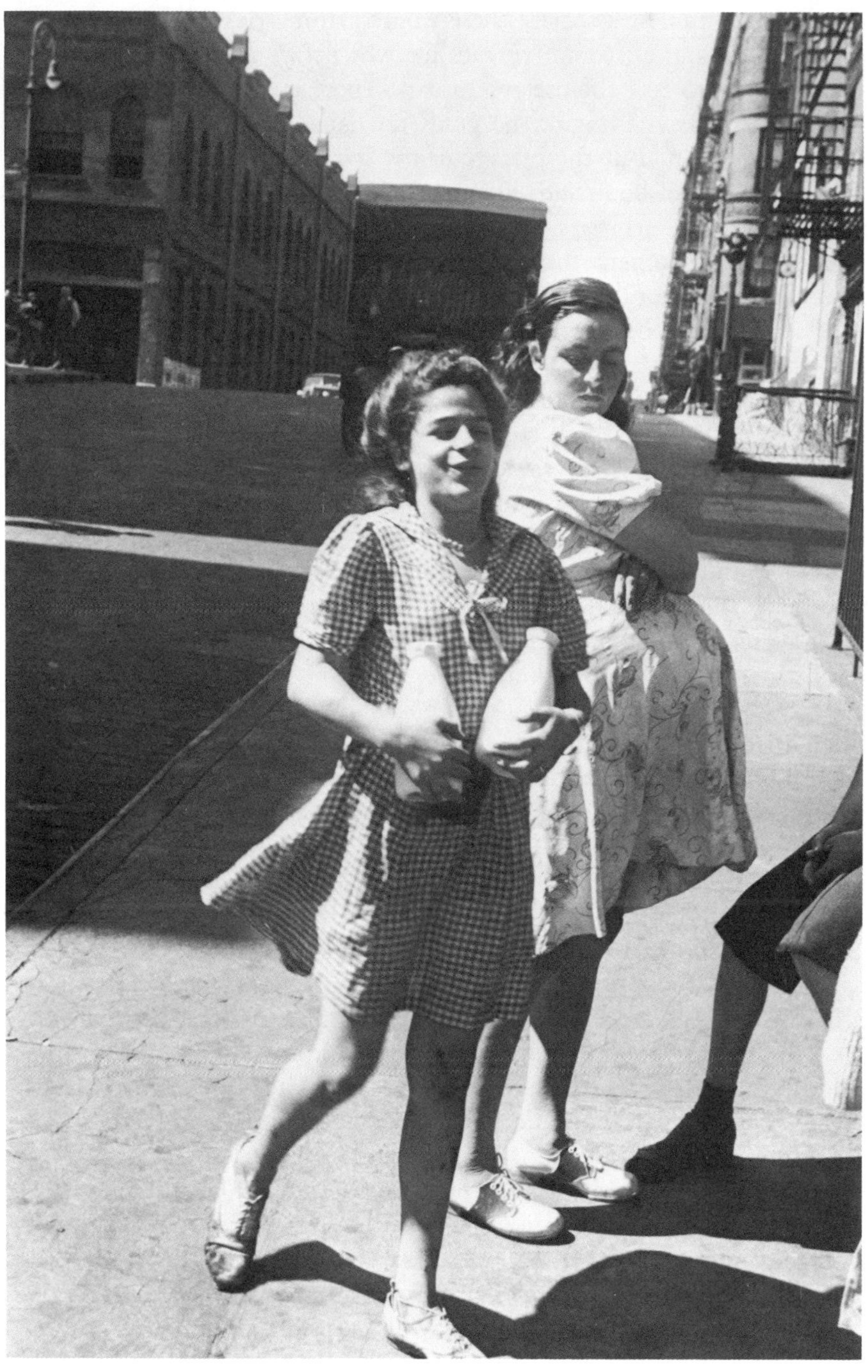

Figure 7. Helen Levitt, *New York, ca. 1945.*

protective. I cannot associate these ironic symmetries with those apple pie comforts and anecdotal verities for which *Life* thought G.I.s were fond enough to risk themselves abroad. There is no domestic witness to the war in Levitt's work, no gold star flags, bond posters, USO clubs, and so on. But the picture of the women is also too vibrant, mischievous, and bouncy to fit into the picture albums of the supposedly miserable thirties. Though rooted in their own, familiar moments, the phenomena that involved Helen Levitt did not need to be assigned any historical epoch.

"Specialized as her world is," wrote James Agee, ". . . Miss Levitt has worked it in such a way that it stands for much more than itself; . . . a whole and round image of existence." He went on to speak of her subjects, of pastoral stock, as the embodiment of "a natural history of the soul . . . fantastically misplanted in the urgent metropolis of the body." In Agee's passion-play, only the rural folk had virtue (soul) enough to survive in the physical rottenness of the city. And Levitt's pictures had a redemptive value on two interrelated counts: first, they showed such survival in all its pity, terror, and grace, and second, because the photographs were close to folk art, the product of an instinctual and pure vision.

Agee's argument, however, does not claim that Levitt's art is naive, but rather that it is occupied with innocence as subject, a very different thing. Be that as it may, he does attribute a high level of sophistication to work that could only have stemmed from urban culture. In fact, Helen Levitt met Agee in New York in 1938, at the same time that she introduced herself to his friend, Walker Evans, the most reflective and disciplined mind just then in American photography.[4] Evans was committed to projecting a study of American consciousness as embodied through its land, faces, and artifacts. Though he, himself, was only partly a street photographer, he seems to have communicated almost osmotically the rigor of his ideas to Ben Shahn in the middle thirties, and to Helen Levitt a decade later. It is instructive to compare her playgrounds and tenement scenes with their counterparts by Shahn. (Both photographers, incidentally, had used right-angle viewfinders to avoid disturbing the street life that interested them.) His earlier pictures are more unbuttoned and grimmer, but not less humane and visually rich than Levitt's.[5] As for Evans himself, Lincoln Kirstein had quite accurately written that his was a "purely protestant attitude: meager, stripped, cold and, on occasion, humorous." If we recall the gritty ebullience and pathos of Shahn, the epicurean speed of Cartier-Bresson, and what Kirstein called the "unsparing frankness" and puritanical eye of Evans, they suggest the conflicting models from which Helen Levitt, still in her early twenties, fused her *thoroughbred* way of seeing.[6]

If it had been necessary to talk around its empathies, it is certainly proper, now, to stress the detachment of Levitt's art. Her book can transfigure the ordinary circuits of human worry and pleasure because it is not engaged with them—not engaged with any moral statement before it has satisfied its zeal for poetic beauty. Or is it that the undeniable poetic beauty Levitt discovered on the streets inevitably had a moral significance—not the least of the questions asked by her work?

Levitt's photographs were not intended for any context, nor for any original use other than the one we presently see. Her images maintain their freshness as a result, and also a certain distance.[7] At the same time, it's an extraordinarily affirmative distance. After having advanced in order visually to comprehend the people of the street, the photographer receded to let them be themselves and to speak. In other genres, content tends to determine itself through whole artifices of stagecraft that are variously photographed as a durable statement of affairs. Street photography, however, is concerned with an artless, involuntary reality of cryptic scraps and bits of visual evidence, taken for what they are. If it seems that such partial views express internal truths about the human situation, it's to the extent that the photographer, alone, reflecting upon experience, knew how to time and project, musically shape and summarize them.

The inextricable gravity, poise, mystery, and charm of Helen Levitt's scenes did not preexist on their own. They came into being as the products of a melodic desire whose aim was to do no more than justice to the moments of its best perceptions. In their articulated setting, their vulnerable embraces, the sense they give of literal kinship, and all the delicacy with which such things resonate, these recurring moments confess their faithfulnes to each other and earn for the book its miraculous unity.

From Observations, *edited by David Featherstone,* Untitled *no. 35 (Carmel, Cal.: The Friends of Photography, 1984).*

1. "Normal deceits" presupposes a semantic environment in which the typical transmission is not a false statement, but a lie. Sisela Bok (*Lying,* [New York: Vintage, 1979], p. 14), defines a lie as "any intentionally deceptive message which is staged." Commercial photography is an environment known for its high incidence of such messages, which deliberately confuse beauty or glamour (that is, desirability)

with the "truth" of their objects. The hubris of street photography is its assumption of an "honest" semantic environment which it would visualize by continually acknowledging the imperfect and limited means at its disposal for apprehending truth. In admitting the relativity of its perceptions, street photography announces the objectivity of its stance. It allows for misleading statements, but proscribes their being intentional.

2. The contrast here can also be expressed in more subjective terms. Working on a principle of representational sufficiency, "the traditional organizing scheme" wants one to conclude that everything can eventually be given that is necessary to know about a topic. The need to know is a practical and exhaustible category. The psychology of nonrepeating events, on the other hand, asserts that one can never gather enough cases to be assured of that knowledge, and that the real necessity is that of intense feeling evoked in response to whatever *is* given. This is the main reason, incidentally, why modern street photographs do not propose topics that can be inventoried. When they appear in books, in their own right, they are *not* compiled, they are cadenced.

3. The initial book was to be brought out by Reynolds and Hitchcock in the forties, but was shelved when one of the partners died. Helen Levitt states that she thought little more about the project for twenty years, until it was suggested that Viking produce it. The title, from a sentence in the accompanying unpublished essay by James Agee, was proposed by Catherine Carver at Viking. All the following comments on *A Way of Seeing* in this essay are based, however, on the 1981 edition (Horizon Press), which includes twenty-four more plates than the original Viking/ Museum of Modern Art book. I concentrate on this body of work because I consider it exemplary in the history of the street tradition. But I do not wish to imply that it represents anything more than a tiny fraction of what Helen Levitt created in the forties, nor am I able to discuss her productive and continuous career since then. These images, particularly her later work in color, are subjects for a much-needed monograph.

4. Interestingly, Helen Levitt's first contact with Evans's work was the folio illustrating Carleton Beals's *The Crime of Cuba,* an account of U.S. involvement with the Machado dictatorship of the thirties. It is suggestive, but probably only coincidental, that Evans had described a tropical locale, with its multiracial communities, bearing up in poverty and heat rather like Levitt's New Yorkers.

5. In *The Photographic eye of Ben Shahn,* edited by David Pratt (Cambridge: Harvard University Press, 1975), compare, for instance, number 1 with Levitt's number 24, and Shahn's number 15 with numbers 58 and 62 in *A Way of Seeing.* The parallels are very intimate.

6. It is appropriate here to stress how closely mutated are the affinities among the important street photographers of New York. Helen Levitt's work crystallizes certain elements from her immediate predecessors. It then takes its place in a tradition that also includes the later images of Lou Faurer, William Klein, Roy DeCarava, Robert Frank, and Bruce Davidson, who were to explore, all quite individually, yet convergingly, the poetic dissonance of New York streets.

7. Ben Lifson has formulated this dynamic quite well: "Levitt's style respects it all and tactfully keeps its distance, neither permitting an emotion to overwhelm the world of a picture nor the world's loveliness or shabbiness to trivialize an emotion" (*Village Voice,* May 26, 1980).

William Klein and the Radioactive Fifties

The photographer William Klein had initially been a painter embroiled in experimental Parisian abstraction of the 1950s. Later, in the 1960s, among his many careers, he became known as one of the most successful photographers of international high fashion. At the peripheries, then, of the work for which he's justly famous—gutsy reports of the megapolis twenty-five years ago—there are analogies to the efforts of two other Kleins, Yves and Calvin.

This displaced New Yorker, whose enunciation is disconcertingly suave and whose face recalls that of Antonin Artaud, was enchanted with sleaziness. Until Klein came along it was not widely imagined that that which was contemptibly low, mean, and tacky in our urban environment could be enjoyed for its own sake. I get my definition of sleaziness from the dictionary which doesn't take one very far. In Klein's photos the condition is much more vividly described as the raucous, debased, lurid, vulgar, and slovenly perspectives of the modern city, a locale indecent and unpresentable, therefore unfit for and ill-used by its inhabitants. His pictures of the 1950s gave news—little of it actually sensational—one didn't want to know, though its abrasive presence was hard to avoid.

Sleaziness is not the same as poverty, for all that they're compatible deficits and Klein's furor is not the same as social engagement. The world he depicts, which has come apart—fissures everywhere and eruptions of crud—was for him a visual discovery. He can be said, almost, to have invented it—at a propitious moment of our cultural history. For him, the streets were populated by hotshots, wiseacres, and meatballs, though a longer look shows that such thoroughfares teemed with harassed or strained people and anxious kids. Isn't this like the first impression one gets when returning from Europe to New

York: an indescribable filth, an unbearable pressure, and a disproportionate number of crackups aimlessly wandering about?

"On Forty-second street, posters in violent colors announced thriller-films—horror films—gay films. I stopped there. On either side of the box office, distorting mirrors reflected the passersby; they were long and broad. I looked at myself; I was on the point of making faces; fog rolled in my brain. . . ." The above, by Simone de Beauvoir from her journal of the 1950s, *America Day by Day,* sums up quite well the wide-angle atmosphere of Klein's New York. More than that, it suggests the vertigo induced by the spectacle he makes of it.

Klein certainly had as much of de Beauvoir's wonder, none of her sour crotchets, and a different sort of animus. While he soft-pedals it now, he must have been affected by the anti-Americanism of the French left, though not by its brittle Stalinism. Everything about him suggests an anarchic temperament, capable of playing any worldly system to the hilt and then of throwing away its benefits. With his hometown, New York, to which he returned at the age of twenty-six, he appears to have had a score to settle, expressed through a photography of ecstatic and ravished vengeance.

He literally blitzed the place in about three months. The full title of the book containing the results of this astonishing campaign (published only in Europe, 1956, and usually referred to simply as *New York*) is *Life is Good and Good for you in New York: Trance Witness Revels.*[1] Mangling a tabloid phrase that might have been "Chance Witness Reveals," the words signal not only a playful mind but a surreal impact that must have been much more concrete for Klein here than in postwar Paris.

"This city of headlines and gossip and sensation," Klein said. ". . . needed a kick in the balls." As he told John Heilpern, for an essay in *William Klein: Photographs,* the *Aperture* monograph on his work:

> I saw the book as a monster big-city Daily Bugle with its scandals and scoops that you'd find blowing in the streets at three in the morning. . . . For me photography was good old-fashioned muckraking and sociology. . . . I could imagine my pictures lying in the gutter. . . . I was a newspaperman! Or a Frenchman. One time in Harlem I cooled things down by saying I was French. "Hey! This guy ain't white. He's French!"

It's interesting to make the obvious comparison between Klein and Weegee, who had a comparable stake in a squalid New York and who really was from the *News*. Linking them like this, one sees immediately that—aside from the similarity of their supreme voyeurist chutzpah—one was a primitive putting on airs, while the other was a modernist slumming with jazzy abandon. There is hardly anything like the real-life murder-and-mayhem of the journalist in Klein (only toy guns and charades of violence), and there is nothing of Klein's extreme artistic rawness visually decomposing before your eyes in Weegee. This is not simply the difference between a parochial spirit and cosmopolitan vision. The real contrast emerges in their attitudes toward the media, which both exploited, but for opposite reasons.

That to which Weegee frustratedly aspired, the status of an artist, was the easiest thing for Klein to shuck off, because he had an artistic identity as a painter from the first. Weegee blazed out space for his Expressionism in a genre that, for all outward appearances, kept him a colorful hack. Klein, for his part, was an uncontainable aesthetic guerilla who made use of coprorate sponsors for purposes at the edge of their taste, testing the axiom that the more they funded the more he could provoke. The entry of both men into the fashion world (a few shots by Weegee and a longer stint by Klein) coincided with the moment when editors decided they liked the *frisson* of models seen in working-class milieux. Coming from such precincts themselves, the photographers could have had only a volatile response toward such a condescending program (the have-nots as backdrop).

Weegee worked within the illustrative confines of tabloid graphics with hypertensive pointedness, while Klein diffused their headline and layout strategies into his street shots. Abounding with billboards, signs, and hard-sell messages of every sort, his pictures are, in fact *about* media as much as they deal with the people who are targeted by them (Fig. 8). Everything within his frames grabs at your attention, the more incongruous, grotesque, or disjointed the presence, the better. At the same time, he was no more a muckraker than a Frenchman, just as it's clear that he had great aptitude but no final calling for painting or fashion photography. Like Weegee in his fun-house mood, ultraquick reflexes and unstanchable energy that spilled over into such modes as film, Klein differed in that he had no psychic base. No one acted the *poseur* with more conviction.

We're entitled to ask what a figure with such equivocal resources contributed to the art of photography. Of late, the medium, during the 1950s, has been considered to have been pretty much a one-chicken town—the chicken being Robert Frank. Photographers of a generation older than Frank's—André Kertész, Lisette Model, John

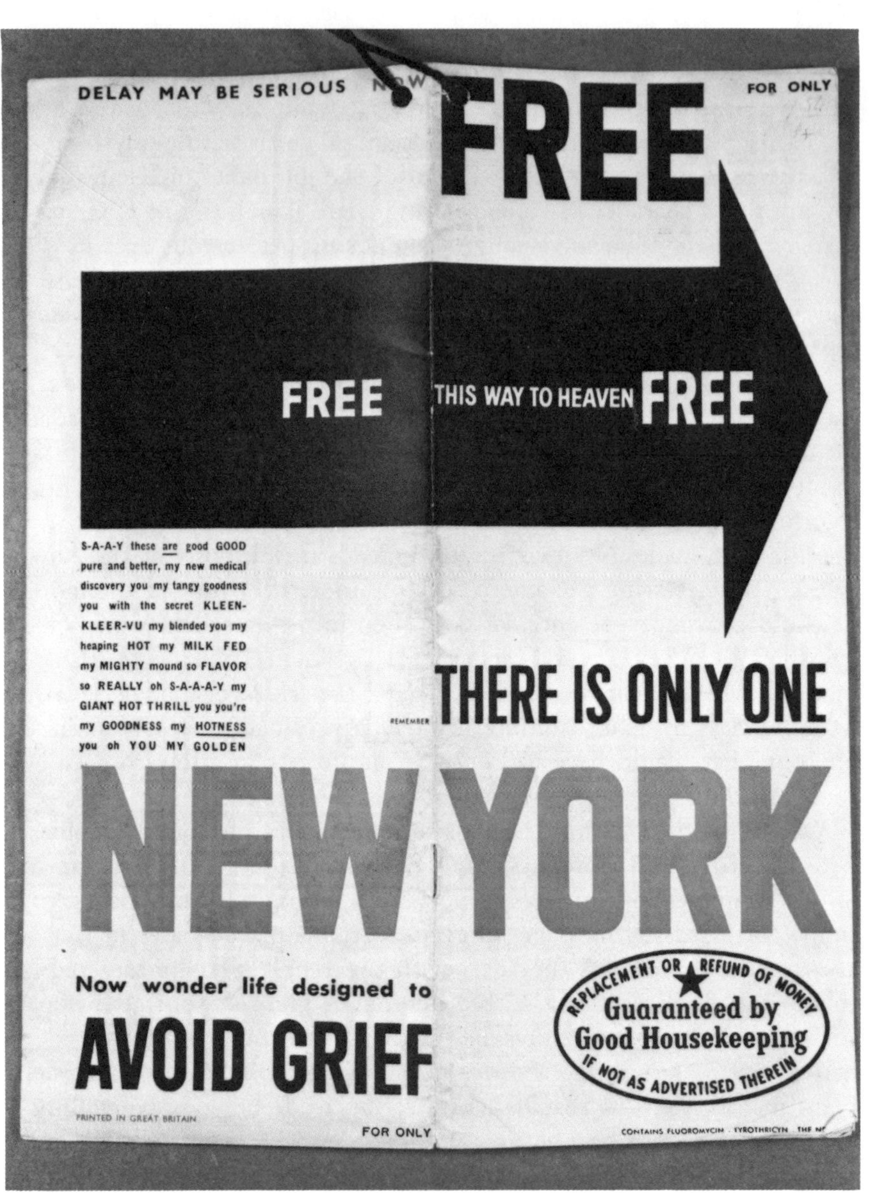

Figure 8. William Klein, cover for *New York*, 1956.

Guttman, Harry Callahan, and Eugene Smith—certainly did not hesitate to exist during the 1950s, which they accented memorably. Frank, though, *and* Klein brought to the decade a feeling for its woes which, in retrospect, synthesizes it for us. There hovers in their work an oppressive sense of the odds against which people struggled, the dismal mood and chance of defeat that lowered the emotional horizon. This was all the more striking because of the general affluence of the period, underway shortly before the start of Frank's and Klein's major efforts, in the great boom of 1955. These transplanted photographers found live and visual metaphors for the bleakness of this Cold War moment, and the deadness of the things in it. For those who remember the era, these photographic evocations of it have the keenest resonance; for those who came later, *The Americans* and *New York* offer a wondrous guide. One cannot suppose that the photographers had anything as simple as sympathy for what they saw. It's a question, rather, of their having developed an unlikely poetry as they came of age, to express their awareness of their time.

The nominal technical innovations that characterize these two books have been misleadingly heroicized. It has been imagined that virtue resides in the unexpected looseness with which they demonstrated that a 35mm camera could be handled. Untidy framing, blurry or grainy description, overcharged contrasts, abrupt or gauche shifts in compositional weight; these have been celebrated as signs of instinctual release which were somehow, in the end, good for photography. I've nothing against an argument that approves of mutinies against an otherwise convention-bound professional environment. But the trouble with this reasoning is that it tends to reduce meaning to a set of strategies rather than understand the form of a photograph as being at the service of a human consciousness. The photographs in question are simply *not about* being faster in their timing, or more gestural, or less prejudiced toward clear focus than earlier practice. Some of Bill Brandt's and Walker Evans's work, and a large measure of Ben Shan's, had already led the way in that direction anyway. No doubt Klein and Frank were more radical in their dependence on chance. The accelerated tempos of their art have suggested to some writers a risk-taking mentality akin to Action Painting. Recently, for instance, Klein's "insistence on physicality" reminded Ben Lifson of Willem de Kooning and Jackson Pollock. Without denying the parallel, I see these photographers putting their "action" to use in a very special way as a means of providing recognitions of a whole historical period.

A 35mm street shot was generally apprehended as a glimpse, a partial view only, whether snatched or studied. To make it count, despite its narrative limitations, one had either to assume something like "the decisive moment,"or build up a story or a theme through an accretion of related frames, much like a stilted movie. Frank and Klein, contrary to both methods, developed a form of witness in which the whole of their perception is implied or evident in the single fugitive glance. Or rather, the avidity of their feeling tenaciously charges subjects they could not predict. There is a constancy in the way, but not in what, they saw. They breathed the air about them, and their task was to find the means to invoke the effect of that air upon social behavior. Once this mission was grasped—and one reckons it happened early on—there was no need for them to generalize or homogenize anything. In fact, they freed themselves to concentrate on the most minute slivers of conduct, throwaway episodes, confident in the unanticipated but exemplary value of such subjects. Call it aura or mood, the matters with which they dealt are enveloped by it. I am talking about a tendentious response to conditions of life in all their various reflexes and textures, that is, in their intangible as well as their material guise. Confronting the culture of 1950s America, the two photographers sensed it uneasily as everywhere and nowhere. . . almost as it it were a kind of expressive dust that settled into the pores of their film, now heavily, now lightly. Weegee could show a bunch of street kids who had opened a hydrant, and the scene would result in nothing more than "human interest." Klein and Frank, with similarly effusive material can haunt you, on the other hand, with a sense of desolation. Empathetic and distanced at the same time, their work broadened in range, transfiguring the myriad circumstances of people into a myth of their present.

Robert Frank, I'm convinced, worked in a pastoral mode. But it was an abused pastoral, lonely and tedious in its reaches, so that when he brought his concerns to bear on city life the metropolis had a great deal to tell us of the sadness he saw in the country. His subjects may have been attached to each other but are dissociated in space. Even when working up close, he reveals how little they command that space, and the unresigned but apprehensive look of lostness is stamped on their faces. With William Klein, though, there is just as much melancholy, but it's filtered through a visual war of nerves, a fact which makes it quite outrageous. The complete city man, both intrusive and obtrusive, Klein often incited his subjects, who hammed it up or looked annoyed or puzzled. When you view his books, you feel that you yourself are a conspicuously uncalled-for presence, hurried in and out of bitter districts in which you have no business.

The experience of paging through *New York* comes to seem almost one of being on the run, of stumbling over obstacles, ending finally in visual fatigue. The big city often does that to its denizens, bombards them with a feckless montage. This effect is brilliantly managed by Klein in a layout that allows the eye no place to rest and hardly any stop (Fig. 9). Initially resembling a magazine, with its double spreads, scattered frames, and multiple image scales, the design of the book quickly goes haywire. There are no adjacent captions, for instance, and the double spreads—two pictures—often run smack together, separated only by the gutter. When two such images are loaded with type, as in window displays, the effect they have on each other is one of mutual violation. Klein will act out a great deal, in fact, to cancel the integrity of single shots—by arranging them in vertical bands or deploying them in checkerboard configurations, by setting them in black margins that break up the white page, by suggesting possible bleeds or sudden crops, by mimicking family albums or comic strips—anything to introduce extraneous ideas, aspects of photo-culture to the side of what he's doing.

In terms of grammatical structure, the photographic *divertissement* is a text without commas, though it has plenty of exclamation points. It swims with verbs and adverbs, some adjectives, and fewer nouns. Phrases and clauses dangle in odd places. Momentum is stalled by repetitions and is then hastened on by feverish "lists." About 42nd Street, in notes for the book, Klein himself writes as he shoots and designs:

> Street looks like a pin-ball machine, all bumpers lit and bonus and billion and tilt . . . chili-chowder soup from Breughel-Chaplin Studios . . . all back numbers of Drool, Quiver, and Queer . . . Stink-O-Matic, Vomitoriums, Pokerino. . . . Films that have disappeared from every screen except Ankara's or Bangkok's.

One has to flag down the activity of his mind just as one has to catch up with the sense of his pictures. Weird equivalents of each other, words and images comprise a stenography of dazzle, which is perfectly lucid though it lacks logic. Klein's excitement is braced with a sensibility that verges on Pop and is precocious for its time. It was some years later that Oldenburg jotted down these comparable thoughts: "I sing the bawdy electric. I sew the Broadway galactic. I slang the body

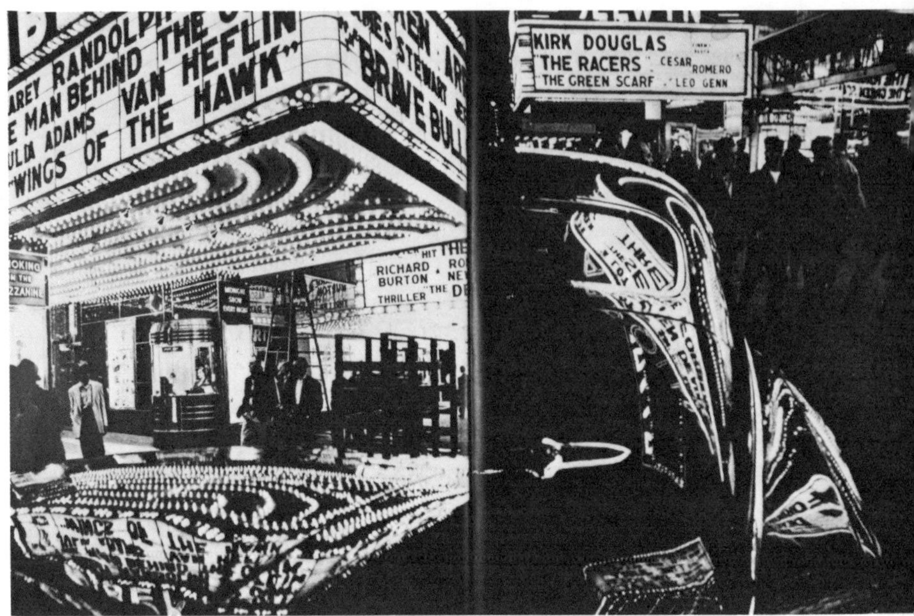

Figure 9. William Klein, *Once the Great White Way, Now a strange kind of side-street side-show* (page spread and abbreviated caption from *New York,* London, 1956).

eclectic. . . . I am for the art of bar-babble, tooth-picking, beer drinking, egg-salting, in-sulting."

To make sense of Klein's first book, I'd have to judge it as a mass of contradictions, some deliberate, others perhaps not. His stance toward his subjects and his viewers is loaded with an antagonism—literally iconoclastic—that is inseparable from a playful punnishness (punishment?). He explodes the sign systems of book design with maximum polemical force, but at the cost of depreciating a number of images which were meant seriously and suffer at the hands of his exposition. Manifest on every page, his gift for parody is not so complacently ironic as that of Pop, nor is it single-mindedly dissident, as is that of John Heartfield, a precursor he may not have known about. Scorn for the intact image and the well-made print is, of course, a feature of the attack against the bourgeois art market that runs through a good many of the modernisms. But because Klein was already an authentic photographer, pictorial ideas of simultaneity and synesthesia involved in, say, the code language of Futurism, could be only an inflammatory overlay.

He came too late to express the Futurist euphoria for the grinding aspects of the city, yet a part of his style is decidedly Futurist in origin. It seems to me that blur, in Klein's pictures, has some of the old scientific rationale. That is, it functions as the optical residue of the motion of bodies in space, alluded to here as a kind of distended placement. It's enough to recall that in Milan in 1952 he aligned a series of vertical abstract paintings that were pivoted to create chance combinations in motion.

It doesn't make much difference whether the effects he achieved in photography are called tonal or linear. Of great interest is the fact that the evident realism of his approach, accentuated by the grittiest motifs, seems in the process of being "steamed out." The power of material comprehension is undermined and countermanded by a vaporous reverie. So the photographic act, for Klein, was a possessive gesture, and its result was a dwindling away, a gradual vanishing of things from sight. These psychic advances and recessions occur in a frame which is activated over and across to its furthest corners. Not people within an urbanscape, not architecture with signs of life, but the whole populated setting, far or close, draws his regard.

To describe the actual situations in his photos is to explain nothing about their capacity to move us. A man walks under the El on a sunny day. A bride opens the door of a car in an outlying neighbor-

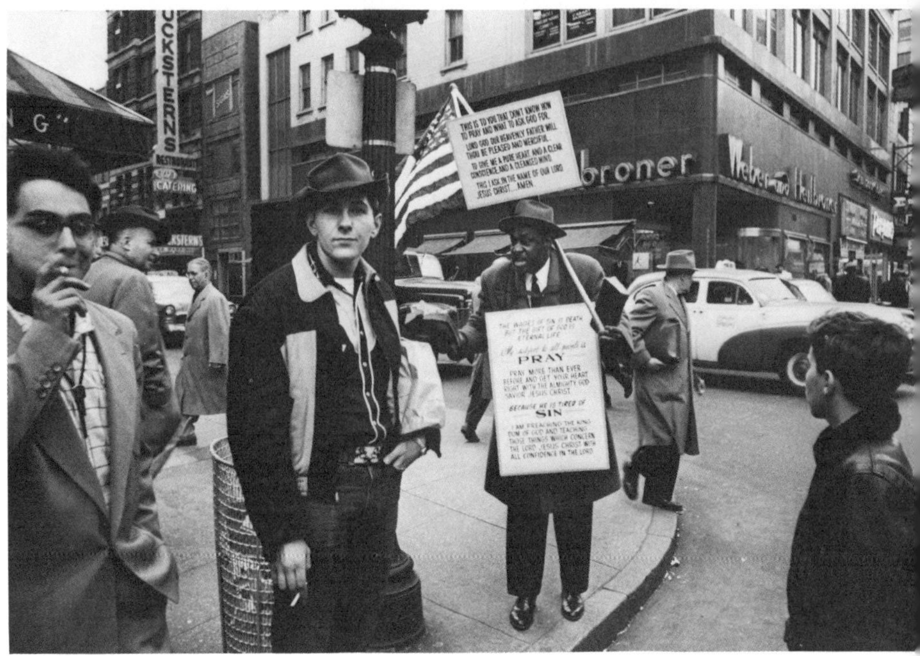

Figure 10. William Klein, *Broadway and 48th Street, 1954–55.*

hood. A black boy, with a floral sport shirt, crouches for his portrait in front of a checkerboard storefront (Fig. 11). And in his book on Rome, there are loafers clowning at a beach, and bemused men looking out from a barbershop at a passerby with a camera. Later, in his Moscow book, there's an oppressive railway station, "Lenin and still Stalin," as he calls it. In an alley, in his Tokyo book, a half-naked man in a hood twists towards us as if in some arcane ritual. These are individual observations, expounding no particular ideas, yet, like scores of others from Klein's travels, they exert an uncanny grip on the imagining mind (Fig. 12). They are strangely noiseless but savage, memorable but not arresting. They give the impression of a bodiless life, other than our own, of societies not exactly alien to those we know or can remember, though they differ from them, as if they existed in a netherworld that corresponds only in its surfaces, not its substance, to the one that sustains us. The poignance of these visions issues from their insubstantiality, for the longer our acquaintance with them the more they appear to transmute everything solid into shadows—until earthiness itself dissolves into little more than flickering light and shade.

The exile of William Klein, I mean from photographic discussion in the United States, strikes me as hard to justify, and the revival of interest in him just now is, I think, very curious. Someone who grasped the medium so easily without prior experience, and who had so many other fish to fry later, has not been treated kindly by our professionals. (Not being one of them, Klein's great advantage lay in not having to unlearn proper photographic conduct. To obtain his freshness Robert Frank had to exert greater effort.) Klein's continued involvement with the international set and anti-Vietnam War politics, his chronic lamination of public opposites, was indigestible to our privatizing 1970s. They did him no justice. In Europe, however, his influence only grew stronger, in the work of Dutch photographer Ed van der Elsken, the Englishman Donald McCullin, and the Czech Josef Koudelka. In Japan those he's affected are numerous. Through his example, the modes of public photojournalism grew seamier and darker in mood, while ambitious photographers were increasingly defecting from it here. The recent exhibitions of William Klein at the Museum of Modern Art (curated by Susan Kismaric) and at Light Gallery in New York, along with the publication of the *Aperture* monograph, offer a glossy restitution for his neglect. One is very thankful for them. They replace the fuse and run the projector for his silent movie. But as the film spools out, it's not at all clear if the timing of

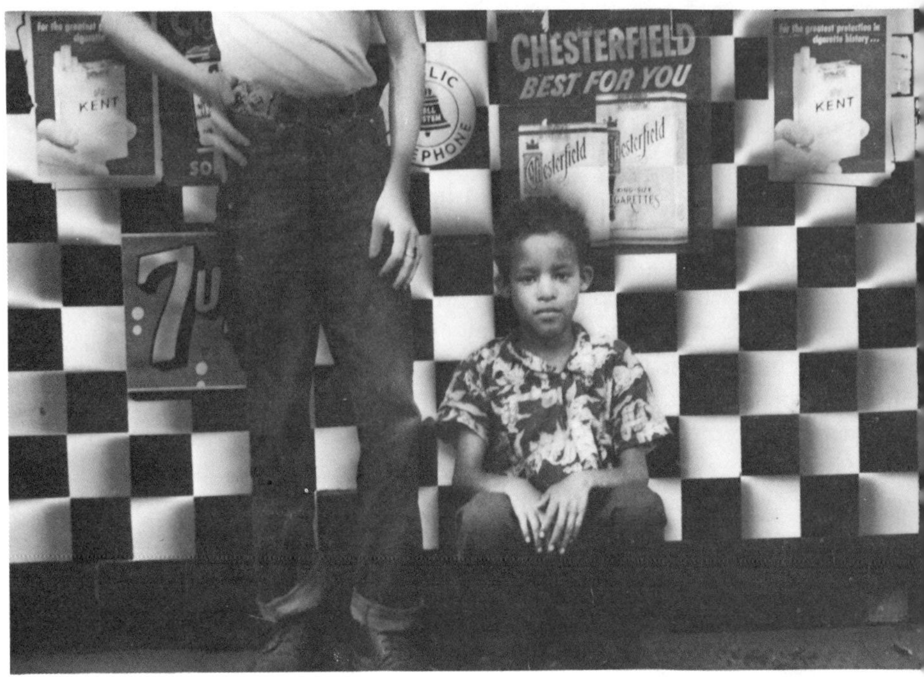

Figure 11. William Klein, *Candy store, Amsterdam Avenue,* 1954.

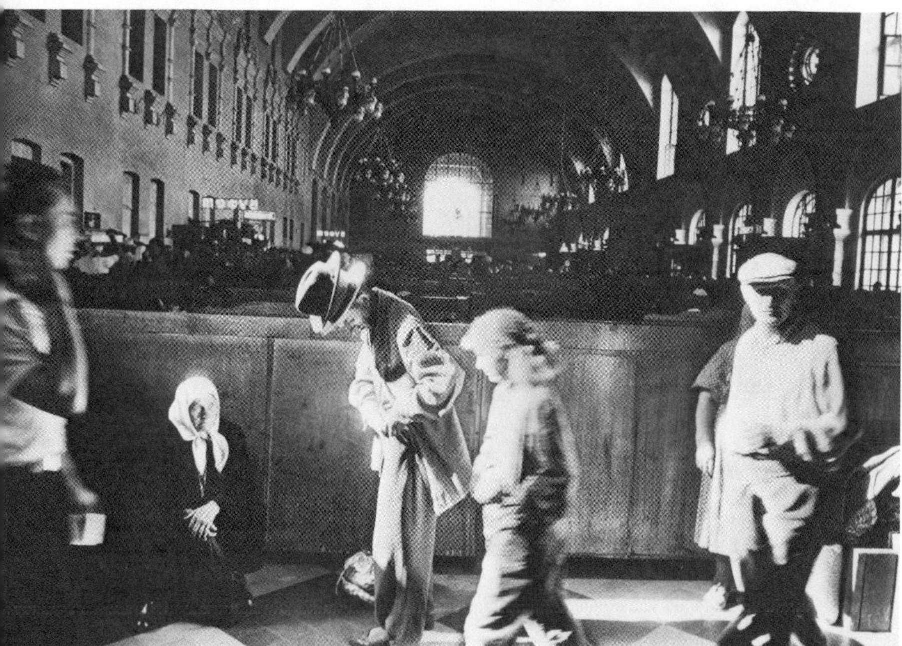

Figure 12. William Klein, *Gare de Kiev, Moscow,* 1959.

this revival reflects consciousness of its real political irony. This poet of the epoch of McCarthy and the bomb is given a long delayed revival during the even more menacing age of Reagan. And the lesson the artist has to teach us is as explicit as ever.

Artforum, *May 1981.*

1. The major photo books published by William Klein are: *Life Is Good and Good for You in New York: Trance Witness Revels* (Great Britain: Photography Magazine, 1956), text in French; *Rome* (New York: Viking Press, 1958); *Moscow* (New York: Crown Publishers, 1964); and *Tokyo* (New York: Crown Publishers, 1964).

The Lights and Darks of Living It Up

So routinely does photography establish banal genres of subject and style that a great deal of valuable turbulence is sometimes released when they are violated. Increasingly, workers seek the tender surfaces of fashion photography, for instance, or advertising, make their incisions, and let the unctuous content squirt out. Some of the iconography and certainly the husk of the older mode remain, but a disturbing, ill-defined expressiveness sets in.

One of the modes in which this has happened is the photography of parties, balls, club dances or cotillions, and openings. Whether formally dressed, or even more aristocratically in casual wear, people at these functions would appear to be mingling among their own kind, with the consciousness of the happy few. A photographer in their midst could only be there, surely, to certify their good manners or high spirits. It's taken for granted that such an outsider is a paid collaborator with the mood to which everyone nominally contributes. If, however, the stranger turns out to be Larry Fink, the results can be unexpected in the extreme.

This New York artist has a knack for probing under the apparently breezy confidence of such occasions. He dissects them visually so that his pictures reveal the more intimately seductive and ephemerally anxious tremors that can rise up in groups. If they solely treated private, funky episodes within semipublic gatherings, they would not be as gripping as they are. More to the point, Fink's work transgresses it "proper" boundaries by a convulsive empathy. One is taken back by the intense, point-blank carnal drama of these society vignettes: the flickering, possessive or dangling hands, the glistening eyes, and the moist hair. At such genteel places as the Colony Club, an unforgettable urgency charges the air. Whenever bold and accepting flesh touch together, or even when there's the silkiest innuendo of it, Fink seems to have been voyeuristically present, handy with his flash. Where is the hired, decorous photographer who would care to show that kind of appetite, behind as well as before the lens?

Parties do offer spectacular opportunities for the cunningly handled camera. A decade ago, Lee Friedlander and Garry Winogrand exploited the centrifugal diffusions and impingements of crowded good times; they took a liking to that kind of chaos. Like the hip street photographers they are, they entangled the scene with sudden openings of near and far, and a whole slew of marginal, mutually divisible episodes bending with the wide angle. All these promiscuous interactions were choreographed with an agility that does credit to the speed of their eyes and the bold dissonance of their compositional sense. Beyond this, though, they had neither ideas nor anything purposeful to say about the specific behavior that froths at parties. Not for a moment did they relinquish their detachment as observers, even at very close quarters. Though deliriously more resourceful than their commercial brethren, they kept to the same social side and distinguished themselves by a brilliant iciness.

Larry Fink, working with similar subjects much more recently, stands in utter contrast to such attitudes. What were spatial connections or disconnections for the others are also psychic ones for him. In his hands, the flashlight is the instrument to gather moral understanding and emotional knowledge. He uses it as a luminous probe that transforms small incident into momentous event. Nevertheless, it veils the action we think we know as much as it serves to highlight it. Above or beneath, to the left or right of a critical business, the light may throw us off the scent. It's as if the animal reflexes and sly plans of his unwitting models are nurtured by a darkness which he has willfully created himself by blazing away elsewhere.

Aside from the astonishing relief and the off-balanced character it gives to the frame, this light converts a momentary glimpse into what looks like a concisely studied theatrical effect. It impresses us not at all as newsy and nosey, as in Weegee, but as voluptuous and even ecstatic. If Fink has a tendency to caricature, it is also wrestled down by his sensuality. These are the two key ingredients of an unstable mixture that infuses a real excitement into his art. From shot to shot, and often within the same picture, he seems possessed by a lively desire to satirize and to embrace the actors on his stage. Then, too, as I mentioned, one notices his tact.

In the early 1960s, Larry Fink studied with Alexey Brodovitch and

Lisette Model. From the one he could have gotten first-hand intimations of high style, and from the second, a decided taste for the grotesque. Earlier than this, while still a teenager in the late 1950s, he had been with his camera among a youth gang in lower Manhattan—"unbelievably angry street poets," as he called them—blowing up cars and taking rough junk. Attracted to their beat mystique, he neither felt like one of them nor "anything else." He had been raised in a middle-class Jewish family of extreme left wing convictions. His own personal rebellion and ideological dissent boiled up furiously during the next several years, alienating him from most of the academic, commercial, and corporate channels beckoning those in his field. Fink regarded himself—because he had given himself no other choice—as a photographer working with people rather than as someone linked by career to a professional community.

In the mid-sixties, he worked for Har-You-Act. When it came under increasingly direct federal sponsorship, the agency and the photographer grew quite suspicious of each other and parted ways. Fink then tried to go slick and self-destructive, hiring himself out to Warhol and *Harper's Bazaar.* "In the final analysis," he reported, "they said come back later when your work isn't so human." Meanwhile, he had gotten to know Diane Arbus, another one-time Model student, and he was aware of Weegee's pictures, whose shots of Harlem and Sammy's bar on the Bowery impressed him particularly. All this was very volatile experience.

There tends to be something—for want of a better word—"romantic" in the make-up of the estranged, politically conscious American photographer, a Danny Lyon, a Gene Smith, a Bruce Davidson. Fink has a whiff of this sensibility as well. Yet, in place of their pity and sadness, which was spurred by the influence of Robert Frank, he expresses his much touchier social ambivalence. He could not heroize poetic outcasts and underdogs. Nor was he out merely to scourge the privileged and monied classes. Much more unprotected in his knockabout youth than Arbus, he felt the powerful allure of the rich, his class enemies. In time, his theme would become the pathos of desire, envy, and ambition. During the 1970s, he discovered a style in which to perfect it.

I first came into contact with his art in a 1972 show at the Diana Gallery, where he posted photos of his family, neighbors, and bar mitzvah celebrations. At the end of protest journalism, he'd felt overextended, far from his inner vision. These tight and hot, homey images were perhaps the first in which he had given himself license to be an artist. And it's significant that whatever his locales since then, ranging from Parsons School art student bashes to beery doings at American Legion halls in rural Pennsylvania, he betrays an almost sibling intimacy with the groups he photographs. It must have been necessary for this trespasser to blend in, with tuxedo or T-shirt as the occasions demanded. Still, one feels that he established a greater rapport with all of them than what mere camouflage allowed. This photography moves with the tide that swelled around it. Merrymakers are not simply objects of his ironic or snide curiosity. Rather, they are fellow human creatures, with their needs hanging out, like his own.

Before saying why I feel that way, let me discuss the view of parties brought out in these photographs. Fink doesn't seem to care what these affairs looked like or even where they were. He takes no inventory of the guests. If there happened to be some main event, he doesn't show it. All these bits of information exist, when they do, only as peripheral fill-up. The theme of which he gives the variations may be high-energy drinking or dancing, but even those are shattered into incandescent fragments. There may have been rock music blasting about or raucous clatter. He provides us dark zones emergent with lighted bodies hearing their own, inner beat.

The party takes shape, then, in a rather ominous space inhabited by introspective beings. The peculiar gravity of that introspection affects even the most fugitive expressions or movements. Weighty matters appear to be pondered in mid-stroke and communication seems to be effectuated only across voids, and with difficulty. Yet the actual gestures are relaxed, entertained, or bemused. We recognize the conviviality of the gathering at the same time that we're baffled by the slowness, or rather the weird suspendedness of its banter. No one poses or gets ruffled—the photographer enjoys an easy passage through the proceedings—and yet the scene, from frame to frame, appears as the most transparent charade of sociability. One senses insecure instinct, or the presence of uncertain or equivocal feeling as it comes through and wins out over assured manner. A party is here visually defined as an array of individual egos in chance conjunction, sometimes pocketed with clandestine anxiety. Real parties as we know or can imagine them, in their dull charm, do not conform to such a reading. Yet for the moment, all humdrum evidence has rhetorically vanished. It is the complete triumph of rampant style over situation.

Nevertheless, Fink's photos, while they slur fairly obvious appearances, also recognize and isolate some concealed social truths. The larger the party, for instance, the more the exchanges within it are

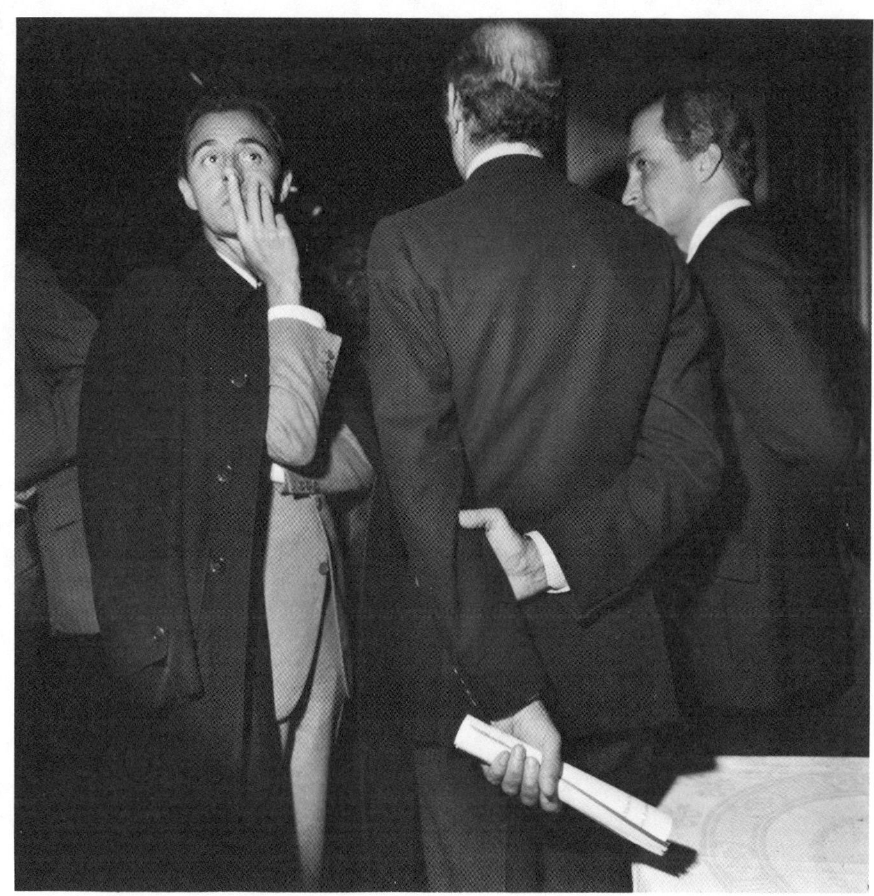

Figure 13. Larry Fink, *Opening of the Rauschenberg retrospective, National Collection of Fine Arts,* 1976.

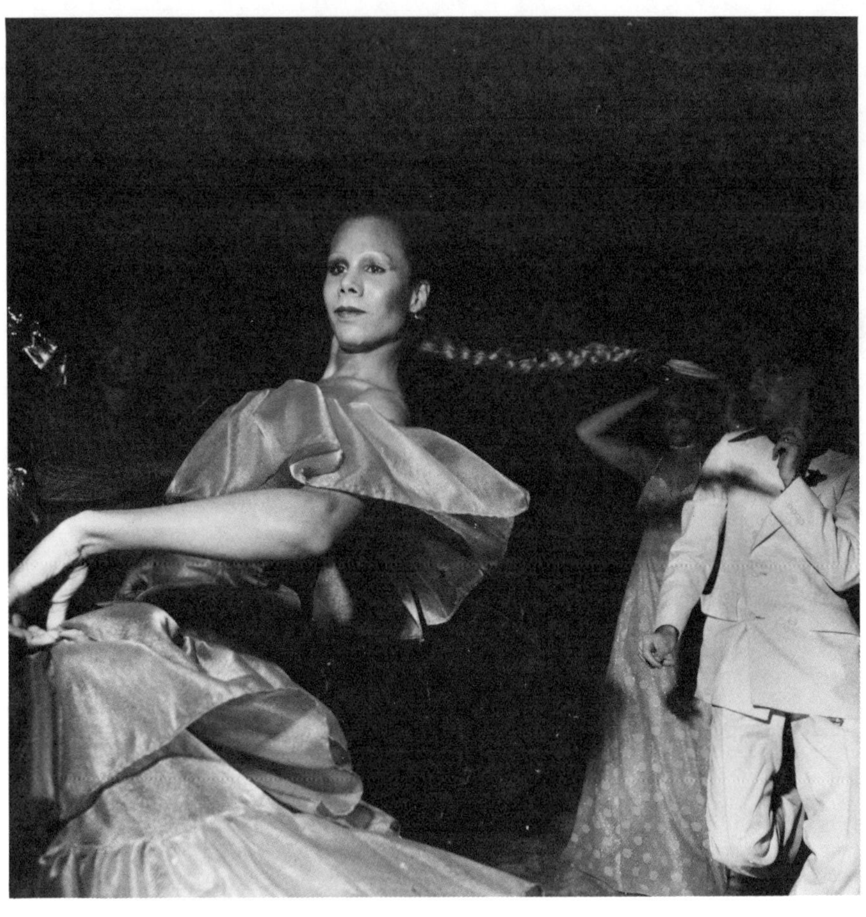

Figure 14. Larry Fink, *Studio 54, New York City,* 1978.

likely to be derailed and unconsummated. People are visibly forced to change psychological gears. Moments of hectic confusion and chinks of unrelatedness open up all around. Fink studies the poignant intervals hemmed in by the fading and blooming of smiles. We can talk about the rhetoric of these pictures, but we can also see how it's responsible for the split-second insights breathed into his subject . . . and our experience.

As the folks at Regine's and Studio 54 kick up their heels, the photographer makes us aware, too, of what's been called the "me first" narcissicism of the seventies (Fig. 14). He maneuvers with his historical consciousness, which is just as important as his photographic timing. And he's not bashful in showing his personal animus. The cheery grimaces, stifled yawns and decadent emptiness which he shows doubtless existed subliminally when he happened upon them. But he inscribes them with such hyperbolic ease that they seem to us astonishing fictions. Contrarily, his manic tempo also serves the exposure of grace, a quality he couldn't have dreamed up either, though how it could have been as emphatically visible in the flesh as he shows it in his work, one doesn't know.

It's not enough, of course, to speak of this art as having pungent graphic contrasts, fluently arranged. His flash casts the privileged set into the most luridly sinister depths, where the fruitiest scandals are hatched. At the same time, the light caressingly beautifies all sorts of bodily features ejected from that darkness. Here, the photographer's chiaroscuro works judgmentally as much as it does formally.

Fink is fascinated by a gentility whose languor he fashions into arabesques of startling iconic strength. He catches, for instance, the obeisant face of a woman in the custody of male conversation and places her under the drooping neck of a deceased swan or goose in a Baroque painting on the wall behind. Actually, the very form of these photographs recalls Baroque luminism, Caravaggio's especially. Certainly Fink, in his own way, is as vehement, tendentious, and profane. Oddly enough, these qualities of temperament and style do not sensationalize his theme. Rather, they work to normalize the flawed humanity of his subjects, and to make them, in the end, less remarkable and more like ourselves.

This imagery has to be located, too, in its more immediate tradition, that of Weegee and Arbus, whose artistic potentialities he mingles into a dazzling new amalgam. Instead of the comic hysteria of Weegee's losers, or the self-implicating hardness with which Arbus lighted her defective subjects, Fink impulsively wants to close the

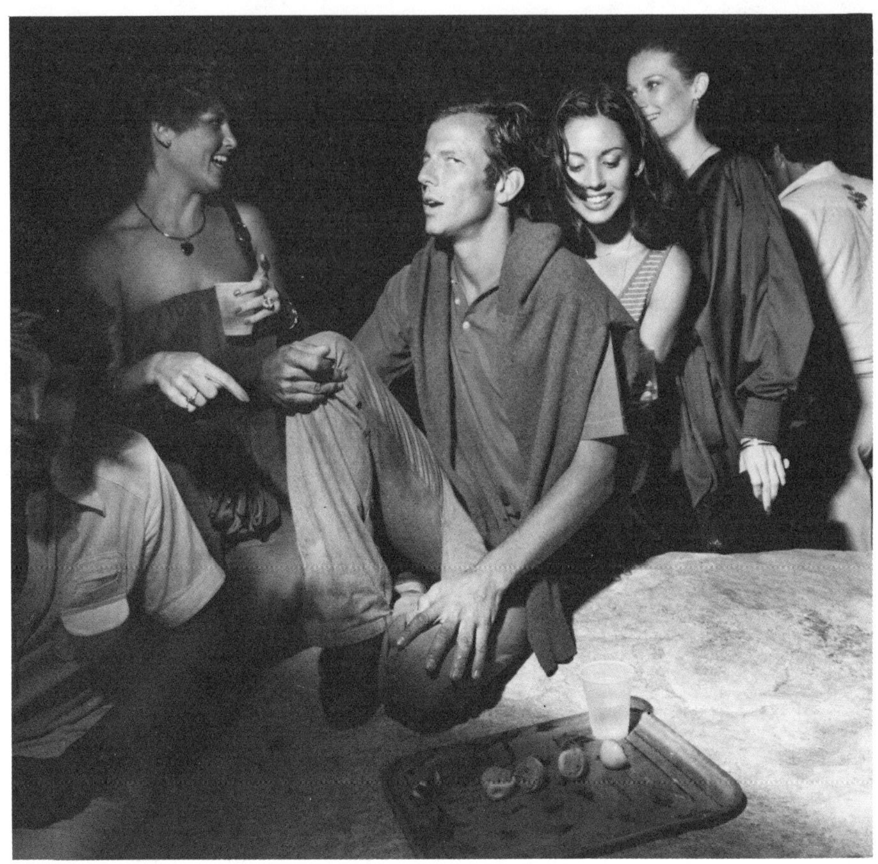

Figure 15. Larry Fink, *Peter Beard, Montauk Point, Long Island,* 1977.

psychic distance between himself and those "others." It's as if the more he becomes aware of his outside status, the more he aims to shed it and to wallow in the action. He carries on, incredibly, as one who has special, uncomfortable knowledge of, and long ties of affection with, those in the milieus he photographs. His visceral identification with his figures is strong, yet Fink maintains a crucial detachment, one of consciousness and intent. For while they play he is at work.

Art in America, *September 1979.*

II

The Illusions of the Pose

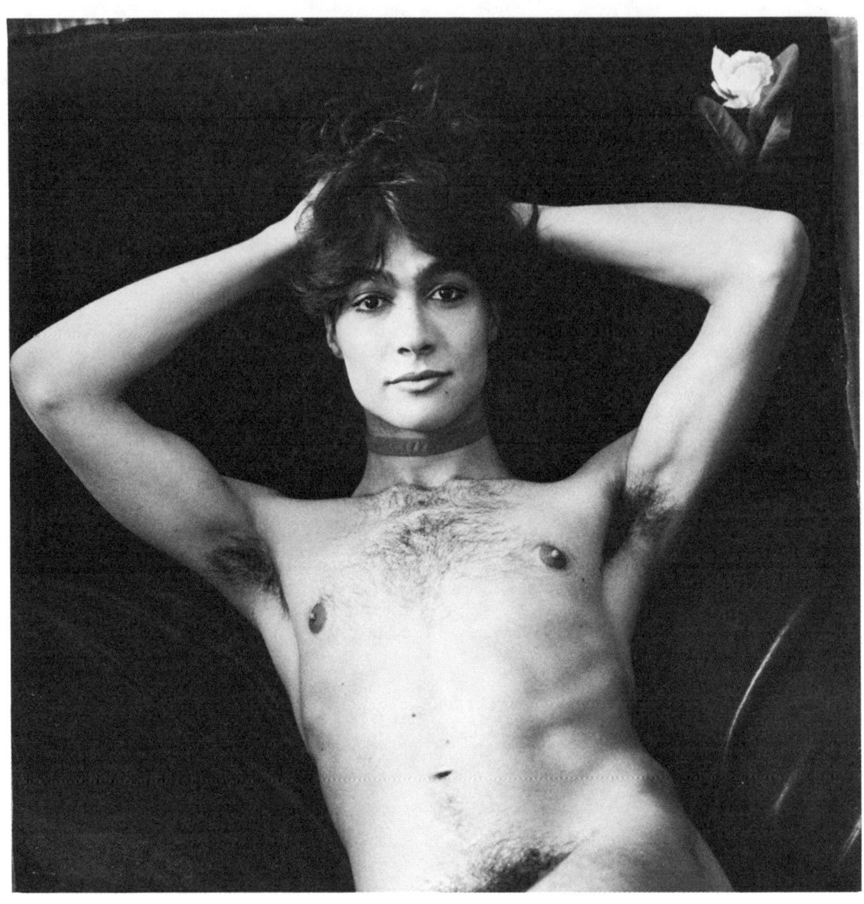

Figure 16. Joel-Peter Witkin, *The Beautiful Man,* 1982 (Copyright © 1986 by Joel-Peter Witkin, courtesy Pace/MacGill Gallery, New York, and Fraenkel Gallery, San Francisco).

Contention Between Two Critics About a Disagreeable Beauty

Critic 1: It seems that we're slated to disagree again. We just came away from a session with Joel Peter Witkin's photographs, but it's as if we had been at a movie, and as we left, looking into each other's face, I saw in yours the wrong expression. I'm dumbfounded that you're able to smile.

Critic 2: I know what you mean about the movie because I've often sauntered out from one with friends and been astonished, in the light, that they were frowning. *So many feuds start out that way, with a flick. Just when you think you know a person very well, it turns out that you don't, especially when it comes to something as considerable as a taste preference. But I don't want to make an issue of it. Witkin's subject matter, alone, is so reflex-jabbing and sensational that I can well understand people recoiling from it. In any event, there's much more to his work than subject, and, as I haven't sorted out why I feel as positively as I do, we can just chalk this one down to instinctive differences and let it go.*

No, it's too big a mystery. This is self-evidently meretricious art, and I want to know how you can possibly defend it. Incompatible ideas should be compelled to fight one another rather than be permitted to coexist peacefully.

What a heavy thing to say, not least because it was touched off by a smile! Besides, I'm rather a pacific person, and I turn reluctant and defensive when someone invites me to lock horns.

This isn't a setup. If I know you as I think I do, it's just staggering that an unaggressive man, with your values, should be attracted by the photography of Joel Peter Witkin. The two of you are quite miscast for each other. It's hard-core stuff, and you've got such elusive, oblique critical strategies. I know that you've been thinking and are prepared to write about his work. Here you are, an upstanding type with a positive outlook, a humanist who likes virtue and deplores vice. Above all, a spokesman for a gentle and civil conduct of affairs. Yes? Now, it appears, you're turned on by a photographer who employs every belligerent, sick trick in the book. We won't even talk about how his doctoring and doping of negatives offends your well-known rhetoric in favor of straight photography. It's enough to list his subject concerns: necrophilia, homosexuality, masochism, sadism—those photos just screech and reek of sheer degeneracy—from your point of view. If photographs could smell, Witkin's would stink of semen and formaldehyde! There appears to be enough hot hatred there of women, life, and loving to sizzle all your good intentions right off the page. If you endorse his work, you approve of imagery you understand to be antisocial. If your friends don't tell you that, I don't know who will.

The truth is, I'm not "attracted" by Witkin's art, but I'm certainly drawn to it. And you've missed a few of his other interests in your list: blasphemy, transvestism, fetishism, and other assorted depravities. It's a smorgasbord of crazes and, come to think of it, it's wonderful work.

I'm genuinely surprised. That's very unequivocal. Could I have underestimated you? Instead of being a prevaricator you may be a provocateur.

Me, provocative? I'm a critic. But, as a civilian, I suppose I have all the conventional horrified reactions to the cruel themes of Witkins's work. If I was attuned to the infliction of pain I wouldn't trust my reactions as much as I do.

I take your point that a personal interest or a prior erotic attachment leads to a form of critical overalignment (though an experienced person might just have something more revealing to say about Witkin than you). Still, it seems to me that with this you verge dangerously close to a critical theory of art that keeps you insulated from the psychology to which the work alludes. By that reckoning, you'd feel freer to react the less relevant worldly experience you had, and you'd feel freest if you had none. That's—no, let me go on—that's obviously impossible, or, better, foolish. Who would want to trust a know-nothing as a critical guide? We're not in a court of law, though even there the assumption is that juror inexperience—meaning incompetence—leads toward objectivity. A fatuous idea. Instead of setting you up as an authority, I would have thought that your innocence of Witkin's world, or ignorant repugnance, would tend to disqualify you.

Are you any more "qualified" in that respect?

No.

Then let me explain myself. I make no pretense to be "objective." And as for my conventional, and therefore nonexistent, background in Witkin's iconography, it can't be helped. I have to start looking from where I am, and if at the end of my contact with the art I'm somewhere else, well, something has happened. (I know these remarks have as much piquancy as beancurd.) If Witkin's work simply confirmed what I already knew, or reinforced my special tastes, very little would have happened. Not that increased knowledge was ever a chief goal of art (though it often is of photography not intended as art).

And can there be any doubt that these photographs are artistic creations, almost rabidly artistic, rotten with old-master references and poetic at all costs? To strip art down to its so-called informational content or ideological components is a philistine error—however much the artistic aim may be embroiled with them. The same applies to the idea that the depiction of real nastiness, let us say, incriminates the picture maker. Reciprocally, you're in no position to say that a viewer moved by such work has some covert allegiance to wickedness, or behaves hypocritically by aestheticizing it. You're a sophisticated member of the art world, so you know the difference between a moral outlook and an artistic message. It's always a question of finding one's own morality, rather than imposing it. Imagine how little modern art we'd have if it were restricted to those areas where people were consistently upbeat in their lives, and never caused each other grief. We wouldn't have any tragedy, either, or even worse, any comedy. As for Witkin's art, what's really disturbing is that his mode is neither tragic nor comic, but lyric—and rapturously lyric at that.

It sounds as if you've come over to my viewpoint now, and have defected from your usual theory about ripped-off people in photographs implicating their viewers, instilling us with guilt. By the way, what do you mean when you say you're disturbed by Witkin's rapturous lyricism (not that I agree with the epithet)?

Heaven knows, we've seen a lot of grimness and gore in photography—the usual context being that they're reported on. The sad canon of such work makes you wonder about people's inhumanity to each other—it can cause indignation, get you angry at violence and malaise (Robert Capa, Ron Haeberle, the Auschwitz album, and so on). The resonance is tragic. And there are inflammatory political lessons that are learned or repeated. But don't you think that Witkin exhibits a positively glandular euphoria over such noxious stuff? He's an authentically Sadean artist of high ambition—someone I'm reluctant to deal with, and who is fortunately rare. It's not his subject matter alone that upsets me, it's his processing of it—and the circumstances that contribute to his style, or are necessary to his impact.

How should I put it? His artistic form is "on the side of" pain—a world that comes into its own for his lens. He is electrified by death and is in conspiracy with the torturers. I look and am taken into their shameless confidence. At the same time, this is a very serious affirmation, not at all an entertainment, cynical or otherwise. In horror movies, we can derive a pleasure from being scared; in Witkin, I'm scared because of his pleasure! And he'll do anything he can to make me accept it, not because he's socially inclined toward me or anyone else, but because he's so radically self-absorbed, like an artist.

You say the artist scares you, by virtue of his pleasure, no less. What is this, hypersensitivity or garden-variety paranoia? Whichever, your condition sounds pretty regressive. It's an artist's right to be absorbed in artistic processes—we don't expect and don't like an artist's indifference to the execution of the work. Apparently you can accept the condition of a photograph as a report on gore, but you take issue when an *artist* internalizes a gory theme. Somehow the reporter is innocent while the artist can be reprehensible. Yet, if the difference is between witnessing something and metaphorical engagement with it, what has Witkin actually shown that compares in the least, say, with Donald McCullin's photographs in Africa, Cyprus, or Vietnam? I don't have to tell you that the spilling of real blood is on another level of existence from kinky charade.

You mean that the one is entirely disproportionate to the other, and, of course, I agree . . . as a general statement. The act of bearing witness to war doesn't ordinarily implicate the witness or viewers by any rapport with the atrocity. Even when the photographers belong to the same party as those who have slain. What is the relation of the one who records to the things that have been recorded? We can't say that the photographer has caused or even permitted terrible events (their effect is another matter entirely). If it were not a literal outsider in its dealing with such events, the photograph could not be called a report. Such a report is intensified by the way it signifies that reality is a fait accompli, that the awfulness would have occurred—did occur—regardless of whether the photographer was there or not. (Naturally, the framing editorializes it, and the eventual context prejudices that reality through and through—but that's a different question.)

It's obvious what's coming next. The artist photographer, you will say, takes reponsibility for the subject, either through having brought it about or through an arrangment and encouragement of it, and therefore has *created* a reality. But I can't call the result a reality; nor can you. Witkin's scenes are fictions, his people are actors playing a role, with the exception of the cadavers—whom, I presume, he has not bumped off ahead of time. It would be ridiculous to say that they were playing the role of dead people. Witkin's work approaches still life or, at best, a tableau-vivant, not action. He may be largely in control of the proceedings, but they are not of *consequence.* At least not of any historical consequence. Even if there are moral provocations, they are strictly bound up, and subservient to, his metaphorical strategies. So I fail to see why you're still spooked, as if there were things that actually happened in these photos.

Work of this sort strikes me as an antidote to the numbing effects of photoreportage. We become desensitized to fatality, for it's photographed every hour by those whose professional detachment becomes, in the end, infectious. Oh, I don't know. Maybe we need to protect ourselves from this kind of everyday nightmare. But I didn't feel protected or prepared for the magnitude of what Witkin has to offer—because of his revelation of the desire *for cruelty. Certainly he hasn't given us a "snuff" movie, but that is no cause for gratitude, only a restraint that makes him discussable. The war photograph inflicts me with my very real helplessness in the face of what it presents. It's like a crime photograph writ large, even if it happens to frame fewer bodies. War is sanctioned and escalated crime—historical enough—but in still photography, the carnage of it recedes. You ask, "Why had it come to that?" A good question. Lebanon, for example. But in Witkin's work you can almost ask, "How can* he *come to that?"—the kind of attitude that leads to bodies, the production of dead bodies. You're in a universe in which things seem to go wrong genetically. No war photograph quite gives you such unusual access to morbid states. . . .*

Of what?

Of consciousness, of animal release that isn't good. There's a difference between seeing the results of the killer instinct and anticipating them. In that sense, the bodies in these photographs might be the most terrible images, but they are the least frightening.

For me, you know, it's the contrary. With the bodies (deceased through natural causes or not), Witkin realizes his aesthetic goals with the least amount of artifice. It's possible to be skeptical about a dramaturgy that has to extend itself too far in order to match the apparent

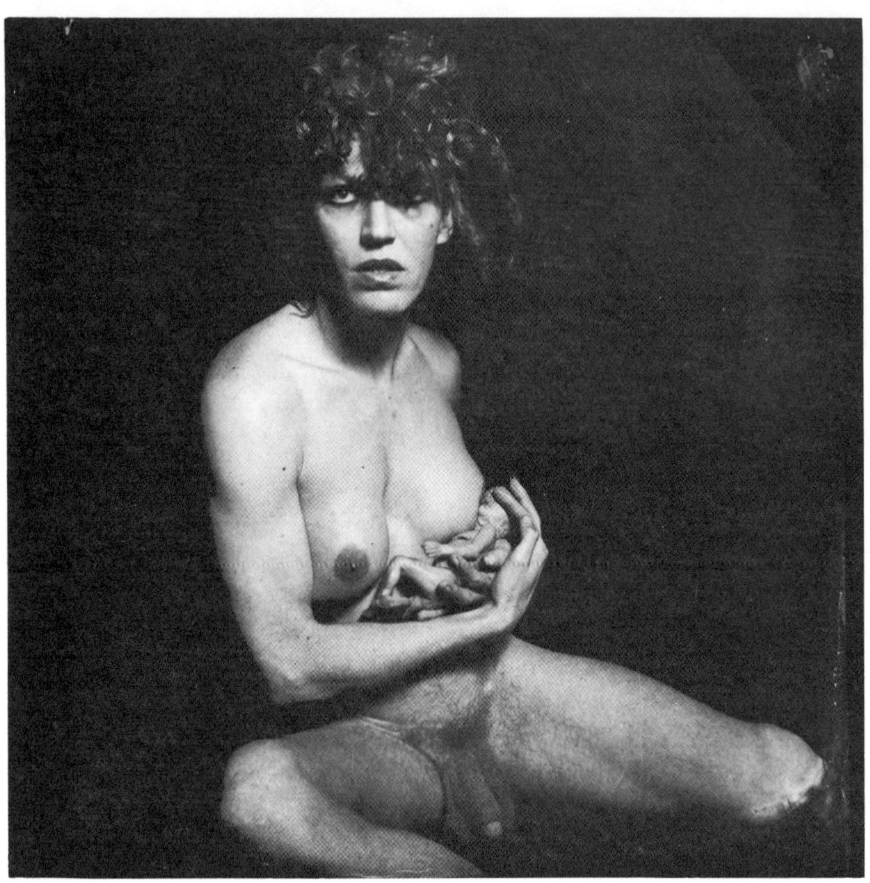

Figure 17. Joel-Peter Witkin, *Androgyny Breastfeeding a Fetus,* 1981 (Copyright © 1986 by Joel-Peter Witkin, courtesy Pace/MacGill Gallery, New York, and Fraenkel Gallery, San Francisco).

extremity of the subject matter. But Witkin protests his aestheticism instead of activating it. In the play of dramatic personages only the dissected ones strike home into my feelings, give me an irreducible shock. I am in the presence of ghastly images that have been discovered and not contrived. The medical circumstances are conflated with far older medieval and Mannerist descriptions of ravenous, wormy decay. These are, no doubt, autopsy specimens that have been roughly cut or sliced by metal. Just the same, Witkin has arranged the vertically split head of an old man so that it appears to kiss itself on velvet, and he photographed the profile of an opened OD'd young woman close-up, and tenderly. Compared to this loveliness among the maggots, how am I to respect the merely Guignol effects of all the rest? The hot breath of the apparent doesn't compete with the cool beauty of the actual.

Were it only so simple! I don't find anything "apparent" about the quite real fetuses that crop up in some of his pictures, and that singular creature who sports a penis as well as mammaries, a legless man, or Fist Fuck, *where half an amputated arm vanishes into an anus. Were he to have* painted *any of these subjects they would have been more or less sensational invented icons; here he does much worse and bears witness to them.*

Having said that, I'd also say that he gives us a mix in which irremediable states are mated with transitory or inferential ones. The Wife of Cain, *I presume, has ceased being pregnant since 1980. And it's hard to imagine that man's testicles still being stretched by a pullied weight over his head a year later. As for the inferential, how about the expression of the naked androgyne, suckling a fetus* (Fig. 17), *so concerned it reminds me of Dorothea Lange's* Migrant Mother? *Call them one-shot abominations, if you will. Call them setups! Whether directed by the model or imposed by the photographer, decked with symbolic trappings or not, these scenes once existed and now engage me in a war of nerves. "The actual" and "the apparent" do incest before my eyes. Show me where these images are only hot-breathed or cold. Far from being one or the other, they're feverishly both.*

Well, I see that more credit than I thought has to be given Witkin for exploring what you call "the irremediable." That takes him well past Diane Arbus, Hans Bellmer, George Platt Lynes, Les Krims, and Robert Mapplethorpe, I grant you. He's an authentic bad boy. But in raising their stakes he also magnifies their problems. His subjects are so inherently abused in the flesh that he has to serve them up with an allegorical gravy in order to make them palatable. Such titles as *Expulsion from Paradise of Adam and Eve* (Fig. 18), *The Capitulation of France*

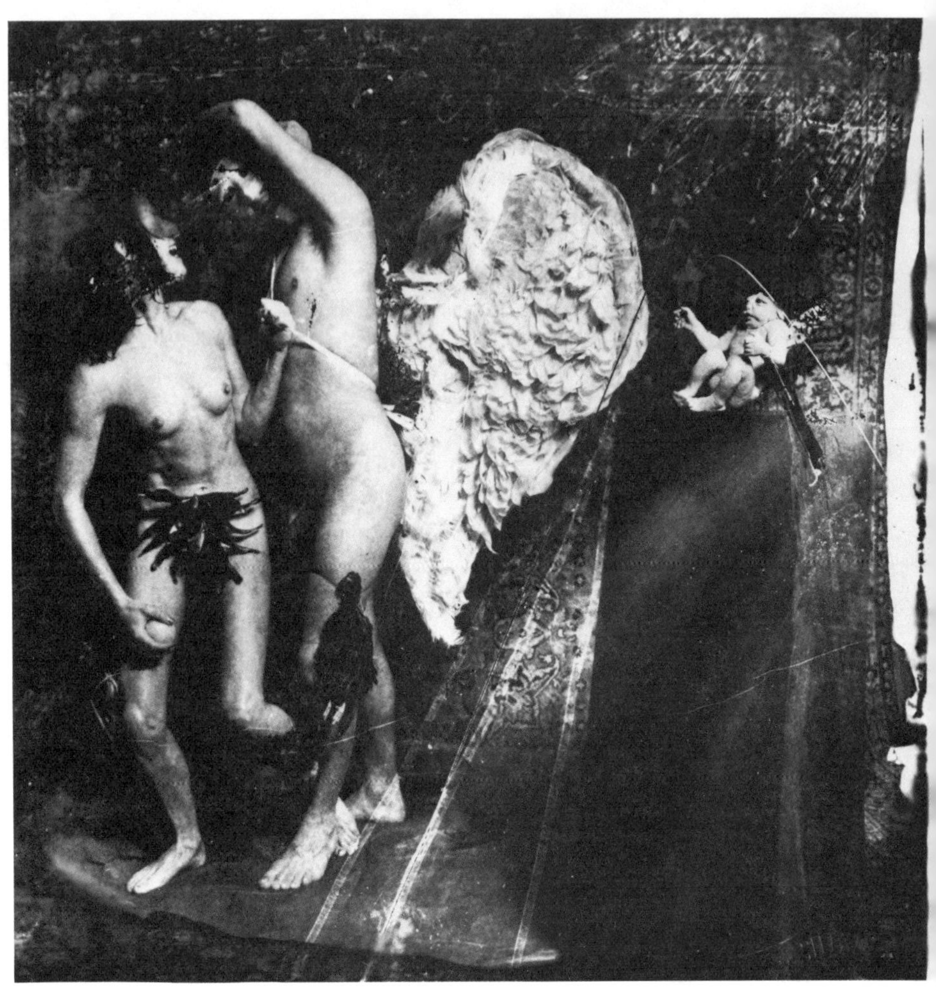

Figure 18. Joel-Peter Witkin, *Expulsion from Paradise of Adam and Eve,* 1981 (Copyright © 1986 by Joel-Peter Witkin, courtesy Pace/MacGill Gallery, New York, and Fraenkel Gallery, San Francisco).

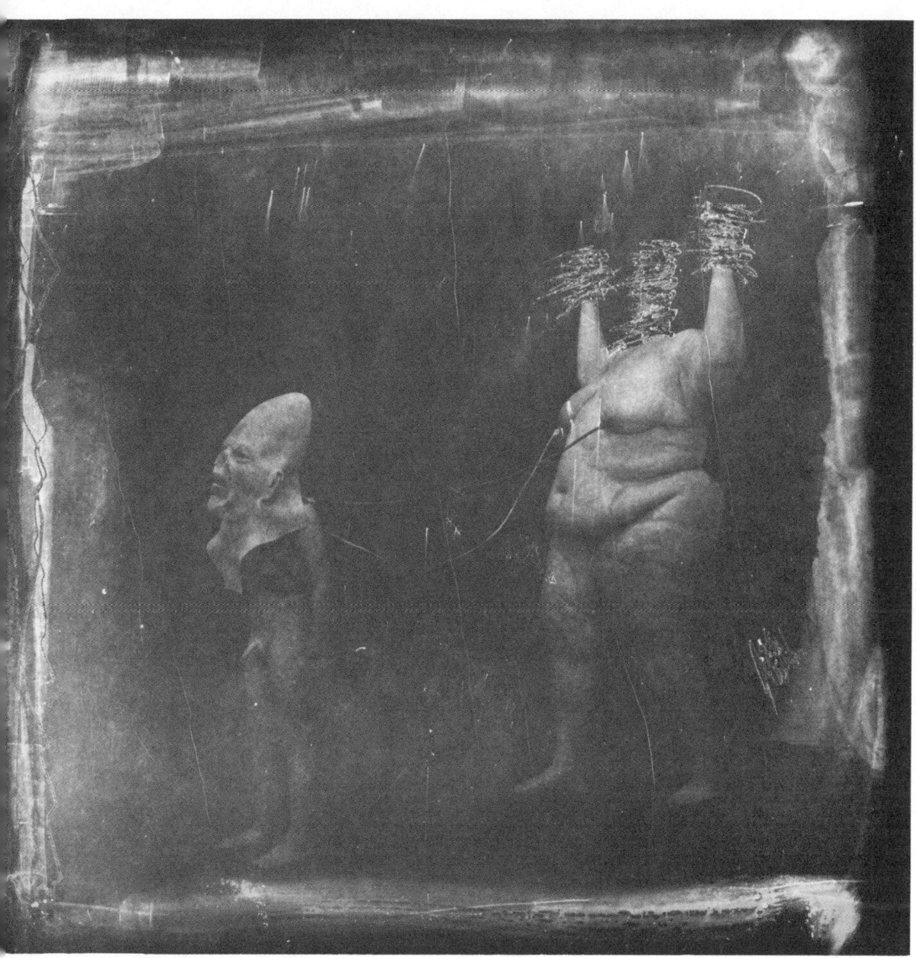

Figure 19. Joel-Peter Witkin, *The Capitulation of France,* 1983 (Copyright © 1986 by Joel-Peter Witkin, courtesy Pace/MacGill Gallery, New York, and Fraenkel Gallery, San Francisco).

(Fig. 19), or *Pygmalion and Galatea,* to take only a few, indicate his pretensions. That's the trouble with so many of these people: involved with gamey material, they have to demonstrate how *raffiné* they are. It's not surprising how easily these naughty men, and a nervy woman—or rather, their work—get on with *chic,* the chic crowd. It's a chain reaction, downward, into the furbelows of tastefulness. If I don't sympathize with Witkin's art-historical posturing it's because I find it dispensable—and the moments in which he really gets me are free of it.

I can't help noticing that the work has negative attributes for you, partly because it is appreciated by people whom you disapprove of—the "chic" crowd. Even when stigmatized by fashion, some art, don't you think, can still retain merit? More important, haven't you allowed your attitudes toward an artist's (assumed) public to affect your judgment, so that—well—it may not be just your unique organism I'm dealing with, but some highly socialized class biases.

I see no reason to revise my opinion about a market environment in which a certain kind of art makes a strong appeal. That may just be a handy way of confirming the instinctive reaction that I do have.

How, even if true, does that really bear on the problem—my uncertainties and your convictions?

Because art is tagged by its patrons, and their identity can illuminate its rhetoric. There's nothing to restrain me from reading backward like this and discovering how an artist's intentions can be reflected quite accurately by their coterie, and their specific institutional network. These are social exchanges, the artist and his audience are in the world, and am I not, too, in the social world?

I thought you'd never ask!

Oh Oh! That was particularly devious of you.

Maybe. But my point was a general one, you see, because it's necessary to stress how very impure our reactions are—that our 'instincts" are already highly socialized, to begin with, and that even if we were to make some reductive definition of them, as you did, they rarely operate in isolation from other factors that push us on. Our drives are affected by and affect our reasoning and our sociality. Just the same, the social projection is by no means the whole story.

I assert that this man has *pandered* to an audience, which is an inauthentic position for an artist. You hedge on the social aura of these pictures, yet you deny any instinctual priority—you're in limbo.

I have to acknowledge that I'm glad you said that, even though it emphasizes what's hard to follow in my argument. I find it hard, curiously hard, to empathize with people in photographs who flirt, as you say, with the enactment of their own pain, or who undergo pain willingly for a photographer. Photography brings us faraway peoples, remote customs, bizarre practices of other cultures, dead acts. That is, it habitually acquaints us with communities that are strange to us, or out and out different. Yet the citizens of Cuzco in 1929, or of Madagascar in 1859, are well within my family, compared to these self-punishers in San Francisco in 1981! To me, they are the ultimate others. By excluding everything else, Witkin says to me, this is the present and the imminent future.

What I would want never to happen to me his people mime or undertake—as Witkin insists—with large good humor and complaisance. Such a divide takes my breath away. It makes me feel closer with everyone else in the world—an unexpected and valuable solidarity. You know I'm pretty concerned with the transactional character of photographic experience. How does a viewer relate to the material in the picture as something that actually happened, as human and social action? If it were a question of one more exotic group of outsiders, relative to me as to other insular viewers, I could accommodate his art—and there would be no limbo. On the contrary, he gives me to understand that I'm *an outsider to those who collaborate with him in these unspeakable practices, these frightful and aboriginal rites. And then, with amazing chutzpah, he implies that I'm missing something—that he and they are having all the fun! At the precise instant that I realize my strong alienation from his subjects (that is, right away), he blithely, though with considerable art, works to dissolve it by his invitational stance. As soon as I know that I will not empathize, the photographs declare that I can and even that I should. He anticipates or outflanks my desire to disconnect from subject matter with which it's impossible for me to be engaged. That is the limbo and you will admit that it is unusual.*

Tell me, then, are you having any fun? . . . No answer. You're foundering, really, in your own ambivalence.

It's certainly no fun to try to given an account of myself to you. Yes—no—I'm not having fun. Who enjoys being blocked like this, and who can fail to be moved by it?

Many! Your introspection, apropos Witkin, resembles run-ins you've had with the avant-garde, which in the past you've often rejected because of its obscurity and arrogance.

Not so in this case. When I complained then, it was because I felt depreciated or demeaned and used. Chris Burden, for instance. His documentary (really publicity) photographs—completely insignficant in themselves—reported self-abusive acts: shooting or crucifying himself. I hope I don't sound callous when I say there was no return in that. Burden was merely gesturing within a context that had an avant-garde structure. Witkin is no avant-gardist. He's not testing how far he can go, in an utterly detached way. Witkin is a romantic. He's contemporary, very 1980s. He doesn't depreciate himself or his people or me by what he does—no matter how depraved the tone. And the photographs are highly significant in their processing.

Well, the limbo still exists, by your own admission. And I'll put on file that strange bit—strange, coming from you—that no depreciation is involved in the experience of his work. In your terms, he seems to have deprived you of the luxury of feeling guilt over the sadness of his people, and then of expiating your privileged remorse by admiring the photography. What I see in your argument is a quickly improvised scheme to salvage intellectually the disintegrative liking you have for this guy's art. It doesn't give me pleasure to see you in this fix.

I suppose the *ideal* shock of Witkin's photography would derive from its character of revelation. He himself often chooses to interpret it as religious revelation, but we're talking about the psychosocial response to his images. Or your response. You discover that you cannot accommodate this work because it postpones and twists the notion you have that Witkin's subjects should be outsiders to your experience, and therefore in a more or less pitiable state. Suddenly, the artist makes you think that you may be in the pitiable, powerless state. I think it's novel for you to entertain the idea, that it's strangely comfortable.

Any disequilibrium in the power relation between myself, as a viewer, and photographed subjects makes me uneasy and is probably inevitable. I'm anxious when I can intuit an advantageous or disadvantageous position for myself—and I'm bored when I can't. Witkin really tips the scales in a problematic way, so that naturally, I'm very interested.

Obviously, outsider status is not my exclusive prerogative when looking at photographs. Nor is it yours. I've gone into this, off and on. "Outsiderness," if you excuse the term, is our lot in this context. I mean simply that we weren't there, and I also mean that we don't know what happened (although, in Witkin, we can well guess). So this is an automatic alienation, which we all share and which unites us. Our physical insulation from the pictured scene, even if the setting is familiar to us, is a given. No doubt this is to trivialize the word "alienation," but this is nevertheless the estranging rule from which we all have to start when we look at these pictures. Special empathies, knowledge, or prior exposure to the subject, depending on personal circumstances, will bring some of us closer to (or take us further from) the content of the photograph. I'm interested in the mutual foundations of our regard. And, therefore, I search out what is nominally common in our approach—something that levels us when we start treating photographic culture itself. I think we start by recognizing that we're external to the depicted scene. And that implies that another reality, not the one we're in, has been presented to us. It can look just like ours, but it isn't. Meanwhile, we do know that it once existed, and this awareness produces a kind of suction. It draws us in.

Why on earth are you interested in leveling? It really bothers me that you use so liberally those words "us," "we," "our." Don't you see that your readers can be put off by your assumptions? I'm equally put off by your equation of your "conventional" and "insular" self with other viewers—in the teeth of your very peculiar involvement with this art. It's a rhetoric of false inclusiveness. Count me out!

I hope not. For one thing, I want to be able to talk to you—or to talk out of, and past, myself. What does the relation of the writer to the reader amount to if it is not based on a social contract, an assumed possibility of communication, and understandable terms of reference? As viewers all *of us are outsiders to the pictured events. That's why I can use the word "we"—the vast number of us who weren't there. Witkin's extremists excite interest, not because they're the center of attention, but because they disport themselves as if their desire is unexceptionable—and we're at the margins. I want to be able to convey this topsy-turvy matter—with all its disturbances—to readers.*

In order to do that, I have to assume not only that we confront photography, and its unique challenges as a medium, together, but that my sexual makeup and my morality are clear to those who hear me or read me. It's not so terrible to be a sounding board, to have average responses, believe me. They allow me to be grated like mad by Witkin, to experience the full, disagreeable beauty of his work.

Do you, then, in the "full" presumption of your averageness, imagine that you are some arch-representative of the majority of audience attitudes, that you can speak on behalf of people you don't know? That they must agree with you because *you* have taken on for yourself, and headed off, their unspoken sexual makeup and morality?

Oh. No . . . no, no!

One "no" would have been enough.

I didn't mean . . .

Don't get embarrassed. You just don't want to feel too alone. We know about that, we critics. How often do we extend ourselves or expose ourselves without any kind of visible repercussion or sense that it makes a difference, that people are interested or listening? Of course, I'll concede that if critics don't seek support and credence beyond the immediately interested party they won't deserve much response, either. But you see how self-entangled you get when you try to build bridges. You're a white, middle-aged, heterosexual male; but I could easily show you how less and less typical you are of those around you. What a strange perspective—your humble grandiosity! There's a kind of sympathy that overreaches itself and becomes obtuse. Actually, your ego is strongest and most authentic, most valuable to your fellows, only when it does not imagine there are others like it. You felt you had to get the audience on your side *against* Witkin's subjects. There's a writer, Hugh Prather, who's worth quoting here: "The principle seems to be: It's a 'fault' if I am also capable of it, a disease if I am not."

I stand corrected. Yes, we're all encapsulated in our idiosyncracies, which surpass the understanding and can't be leveled. Maybe your phrase my "humble grandiosity" catches something idiosyncratic about me that I haven't considered. I wonder if it isn't possible to see sadomasochism, Witkin's thematic, as oxymoronic, too. That figure of speech comes very close to evoking what is dreamlike in Witkins's work, its use of opposite and self-cancelling terms.

Since you mention it, we can get back to the work, which you still haven't slapped into life for me. Would you please explain what you meant about the art being "very contemporary, very 1980s"? It seems quite passé to me. You talk about this photography as simultaneously embracing you in it psychic pull and putting you off. I see it as very nineteenth-century in its references—and therefore very far from suggesting questions like "How can he come to that?" Witkin's processing, his use of tissue over the paper in enlargement, his dribbling and soiling of the negative with potassium ferrocyanide, his sepia toning, the way he scratches and scrawls on the negative—all this suggests his infatuation with age, the mortality of that object which is the image. Nothing could be further from *anticipating* the killer instinct, as you put it. On the contrary, he gazes backward, and elaborates the conceit that his work has survived accidently, like E.J. Bellocq's, in a distressed and battered state. The more these photos seem to have gone through a hard time, the more they aspire to a retro-justification—as if earlier, obviously benighted viewers, compared to us, had wanted to kill them. The only interesting thing to come out of this is the impression that to view Witkin's pictures in the present is to rescue them from an undeserved oblivion.

Oh, and one further idea. Nineteenth-century photographers tended to scrutinize their subjects, while twentieth-century ones glance at theirs. The scrutiny is imperious and encyclopedic, a protracted and relentless visual exam which assumes that things are indefinitely available for study. It's acquisitive and yet clinical. The glance is a much more nervous affair, nervous in its interestedness because it doesn't know itself to be honorable. We have shorter attention spans now; we're not so much interested in descriptions as in mood. We crave fast intimacies. The moderns are bewitched by sensations and events that dissolve before their eyes, so that they tend to evoke an unstable environment of partial action and psychological nuance. Witkin employs the scrutiny, so much so that he looks positively Victorian. At the same time, he fussily murks the space, and the light, or vignettes his scenes, to invoke a special mental agitation. . . .

Wait. You know, as you were talking—oh, excuse me for interrupting—but, as you were talking I thought of something peculiar. Transparence. There is one sort of photograph, isn't there?, where the last thing you want to deal with or care about is that it's a photograph: pornography. Who cares about the filtering mind that produces these studies? Pornography, or for that matter slides of paintings. The use, the showing forth, is so evident that the photograph figuratively dissolves. If looks could touch, in pornographic photography they'd do it. However, I want to speak technically about a psychological transaction. Not necessarily mine. Desire, supposedly invoked by the pornographic shot, and knowledge, apparently confirmed by the art slide—both are given through modes that operate as visually sufficient. The immediately accessible subject is yielded up to satisfaction right away, short-term, or else it fails . . . the picture fails. That is what I mean by transparence. When it succeeds, the pornographic photograph or the art copy substitutes for the object. God forbid anything should get in the way. The photograph can't be seen to interpret anything. No one wants to read the photograph that reads the Michelangelo. The more there is a need to understand the picture as a compensatory image—to reward *one with a substitute when the real thing isn't there—the more the picture ostensibly thins away. I'm not talking about naturalism here, but rather the uninterrupted illusion of the viewer's proximity to the subject. One can either "scrutinize" or "glance" and still be concerned, above all, with proximity. This is very social of the pornographer and the slide maker. To serve the sensation required by the mode is to imply an exemption of the image from the photographic process—on behalf of a specific use.*

Witkin, absorbed in art and sex, as I said, is not *social. His work isn't compensatory, in the manner of the pornographic photo. He told me that, in the past, he sometimes used to join in, after photo sessions, just to continue the sexual energy, but that now he puts all his energy into the negatives. As soon as that happened, I bet his work started to get more opaque and took on a certain body. By the way, I think you're wrong about the scrutiny being marooned in his work; there are all sorts of glances there, too, and* both *are very moody.*

How can a photographer be antisocial and invitational? If you invite, you invite someone—it's transitive. Any verb that implies a human object is virtually social.

Well, I could point to the fact that the pornographic or art-copy photo is abrupt and quick whereas our photographer is postponed and obscure in his effects. We tend to look "through" the utilitarian pictures and at *the self-consciously artistic ones. Use implies a subordinate relation of means to ends; the picture is supposed to be delivered with as little mediation as possible, although that is rarely, no, never, the case. Pornographers are constrained to be pretty formulaic and self-effacing, on pain of being taken as artists—and having to perform like them. If they were artists, they would be far more concerned to gratify their own narcissism than to craft the visual metaphor of their sitter's narcissism. I have to interrogate the way Witkin pictures things before I can make any sense of them.*

Meanwhile, his adrenalized flare-up sieves back through the murk, but delayed and oddly filtered. I can't think of this as being compensatory or useful. These people turn into icons, finally. Or maybe they were iconic from the start and I was confused. But I have a right to be! Witkin's genre suggests pornographic or, better, obscene intimacy, yet most of the eroticism goes into the handling. The iconic ends are surrendered to the means, safely enough since the icons have already been derived from the real evidence, out there. I can't strike that evidence from my mind, yet I also can't ignore the strange transformation that has occurred.

What ironies! The "out there" that I mentioned comes back to me now as the matrix of another world, an art zone that I can never enter but can certainly appreciate. Just when I, as a spectator, can count on the model's flagrant exhibitionism, the artist inscribes it with his own. If I am brought close to anything it's to his portentous sensuality, which has taken a soft, though objectified, form. His hand touches the negative. Look how he tinctures it. But the "it" is the two-dimensional image, not the person pictured. Frankly, you know, that's a relief. I am back in the familiar area of the artist's self-regard, that is, the regard for his object, the secretion of his ego. That is something that I can cope with and that includes me, as an art lover. Witkin returns the image from the photo-land, where it was potentially unbearable, to some intermediate district, where it appeals to me actively as an invention. The more enigmatic the final product, the more domesticated the effect. I consider this invitational. I begin to think he sides with me, against explicitness. Naturally, I don't mean explicitness of act and behavior, but of description and setting. His treatment of the negative and the depth of his printing are intrusive and violent only in the sense that wounds can sometimes be understood—in poetry, of course—as tender. So, here again is another use of the oxymoron, that figure of speech to which I'm sympathetic. I have seen one of his photographs in the studio, a picture that won't go out. Probably a test shot. It showed a rather trussed-up figure against the bare wall, under a hot, glaring light, and it left nothing to the imagination. It was naked. And I saw in a flash how the darkening and the vignette clothed the nightmare in a fantasy that was delicate and, yes, redolent of the past. When other artists do that—and there have been many, but with less extreme subject matter—the nostalgic softening seems excessive and unearned, a mushy overlay. There was nothing really that significant or sensational for them to cover, and they became too invitational.

You wear me out with your finical qualifications and your loose dialectic. Evidently, the more asocial an artist is, the more he engages your fellow feeling. At one moment you applaud his raw, unpleasant shockingness; at another, you admire his euphemistic procedures. If Witkin isn't "transparent," that is, useful, nor is he altogether opaque, then what is he—translucent? Maybe he just has to wipe more of the excretions off his lens. Here we go again, with your wavering, your inconsistency. I'll say one thing for Witkin: he's less digressive than you are.

Am I required to be logical about this business? Oh, I didn't know. As for my inconsistency and wavering, I'd like to quote Diderot in my defense: "Look, my friend," he said, ". . . you will find that in everything our true opinion is not that from which we have never wavered, but that to which we have most habitually returned." You and I see things very differently. I perceive myself as always coming back, maybe from different angles, to the same tension, the same disturbance that Witkins's work has generated within me.

Naturally, I'm talking around it, but everything I say has the purpose of respecting the unreasonable contradictoriness, the at-odds quality of the experience. Is there, in the name of psychological realism, a more appropriate . . . ?

That's just it. This whole argument smells of psychological reductivism, spiced, if you can call it that, by liberal morality and effete connoisseurship. And even on the comparatively trivial level of psychology, you trip over your feet and don't make sense. You call yourself a civil person, concerned with civil conduct, and yet you hanker after violent and abusive art.

Can you think of anything more bland than art whose ideal is civility?

Look, psychological realism is a minor issue compared to the actual values we ought to be talking about. Where is your awareness of the fact that this guy shows work that has horrible problems, among them the depiction of women? The women are grotesque or monstrous, suffocatingly ominous and castrating. They produce or sprout succubi. One of them serves a man's head on a platter. Witkin's women play with carrots at the wrong orifice or suckle eels. Come on! You call this world enigmatic? The fin-de-siècle viciousness of it drives me up the wall. You're a boob for backing it.

OK. No doubt, if you get a culture like ours, you're bound to get unwholesome art like his and strident talk like yours. I wish it were different—let me tell you! But, do we really know that his ambiguous work has outright sexist messages, or worse, when, for example, it shows that most of his men want to achieve the illusion of being beautiful women while the actual women in the work are often gorgons. And if it's hard to say that works of art have obvious messages it isn't so easy to characterize some human beings, either. You speak out against aggression in this world, which presumably would include the aggression of men against other men, and therefore the endless production of innocent male victims, too. No? So what about your aggression toward me, the way you demean me?

What are you talking about?

What you permit yourself to say to me. You've needled me, you know, you've sneered, you're a virtuoso of condescension. It's not as if you're speaking to a colleague and a peer, but someone you can call a "boob," and therefore a person who doesn't have much human dignity, or self-respect. An object. Criticism has every right to be tendentious, but it shouldn't be a blood sport. You initiated this topic not to engage in mutual exploration or to offer corrective ideas, but to provoke me, as I now see. Relating to you turns out to be much more damag-

ing than relating to Witkin's work, which is to say a great deal.

If your feelings have been hurt, I'm sorry. And I wasn't trying to provoke you, but to hold you to account for vagaries that you haven't thought out very well.

Apparently Witkin's work (or my espousal of it), does *have consequence, since you're so riled by the whole thing. Come to think of it, our personal dynamic grew out of tangling with his program, so that it's not just art moves but life events that we're reacting to.*

But I can't simply interpret this photography as a misogynist tract or evangelical sadism.

Don't you see the great deal in his work about nurturing and wonder? Oh, you raise an eyebrow. But just as you say there is a sympathy that's obtuse, I reply that there is a skepticism that's blind. Look at the nursing and kissing and bodily pride and ecstasy in these pictures. The Beautiful Man *happens to be an image . . . of sweetness . . . of such seraphic excellence and charm (Fig. 16). The demonic character of its grimmer cousins undoubtedly enhances that effect, but even those grimmer ones share in a kind of astonishment. Someone has taken risks and plunged into a distorted world. There he had encounters from which I would shrink. And he comes back with emblems of the marvels he saw or contrived, and of the trust he inspired.*

Truly the whole atmosphere is more innocent than in Arbus's work. With her milder tableaux, the effect arises out of an element of broken trust, which creates great moral seaminess. She does not destroy her subjects' confidence, but in order to get her kind of distressing pictures, she breaks their trust, the trust they had in her. With Witkin, trust is simply taken for granted in the collaboration of photographer and subjects as performance artists. I'll admit that I didn't sense this at first, because I was put off by the freakish display. It's true I spoke of him as a Sadean artist, but he has a childish amazement, a desire to see unheard of things that's terrifically fresh in itself. The pain of these scenes loses out to the life in them. And then, though there's very little irony in his work, despite the titles, I find a lot of comedy. . . .

You've got a brain that foams, you know that? It's maybe one of the endearing things about you. But I can't keep up. And this bit about comedy—in a minute you'll be saying that Jack the Ripper was really Woody Allen in disguise!

Well, these pictures operate by hyperbole, they have an outrageousness which is burlesque, a "bad taste" which is humorous in the end. He can call a picture of a man with an amputated arm and many kinds of artificial limbs—Deviated. *This is the humor of insiders who are the only ones allowed to get away with the put-downs by the outsiders. And he pokes fun at Renaissance, Baroque, and Modern art all the time, in an affectionate way. He has it in particularly for the Venus figures. Art history is a caricature of desire, a field for sexual inversions. Witkin possesses a lively sense of the ignoble and the most profane instincts, which have a critical value as well as a comic aura. I like his frivolous morbidity—which doesn't prevent me from being grossed out!*

So what do I do with my "blind skepticism," which hobbles my appreciation of this fine, ignoble artist? Where you notice the burlesque, I spot the ridiculous. That is, an archly conceited attempt to be clever, as if to misdirect what is only too obvious. Daumier disparaged the classic tradition by turning its heroes and heroines into flitch figures for the good reason that such idealism was really dessicated in his day. Witkin plumps for a classic tradition of "the nude," but in drag, for no better reason than to aspire to its authority within his terms of reference. In any event, the accent is still phallic. As for comedy, if this stuff is to have any impact it can't be intended as spoof. I refuse to believe it.

In the name of your disbelief you can perform prodigies of rejection. I think it's funny that you've just tried to rescue Witkin from my defense of him as a comic spirit. Comedians frequently get away with murder. Humor is just one more potential used in a strategy that siphons us into the dream world, or the limbo that I talked about. I think that this is a zone where people exhibit, in the most pronounced way, their failure to conform to certain things or to be certain creatures. Only the very beautiful or the very dead are what they are—and then only temporarily before they vanish. Most of the rest are in some onanistic drive or mortifying process, enacted out of an impulse that can never be fulfilled; their offspring have died before they were born. Perhaps the fact that so many of them wear masks, or their faces are obscured by Witkin, bears on this point. You remember Oscar Wilde saying, "Man is least himself when he talks in his own person. Give him a mask and he will tell the truth." And it is the truth of their fantasies (or Witkin's) that exposes them, far more than the fact that they are disrobed. I remember years ago, in the 1950s, the film based on the Broadway play The Moon is Blue; *the ingenue in it, Maggie McNamara, is criticized for always being preoccupied with sex, and her snappy reply is, "Better to be preoccupied than occupied."*

Well, times have changed. But this "preoccupation" homes in now, with delirious comeuppance. Partners are not generally available in Witkin's images, sex identities (whether pre- or post-op) are not what they seem, pain is not what it's supposed to be. The whole universe of S and M revolves around a kind of charade, an elaborate counterfeit, in which the mental gratification far outweighs the physical one, and yet eggs on the pleasure of the body. And in photography, that pleasure can come from outside in, from the subject's awareness of being looked at. These people have got it all wrong, I keep on saying. They've got it backward. They should be looking out at the world for their pleasure, but, of course, the camera does the reverse to anyone who poses. It saturates them with the pain or pleasure of being looked at. In that sense, these weird people are doing what comes naturally—in fact they're very pure, super camera subjects, except they can never do what they do in public.

And what about Witkin? That waiter in an Albuquerque restaurant, whose horrid pictures we've been discussing all this time under the sun and among the palms of California. What about his makeup or mix-up?

I don't really know the man and can only retail what he tells me of his life.

Which is?

That he was born in Brooklyn, an identical twin (though a fraternal triplet died), to a Russian Jewish father and an Italian Catholic mother, who divorced when he was a baby. This was about forty years ago, I'd say. On the weekly appearance of a mysterious stranger he would ask his mother, "Who is this Al Mony?" He remembers coming upon an automobile accident when he was six, when an object rolled out over to him across the street, a little girl's head, which amazed him. He seems to have been trained as a sculptor. He spent four months in India meditating, studying Buddhism, photographing temples. Somewhere along the line, in the early 1960s, he'd been in the army, with an M.O.S. as a combat photographer. Later, for many years, he was involved in primal-scream therapy, during which a padded room in New Jersey graved itself in his memory. He wants to do a graduate thesis show at the University of New Mexico entitled "Pictures That Changed People's Lives," of adultery photos from detective-agency files. He assures me that one such picture changed his life. A few critics say he's been influenced by the old Penitentes of New Mexico, but frankly, the Jews invented tsouris *and guilt before the Penitentes. Some photographers need refrigerators to keep their film cool; this one has used a freezer to prevent his props from decomposing. A further or final note: he's married and has a child.*

It doesn't at all sound like there needs be a final note. This story of a life, that explains everything and nothing, is very much in progress. What a protean fellow!

Yes, I think I sometimes get preoccupied with protean personalities.

Better to be preoccupied than occupied.

Well, I can't prove you wrong. But then, it never was a question of proof.

Agreed . . .

That word! That blessed word!

No big deal. But all this talk has made me thirsty. Come on, let's have a drink. Whaddya say . . . a Bloody Mary?

Artforum, *February 1984.*

Through the Narrative Portal

Our mind is a moving scene, which we are perpetually copying.

—Denis Diderot

As artistic traditions go, the modernist belief in a work's autonomy had a strong grip but was of short standing. No one over forty has any trouble remembering the strictures against programmatic music or figurative, and before that, narrative painting. Such bans on external references ruled the aesthetic life of the nondiscursive arts at mid-century, and they had a knack for seeming to be unbudgeable rocks of purist principle. If you aspired to serious modernism, you could make signs and evoke symbolic meanings, but you were prohibited from regressing so far as to tell a story. Here were strategies and gestures that asserted the work's presence though they did not presuppose a general audience. Here were self-reflexive states of being that did not allude to any historical process, past or present. On no account was the modernist work of art to be understood as an account, as an allusion to events that were interwoven or sequenced, possibly with an eye to human cause and effect.

This was, of course, the route taken in older culture, the middlebrow arts and the media, the movies, popular fiction, songs, legitimate theater, soaps, and the comics. And it was the implied structure of a great deal of advertising. Embodied by its deeply coded and disjointed forms, modern art stood in contrast to the media, with their seemingly continuous techniques of exposition. Nowadays, long after the two cultures have expressively dallied with each other, their characteristic modes of control ironically accommodated, crossed-over, and mutated, these distinctions of high and low have been rendered thoroughly out of date. It is hardly news that contemporary artists have enthusiastically rediscovered their premodern traditions and that some consumer imagery has embraced the "avant-garde." Just about the only trace of the old hierarchical rule in such matters is the still current habit of referring to the artistic "colonization" of the media, and of the media's aspiration to art.

In that transforming sweep, the photograph, an inherently social yet enigmatic image, had perhaps been the chief catalyst. Each culture could tour freely within the other's territory, sanctioned by photography's neutral passport. Photography spoke more of the world than of a self, yet its realism was only fragmentary. It had a most immediate power of historical engagement, but it was inanimate and did not work through actual time. Its original purposes or uses could be easily sloughed off and reinvented, depending on the spectrum of endless contexts to which it had natural access. Photography happened to be malleable but also highly unstable, a kind of visual plastique. In promiscuously making headway for itself through an image-hungry environment, it could detonate all kinds of genre molds. Part of its success in this project was owed to the impassivity of the photographic image as a conductor of messages. There has always been a much greater social interest in maintaining photography as an expedient form of communication than in establishing it as a privileged, class-bound discourse. With such a cover, it was granted any occasion to be as obscure, banal, or disturbing as the world itself.

Not long ago, I needed to step only a short distance to my local bus stop to see how this situation could be illustrated with considerable but ordinary depth. The ad-display case in the stop's shelter housed a large, melodramatic photograph of an anguished little girl, whose legs seemed to wedge open the doors of a refrigerator in the bottom part of the image (which had been turned upside down). There was no legend and not one word to explain this upsetting tableau. Yet such an absence acted as a kind of caption in itself, a sign that I was in the presence of art, the kind of art proud in its defiance of the tyranny of words. For, however "literary," the image was thoroughly unsolicitous and self-contained. Anyone waiting for the Number 5 bus had this horrendous non sequitur to keep him company and in suspense. Far from being circumstantial, the effect, of course, was highly calculated. And it had a double provocation, not only that it muted its own implied narrative, but that it usurped a place normally given over to advertising.

Such photographic infiltrators crop up frequently in New York, a city where art and corporate communications coexist in such dense visual intimacy, chic by jowl, that it is one of the finer spectator sports to see how they mimic each other. Recently strap-hangers could gaze upon the faces of an alarmed Asiatic couple selling nothing among the subway placards, and Senator Joseph McCarthy admonished passersby—though to what end?—from his limbo at the Lincoln Center bus stop. Where these art pieces differed from their commercial brethren was in the way they intimated bad news rather than behaved as the harbingers of good news. Even as they declined to spell it out, they told of a nameless malignance that surrounded us, and of personal danger. Installed as normal examples of sign culture, they refused to be assimilated by it, and this made their mood all the more cryptic. It could have been that their function was to resist, delay, and foil a quick "reading," that is, the usual fast sell. With their odd mixture of the surreptitious and the overt, they might even warn that those who live under the sway of programmed images are likely to be deadened by them. But this is to underestimate the cunning of publicity itself, which has never hesitated to turn art strategies to its own purposes.

The next time I took a bus, for instance, the art photo of the young girl in peril had been replaced by that of a young couple under stress. It shared with its predecessor something of the same style, though more from the Helmut Newton or Robert Mapplethorpe end of the spectrum than the *Citizen Kane.* In a desiccated wood or jungle, the young man is seated in a dejected and worn-out crouch while, with work shirt floppily open from her naked chest, his companion assumes a fully erect and heroic stance above him. They wear heavy-duty canvas gloves and their denims have been torn. For a moment, one might have thought such subjects were a blue-collar Hansel and Gretel who had lost their way, rather than highly paid models for Calvin Klein Jeans, the cabalistic words that run across the bottom of their frame.

The scene illustrates a possible sexual contretemps that has been calculated to appeal to both genders. Asking us to speculate on the fascinating pass to which the couple has been brought, the image switches its narrative lure to an object display that conveys, in fact, the real story message. Ours not so much to wonder about the history of this tense, mysterious pair, as to acknowledge that wearers of Calvins are likely to have such a history. Suitably denimed, we, too (waiting for transport), can embark on the sensual and other adventures of role reversal.

The more advanced forms of fashion photography had sought glamour for the product, not in depicting the propriety but the implied license of those who could afford expensive clothes. So-called designer jeans or house-line cotton underwear are not luxury merchandise, and

Calvin Kleins are only marginally distinguishable from a range of competitors. It was a question of proposing a very singular gravitation for consumership of a mass-produced article, in which the illusion of mildly kinky status could be purchased at reasonable cost. What you buy—traditionally enough—is the aura of a certain kind of behavior, rather than the specialness of any goods. The characteristic somnolence and alertness, passivity and assertion of the Klein personnel are iconic traits in theoretical search of a narrative which they don't need. With its muscular arpeggios, the ruggedness of these figures is understood, not as a biographical outcome of work or a sportive life, but solely as an attribute of those who function as objects of *private* desire.

Bruce Weber, the photographer responsible for this and other celebrated images of ripe bodies wearing new Calvin Klein underthings, specializes in pictures of Aryan beefcake. The convergence of his ordinary work and the Klein campaign is located in the theme of a flaunted sexuality that may be inverted. A young woman who wears a man's under-briefs sports this idea and also implies how to read between the lines of fashion photography. Before they appeal to men, the women illustrated in the fashion magazines must first be attractive to women, that is, they must act as objects to their own sex. And the same goes for men's fashion. It is not the opposite sex that buys the clothes, but it's for the approval of the opposite sex that the clothes are generally bought. Inevitably, in sexually expressive fashion photography, there is a confusion between the role of the erotic viewer and the potential buyer. Unquestionably these need to be combined in the same individual, even though the two roles are considered to be sexually distinct. It's beyond the power of the fashion image, any single image, actually, to define the connection between a viewer's means and goals. Yet fashion constantly suggests how they might be transfused by the pronounced self-regard of its models, which places them *hors combat,* as it were, in a zone where they are supposed to be envied rather than lusted after. Such icons teach the worldly virtues of narcissism. What Calvin Klein seems to have done is to draw out some of the filiations between classic fashion hauteur and homophile sensibility.

The historical moment of that liaison came when it could take successfully to the streets. All the more resounding was that success in view of the virtual stylelessness of its product. It used to be that modern fashion was determined by high social placement, or its illusion, achieved earliest by certain elites through birth and then wealth. The buyers of Calvins, on the other hand, are told they need neither be the one nor have the other in order to enter a world of special privilege. Consider these pictures once again. Epidermis alone and cotton underwear do not speak of an affluent life-style, but something else about these pictures does.

The imagery asks its audience to speculate that Calvin Klein "people" are looked after, well taken care of, or, to talk plain, that they're kept. What is actually performed to earn the keep, and for whose benefit: these are matters that remain behind the scene. But the angle of vision, suggestively from below, combined with the exhibitionistic tensility of these figures, dramatizes their awareness of being surveyed, and not just by the camera. Or rather, the camera is used as an instrument that extolls a very presumptuous relationship between the seer and the seen.

The models are posing. There is nothing about the act of posing that should surprise any observer by its self-consciousness. Posing is associated with performance on one hand, and a more static display, on the other: that is, with a theatrical mode, and with its opposite, the figure as still life. Let the first be exemplified by portraiture and the second, say, by the tradition of the nude. It would be fair to state, in either case, that the posed image is one in which an active will from the outside has intervened to exercise its rule upon the behavior of those within the frame. They had not only been caught by the instantaneity of the exposure, but drastically restrained by the convention to which they submitted. Even if certain physical details were self-directed, the subject had been deprived of overall initiative and self-absorption. What we have at the most is only a charade of these possibilities, established through the gradients of the pictorial genres themselves, from energetic to inert. Legibility of gesture is gained at the expense of unself-conscious conduct. These are the costs of the "presenting" modes, as compared with the more spontaneous action modes. But posing—formally impersonated behavior—happens to be a perfectly authentic activity if apprehended as the service it provides for a visual occasion that could not be realized in any other way. When looking at a posed image, I am gazing at the appearance of someone who confronted a camera, and it was that someone's contact with the apparatus, the requirement to deal with it, that initiated the specific acting out, long a ritualized product of photographic culture.

Please now hold in mind all those photographs that were primarily made to illustrate the domestic attachments of those involved and would tell of a history shared by photographer and subject. It was not a question of the machine that held the figures in thrall, not the photographer who called the shots, but a familiar person who would visualize some mutually asserted intimacy. The subjects might still obviously be posed creatures (acting within their lives, rather than as if disassociated from them), but that fact would be secondary to a new dimension that enters into one's current dealing with the picture. If it hadn't been intended for my nominal regard as a member of the public, the arrangement or display of the photographed figures must have a private content, not necessarily an esoteric or alien one. We have that illegitimately included feeling often when family album photographs are published, for they were not addressed to those who now receive them. To view such material is mildly like opening someone else's mail. Why, then, should the Calvin Klein ads, intended for *public* consumption, look far more indiscreet?

For one thing, instead of being jobbed and misused, they were designed to have that eruptive effect. What appears to be very private memorabilia has been deliberately amplified and inserted in the public arena, where strangers mill around. I have an unexplained entree to the mutual fondness ascribed to the collaborators of these pictures. It's as if I—and you, too, if you're a bystander—intrude at that phase of a relationship of which the photograph is a studied, seductive memento. Its softly pornographic display and diaristic mood are not in themselves provocative; what makes them brazen is being posted out in the street, anyone's fantasy.

Broken in by an indefinite number of gestures similar to the Klein campaign, the megapolitan street operates as a zone of illicit visual inclusions. All citizens who circulate there receive such bogus intimacies as a joint, unearned experience. There will naturally have grown up a class of viewers that has become immune to it. Such people are reluctant to be let indiscriminately into any picture's confidence. Or they're just tired of it. But there are nevertheless psychic entrances or exits, if you will, everywhere, and viewers who cannot help being alive to them. At any moment the metaphorical insinuations of the imagery can be engaged with or sparked off, like magical phenomena, defined by T. H. Huxley as effects perceived to be visibly disproportionate to their apparent cause.

Rather than invited only to study flesh, or how models have been choreographed for the lens, I feel set in motion by an intrigue, a sense that the beautiful figures are turning into the characters of some embryonic play. And yet it is not the subjects who have changed, but the viewer. Instead of remaining an undetermined unit of the public,

I am personified as a member of an audience. A part of me has grown animal, spirited, and credulous, active in a new, disquieting fancy.

At this point, a rather unsettling question has to be asked. One wants to know, not so much who, literally, regards the images of those desirable bodies, but rather, for whom, underneath, it is imagined that the subjects were complaisant. I am talking about strange matters—at least as far as photography is concerned: the power of the image to evoke an *imagined* time, distinct or even opposed to the moment of its execution and of its ability to "insert" the spectator into that fictive time zone, and therefore to create a new kind of onlooker, in league with the camera but less innocent.

To ask about this rather ill-defined viewer, still so little known, is to inquire into one of the key issues of the eighties: how the media use the tool of narrative for psychic programming.

If I were interested in story line, wanted that sort of narrative exposition from my art or cultural products, ordinarily the last place to turn would be still photography. The other arts commend themselves more easily for this purpose because they are fictive from the start, alternative or speculative constructions about what has happened or could happen out there. Life, it must be said, doesn't *tell* stories; stories are told about life, and the traditional forms we have to recount such stories are necessarily separate from their referents. My understanding of situations, comprised of events or looking forward to becoming events, evolves from our means of representing things. But no one has ever proved that photographs, howsoever they depict, actually *do* representations of life. Such images are, of course, at a definite physical remove from what is configured in them, but they are nevertheless traceable to a light that occurred. A photograph is an image we understand as crucially generated and therefore determined by an aspect of those external sensations which it records. And while obviously useful as evidence, this turns out to be a quite devastating mark against photography as a narrative vehicle.

That is, a photograph is implicated in the reality which it witnesses, enough, at least, to be lost in it from the viewpoint of cause and effect. Worse still, it is immobilized in its material ground. Whoever heard of a single photograph that unfolded its own description? Narrated events, to deserve the name, cannot be "of" themselves, that is, identified with that which tells them. No one, for (a contrary) example, expects a historical text to be what it says. It makes a great deal of weird sense, on the other hand, to say that photographs are "of" (stem from) whatever it is they reveal and, that being the case, they can't be "about" it; they can't, as we recognize, *tell* it. In ordinary language, it's perfectly acceptable to ask what a painting is "about"; the equivalent query of a photograph is to ask what it *shows*. For the negative of the photo picture is characteristically factual from the start, never so ideal in its allusions as to escape being genetically splotched by the world.

I think incidents in the visual field of the photograph, processed though they are, retain a great measure of the status of phenomena, with the casual order or disorder of appearance that phenomena bring to the senses. In setting forth the picture field, a frame puts the viewer on notice, discriminates, usurps, or buffers the casualness of optical phenomena. While this relays, it does not exactly create information. If the motif is a rumpled bed, the frame does not act to smooth it out or rumple it more but only to put a fence around the whole or a part of it. Suppose one was given an unmade bed, but one really wanted a picture of a made bed, the same object in another condition. It would have to be attended to, and the results photographed. Photography is in many respects an initiating or imposing act, but on this level of the scenographic, it discloses itself as a reactive effort.

That to which it reacts may, of course, be randomly flung about, in a potluck constellation, or set up beforehand quite rigidly. For over a century, with the advent of fast films and lenses, we've been accustomed to a photographic view of the environment as a flux, ceaseless in the process of *unmaking* and reconstituting itself. A notion of the unseizable and evanescent quality of experience had been a modernist perception. Reinforced by street photography, it was now intimated that however we tossed and turned, we would never grasp the reality of our messy surroundings other than in cryptic, unconnected, and frustrating glimpses. By a curious twist, their very inadequacy on this score was what made ruffled street photographs credible to the unworldly doctrines of modernism.

But a strong counter-tradition exists in the photographic medium, or perhaps it should be called the main tradition because it was powerfully articulated before the moderns, and continues still. This is the mode of the directed image (or the directorial mode, as A. D. Coleman called it): the subjects beckoned out of their own moments to participate in a pseudo-moment—the moment of the pose. Every person caught in such a moment functioned as two people simultaneously: the one who was there and the one who was impersonated, according to circumstances at a closer or further range from the first. (As a rule, the more elaborate the role-playing, the more it conformed to media usage, whether official or commercial.) Quite early on, a symbolic value was inevitably ascribed to the frame as a sufficient border for a preexisting content. Instead of random passages through space, we have, as in much portraiture, territorial assertions. Rather than lightsome and fluid, unrooted appearances, we're given strenuous and weighted presences projecting themselves for further scrutiny. With its accent on the contingent, its short-term implication of events that preceded or will succeed the phenomenal moment, street photography would seem to have a greater narrative reach than posed photographs. In these far more insular proceedings, on the contrary, all the psychic forces seem to coalesce, as if directed to a still point. Even when expansive, the pose is still a literally *corrupted* form of momentum. It can do no more than hold in one hopeful breath the sum of an individual's rash desires to embody a role or distill character.

The unreasonable assumption behind a directed image is that it gives all that is needed to know to form a judgment about a human moment. If it protests too much in that direction, forcing signs of its content, we often call the outcome staged, or stagey. The more convincing premise of street photography is that visual experience always uncontainably spills past what can be depicted, though if the gap between what is seen and what can be emotionally satisfying or socially useful opens up too graphically, we might think the results inopportune. The feeling arises that they have been settled for rather than selected. *Inopportune* then is merely a polite term for appearances so routinely unpointed as to look banal. Photographers would here seem to have followed the deadbeat advice offered by Ashleigh Brilliant, writing in another context: "To be sure of hitting the target, shoot first, and, whatever you hit, call it the target."

If visual narrative is the issue, however, the real target is far less an actual or fancied incident than the spectator's mind. It is all very well for a spatial image to quiver with some slight temporal vibration, as does a street photograph, but unless the sense of the subject's time illusorily takes precedence over the way I feel situated in my own, it will not narrate. When I look at a street photograph, I meditate upon a phenomenal moment of the past, which I compare with my own grasp of the present. The interval that has been "framed" does not presuppose my awareness or anyone else's. It comes to me with a beautiful and chilling indifference to any pattern that may be imposed, any story that can be construed from it. It's a sign of a street photograph's persuasiveness that it will concede any number of interpretations and be pinned down by none.

As for the directed image, it, too, appeals out of the past, but through the eyes and gestures of those for whom a spectator existed. The very fact of theatrical artifice or charade implies a longing for a world of visual consumers, so that the transactional gears want to be engaged on visual contact. No one, as I said, has proven that photographs *represent* life, but some of those images, with the help of the pose, show us human beings involved in *their* act of representation. The act may be covert, as in commercial genres, frequently, or acknowledged, as in portraits and family snapshots, but in either case it transforms the photograph into a psychological portal opened on to a narrative horizon.

In a movie called *Black Sunday,* there occurs an instance of someone who stepped through that threshold and lost his mind. A psychotic veteran recounts his trauma at having received a snapshot of his wife and child when he was a prisoner of the Viet Cong. What should ordinarily have comforted him—the smiling faces of his loved ones—exploded his emotions. It would have dawned on us filmgoers that the long shadow in the picture's foreground was the photographer's. That same form brought forth to the husband the presence of his wife's lover.

This particular viewer had opened up his own mail, to be sure, but only to discover, as he thought, someone else's message. I should like to put to you—in fact I've already suggested—that this is a common episode, more our lot than not when walking the streets. As long as we don't know who, precisely, is being addressed by the solicitous face—the smiling lips—we are made dubious in our response to the image. The smile itself declares the certainty of *two* sorts of recipients. Clearly the expression had been performed at the behest of the photographer, who acted rather like the first outside reader of a manuscript. Just as definitely, the performance of the smile was to be recorded and transmitted for the benefit of known or possibly unknown spectators, the readership. The prisoner in the film read *through* that benefit, discounted it for himself, and transferred it back to the photographer—empathy on the rebound, and vicious.

No one disputes that the woman had smiled. This, after all, was part of the genetic splotch that made that particular image. But a great deal pivots, to put it crudely, on who was to gain from that smile, or what kindled it. Given my state of doubt, it is always conceivable that the snapshot photograph eventuated from goings-on that anticipated viewers but did not broker my particular interests. If I am in the least tempted by that idea—and why shouldn't I be?—I begin to be drawn into the photographic occasion. It becomes reasonable to think that such a moment might have a past history and that it also indicates something about the immediate future of those who collaborated in the production of the picture. Once that happens, my own placement in time is clouded over and I am all ears and eyes to that of the participants. Instead of a scenario conventionally understood as removed from their real lives, the photo symbolizes only a momentary pause in their day. The image is still the end-product of the posed occasion, but the occasion itself takes a bow for a social reality that continued off-camera and outside the frame.

In the family snapshot, regardless of how inert, the poses are incipiently alive because they emerged from a lived situation appointed everywhere with specific historic details. What had been consciously taken from (represented of) that situation is about to be given back and diffused into it. From a narrative point of view, the snapshot has a certain immanence, of which there may well be hints along the margins. Snapshots and many portraits differ from publicity photographs in the way they are matrixed in their subjects' time. If the purpose of the image was commercial, then concrete elapsed time was meaningful only to those from whom it had been bought, the people who were there. It takes only the slightest glimpse, on the other hand, to see that time was of no moment to the ones who were impersonated. Their historical experience was as illusive as their pantomime was fictional. Their whole guise is of a remarkably static no-time, an immobilized timelessness, no matter how many heels were kicked up. (Richard Avedon's leaping models are an apt illustration.) But snapshot people impersonated themselves in a time zone which they shared, not only with their everyday selves, but explicitly with the unseen photographer.

Such was what the character in the film had focused on, and it unhinged him. To say that he was a radically interested spectator, unlike the rest of us, is to put it mildly. But there is a critical sense in which we're all joined together, here no less than anywhere else in the world depicted by photography. That sense has been generally described by Stanley Cavell. "Photography," he writes, in a well-known passage, "maintains the presentness of a world by accepting our absence from it. The reality in a photograph is present to me while I am not present to it; and a world I know and am seeing, but to which I am nevertheless not present, through no fault of my subjectivity, is a world past."[1] With a play or any other temporal performance, players and audience are present to each other in almost synchronous interaction. With any directed photograph, contrarily, the interaction, as far as the performers are concerned, will be postponed; they themselves will not be present to be received into it. By the same token, we outsiders will never have gotten close enough in time and space to have heartened or inflected the action that went into the picture. What separates us is the gap opened up between its quite definite "then" and our very palpable "now." And this gap can have poignance, as Cavell's remarks suggest. In fact, a whole book has been written on the subject by Roland Barthes—*Camera Lucida,* a book fixated on wounds suffered by the ego when it contemplates the past in photographs. An extreme case of such wounded consciousness is represented by *Black Sunday*'s husband, forever prevented from heading off "that which has been."

Unfortunately, when I recognize that the photographed scene is not concurrent with my view of it, I do mischief to arguments about the narrative potential of the still shot. A spectator will be generally aware of the fact that the reference of which there is only a fragment in the photograph had already taken place, from "start" to "finish." And it will make no difference at what chronological point along the natural track of any activity the camera had intervened. The abortive-looking result will carry no narrative suspense. Retrospective historical knowledge of what really happened is interesting but irrelevant to the experience of a tale unfolded and now over with. Since the doings in question (the ones framed) were concluded, they could not have turned out other than the way they did. Now, all truly narrative photographic work is a protest against this time closure, the literal, distanced character of photographic implications as *faits accomplis.*

This is a problem endemic to still photography as a communicative and artistic medium. For no other spatial medium functions as a delayed record-trace of real appearances and true incidents, incurably receding from us in time. The job of the narrative photographer is to suspend our sense of the irreversible lateness of our arrival at the scenes depicted, and to try to resituate viewers within an apparently emergent process, still unconsummated at the moment of perception. In order to bring off that tricky metaphor of spinning the temporal wheels, photographers have imbued their content with a kind of backward progressive motion—one goes backward into a new present, that starts fictively over again and finishes. Looking out at the train "speeding" next to mine, I do not realize for a moment that I am the one in motion. Something like that appears to happen when I am furthered through stationary photo images that have been sequenced as if chronologically and am guided to their meaning with the help of titles and texts.

With such traditional aids, which the visual arts have often drawn from the discursive ones, photography could officially adopt a quasi-narrative structure. It hardly needs to be pointed out what storytelling advantages were thereby programmed into the photographic act, lending it an apparent wholeness that individual and uncaptioned frames themselves would never possess. Consider, for example, Erich Salomon's suite of six photographs, entitled "Marlene Dietrich telephones her daughter," 1930 (Fig. 20). It's not only as a symbolic tribute to the subject's profession, screen star, that the six frames are arranged as if on film strip; the temporality of film is also suggested. These pictures run through a gamut of smallish events—changing facial expressions—that together make up Salomon's anecdote, spun out seemingly in the real time of one fixed, average-length movie shot. The illusion is fostered that at the uppermost left we have the commencement, and the lowest right, the conclusion of a "story," a telephone call, of which there are six smiling installments, each melting into the next. That the frames are relatively distinct from each other (abrupt, therefore), and the poses outrageously fewer in number than would be in the actual script, is neither here nor there. The ensemble aspires to narrative persuasiveness because Salomon has *extended* posed images as occasions within a flux.

Theatrical activity, in fact, spills so easily through this image set that Dietrich appears to have been as much on-stage between Salomon's frames as within them. No one gets the impression that the photographer had obliged his subject to assume the role of warm-hearted mother over again on six separate counts. Let's say, rather, that we think the photographic "moment" was dilated, and as the performance started on its course, Salomon cut into it strategically, netting an attentive Dietrich here, a fond one there, winding up with the young woman cradling her telephone as if in relaxed, amorous bliss.

One can almost imagine that the most repeated word advertised by this performance was *Liebchen,* but whether it was murmured to Dietrich's daughter, agent, or lover, or no one, is another matter. On the lamp table, however, next to the actress in her bed, is a framed photograph of a coquettish little girl (reinforcing the title of the ensemble). The rhetoric of these images by Salomon primitively asserts that the pictured child is the object of Dietrich's involvement on the phone. In

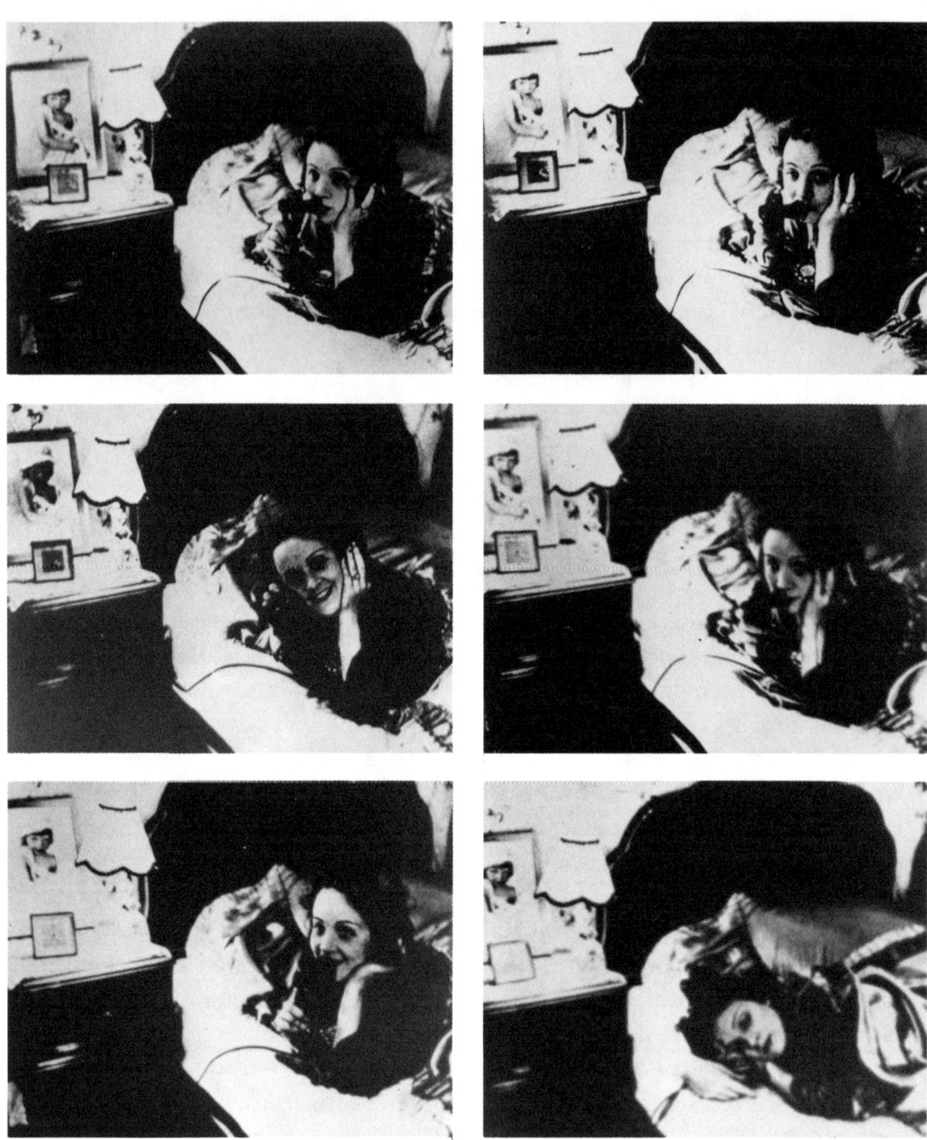

Figure 20. Erich Salomon, *Marlene Dietrich telephones her daughter,* 1930.

the visual juxtaposition of the image of the absent little girl and the physically present adult, Salomon suggests the tides of a dialogue carried right out of and back into the picture he himself has made.

Salomon, however, was not a practitioner of the directed image, but, professionally speaking, a street photographer who often intruded within closed interiors. The social motive of the Marlene Dietrich photographs, though journalistic, shaded off more interestingly into publicity. Supposed to document one of the first calls on the new trans-Atlantic telephone cable, these pictures played into the hands of the film studio. Meanwhile, the reputation of the photographer was that of someone who cleverly transgressed social boundaries, bringing to media publics the off-guard and therefore intimate, "behind-the-scenes" behavior of the famous. The genuineness of his results was certified by their lack of authorization. For that reason, as soon as Salomon gained entry to Dietrich's bedroom, that instant was fatal to his aesthetic, since he was to collaborate with a film star who specialized in projecting performances for delayed interaction. Literally embedded in what passes for her own domestic moment, Dietrich seems impossibly indifferent to the close-range presence of a stranger in her boudoir while she conducts private business.

This particular performance, finally, was a little curious because it invented and dramatized a character modeled after someone who, though always there, had to withdraw further from us: Dietrich herself. Walking into that room, a viewer would have left the indifferent world of phenomena but not yet have been absorbed into the solicitous order of narrative.

If one suspects that such things don't happen readily until the visual ambience of the picture is more thoroughly controlled by words, that would preliminarily be right. Language is the referent that generates, not the factuality but the indicativeness of photographic images, which means that language can change the names of its objects at will, assign different referents to the same things, and orient them in modes of consecutive order, according to the contrasting virtualities of its own logic. However they're conceived, images have to be mediated by words. About images, Vilém Flusser, in his powerful "Towards a Philosophy of Photography," writes that

> they are translations of events into situations . . . omnipresent technical images have begun magically to restructure "reality" into an image-like scenario. What is involved here is a kind of oblivion. Man forgets that he produces images in order to find his way in the world; he now tries to find

his way in images. He no longer deciphers his own images, but lives in their function. Imagination has become hallucination.[2]

But then, about words, or rather writing, Flusser continues, dialectically:

> Inventing writing, man took a further step away from the world. Texts do not mean the world, but the images which they tear up. To decipher texts is to find out what images they refer to. The purpose of texts is to explain images, to transcode image elements and ideas into concepts. Texts are meta-codes of images.[3]

As Flusser points out, history records a long struggle between imaging and conceptualizing, which produced moments in which these conflicting drives were infiltrated by instrumentalities of the other. The more successful visual messages, including narrative ones, head toward highly selective combinations of images and texts which seem exceptionally to warrant each other, taking on a new life in their liaison. The narrative photographer puts a stop to the phenomenal chaos of appearances in order to plant clues that have been anticipated by a text, although in the process, the text, even if it's not actually given, is reimagined. And in the reduced but clue-filled world that is now framed by narrative, a world of matured inferences, the outcome of things can almost be sighted.

Let me turn from this abstract discussion to a concrete example of a photographically illustrated short text, whose outcome happens to be quite alarming. The story at issue is Charles Perrault's "Little Red Riding Hood," depicted by Sarah Moon in a style that is unquestionably her own but also uncannily suggests that of Carol Reed's film *The Third Man.* In visualizing an ominous mood, Moon also illuminates a story on an itinerary that had already been plotted out to a known destination (Figs. 21, 22). For narrative purposes, the still photograph is aligned with others to form a new composite whose images are all interdependent. In this system, no single picture is sufficient in itself, but rather is understood as a *carrier* of meaning that may not be fully evident until the final frame. I can riffle through the few, unevenly weighted pictures without scanning the text and still catch their progressive description of a childish soul led into a bestial trap. The photographer could have chosen other moments in the story than the ones that do appear illustrated in the book, but she could not have shuffled their sequence and be faithful to that story. Its words hold her accountable at least to a structure of happening in time, unlike the nominal

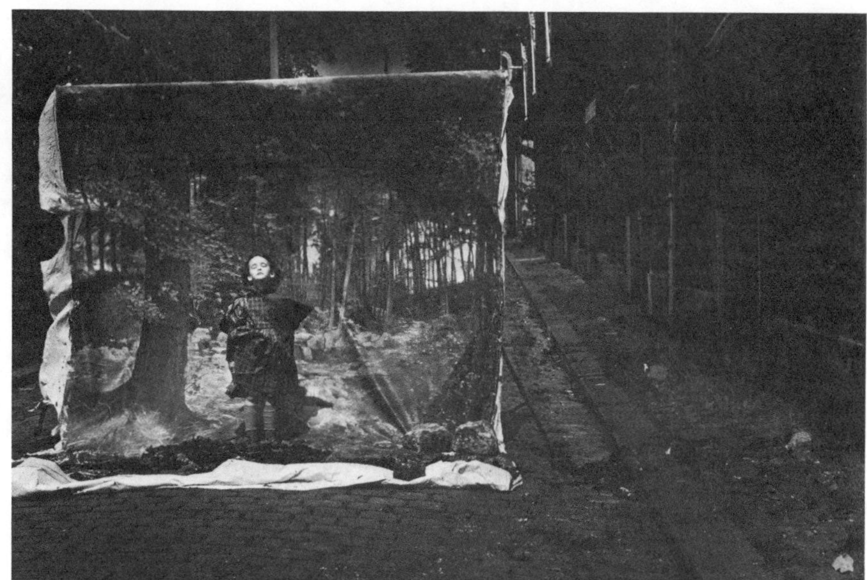

Figure 21. Sarah Moon, *She was the prettiest creature who was ever seen,* 1983.

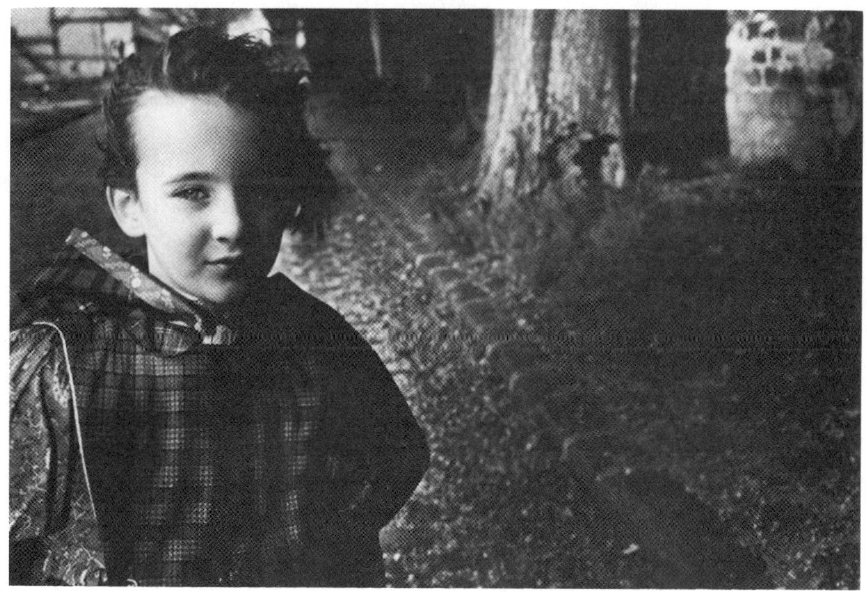

Figure 22. Sarah Moon, *"Does she live far off?" asked the Wolf. "Oh! yes," answered Little Red Riding Hood. "It is beyond that mill you see there,"* 1983.

words of Marlene Dietrich, which did not prefigure a visual sequence to Salomon, and therefore evolved in activity that was glimpsed in completely interchangeable progressions.

"Little Red Riding Hood," as Moon correctly *sees,* is a paradigm of deceit. The wittiness of her illustrations lies in her detailed defections from a textual outline to which she otherwise adheres. Did all this take place in the day? She changes it to the night. Wasn't the setting always understood as pastoral? She transforms it to the city. As for the wolf, instead of skulking through the wood, he drives an old Citroën over wet, cobbled streets. Just the same, as I read the text, the words increasingly ask me to discount what they say. "The poor child," writes Perrault, "who did not know that it was dangerous to stay and hear a wolf talk" is a child who enjoys her knowledge of just how dangerous it is. By the Manichean darkness and lights of her scenes, spotlighting the little girl's figure overwhelmed in portentous space, the photographer justifies the literal sense of the story. But that mock-naive straightness is broken at the point of the first conversation between Riding Hood and the wolf, when she tells him exactly where he can meet her again—at grandmamma's. Here Sarah Moon gives us a close-up of the child, looking directly at the viewer/wolf. There plays over her sweet, angelic face what psychologists would call a "knowing smile." From then on, to the conclusion of this fairy tale, I was reminded of what Djuna Barnes had to say about it in her novel *Nightwood:* that children know something we don't. They like to see Little Red Riding Hood in bed with the wolf!

It's evident by now that one of the chief narrative instruments of the image is the way it materializes, where texts more naturally conceptualize point of view. The fact that the wolf is never seen in Moon's photographic images is but a necessary corollary of the fact that his role is given over to the viewer. Let Riding Hood address herself for just one moment—but here there are several—as if she's on the lookout in my direction, and I'm helplessly animalized. There had never been even a suspicion of this in the original text, and the enhanced crafting of such literal insight into self-consciousness goes further than the words themselves to ferment the story with sexual irony.

"How sour sweet music is when time is broken." This phrase from Shakespeare is used as the epigraph for *Improbable Memories,* a book that collects images from Sarah Moon's main line of work, fashion photography. For *French Vogue* or *Marie-Claire,* and such firms as Cacherel, she constructed elaborate gauzy fictions in which the loveliest women and little girls take tea with wild animals. Lest there be any question about the sex of these creatures, Moon answers by placing the heads of beasts upon the bodies of gentlemen callers. These sugar daddies are by no means teddy bears or pussy cats; though domesticated for the moment, they're carnivores, capable of ugly growls. Red Riding Hood would immediately find herself at home in such surroundings. One eats well and smells fragrant in this prim, dainty world, but it has a hairy lining.

Reciprocally, in Perrault's scary fable, Moon sees to it that the heroine is crisply gotten up and stylish, the daughter of a very fashion-conscious mother indeed. This accent on haute couture in false peril underlines both the invented texts for the magazines and the pictures for the children's story. This poetic consumer's fantasy is further ramified by variously staged effects indicating that all these feminine doings are under outside surveillance, and the nervous edge given to the poses by this idea expresses not only some of the socioeconomic but also the sexual tensions in photographic experience. More and more, that experience should be understood as a kind of mussing up of the power relations suddenly incurred between viewers and subjects. Moon's Red Riding Hood, an understudy auditioning for the role of model, is a narcissist, and with her weak psychic radar is prone to be a victim but also to do seduction. Of course, for Perrault, the seducer was the wolf: "Grandmamma, what big arms you have!" "The better to hug you with, my dear." The sheer extravagance of that drag imposture is famous for having worried but disarmed its childish readers, allowing them to externalize their fears. Sarah Moon accomplishes a visual ambiguity of her own with her epilogue shot of a rumpled bed which may signify the site of the wolf's tasty (and remarkably bloodless) meal or that the story all along had been but a nightmare, though from this adult vantage, either way, a howling success.

In retrospect, sequence photography of this and related narrative types demands to be read through certain conventions that channel appropriate meanings. The notion of an empty, rumpled bed at the end of the Dietrich series is conceivable, for instance, but would be conventionally out of keeping with Salomon's reportage. There would be no newsworthiness to the fact that she had left the room, say, to make a local phone call. Photojournalism concerns itself with where people are present, not the irrelevance of where they're not. And while such photojournalism aims to define a typically informing or climactic moment in the single frame, the multiple images of narrative more often slip around or deliberately avoid critical turns of plot. You might say that they couldn't help doing that because of the haltingness of the form. Gaps and chinks open up inevitably between charades of even adjacent frames. But that would hardly explain how the deliberate extreme of human absence can be used expressively in narrative, as a positive element.

To be sure, we know from experience of such work that even when figures are off stage, the props can still speak. The act of calling exclusive attention to them, in one or more frames, is already a characteristic genre utterance, for they have roles to play in the conveyance of *mood,* still the prime factor in the visual exposition of the text. If they had to make a hard choice between spelling out the nominal happenings of a story, or evoking them through details of facial expression, light, shadow, surfaces, the space of imagination, and the objects within it, photographers, I believe, wouldn't hesitate to choose the latter. Significant omissions from the linear story do not jeopardize its overall import so much as failure of visual stagecraft, and therefore, the rupture of mood. It's through mood rather than through mere faithfulness to plot that the really discursive possibilities of the pictures are triggered. As Sarah Moon conceives it, the mood of "Little Red Riding Hood" is one of enchantment—her rule of priority—of a state in which the headlights of a car can be fancied as glowing lupine eyes, and a rumpled bed can stand as an emblem of hallucination. Bound as they are by the immobile image, narrative photographers insinuate the sentience or animism of things, working their spell for what it's metaphorically worth. When an *author* is found to hanker after that magical sense of the environment, the words used tend to be extraordinarily imagistic. Conversely, when photographers introduce an object for the sake of its power of association, they inevitably hope to add a conceptual overlay to the material constraints of their art.

Something of that order is immediately evident in the "career" of an overcoat in Duane Michals's "The Bogeyman," 1973 (Fig. 23). What appears to happen in this suite of seven pictures wants to be described almost in one sentence. Here is a rather flat go at it: A large overcoat on a rack next to a curious little girl turns out to be a bogeyman the moment she falls asleep and carries her off. This transcription keeps the activity in the present tense, but along the way it's progressively harder to hold on to presentness in the frame sequence. Certain parentheses crop up in the hypothetical sentence structure. Thus, the little girl (who had been reading), the bogeyman (who had been deadened or stiffened in matter and is now released). These principals evolve out of their past, what they had been, which loads them down or lightens them in their progress, shown in episodes of straight and concise proximity.

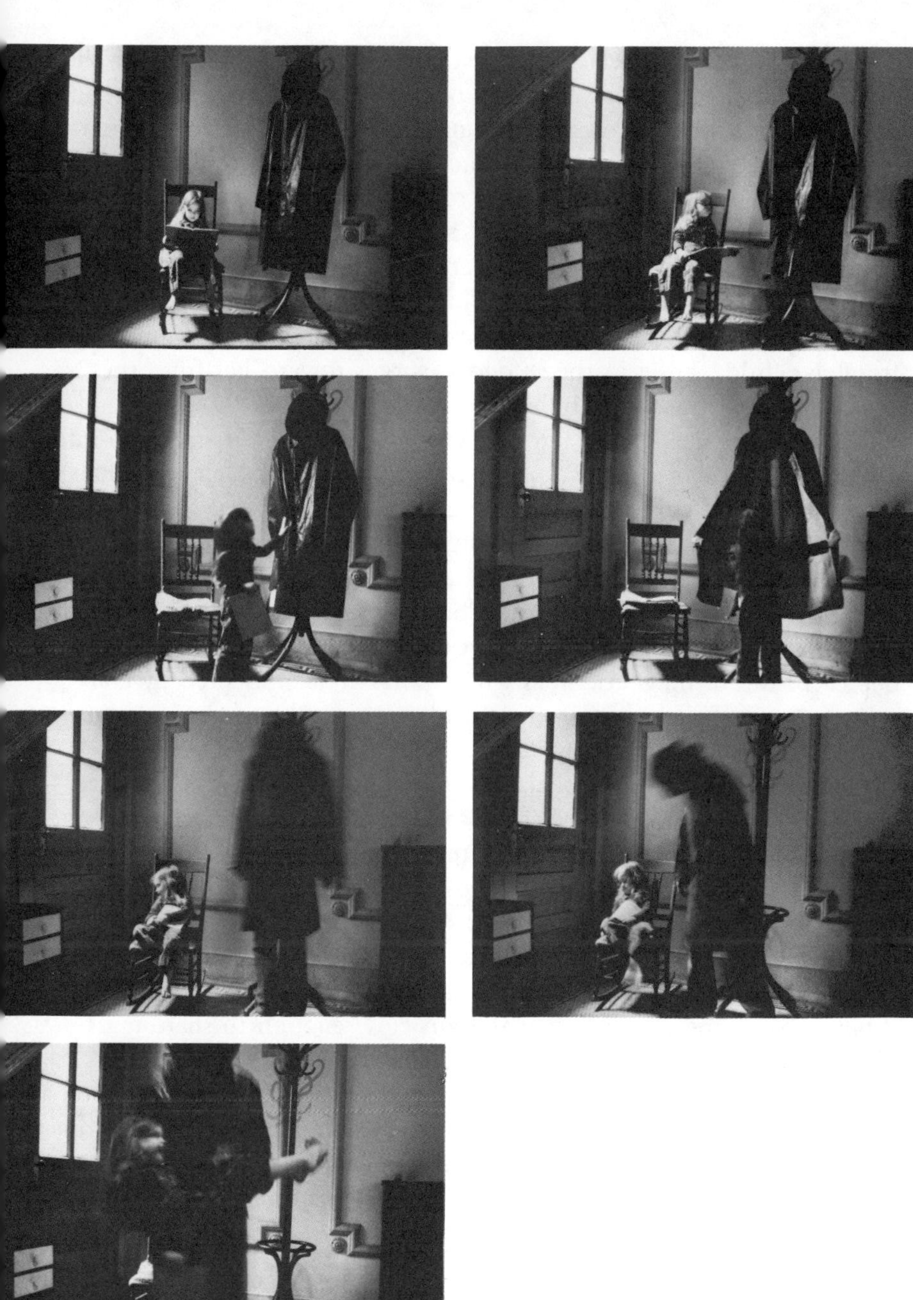

Figure 23. Duane Michals, *The Bogeyman,* 1973.

All right. But as I review my first sentence, I see that it's not the tense of verbs, but the reversibility of subject and object, active and passive agents, that throws the meaning of the piece up for speculation. Let me construct a new sentence to express an alternative drive of the set: A seated little girl stops reading to examine a large hanging coat, after which she returns to her chair, falls asleep, and is abducted by a monster in the guise of the coat. The starter kit consists of the girl and the coat, and the later business between them oscillates almost mechanically, so that impetus in the first half of the work comes from the child, while in the second it surges toward her from the coat/creature, who evidently has the last say.

This scheme describes a fair scenario, perhaps, but it may also infer a hidden agenda in the concept or, rather, conceit of Duane Michals's fable. Instead of being specific characters or even general social types, the figures in his stories function simply as human presences or otherwise, undergoing metamorphosis. I am not asked to care very deeply about them, one way or the other, but I am invited to reflect on a mystery. It seems to me that the artist has gone to some length to depict a kind of magnetic field whose poles are represented by consciousness, with its belief in the world of physical surfaces, and by dream, with its haunting by spirits. Not later than mid-point in many of his sequences, Michals has it that consciousness falls away and loses out to dream, the more powerful source of narrative attraction. Quite often in the picture suites he did in the 1970s, this successful fashion photographer concerns himself with the theme of sleep or hypnosis and the chimeras that rise up in its wake.

When I dream that I am pursued, I am also, more vaguely, the pursuer. Similarly, when I witness the little girl's misadventure, it's difficult to escape the feeling that I am close enough to share it, if only because I identify with the camera. Alter-ego of my eye, the camera unflinchingly records a sinister and uncanny event, as if such a thing were capable of being recorded, in a room that throughout remains the same in all but one of its particulars. A common aspect of photographic experience is the ability of viewers to entertain more visual trajectories within the picture field than were accessible to subjects, with their fixed sightlines. So, here, I see not only the conscious activity of the little girl, but also into her dream, a vista that cannot be, unless I am projecting (into) the situation myself. And this is the conceit of Michals's work, worthy of the art of Magritte, which has inspired it.

Suppose you are a photographer who has been commissioned to portray a writer, not so much the individual, but what that person does. Imagine, for instance, that you are going to make a photographic portrait of me, *as a writer.* If you wish, you can do me seated at my desk, with fingers on the keys. But you reject this boring idea and subsequently decide to photograph me acting the pose "lost in thought." Writers can be reasonably conceived as thinking—sometimes—but the trouble with that pantomime is that it's not particularly visual, and besides, it makes me fidgety and self-conscious. It then suddenly occurs to you that you can photograph my thought! You can substitute it for me and yet not digress from your theme. As a reader, you assume you know what's going on in my mind since it's spooled out in this essay. At the moment, my thoughts are agitated, in a kind of stew because of the difficulty of finding words to do justice to certain visual enigmas. But you are a visual artist, and as you read, you realize images that are encoded by my text. Presently, closing with your subject, you invent a "bogeyman."

Unquestionably you would be following a different script than the one touched upon by Michals. Discreet though he is, either by his exclusion of words or by being very laconic with them when they accompany his pictures, Michals is still a very "writerly" photographer. The medium he has chosen affords us only a special trace of literal surfaces, whereas he conceives his job to penetrate behind them. In materializing his work he does not mumble a hocus-pocus and snap his fingers. Nothing so magical as that. Rather, he superimposes a new mental frame upon the physical border of the photograph. The camera can be counted on to relay information that was presented, but chemistry and optics aside, that information can be variously filtered by known narrative devices. Such, for example, is the interior monologue of the novel or the flashback of movies. Because they are considered part of someone's *else*'s perception or memory, the things photographed are distanced from the viewer, yet they remain just as neighborly as they would have been without the filter. The artist only needs to pronounce that the scene emanates from within the consciousness of another, and you are made to understand that you are *not seeing* what is actually to be seen: rather, you're made present to an idea of it screened in your mind. The scene, in other words, has already been claimed by an intercessor or emissary, so that all the surfaces are strangely discredited as objects of your immediate apprehension. The major character falls asleep, and with that a dissolve takes place that finally has to be judged as a verbal act—the assigning of different referents to the same things.

Certain implications follow from that act, from which Duane Michals has been quick to profit. Call it sleight-of-hand, if you will: the introducing of a wild card within a deal of normal, regulated values. Given the mute and immobile quality of the photographic image, the anxious, destablizing tone with which he can suffuse it is quite remarkable. I don't know what is going to happen next in one of his sequences, what laws of causality his events obey, because they have been internalized. Following from the notion of the "internal," by logical antithesis, is that of the "external," and to back up this pairing in Michals's work are related oppositions: small and larger, framed and framing. Of course the ultimate frame is text (thought), which encompasses the smaller one—not so much the image itself, but what the image purports of reality. Or, as Michals himself puts it: "People believe in the reality of photographs, but not the reality of paintings. This gives photographs an advantage. The disadvantage is that photographers themselves believe in the reality of photographs."[4]

One might gather from this skeptical comment that, for Michals, there was never any possibility of a photo document, that photography's engagement with the real is only a pretense, a sham that could be exploited. The consequences of such an attitude for narrative are plain to see. How very little exists, he might say, apart from the way it is represented, that is, "storied." As a result, objects are less palpable to us than thought, and fulfillment is less apparent to us than desire. I was going to speak further about his antirealist position, but I suddenly understand that if the proposal about objects is very metaphysical, the one about fulfillment is very worldly.

Many an agent in Michals's tableaux is (or gets) stripped for action, but I don't remember seeing any consummation in the flesh. The disrobed condition of his people is but a sign of the overall pithiness of his outlook. As far as the demands of any story are concerned, there is very little material in any Michals sequence that could be judged extraneous to them. Now, photography does not arouse or exert pressure on my will to believe what it shows; it effortlessly warrants its content by displaying more than is necessary for any story. Its vast threshold of gratuitousness and inefficiency, from the strict narrative point of view, does wonders to guarantee its realism. Think of the clutter in Marlene Dietrich's bedroom compared to the spareness in Michals's interiors. The former is all realist triviality, and the latter is all idealist patterning. But, if that's his game, why is Michals a photographer, why has he resorted to this profane medium?

I think the answer must be that he had to give life to his particular ideas, he had to image them, and that their image-life depended on raising doubts that they were fictitious at the same time as he affirmed their mental origin. If the theme of this dialectical artist is transubstantiation, he had to have substance to start with, and where better to credit substance (the stimulus of external sensation) than in the medium of record, the photographic medium? Where other forms of representation all had their symbolic codes, this one hadn't. Where others employed an indigenous syntax, this one couldn't. It must have pleased him to see how these disparate modes, the projection of spirits and the photographic picture, could mate with each other. Even better, he goes the route, stylistically, not of the overtly directed and posed image, but of the street tradition. One notices right away that there is an apparently hurried manner to the tone and a blurred quality to some of the images in Michals's series, as if he had to act quickly in order to catch the demonic and split-second metamorphosis of an object into a creature. Moreover, the light in these delusional rooms has to be described as "available," and most often as natural. Michals shuns techniques of high drama and forboding while, just as consistently, he adopts methods of startled-looking observation. The more that I feel I can't keep up, that my camera eye is too slow to make out the swift pace of every development, the more I'm drawn into what appears to be a sequence of phenomenal moments.

In themselves, some of those moments might conceivably pass as intervals that were happened upon rather than planned. By delirious coincidences, as it seems, the photographer turned out to be in the right place at almost the right time. However, above and beneath the frames of sequences like "Take One and See Mt. Fujiyama," or "The Enormous Mistake," Michals writes a kind of voice-over that determines the inner alarm of his characters and snares them into their fates. I "know," from what I read, that this one's excitement had turned to terror, and that one "felt overcome with anxiety as he waited. Only his desire kept him from fleeing."

The apprehensive ones in the story cannot hear this narrator's voice, just as the actors in a movie canot hear the music on the sound track. Yet Michals's script works not so much as superior comment, orchestrated for my benefit, but as a metaphorical blanket that traps and amplifies the body warmth of his bedeviled players. Their supposed bafflement at the plight in store for them is charged by the issue of whether they can or should resist an erotic psychodrama just around the corner. In a Michals scenario, however, the energy or will needed to deny eros is always in short supply.

For his subjects, even the act of looking is suffused with erotic helplessness and thrilled by the animism of matter. Where the camera cannot show it, *words* will indicate precisely the randy tropism of things and people. In *The Pleasure of the Glove,* 1974, a young man's hand approaches a fleecy-lined glove, in one frame, and enters it, in the next. Yet the glove, says the text, "swallowed his hand." After that, when the hand tenderly pinches a woman's nipple, it's the culprit glove that did "what it wanted to do." Explicit as they are, words cannot verify the physical presence of the obsessive object. Illustrative as it is, the image cannot activate a magical effect. It's as if words and images reach toward each other in a Surrealist *folie à deux,* imbued by Michals with affection and grace. Gloves, coats, shoes, cups: all these plain, friendly, or protective objects, which we mold or touch, touch us in turn. It's a wonderful narrative conceit to have imagined that they, too, don't know their place and can't help themselves. Something about them arouses suspicion. As they are inspected, they slowly begin to fail their test for immobility. Most often, it's the third person who looks, the "he" or "she" of the script, whose glance innervates the surroundings. The artist, though, is not above slipping his proceeding into the first person, apparently without the text being the wiser. When it states that "The book was dull. He was bored," the picture contrarily insists that the reading head is that of the viewer, whichever "I" that happens to be. And who can say the artist no?

Unfortunately, in English, there's a confusion in usage of the words *object* and *subject,* a confusion that has certainly found its way into this essay. The figures in the photograph, for example, are *its* subjects, but they are the objects of the spectator's view. And, if that is the case, as it definitely is, then the spectator is the subject who perceives [other] objects, including—and this is horrible—the *subjects* of a photograph. In actual parlance, these differentials sort themselves out according to the local sense of who or what is considered, by whom, and from what vantage. Pictures, though, don't commit themselves, as does the possessive pronoun, to a practical distinction between subject and object, and that noncommital state can be conducive to narrative.

Michals, as an instance, provides a photograph of a couple seated on a bed, she embracing him from behind, and both looking outward, smiling (Fig. 24). Beneath this little play, one reads: "This photograph is my proof. There was that afternoon when things were still good between us . . . and we were so happy. It had happened. She

This photograph is my proof.

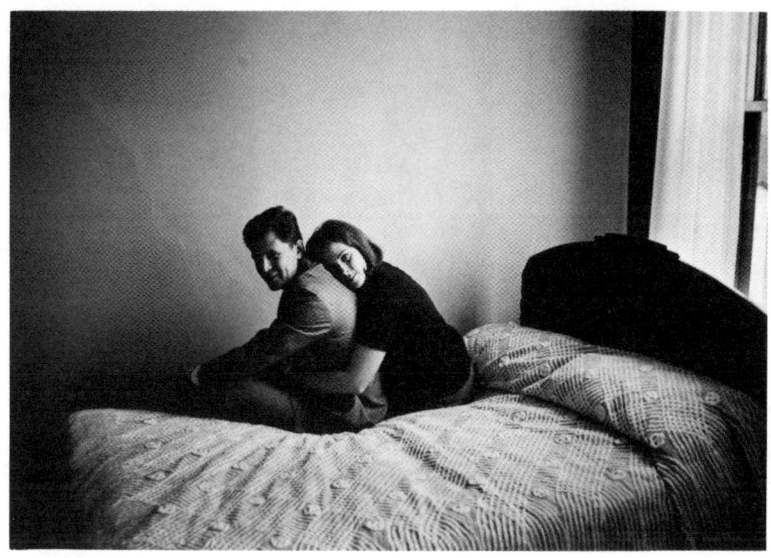

This photograph is my proof. There was that afternoon when things
re still good between us, and she embraced me and we were
so happy. It did happen, she did love me. Look see for yourself

Figure 24. Duane Michals, *This photograph is my proof,* 1974.

did love me. Look, see for yourself!" With these words, the writer is naturally identified with the image of the man in the photograph. He is projected as both the object of his own regard and the subject of the photograph, as both an actor who figured in his own story and the one who now furnishes it to the viewer. Previously, the text had not alluded to any historical time or determined place; it simply existed as dissociated comment, presumably elucidating what the equally timeless and bodiless pictures could not disclose. Thoughts and appearances that came from nowhere and lapsed into a void were partners in a narrative game. All that changes when it's a matter of a writer who has a face.

The time of perception is "now" and the written message is autobiographical, distinctly a question of someone's past. It's stated that from his vantage in our present a man remembers his past joy, the moment when a woman loved him. "That which had been" was good. No doubt, the tone of voice is a little desperate as the words urgently make out a case for memory. As evidence, a photograph is produced to substantiate that memory. But the image is so overly protected that it is smothered and consumed by the text. It's as if a whole life's meaning is being staked on the interpretation of a particular moment, the moment, only, of a photograph. In all this I am not so much moved by the implied feeling of loss or hope of fruitless redemption from the past, as by the appeal to my belief, an appeal which is quite misplaced. "Look, see for yourself!" What makes up the human need that wants to win me over in that way? Or, alternatively, who is it who would offer me such treacherous ground for such a large judgment? To ask such questions is to be taken further into the narrative.

Nevertheless, simply from the viewpoint of photography's folklore, Michals's character was quite within his rights to have broached his claim. After all, he would not have said: "Look at my *words,* trust them, they show that she loved me," for everyone knows they do nothing of the sort. If we discuss writing, with pictorial experience in mind, we must say that words only *show* that something has been written or printed. They cannot display their allusions, as pictures can, and they cannot come imprinted extrinsically by the world, as photographs do. Of course, the world is partly manifested by writing because some of the world's ink is deposited there, but I don't think the writer would be edified by that observation. As the piece intimates, it was the need to escape from the chronic egocentrism of telling, to be able to point at something issued from outside himself, to show it, that motivated him.

A photograph is not only an independent corroborative source, it's a form of witness, confirming itself by bringing some trace of that which was seen. The text here apparently yields to the superior, evidentiary power of the image, a little sycophantishly, but only to the extent it's to the text's great interest to do so—that is, to further a concept. So, the picture is explained in the narrative, but it isn't justified until its literally vagrant meaning is repossessed by the word *proof,* a concept that is alien to this, as to all visual images. In this sense, the priority of telling is reaffirmed even as text confesses that it is helpless to convince readers by its own means.

I've dwelled on such an issue in order to suggest how the aesthetics of photography, and particularly narrative photography are entangled with a special kind of pleading for the capacity of the image to visualize fact. In the art of Mac Adams, this aesthetic is incarnated perhaps not as elegantly as with Duane Michals, but with even more dispatch. This sculptor, working in New York, produced a number of photo diptychs during the 1970s. In such pieces, two images are butted together for a reason that is not immediately apparent, though it pays off in pleasurable anxiety. The more habituated I get to these *Mysteries,* as Adams calls them, the more it dawns on me that they anticipate or reflect, but never in themselves describe—put down for record in their present—the climactic violence that would be their subject. Fashion imagery had always been about the future, how one ought to look forward to a state of affairs it could realize with panache; these mysteries invoke a future, too, but it's the kind made familiar in horror films and thrillers. They are nasty in that conventional way, and gorey-minded. At the same time, they're stringently controlled by an invisible text that coldly insists upon the veracity of the material in the frame, its status as "proof" of foul play.

Malraux once wrote: "The Dutch were not the first to paint fish on a plate, but they were the first to stop treating it as food for the apostles." By the same token, it could be said of Mac Adams that he was not the first to depict sinister objects, but that he pioneered an artistic idea of still life as incrimination. The things in these photographs derive their importance from once having been owned by victims and from "now" being possessed or left as clues by murderers. The transfer of property in this world is totally grasping and ruthless, so much the outcome of endless rip-offs, muggings, betrayals, rapes, and homicides, that every single object comes through tainted by its inclusion in the mystery. Mac Adams shows a traffic in goods, fetish-

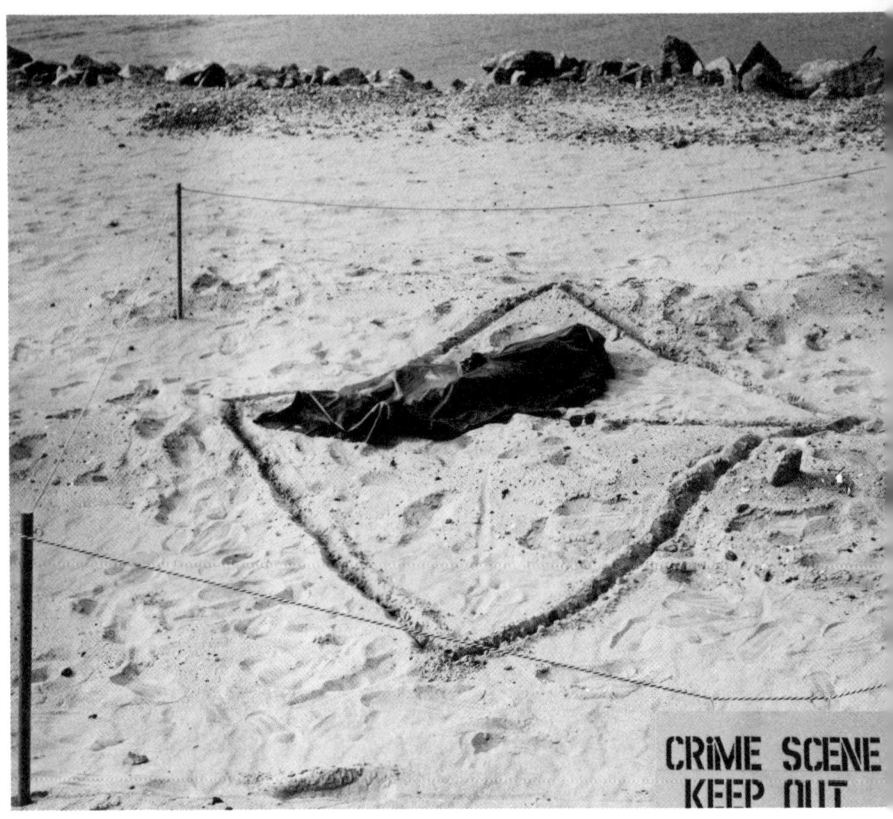

Figure 25. Mac Adams, *The Mystery of the Two Triangles,* 1978.

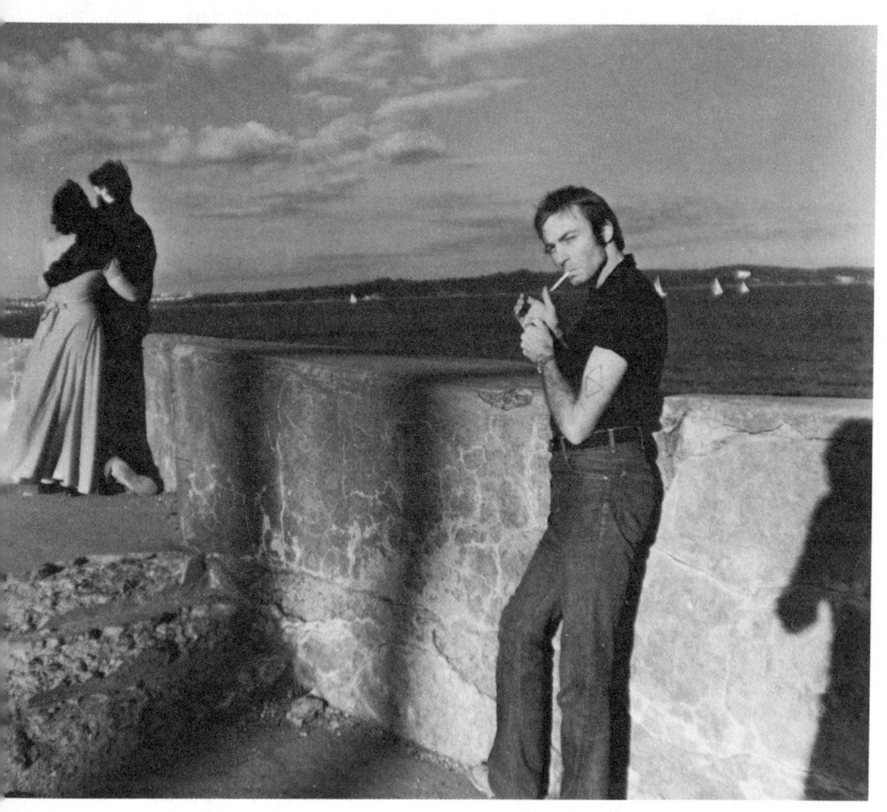

ized in such a way that it would satisfy all self-respecting Marxists and Freudians in the vicinity.

A woman's scarf, first seen on her neck, is later glimpsed dangling from a stump in filthy water. Poison goes into a glass, and then, inevitably, down a throat. In the time it takes for the toaster to do a slice of bread, a woman in deshabille dies. Cigarettes are offered and tatoos are worn by those who are up to no good. Like a trademark, the perpetrator's watch gives the time frame for whatever stealthy and lethal deed is accomplished between the first and the second shot. Bracketed densely at point blank range even when outdoors, each of the objects forensically shown by Mac Adams has something of the memento mori about it and also the Hitchcockian MacGuffin. Through a tantrum of showing, a rage for display at the expense of performance, the photographer achieves an effect of telling, that is, of story.

It is a paranoid's nightmare that has taken permanent form, a world in which there is no room whatever for the *indifferent* existence of things or people or situations. They take on an instant, suffocating meaningfulness. The apparently random information each picture contains is contracted psychologically, as it is physically, by the photographic frame. If that frame intends to leave no choice but an alarmed inference about its contents, it is because the limitations of frames are cunningly equated with the onset of formalized panic. Like a poison squirted by certain insects into their victims, the frame paralyzes action. I can no more intervene into the single picture than I can come back to it and find something else. When Mac Adams shows two frames yoked together, the second not only intimates the worse possible outcome of the first, but retroactively infects it with its fatality. Yet the frames themselves, though easy in their synthesis, imitate two rhetorical forms that deliberately clash.

One of them is the official police photograph that documents the aftermath of a murder and memorializes its grisly leavings. Such images rationalize what I've called the "lateness of our arrival" as witnesses to some state of affairs. This is a condition of all photographic experience, to be sure, though with this mode the state of affairs is exclusively the scene of a crime. Pictures of this sort record a disturbed territory, a place rumpled like the sheets of a bed, that is marked off for study by an investigative team, and which may be used as evidence in court. Yet Adam's reference to photographs that function as sources of authority and control is mainly strategic and would not, in itself, account for the shiver induced by the mystery. It's important to realize that the artist confronts us with two forms of observation simultaneously: the one of detached, impersonal, and bureaucratic scrutiny, and another of intimate involvement with the malignance as it brews. Joining them in this bifocal way, he gives me suspicious access to a moment of great sexual tension and imminent homicide, and then suddenly distances and disconnects me from it (Fig. 25). Were it not for being impressed by my lateness, I would not have been forcibly seduced by the illusion of *prior* entrée to the situation, where it is exciting to know, and apparently to be alone in knowing, that the worst has not *yet* happened. There is only one environment in which it is possible to function as an unseen witness at such awful proximity to the throes of private obsession: the world of movies.

In effect, the melodramatic revelations and the claustrophilic power of the film noir suit Mac Adams perfectly. With his *Smoke and Condensation,* the viewer is placed only inches away from the cruelty of which the images whisper exquisitely (Fig. 26). In the first frame, the curling smoke of a young woman's cigarette is like an arabesque that presages the second frame's wisp of hair, limply uncoiled from the rolled-up window of a car covered with drops of dew. It is as if the evaporation of a life gave off warmth that produced moisture on a cool surface. This artist is very indirect, even in the most explicit management of his scenarios. In the toaster piece, for instance, one never sees the victim, but only her reflection—and a fragment of it at that—on the shiny side of an appliance. Glass, chrome, wrinkled cloth, and spilled drinks: all these play their tactile role in the mystery, either by recollecting the flesh or repelling the sense of touch. Evidently these objects themselves are poseurs, representing something other than what they are: that is, they're props. In a Mac Adams mystery, human energy is snuffed out, with only the props as acknowledged but silent witnesses. Unlike Michals, who speaks of the sudden animation of objects into sentient life, Adams deal with the degradation of life into matter. Given this chillier theme, it's appropriate that the diptychs have a heated gaffing and staging, to compensate, with the artifice of the movie thriller, for the actual muteness of the still photograph. The "mystery," of course, is a dumb show compared to its genre reference. But what it lacks in scale, sound, and action through time, which convey the kinetics of film, it regains in the cryptic presence of the immobilized image, which eliminates all distractions from committed, self-interested looking.

Tapped in this way, film conventions provide a curious narrative advantage to the photographer, an incitement to "reading" where none

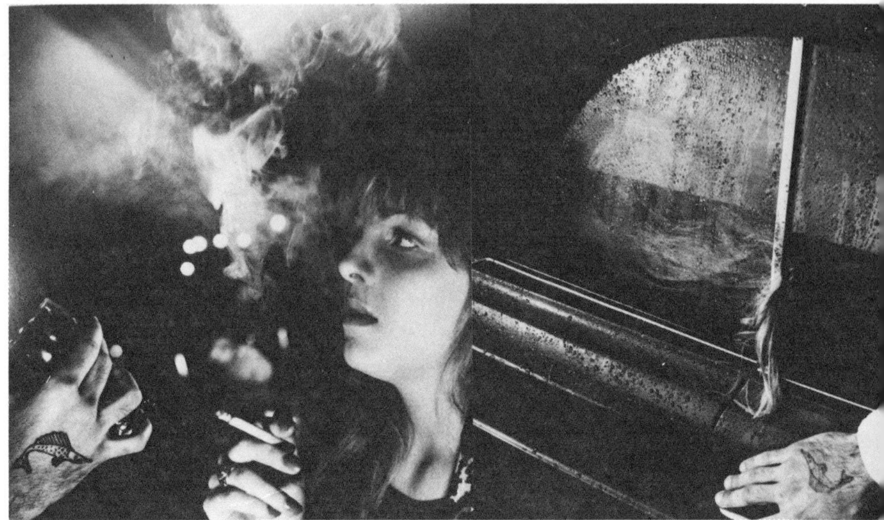

Figure 26. Mac Adams, *Smoke and Condensation,* 1978.

literally exists. Modern film, as we know, nominally dissolves any buffer zone between viewers and the immediate personal territory of the subjects, or rather, actors. So taken for granted is their conventional unawareness of viewer surveillance that the vulnerability of the players is all the more shocking when they mime in a photographic frame. I can accept the defenselessness of actors before my gaze much more readily in the film than I can in a photograph. Partially this is because I suddenly have time to think about what their exposure means, but also it's because the acting convention, with its spatial tolerance, is not yet very familiar in photography. Salomon's work with Dietrich did have such dramaturgy mixed in, though with journalistic intent. Film stills are purer examples of the type, but are popularly misunderstood to be teasing extracts (rather than paraphrases) of already finished scenes. Adams, however, seizes upon the totally solicitous yet completely fictive unconsciousness of acting in the film mode as a self-contained narrative vehicle in still photography. As a result, he profits enormously from the sense that the images come to us from a prior story, that they are emergent from a "plot." Without the filmic tag, what he shows would look arbitrary and even incoherent; with it, we have the erroneous conviction of voyeurs, keyed by the desire to make good on the invitational script.

He asks very little of his actors, in fact nothing more than the patience that would be required of them as models for advertising work. Instead of reproducing glossy production values from the studio, however, he comes too close for comfort into these grungy scenes and he knocks the lamp over.

At this point, I realize that while the *Mysteries* lack the absorptive power of the movie, as fluid wholes, they are necessarily dense in the single shot. It's not just that, with their fewer means, their material has to count for more than in an equivalent movie frame. How could it be otherwise? Rather, the density is realized in the degree to which the photograph makes me conscious of my own introspection, the work I exert in order to fill in or even to grant meaning. By piggybacking the thriller film, Adams alludes to the absorptive dimension of film but operates with the typical density of the photograph. I want to give and to lose myself, as if with delicious passivity in the movie house, but I cannot.

A bit earlier, I wrote of Mac Adams's *Mysteries* as a paranoid's nightmare made durable. In another context, Norman Bryson, a professor of English who has become an art theorist, describes paranoia as "a representational crisis in which nothing can exist for itself or innocently, for everything is perceived as a sign. To the paranoid, all existence is plot, not only as conspiracy but as narrative; paranoid reality is entire discursive."[5]

We have an informal word to denote a conspiratorial arrangement of possibilities in a life situation, the word *setup*. Both it and the cognate *frame-up* characterize the way an individual's moves are egged on and supervised for the purposes of adversaries. If such words resonate with genre overtones from the entertainment media, it may be because the media often aggrandize themselves through the projection of paranoid fear; they wouldn't be the media we know without that projection. Taking its cue from a literal boundary (conceivably a photograph's), *frame-up* insists upon an aspect of hostile determination so extreme, and covert, as to be called "entrapment." Part of the legal argument that has swirled around such entrapping scams or stings in the political arena has to do with whether they induce felonies that would otherwise not have happened. But in art, which is judged by the internal economy and credibility of its charades, there would be no bait unless it was *bound* to be taken.

All of which is to say that a relationship can exist between the ultra-selectivity of artistic processes, paranoid fear, and the idea of entrapment. Whatever element or motif is introduced, it performs in concert with an ensemble of implied meanings, each indefinitely modulated and inseparable from the others. Let viewers know that the stage has been set and the representation that follows can be said to have designs on them. Assume that the theatrical metaphor is actually in force. Nothing exposed on the pictorial stage, or within its frame, will ever get back to the wings where it can calm down and retire from significance. Of course, this state of affairs is only a temporary illusion produced through the aesthetic experience; in fact, it does not exist apart from the aesthetic experience.

For Bryson's paranoid, consciousness itself would be like this aesthetic experience, but for the key fact that it lacks a frame. If the paranoid's reality is fabricated as if it were art, that would imply a world of indiscriminate encroachment, a world of situations perhaps similar to those referred to in narrative art, except that they run amok. Everything is perfidiously other than what it would be taken for. There springs up, full-born, an untrustworthy and acutely unfriendly environment, an endless prospect of sign after sign, creating a dazzlement of semiotic misery. The paranoid is doomed to a relentless decoding of signs without ever diminishing their potential for harm.

Let us treat the men and women well; treat them as if they were real; perhaps they are.

—Ralph Waldo Emerson

Cut now to the eighties, the age of Reagan, which sees the rise of media evangelism and Calvin Klein, of Star Wars technology and "exhibition wrestling." That is, the era of ridiculous story content and debased narrative structures. Of course, our decade does not cover any new ground in the area of mendacious public performance. How could we deny to so many of our earlier leaders, corporate heads, and media manipulators their claims to distinction in this enterprise? But the present scene does contribute its own accent to these long-term discreditable proceedings. With Nixon, who was always reasonably worried about his credibility, performance and reality were having trouble resembling each other. The "credibility gap"—his phrase—referred to doubts about America's ability to export its paranoia in sufficient force to convince others that they should be scared of us. One remembers very well the performance anxiety of his press conferences, and one can still recall one's few faint flickers of hope that those who spoke were deep down capable of humiliation at the uncovering of their deceit. Nixon was a failed narrator, dismally caught out in the unsocial shortfall of his chosen signifiers. A famous photograph of this unhappy president, by Horst Faas, fixes him just so: in a crowd, shaking hands on his right while at the same time consulting his watch on his left.

Print journalism and electronic and TV news media have frequently exhibited an occupational disease of this sort that's gotten worse. They fail to distinguish enough between the fact that something was said and the fact that the thing said misinforms about the thing done. For reportage is naturally weighted in favor of the given, ready-made story as against the one that does not yet exist, the one reporters have to produce by investigative work. A yeoman part of journalism, therefore, transmits unanalyzed, unsubstantiated representations of interested, self-inflating parties, channeled through small, unconnected units or frames, the spot, the item, the column, the piece. The media, in other words, are effectively willing to be a function of public speakers, provided only that the speakers understand how to be media personalities, that is, competent playactors. Either their performance will bear scrutiny under repeated exposure, or they will lose media status. This is emphatically what happened with the bicameral hijinx of Nixon, the balsa woodenness of Ford, and the decayed smiles of

Carter. It is perhaps not exaggerated to say that they forfeited their continued office through their lack of media savoir faire. With the relaxed amiability of Reagan, on the other hand, it came into its own.

Fortunately for the rabid frothings of neoconservative policy, they could be honied over by the flow of presidential imagery, engineered for an ex-movie actor whose vestiges as a person were long ago incorporated into a public role. (He cannot be unmasked because there is nothing behind the mask.) Realized in terms of a familiar movie routine, the pose of this figure absorbs its audience into the illusion of proximity to the deed, which naturally occurs in the real world and has real consequences, though it is comfortingly presented as if it were only "realistic." Once any detail of the performance is accepted on its own involving level of make-believe, there's a likelihood it will take others with it into the charade. Whatever it may believe, the public subscribes to everything. For it feels itself in the presence of a performance that is naturally fictive, exempt, therefore, from the normal accountability of doings in actual life, as are spectacles and coarse entertainments. Like theirs, the subterfuge of the executive branch can be practiced openly. For reasons of its own, the press is eager to agree, by visibly feeding its source of attraction into its magnetic field. There grows up an acutely indulgent environment, a frameless prospect of sign after sign, instantly decoded according to the desire of the public, the fantasies it wants rather than the knowledge it needs.

In 1983 was published an old Warner Brothers publicity Kodachrome, *Jane Wyman and Ronald Reagan at Home,* 1947 (Plate 1), in which the fantasy is imperfectly executed. Intended as a portrayal of a young, healthy, wholesome Hollywood couple (of medium studio rank), enjoying the sun in their reclining deck chairs, the photographic enactment wobbles off the mark. There can be seen in the tension of their eyes, clamped shut, the rigidity of their bodies, the sucked-in stomach of the man, a strain that for this moment, at least, belies their nominal leisure. On an oppressively sun-baked terrace, placed against an indigestibly green hedge, the two subjects are characterized only by the effort of their pose, not what the pose was meant to signify. There's a discord between the theme and its realization, something not admitted—that could not be admitted—but which is nevertheless perceived.

Quite earlier in this essay, I wrote that the pose was a corrupted form of momentum. Among other things, that implies a dissolution of character, which, rather than being inflected and therefore vitalized by action, was marooned and trapped in a fishy pseudo-moment. But it's the phenomena of such dissolution, the nervously self-conscious gesture, the slip of the shutter, errors of setting, and the psychic detail that *undermines* the charade, which excite an aesthetic interest of the 1980s.

The Reagan photograph comes from a book called *Still Life* (edited by Diane Keaton and Marvin Heiferman), a collection of movie stills and studio shots dating from the forties to the early sixties. To be sure, they are the promotional flotsam of a vulgarity that has not aged well. But when we compare them now with our memories of the period, they have a strangeness that was not expected and that is even breathtaking. Instead of a nostalgic charm, kindled by the look of manners presumably simpler or sweeter than those today, they have a distressing relevance to our own historical moment, manifest through the evident fissure of manners, and the view this gives of civility itself as only the thinnest, brittle veneer over a less speakable consciousness.

The origins of such an effect are not difficult to describe. To leaf through this album is to encounter a series of hyper-formulaic postures, uneasy grimaces, and absurd group pantomimes. See, for example, how George Peppard flubs his vengeful look (or whatever) at a bedroom double murder. One doesn't know whether to be amused or saddened over the plight of these characters, their pictorial bondage to fancied scenes or situations with which they exhibit not the slightest personal engagement. No one's body, much less mind, is animated by the spirit of the part to which it has been assigned. For the issue in *Still Life* is not one of performance—bad as that may be—but the *display*—a kind of mock-up—of performance. Pretending to be a sample frame from the original film, the still is, in fact, either a reconstruction or a thematic alternate to some passage or vignette already in the can. The false colors of the still's concept are inevitably echoed in the fraudulence of its execution, which is a gloss on the artifice of the film itself. No one in a view camera film still is in the throes of an actual performance. Rather, they have lifelessly assumed its attitudes, *as if* they were performing. Hence the relation of such images to dioramas, tableaux vivants, waxworks, or, as the authors of *Still Life* declare, to taxidermy. If the film still miraculously came to us from actual life, as it wants vaguely to signal, its subjects would have been stopped in their tracks by the camera, whereas these subjects have been prearrested before the shot, and the camera only confers upon their phoney mobility an additional, accusatory inertness. From one frame to the other; from one paralytic to the next.

Rarely have such disabilities been made as spectacular as in this case of still photography. In the medium, highly elaborated melodrama is exotic. Since any actor inanimately trying to bring that mode off has only one go at meaning, the pictorial result must stem from extreme compression of "performance," which certainly doesn't wish to avoid hyperbole. There is such a thing as a theatrical concentrate, just as there is a juice concentrate. Movies thin it out and give it the proper suspension. As they subliminally flicker away, they take a great many of their gaffes past us before there's time or will to disbelieve them. I point to the frivolities of their stagecraft, their incoherent cutting, and the gaucheries of their direction. Even these will have the grace that motion bestows on appearances, only too ungainly when considered as static icons.

To my eyes, that ungainliness now inadvertently calls for critical judgment. These photos are self-stigmatizing. They're founded on a psychology that was content to go no more than through the motions of a scene while eagerly pretending that they are larger than life, within a setting visualized in irrelevant physical detail. As Heiferman says: "Everything . . . is displayed too accurately . . . there's no discretion and no escape from the sheer over-abundance of visual facts. There's no cause and no effect."

Just the same, they make their pitch as plot-laden narrative images, whose story line has unfortunately receded from them over the years (assuming that it was ever clearly articulated in the original context). Somewhere, very early in our experience of them, we sense a verbal remote control that we can't figure out anymore. The first impression is extravagantly inviting and the second is that we've missed the punch line. On the strength of the one equivocal frame, showing Mia Farrow, Lawrence Harvey, and Tom Courtenay in dignified but indelicate confrontation, I defy anyone to guess the main thrust of the screenplay in their film *A Dandy in Aspic* (Plate 2). Explicit but no longer expository, it has a fustian quality reminiscent of anecdotal Victorian painting and photos, or even of some eighteenth-century art, of Greuze, for example.

I can imagine being told not to be so hard on these rather slight photo products, spin-offs from larger commercial efforts. They have their conventions, and it would be misguided to impose on them any literalism, any obligation to tell a truth they were not designed to serve. Nonetheless, their conventional incapacity to move a contemporary spectator on their own terms—the backfire of their conventionality, if you will—provides a source for new content. Our habit now is to look past or deeper into what the conventions would screen out from the visual image, either in the photographs discussed so far, or the painting just mentioned. As Norman Bryson says of Greuze:

> We cease to obey the order [to empathize] the moment we recognize that language is not in full control of the image; as soon as an aspect of the image is recognized as incongruent with the discursive control, we reject the whole apparatus of control . . . and instead . . . we attend to the pathology of the image . . . and once we do that it is we ourselves who are in control of the image, and not its official discourse.[6]

Bryson's point includes more than the truism that time erodes art meanings that were once possibly clear; he enjoins us to uncover other meanings, inhibited by social constraints so that they could not have been openly acknowledged: a historical judgment but also a critical act. Greuze's "pathology" impelled him to ascribe a sexual knowingness to his virginal milkmaids. (Moon's Riding Hood belongs to their tribe, too, but explicitly.) These film stills, on the other hand, have only an innocent spuriousness to recommend them. In Greuze's case, more affect seeps through the reading than is nominally stated, while, in the film stills, with a similar, weird tension, affect falls way short of the discursive intent.

Discrepancies of this sort—and they're endemic—make criticism's day. As they're lumberingly worked out, the film stills employ hyperrealist means to achieve symbolic ends, and since they do this unreflectively, they get into trouble. But the breakdown of narrative maneuver is itself the product of a narrative heat more long-standing and intense than any we've seen. Its producers don't care how much of the story nutrients are lost so long as the idea of a story is brought to a boil. Like many other dilemmas of photographic experience, this one is materialized in confusions of time and space.

Being spatial, the single image is perceived in the real time of the spectator. The first concern of a narrative image is to superimpose its temporal metaphors on the actual viewing duration, whatever length the viewer gives it. As long as we look, or as briefly as we look, we have the same allusive moment. It cannot be reduced or extended, and certainly it can't be interrupted, since we have the visual whole of it each time we engage with the image. The film stills naturally obey all this, and, just as naturally, they want to contradict it. They counter as forcefully as they know how, the idea that we have the whole of what there was to see, even as they would give out what was most representative or fetching to see. Without a complex history that preceded it, it was impossible for the characters to have gotten into this particular jam, as distinct from all other jams. Where was it written that their fate had to be that way, except in that absent model up yonder, the movie? Since the entire tale is lodged in the medium that actually has the time to store it, this spatial fragment must surely be aswim somewhere in a finite, continuous narrative. This explains why, as soon as I contact the image, it invariably gives me the sense that it's already "started."

Impossible, of course, but no matter. The look of this Greuze-some visual idiom had been appreciated by contemporary photographers even before the publication of *Still Life.* What the book did was to confirm and reflect a memory of narrative images that didn't have to be freshly constructed, while leaving the artist free to invent on other levels.

In reviving narrative for serious photography, Cindy Sherman and Eileen Cowin have kept the still's priceless sense of appearing in the swim. But they have inverted that image's reason for being. Stills fulsomely push the immediacy of their effect. They ask us to believe that a static mock-up of a performance, which is in turn an interpretation of a script—in other words, an image at three representational removes from experience—is, in fact, absorbing. Cowin and Sherman insist that it is distancing. A great deal of the still's habitual gestures and studio lighting is retained, but the genre's faith in itself, its conventionalized will to convince, is deleted. If it had once stemmed from a parent film, the artistic still is now orphaned. If it had wanted to conceal the filters through which it proposed its theatrical work, these are now made self-evident. What is strange in this otherwise familiar environment is that its own metaphors are suddenly used against it (Plates 3–5).

In short, Cowin and Sherman have compromised the living daylights out of a cheap entertainment mode. Even if their critique is mounted through a mimicry of postures that were already extreme, these artists are not, however, didactic. They assume that since it demanded inauthentic performance, the text was corrupted before the poses, but this premise wants to be *shown* in their work, not told. The showing is open to all sorts of interpretative choices except the original manipulation. A deliberately hollow overstatement is, of course, involved in a self-conflict because it simultaneously confesses to the exhaustedness of its forms and yet hopes for the renewal of meaning. Because of its near resemblance to the psychological conditions through which the media themselves are received (I take film stills and their like to be a sector of media), this is a dangerous game.

Media directors knowingly misrepresent products through the process called hype, which does not attempt to persuade viewers so much as to minimize their skepticism. If you maintain the exorbitance of your transmission, you might regulate and stabilize the level at which it's discounted, until a receiver fatigue sets in, amenable to soft, long-term programming. The media pass themselves off as having a genuine falsity, an honest chicanery. They do lie—they make intentionally deceptive statements—but as a form of socially *expected* hyperbole, privileged by our system of free competition. The redundancy of hype is a social fact of primary importance. It purveys a hallucinatory environment so widespread that it's progressively easier to give into it, to yield, not to the frankness but the cheery zeal of its artifice until the artifice isn't seen or doesn't matter any more, and we are variously naturalized to it. All the more, then, do the singular dreams of art need to be counted as exceptions or as antidotes to the media.

Of course, art is not open to the same potential for falsehood as are the media because art's dynamic is a play of metaphors judged by their interactive synthesis, which may or may not seem to allude to any external state of affairs but is not, in any event, held accountable to them. To see how this contrast between art and the media can be perceived, consider one theme—of the sunbather—first as it was treated in the publicity photograph of the Reagans and then in an image by Eileen Cowin.

In Hollywood, the subjects were illustrated from the point of view of how they were at home, rather than who they impersonated at the office. Rhetorically concerning itself with that which is the case, this is some kind of hack studio approach to candor that did not intend to let go of the hype. Time has made the Reagan's representation of their home life bleed a little, as it might any social charade that tried to imitate domestic happiness. Cowin's "bather," on the other hand, exists as someone who certainly posed in a photographic scenario, as did the movie actors. This young man isn't so much acting, though, as being there, relaxed, and apparently completely indifferent to the fact that he's inside and can't get any sun. Such a figure performs or rather functions dramatically, to be sure, but somehow on the other side of charade, in a zone where the rehearsal of social interactions and the elements of plot are, themselves, objects of study. The situation within the physical frame is clearly controlled by the textual frame but so overtly at the cost of the text itself that behind it another text has to be imagined, one that requires pantomime to be a self-exposing, defeated activity. However everyday in some details of the family going about its various interior business, this is a topsy-turvy environment. At every turn where I might happen upon gaps between intention of the play and performance of the role, I see that they have been anticipated and staged by Cowin. In fact, that's the only way her little theaters come to us, preincriminated by design. Within that totally preemptive framework, she makes her social observations and finds her moral truth. That is, this artist becomes reliable in a manner that transcends the duplicity, off which she feeds.

Cowin deals with the American family, which is seen as a nexus of sexual and sibling intrigue, or of the warfare of parents and children, a domestic version of international espionage. Essentially all this is enacted in the manner of afternoon television soap operas, and as if fashioned in the genre of film stills. Cindy Sherman investigates only one character in dozens of guises borrowed from movies, television, magazine illustration, adolescent comic strips, and cheap supermarket or drugstore romances. The subjects in both artists' work conform to the great ubiquitous mass of cultural programming, the most sentimental and pandering, from whose pulp is squeezed a ludicrous but at the same time, a disquieting melodrama. It is a rude scenography of typed emotions, where groups or single individuals endure a kind of mute, bathetic crisis of disappointment, jealousy, ennui, and betrayal.

I want to find language to imply that this photographic indictment of media culture, while political, has not gone so far as to cease being poetic. In Sherman's case, the heroine falls into a dream imaginable as in the same style as she is visualized. It would appear that her mysteries are as sorry as her situation. Often caught in some strained perplexity or sullen moping, tense, disheveled, expectant, or with a vacant gaze that suggests she is psychologically far removed from where she is, this tough or vulnerable, dry or strangely wet young woman is her own spectator, the artist herself. Here is an art ruled by the emotional polarities of feminine self-sufficiency or helplessness, coded in a limited range of body gestures and facial expressions. In the work since 1981, narrative is understood, not as a sequence of depicted events that elapse within an assumed time, but as the lighting up of an inner life, so intense in its moment that time appears suspended in the brimming eyes of its own fiction. Remarkably, these very large single-figure arrangements are void of noticeable incident, yet they tingle with action. Just the same, if I were to list what is in them, I would be adding up a number of features that would suggest portraiture rather than narrative. What is a photographic portrait if not the record of a deliberate human encounter, in which one or more individuals had presented themselves to the look of another? And what are these photographs if not pictures that resemble but do not function as portraits? That is their paradox: they display the person *despite* the persona. So that we may have a series of fanciful self-portraits, the creator is a ventriloquist of her own sentiments. The story might then consist of the dialogue between the shadowy creature behind the scenes, the one who constructs the tableau, and the physical one who poses under her makeup and wigs. To invent others who may also be vaguely herself—such is the goal—but also to break herself down, to depict the moving scene of her mind.

Of late, the characterizations have become manic and the costuming sketchy—she wears any old rag—in the deepening, Cibachrome murk. The sultrier poses ebb away, and outraged ones come to the fore. The pattern that emerges from this development might be embodied by the gradual assertion of a consciousness opposite to the narcissistic one which began such work. There, the plight of the heroine was constructed from the vantage of the figure who received or occasionally suspected unwelcome attention, and who was the object of stares that transgressed her space. The representation was interesting because it combined the psychology of two countervailing fictions: that the woman could not have been at fault for being victimized and yet that she was seductively prone to it. This was the period of the artist's early "film stills." Sherman recalls that

> I used to put makeup on sometimes . . . experiment and make my face to look like somebody else. . . . Once I started doing it I realized that people were entertained by it and also very confused. . . . But when I moved to New York it seemed almost cliché. There were so many strange looking people on the street . . . I realized that by doing it so many times in a row I felt like I was losing my street identity, which you really need in New York. I was becoming vulnerable by being somebody I didn't identify with.[7]

So, the vulnerability, it might be supposed, was placed into the work, distanced there until the masquerade threatened to disintegrate personality within the frame as it once did beyond the frame. Somewhere, the romantic element of self-pity lost ground in these images to the notion of a person who had a firmer grip on herself, and who stared back, angry, at the impinging spectator. The Sherman who conceived the image, and provided the text for it, is at growing odds with that female pawn and flunky who acted out the role. This is not the same thing as making faces at yourself in the mirror, for it is transcribed permanently as a conflict between the demands of art and of reality, locked together in resentful poise.

Eileen Cowin, too, composes imagery in which she is personally embroiled as an actress. It is not absolutely necessary to know that the artist, her twin sister, husband, and other members of her family perform in these "docudramas," but such knowing enriches her scripts. It's as if she has taken the lid off her own household, or more accurately, removed one of its walls. The result gives quite a formalized viewing station for the proceedings, in contrast to the thrusting camera of Sherman. For all that it violates their apparent privacy, Cowin's perspective does not often trespass her characters' space. Occasionally, a tripod camera is seen within their rooms, and she has even represented herself or her double at work with it, in advertisement of her presence both behind and in front of the lens. *How* the episodes are portrayed sometimes gets equal billing with *what* is portrayed in them. The idea of "docudrama" is just such a hybrid form to match her dual strategies of stagecraft, since it weaves fictional situations around "real" people. Just the same, these people rarely start up in the guise of specific characters, but are immobilized in general roles, frosted along the edges with an almost allegorical presence: the mother, the lover, the victim, the husband. These figures are no more animated than the withdrawn protagonists of a Robert Bresson film. In order to arrive at meaning, she seems to say, mood has to be purged and affect reduced. A fairly uniform deportment and a clear consistency of light illuminate scenes that could be described as explosive. Cindy Sherman kept the meretricious at bay by overcharging it; Eileen Cowin, by understating it. This is what knocks me off balance as I look: the promise of flashy indiscretion combined with the poker-faced performances and nerveless photographic style.

In fact, Cowin's scenarios have the look of situations without any of the convergence of purpose that define situation. Many of her tableaux collect miscellaneous activities that could not have taken place in that one time and that one room. I have a choice of thinking that these adulterous ones (if that's what they are), and television watchers, sleepers awakened, and birthday celebrants are either astonishingly indifferent to each other, oblivious really, or else consciously estranged from those around them. In one picture, two standing people, kissing each other, are inexplicably bordered off at head level with a frame while the man bestows a rose to a seated woman to his right and kids play Clue on the floor. In another, kitchen work goes on, along with sunbathing, housepainting, and primping for some evening occasion. Certainly all this incongruity is the product of synchronous presentation, the fact that disparate, temporary separate things were crowded together. Many of these images are anthologies pretending to be unique selections. Loading the material in one shot, the artist achieves a phenomenal, speechless concentration, asserting that all the life one needs to know is quarantined in these sheet-rock rooms with their matte shadows.

Though they live together, are mutually dependent and intimately related, the characters in these scenes interact only partially and poorly. They exist side by side, but not with each other, so their inwardness tends to cancel the domestic moment, which falls apart as it is examined. When something promises to warm up a little bit, such as an adult tryst, Cowin ensures that it be discovered; when the son is about to blow out his birthday candles, the father is distracted. Nothing's followed through; the whole vignette is a series of stoppages and of energy draining away in anticlimax. Rather than comparing levels of psychic connection or disconnection—which, on one plane she certainly does—Cowin seems more interested in showing that cross purposes organize the family, that people either quietly get in each other's way or that the family is a club whose members demonstrate a fatal lack of consideration toward each other at moments of need. These misalliances of impulse could have been described in a comic light or with tragic overtones. Cowin, however, expresses a fondness for statuesque occasions.

The sculptural, a feeling for studied volumes and spaces, inhibits the narrative, and this, by and large, is a very curious outcome for a series titled *Docudramas*. It took me a while to get acclimated to this atmosphere and to feel my way into the performance that it exhibits. Cowin's texts are hackneyed enough and also complex; they don't lend themselves to advantageous treatment in a visual mode that is only spatial. How does one visualize, say, the shriveling of a person through emotional neglect—a condition that begs to be unfolded by words, but one that resists being imaged? (Compare the level of difficulty here with an easier representation—a resigned soul.) Then I noticed that this artist and Cindy Sherman, too, employ a repertoire of sight lines and eye contacts, converging or deflecting, that excites the narrative appetite at a point where literature itself falls off and can't compete. An intensity flares in the eyes. Someone wants to parry it or doesn't pick up on it; others show that they're witnesses—and all this can be articulated without the flailing of arms. That is, I can be made to see, durably, how people regard each other, what judgments are being made at close range. It even happens that some subjects gaze off to the viewer with a look that suggests appraisal.

Sherman shows particular bravura on this level. There is someone just next to me whom she is about to perceive; someone behind me or the left. I am made to feel that I've walked into or run afoul of this kind of awareness, or even that my being there ignites it. Under no circumstances does the same kind of charged perception arise in viewing the *Still Life* book. With the infinitely greater equipment of the studio behind them, film stills produced characterizations that went particularly dead around the eyes. Those actors didn't know how to look at anyone other than as fellow captives locked into the same script. On the contrary, as Sherman emboldens the glance she engages viewers in a suddenly open situation. Breaking through the psychological vitrine of the old stills, the inspective gaze targeted on her heroine is being paid back in kind, as if it were an inflammation of my own thought.

As long as I take in the subject's stare—that is, as long as I, myself, look—I am held in an unnamed story, a creature of someone else's imagination. It weakens me, detains me in its illusory place and motivates me despite my conscious will. Or rather, it insinuates something about my will that I would not have guessed. No doubt the power of this address stems from a much more sophisticated understanding of photographic dynamics than was available to earlier media.

But the real basis of comparison here is probably with novels whose manipulation of the word *you* points to the reader. The author transgresses upon the fact that the fiction is being read, as if to appropriate the reader into the narrative (or breach the narrative into the reader's world). In this case, the device is a soft metaphor, a mental construct alluding to a physical vector. Such indicative movement is, on the contrary, *enacted* by the gaze of photographic subjects when they peer outward. As with the viewer, the way they handle each other visually is chronically penetrating. Let the eyes have that kind of laser excitement and the body can relent in the reach of its performance. Dare I go further and say that such a graphic device, or rather insight, tells as much as it shows, that the activity of telling and of showing are fused in this aspect of the scenario? I cannot "see" anything like it as I read a text, but the carnality of it in the photographs is brought to me by virtue of another sort of text, the mental concept that underlies the degraded charade of the image. As an expressive feature, the

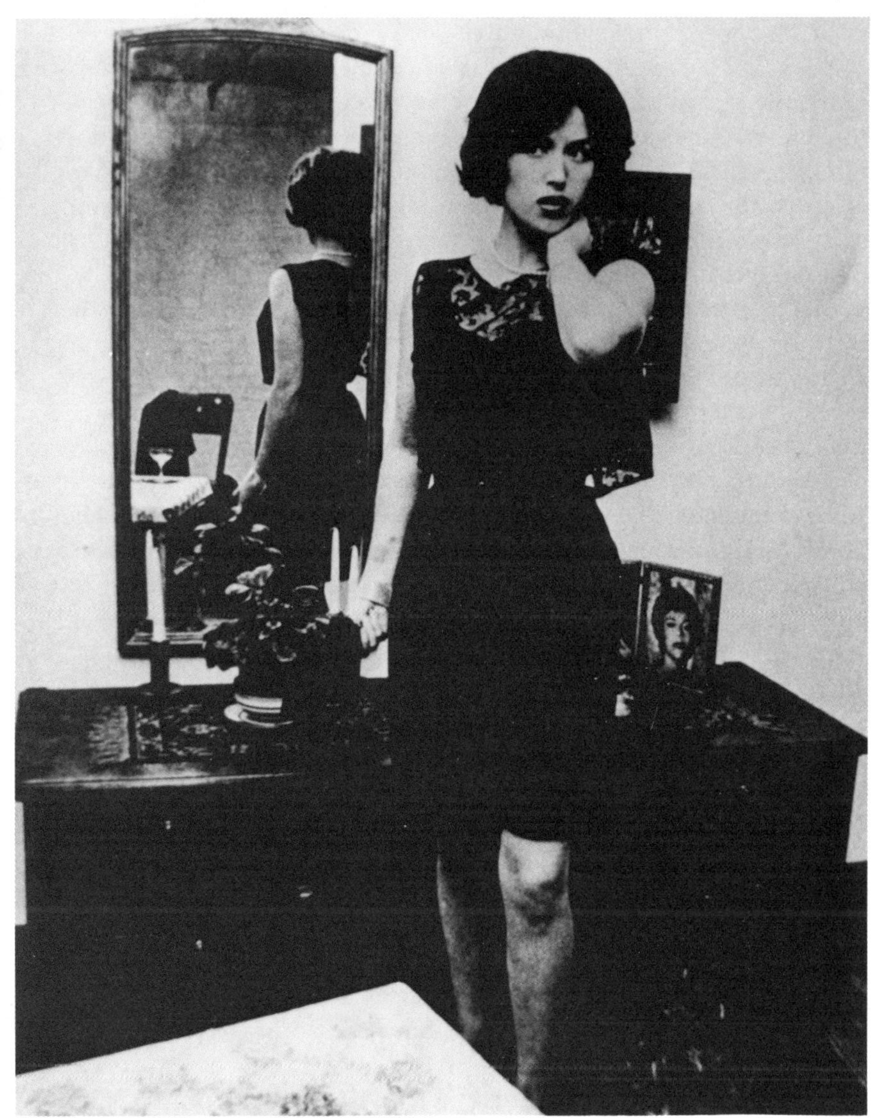

Figure 27. Cindy Sherman, *Untitled Film Still #14,* 1978.

sightline inheres in a thoroughly visual order of perception, and yet it operates as an explicitly discursive phenomenon. Mute as they are, and immobile, these figures had better be watchful, lest they forfeit one of the few dramatic resources that is given to them. This, alone, does not distinguish the work of Cowin and Sherman, or Adams and Michals, for that matter, from painting that may articulate a similar state of affairs. But the art of painting, while it can signify, will never transcribe that moment "out there," when a body is controlled by the vigilance of the one who images it. For the photograph, whatever it may come to mean, is a product of that control, not a hypothesis of it. If we could not apprehend that control as an actual event, we could not speak of the voyeuristic mood of much of photography in general, and of this narrative genre in particular.

The artists of this genre have increasingly emphasized the transgressive potentials of the photographic medium. They had models for doing this in prior imagery, but the idea of probing the inwardness of all concerned, including themselves, is struck off their own bat. So often, the knowing smile, the anxious glance, or the intimidating stare, reinforced by media echoes, and accompanied by stage-whispering props, reflect very evident autobiographical concerns. They are felt, sometimes, as only thinly disguised. It is all very well to accentuate the work's fictive strategies, but the animus behind them seems generated by a lived experience, symptomized by the presence of the artists themselves, the people and the things they know. There is an estranged ardor in this imagery, burning through the everyday pathology of the creator's life. She could have extended out to themes that lie further afield but found, instead, that the larger issues of culture and the politics of looking could be well realized through forms of theatrical introspection. While a distancing effect is one result of this choice, it also works to invade one's own privacy, to acknowledge vulnerability through one's own process.

I could say that this interests me though the truth is that it obviously goes further and *implicates* me in its activity. Now, it's worth asking who is this "me," this person who has written of his implication? When a photographer conveys a story or story fragment through various determinations of subjects' eye contact, she is reflexively illustrating what she does when constructing, editing, and revising the scene. This "me" is the one who has been flustered in thought and also the one who has constructed certain thoughts, as represented in this essay. Every writer is aware of such gradual distinctions in the writing act, though I don't know how many would choose to impose such a schizoid interpretation upon the way it completes itself. But there again, this "I" has been used to leave no doubt that it functions here as a rhetorical pronoun. I can assure you that there is another more or less assuming "I" behind the one that began this sentence. A kind of voice had to be fashioned out of word order and rhythm, and a kind of stance had to be adopted for the one who spoke. An essay devoted to examining the effect of particular images upon the psyche of a viewer would be a very strange exercise in self-cancellation if it did not recognize who is doing the viewing. Bodiless and affectless comment tends either to overawe readers by its authoritarian remoteness or put them to sleep by its impersonal drone.

To accord with this text's needs and aims, the two "I's" had to be brought relatively near each other, but not so close as to efface representation. The difference between viewing and writing (let alone writing and spontaneous thinking) can only be bridged by rhetoric. Something of the same applies to the difference between a monologue with oneself and a social address to others, which takes the form of performance. For these reasons, the "me" spoken of here wants to sound like the so-called real me but would not be satisfied in letting you think it is *only* me. The things said to happen to me, in the course of this writing, are proposed as things that could have happened to you. Really, it's a terrible bore to displace all the time with "one feels" or "we feel" when what is meant is "I feel!" The effect of these subterfuges is either of uncalled-for detachment or premature chumminess. Who could possibly know how "one" feels or what you, whom I haven't met—what you feel? So, the first-person reference sounds preferable, provided it has a kind of generic ring to it. The impression to be avoided was that of a definite ego, bristling with its necessarily idiosyncratic, sovereign, and exclusive opinions. These would be far less rhetorically useful than the passivity of an indefinite ego, capable of being acted upon more demonstratively by the artistic content. What speaks here is perception that asks very simply to be compared and then replaced with that of others.

Where these matters become more intriguing is in the suggestion, all along, that the camera "eye" solicits the viewer's eye, insinuates itself as an alter ego of the viewer. Narrative greatly depends on this primitive transference, so that, case by case, an appropriate viewer personality is formulated within the story. To look at Calvin Klein's ads is to be assigned the role of a consumer titillated by voyeuristic intrusions. To look at Michals's figures is to become a fellow adventurer in the course of their erotic teases, fabulous liberations, and final mundane reckonings. With Mac Adams, it was possible to wonder about the lessened moral stakes and prying interest in the business at hand. To look at those diptychs is to be characterized as someone with premonitory insight, a stalker, a connoisseur of sexual pathology. Above all, one who does not interfere when the extremity of the situation calls for interference. Here is Adams's exemplary viewer, conditioned by the passive aggressions of the media.

If I now ask what kind of viewer is fantasized by the images of Cowin and Sherman, the answer is much harder to arrive at. Perhaps it can be approached, roundabout, with the help of an author investigating a related problem. Jonas Barish, at the end of his book *The Antitheatrical Prejudice,* writes:

> We come into this world encircled by watchful eyes, to whose expressions we quickly learn to adjust our own. Our efforts at self-definition consist of our attempts to cope with this amphitheater of gazes—to accept it, without evasion, as constitutive of us in the first place, but then to refuse to bow to its despotic edicts. . . . The props are ready and the rest of the cast is mustered . . . but the script we must provide for ourselves.[8]

He then goes on to talk about two (schematic) choices made visible in this reckoning:

> . . . to settle for a hand-me-down part, one fashioned for us by others, which we ape by performing "gestures" [or] to perform "acts," to invent ourselves from nothing, neither shamed nor frozen into ineffectuality by the sea of faces that surrounds us.

Whatever the local instance, the cumulative effect of Cowin's and Sherman's work is to show characters who have trouble with the distinction between "gestures" and "acts." (A familiar state of affairs, though the distinction is much easier to make in language than in actual experience.) That uncertainty is depicted through their resistant life in a maiming and baneful environment, programmed by media, that is, an environment that smugly defines normal behavior as hyped behavior. Surely this wavering response of the posing actors, this weaving in and out of personable conduct, accounts for the overall sadness of these pictures, a tone lacking, for instance, in the graceful imagery of Sarah Moon.

Yet this sadness is also a facet of critical consciousness, turning upon itself, and rendering me happily volatile in my own choices. Such art risks looking like its enemy in order to deflate the representations of what it opposes. It does that by means of the open script which induces me to collaborate with the visual fiction in a problematic way. Text being at deliberate variance with performance, my belief is at odds with my subscription to the drama. The outcome, I believe, is a new sort of understanding about the challenges of self-creation, at least as far as photography makes us reflect on shared experience. I sense in many of these pictures a fascinated but also a wrathful look at theatricality as a closure of human potential. On one level, they are about the distortive effects of acting as self-regard. Nonetheless, art that bases itself on the exposure of psychological truth is, like all art, inevitably founded in representational modes. I've been writing about the various poses used by people to represent themselves, including the representation of myself as author. Evidently, our representations would have little point unless they were oriented by a fantasy, either generated more from within or imposed largely from outside an individual.

Be it a domineering fantasy or one of succor, of rapture, of justice, of self-identity, of remembrance, or of havoc, it is sought after in representations. They give back to those who engage with them a measure of their own yearning. As it illuminates what is submerged, our yearning cannot tell itself so much as it demands to be told of, by images and texts held together in necessarily uneasy suspension. This is to talk about that which is impossible to grasp except when it is put at a distance, the distance of the fictive. On the scale from fairly light to heavy fiction, the needle of photography can oscillate with maddening effect, leaving criticism to argue for when that might depress or enhance consciousness. Exposed from frame to frame, the continuum of desire and fear competes with a hesitant, correcting flow of fact, the outcome favoring neither the one nor the other until the self is interrogated. What does the self know? What does it want? What does it need? The still photograph of narrative import, spawned illimitably in exchange between art and the media, agitates those issues as its reasons for being.

A much reduced version of this essay was published in Artforum, *April 1986.*

1. Stanley Cavell, "Some Reflections of the Ontology of Film," in *New American Review* 12, edited by Ted Solotaroff (New York: Simon and Schuster, 1971), p. 147.
2. Vilém Flusser, "Towards a Philosophy of Photography," *European Photography* (Gottingen, 1984), pp. 7–8.

3. *Ibid.*

4. Duane Michals, quoted by Michel Foucault in *Duane Michals, Photographies de 1958 à 1982* (Musée d'Art de la Ville de Paris, 1982), p. ix.

5. Norman Bryson, *Word and Image: French Painting of the Ancien Regime* (Cambridge: Cambridge University Press, 1981), p. 40.

6. *Ibid.*, p. 153.

7. Quoted by Els Barents in *Cindy Sherman* (Munich: Schirmer/Mosel, 1982), pp. 13–14.

8. Jonas Barish, *The Antitheatrical Prejudice* (Berkeley and Los Angeles: University of California Press, 1981), pp. 475–76.

Plates

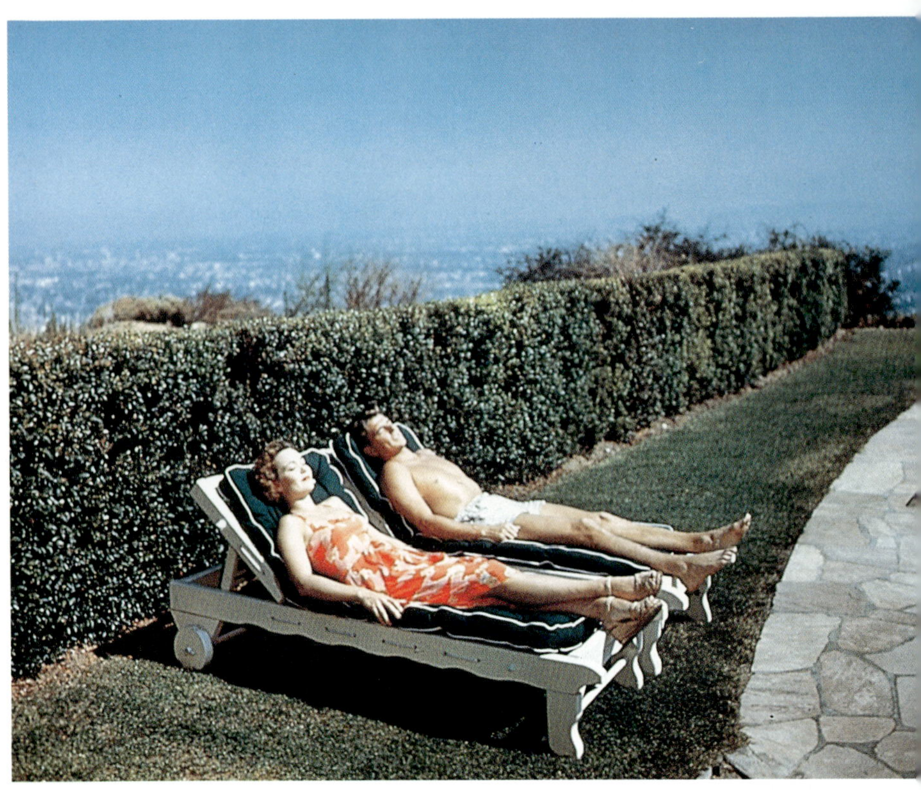

Plate 1. Anonymous, *Jane Wyman and Ronald Reagan at Home,* 1947 (Warner Brothers publicity photo).

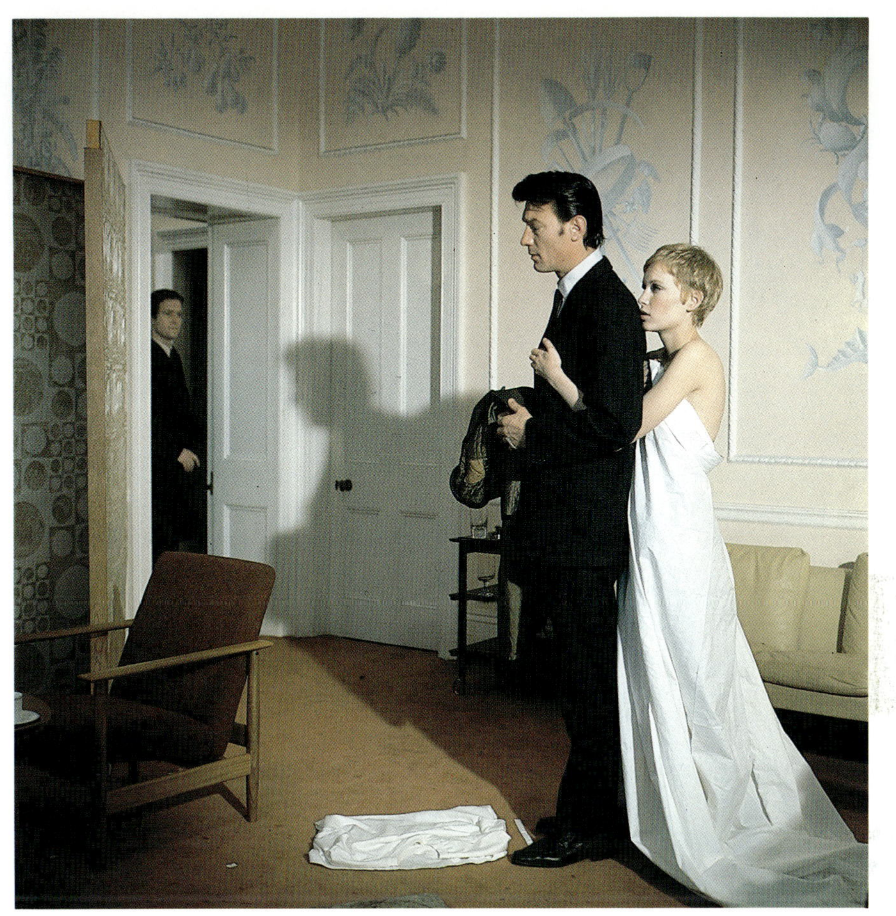

Plate 2. Anonymous, *A Dandy in Aspic,* 1968 (Columbia Pictures).

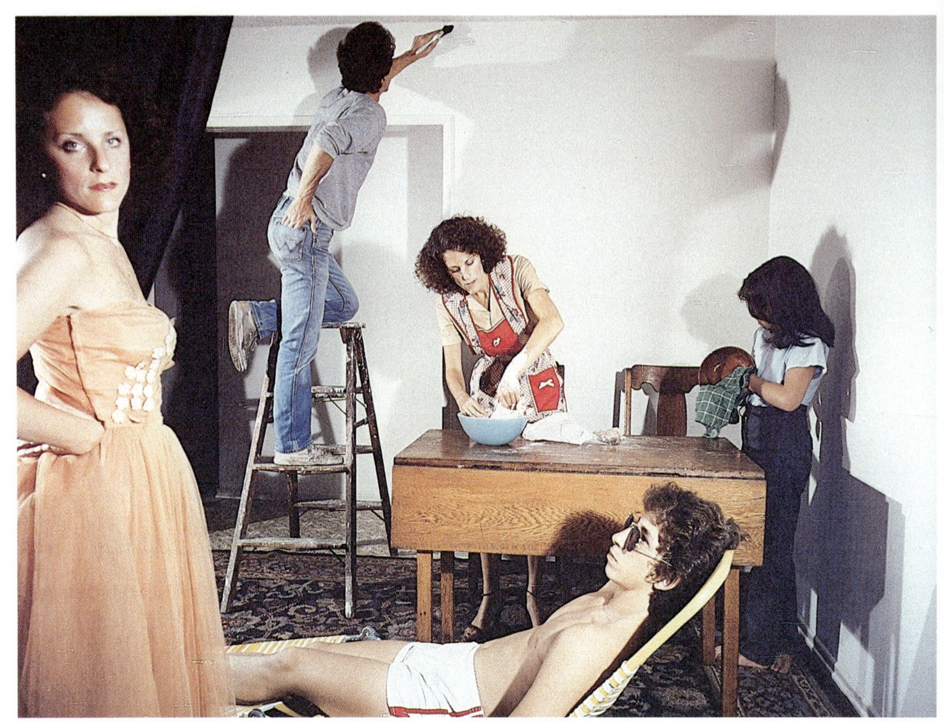

Plate 3. Eileen Cowin, Untitled, 1980.

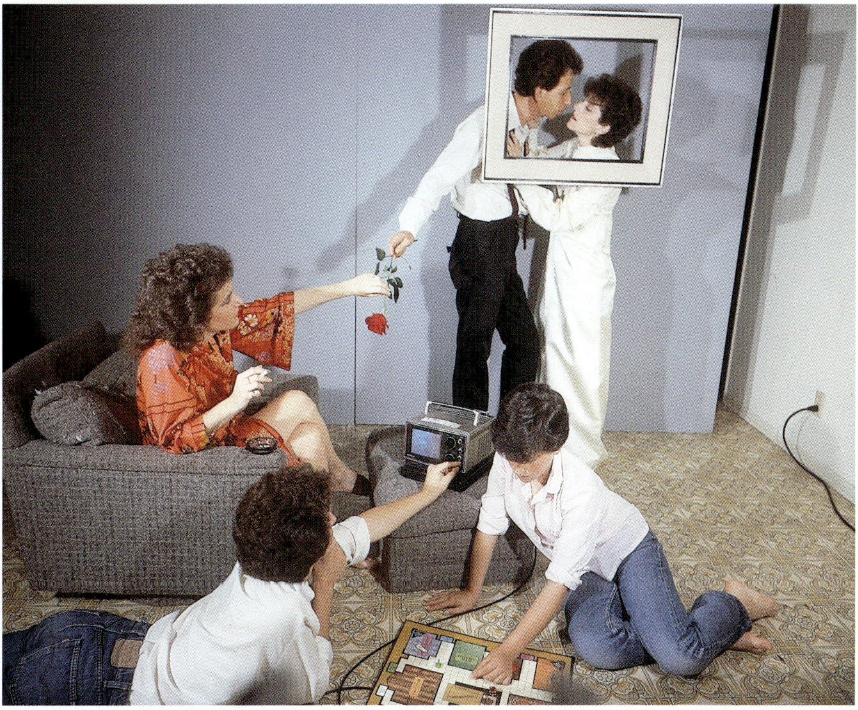

Plate 4. Eileen Cowin, Untitled, 1983.

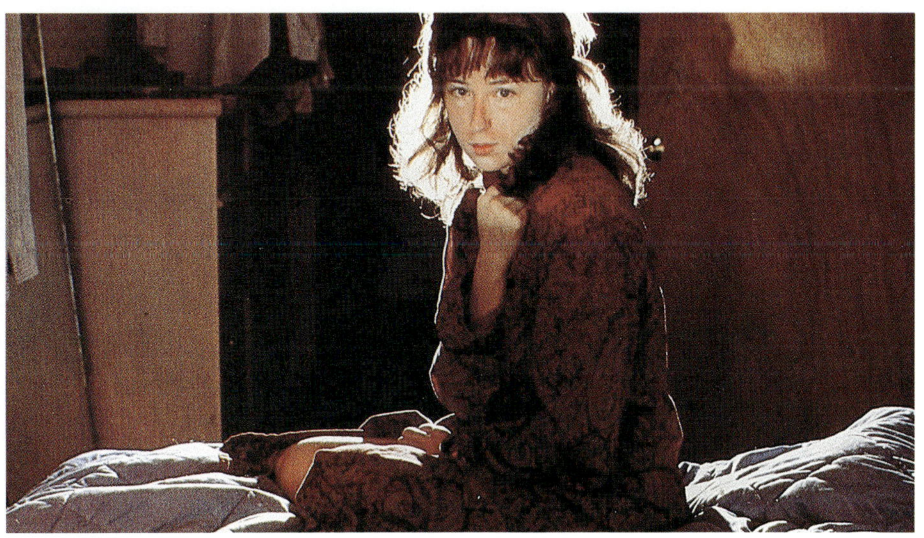

Plate 5. Cindy Sherman, Untitled #95, 1981.

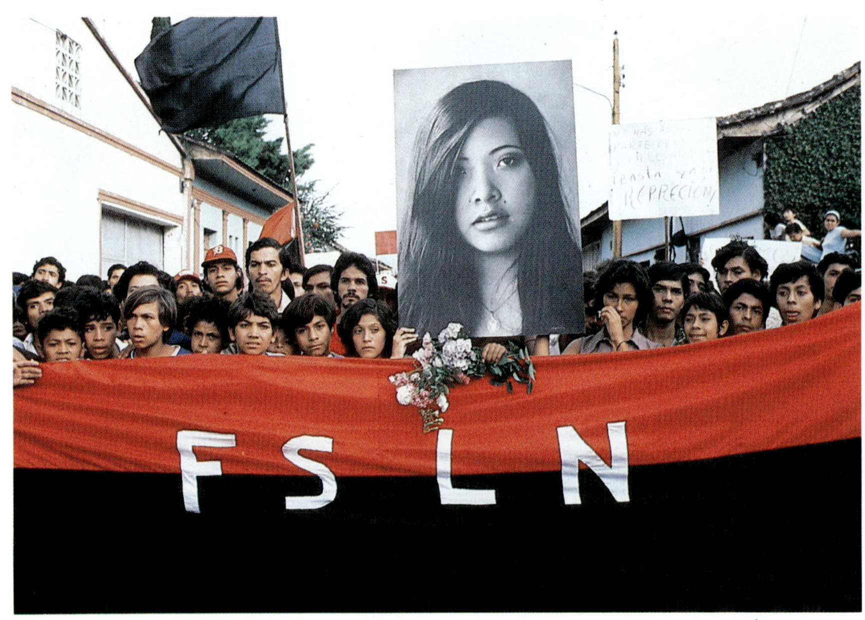

Plate 6. Susan Meiselas, *Nicaragua,* 1978–79 (© 1981 Susan Meiselas/Magnum).

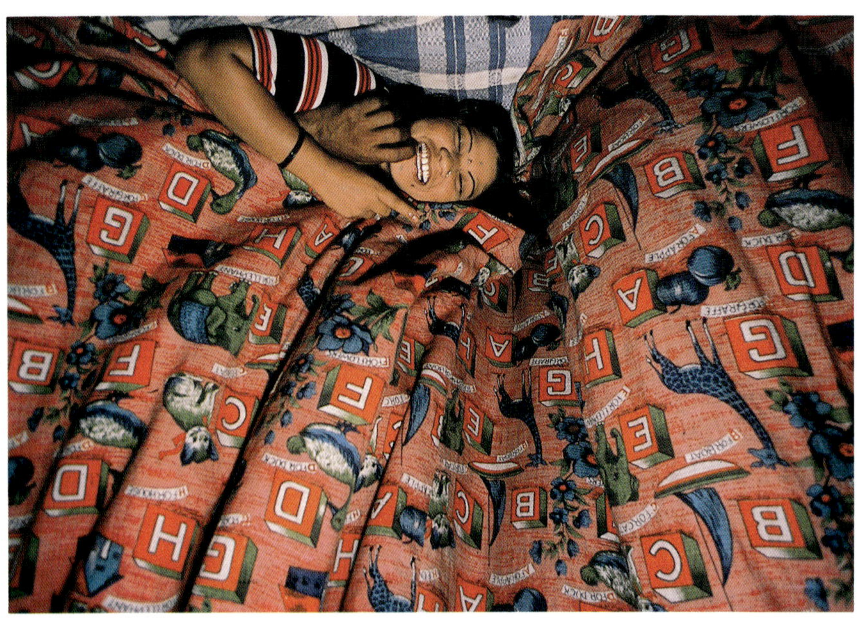

Plate 7. Mary Ellen Mark, *Falkland Road* (© Mary Ellen Mark/ Archive).

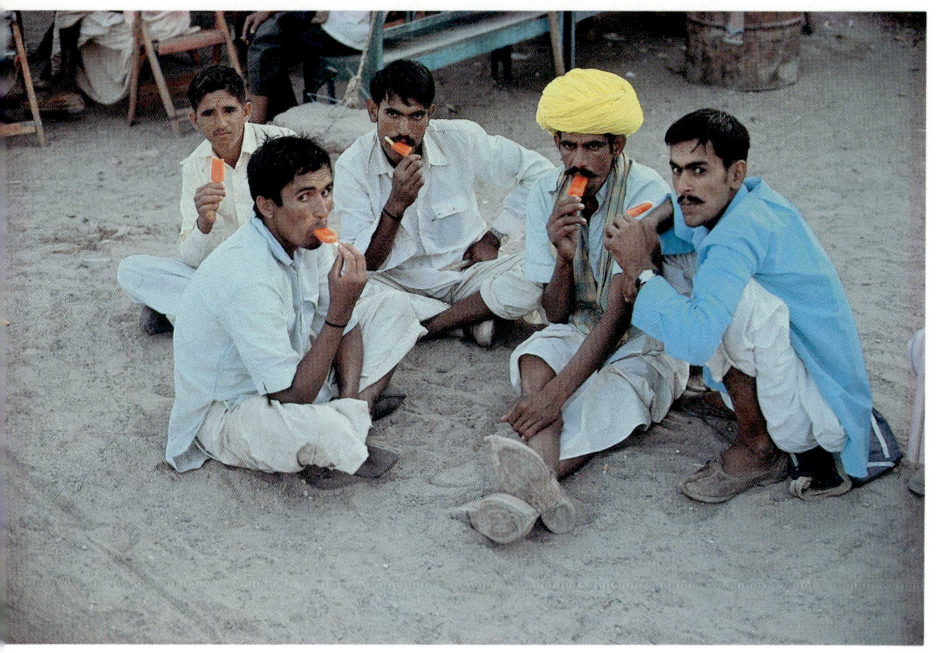

Plate 8. Raghubir Singh, *Villagers visiting Jodhpur enjoying iced sweets*, 1985 (© 1985 Raghubir Singh).

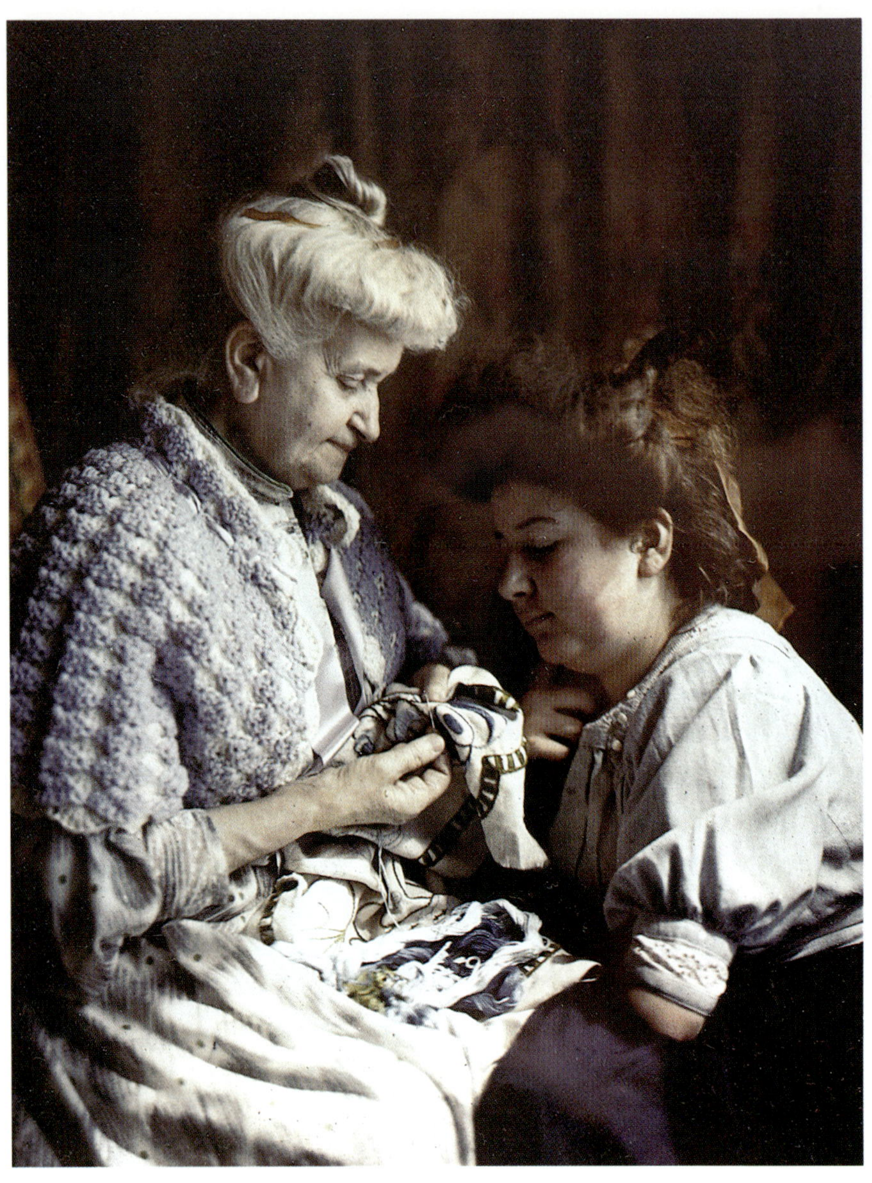

Plate 9. Louis Lumière, *Madame Antoine Lumière and Her Granddaughter Andrée,* 1908 (Ilford-Lumière Collection).

III

Images at Political Work

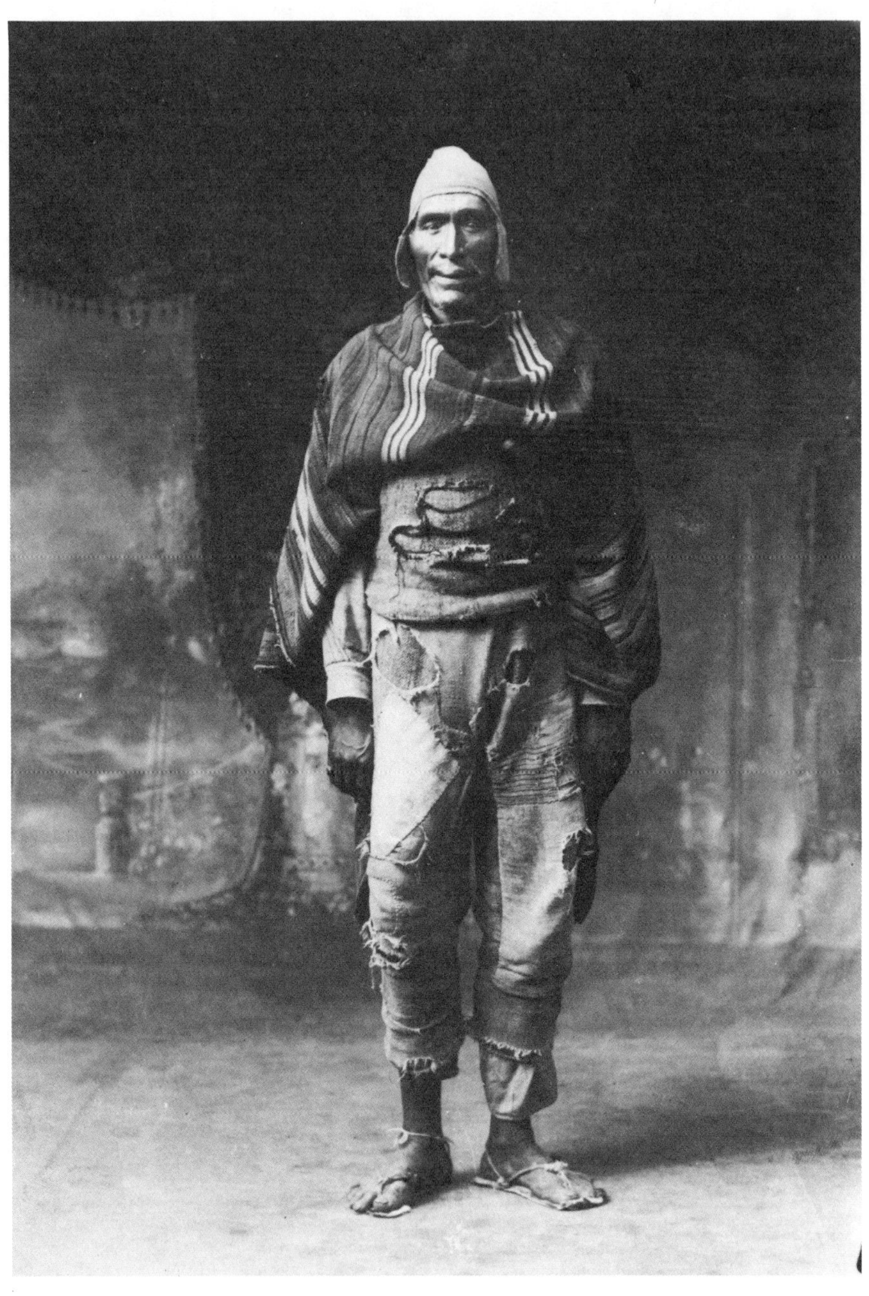

Figure 28. Martín Chambi, *Indian from Paruro in Chambi studio,* c. 1932 (Courtesy Edward Ranney and the Chambi family).

Chambi of Cuzco

Martín Chambi was a Peruvian photographer active in Cuzco from roughly 1920 to the early 1950s. His 1979 exhibition at the Museum of Modern Art revealed a sensibility as communicative and arresting as that of E. J. Bellocq in New Orleans and Mike Disfarmer in Heber Springs, Arkansas. Working within a more ambiguous community, Chambi also had a longer career and a more searching temperament. Like the others, he practiced as a local and commercial portrait photographer. Like those photographers, too, he observed the conservative rules of his trade and exceeded them. In each case the variety and acuity of Chambi's perceptions enliven the archaic performance of his subjects. Here the details of their dated clothes and behavior become a guarantee that their obvious humanity was bounded by mores as peculiar as our own.

Take Chambi's picture of the Gadea wedding (Fig. 29). There's nothing like an old wedding photo to acquaint later viewers with the stiltedness of amateur ceremony and the sappiness of Victorian sentiment. Gazing into this scene at Cuzco, one almost sniffs its inevitably musty odor. The bride's bouquet appears pre-wilted, and the cadaverous bridegroom, with his bleached face, top hat, gloved hands, cutaway, and pinstripe pants, looks like a worried mortician. In the family group behind the wedding couple, where girls hold the train, someone cranes her head to get into the picture. But this picture lives, disturbingly, because outside the natural light in which the young man and woman huddle, the environment is shrouded in an astonishing murk. Using only available luminosity—either on principle or because there was often no alternative—Chambi sticks to the facts, but creates a dreamlike marriage, surrounded by a void.

How did they pluck their eyebrows in Cuzco, or design their court-

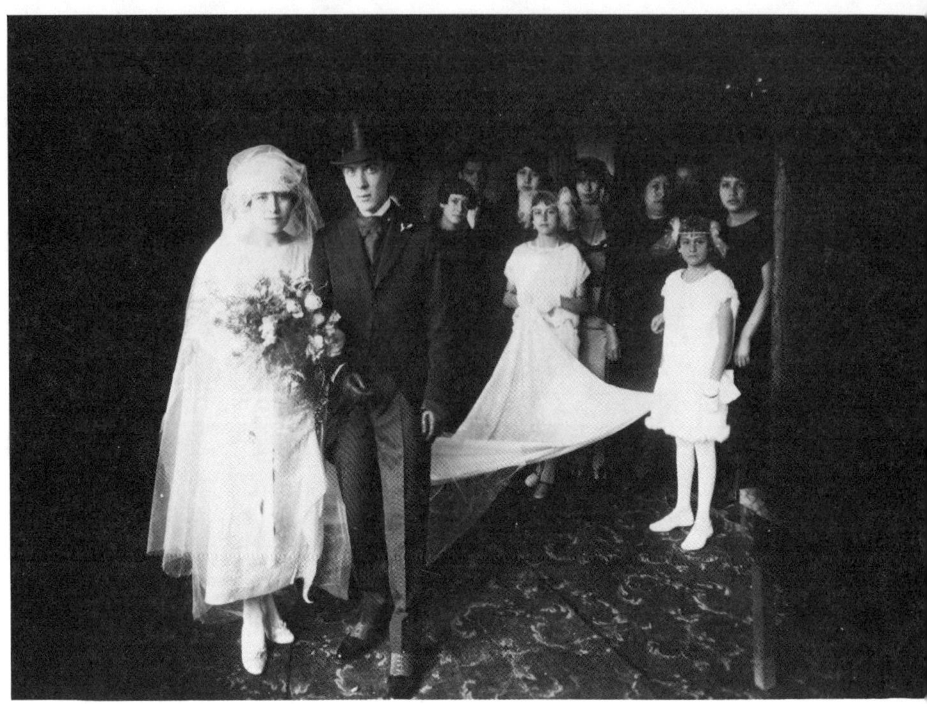

Figure 29. Martín Chambi, *Gadea Wedding, Cuzco,* c. 1930 (Courtesy Edward Ranney and the Chambi family).

rooms? To tally these and endless other living arrangements is not yet to speak of social history, but of obscure and trivial facts endlessly generated in the past and retrievable now, partially if at all, only by some hazard: a text, an album, or a cache of photographs that accidentally comes to light. A photographer from New Mexico, Ed Ranney, goes to Cuzco in the 1960s, to do work on the Inca monuments and highland landscape. On a later visit he becomes friendly with a photographer named Victor Chambi, whose father worked as the town portraitist more than a generation earlier. Martín Chambi had been a local celebrity, the Nadar of Cuzco (as popular but more modest), still remembered by neighbors but virtually unknown outside Peru. The younger men decide to organize and restore the archive of the older one.

This event takes place in 1975. Two years later, under the auspices of Earthwatch, an organization designed to further scientific exploration, a team of ten North Americans led by Ranney descends on Cuzco to clean, file, and print from the 14,000 negatives (mostly 5-by-7 and 8-by-10-inch glass plates) in the Chambi studio. Made by Ranney, the images we now see demonstrate that more was at stake in their restitution than the visual memory of past customs. We should have been happy to get clear, nonevaluating documentary returns, such as those of Florence by the Alinari, or of Harlem by James Van Der Zee. Chambi, however, not only respected his reality, he shaped it as well. He analyzed its tensions. He was a contemporary historian, at least by instinct, and not solely a record-maker.

The stereotyical Peru is a mountainscape sprouting llamas and "natives" in their ragged clothes and shawls. Their heads are snug under picturesque bonnets or fedoras as they carry on at market. Of course there would have to be moldering Inca fortifications and fabulous colonial churches. These tourist stereotypes, seconded by thousands of their kind, remain unchallenged even now, though Chambi's very different assessment might work to change them.

The Inca past, the Hispanic overlay, and the Indian life of his time certainly figure in Chambi's photographs, minus the llamas. They occupy a large place in his output more by virtue of his alert consciousness of his environment than as a market response. He was among the earliest to have done real photographic justice to Machu Picchu (discovered by Hiram Bingham in 1911). We also have pictures from his studio that are the first to describe the habits and regalia of outlying mountain communities. These turn out to be rare images, their subjects apparently not willing to be photographed except by one who spoke the Quechua language and was of their own race. A good deal more is therefore involved in this photographic campaign than ethnographic curiosity. Beyond their reserve, a certain pride animates the faces of these mountaineers, as if encouraged by a traveler whose origins and social footing had once been similar to their own.

Chambi, in fact, had been born the son of a *campesino,* in Coaza, Puno province, in 1891. By exceptional good fortune he learned the elements of his trade from a photographer in a British gold mining company. After further training in Arequipa, he eventually settled in Cuzco, whose commercial promise and cultural history, as the capital of the once great Inca empire, strongly attracted him. Traveling widely in this and other regions for several years, he participated in the rise of *indigenista* consciousness which had come to Peru in the 1920s, later and more falteringly than it had to Mexico. There can be no question of Chambi nostalgically memorializing a civilization on the verge of disappearance, as was true of Curtis and Vroman in our Southwest. More than 90 percent of Peru's inhabitants were of Indian stock. They were not slated to dwindle away. But those of the sierra lacked an understanding of their heritage, while their sense of cultural identity, as viewed by the power structure and coastal society, was hardly a positive one.

There were ample reasons for this pejorative self-image. Within only a century after Pizarro's conquest, six-sevenths of the Indian population of the country had been wiped out. Denied their legal and human rights, the Indians continued to be neglected, wasted, and exploited right on through the 1950s and 1960s. The dictator Augusto Leguia (1919–30) forced many, as indentured laborers, to build penetration roads from the coast to the interior. The hacienda owners employed them as a practically wageless work force kept on a subsistence economic level from which there was no appeal. Only in 1920 did a new constitution recognize the legal existence of the indigenous communities, followed somewhat later by the reluctant establishment of a do-nothing section of Indian affairs. And only in 1930 was property ownership removed as a requirement for the vote, allowing a few small farmers the franchise provided they were also literate in Spanish. These developments were not calculated to dissolve the stigma of the Indian as a nonperson. Cuzco, fifty years ago, was a typical provincial center of judicial corruption, economic repression, and mestizo domination.

The town also happened to breed folklorists, artists, intellectuals, and radicals. An academy of art and the Peruvian Communist party were founded there. Many, perhaps most of the people in these circles, were Chambi's friends and peers. One of the closest, José Uriel Garcia, published a book titled *El Nuevo Indio,* a call for cultural resurgence. The link between polemics on this front and dissident politics can be seen in the formation in 1924 of the APRA party (Alianza Popular Revolucionario Americana), by Haya de la Torre. Haya originally emphasized *indigenista* goals for Peru, quite in line with his anti-Yankee attitudes and his program for nationalization of the land. But in order to build party strength, he had to appeal more to the coastal proletariat than to the plantation workers and the obviously unorganized Andean villagers. There is some reason to think that Chambi sympathized with APRA goals.

The audience of the Marxist José Carlos Mariategui, who issued a harsh diatribe against the hacienda system (*Seven Interpretive Essays on the Peruvian Reality,* 1928), must have been confined to a few educated radicals. In contrast, those who paid for the work of Chambi came mostly from the bourgeoisie, who were happy to have it for family or civic reasons. Working within that society and across its divisions, Chambi portrayed its class strata, its hopes of upward mobility, and its relations with the "lower orders."

A group shot of a hacienda court shows not only its staff, but musicians with their fifes and tambours, clowns, highlanders, troops, a religious brotherhood, and either the straw boss or owner and his white family, conspicuous in this amazing throng. Whatever the occasion that drew them together, the image acts as an institutional medley of types and power interactions. Beyond being blessed, as every group photo should be, by the phenomenon of its subjects posing "in uniform," the frame is marvelously dense, yet informal.

This same kind of orchestration he applied to other, more integrated crowds, such as an outing of the Guardia Civil at Sacsayhuaman, the Inca citadel dominating Cuzco, in 1930 (Fig. 30). These National Police are in a relaxed, affectionate mood. The wave of smiling faces seems to be sucked in toward a pass in the ancestral masonry. To have gotten them all to respond with such fresh sweetness and swagger implies a considerable charm on the part of the photographer. (Chambi was expert in posing people *al fresco,* on sloping grassy ground, as they propped their feet or found little humps on which to sit.) The upbeat character of the scene may also have something to do with the fact that the military provided one of the very few access routes for the peasantry to attain higher social status. The privileges they were accorded arose out of the increased nationalism of the new

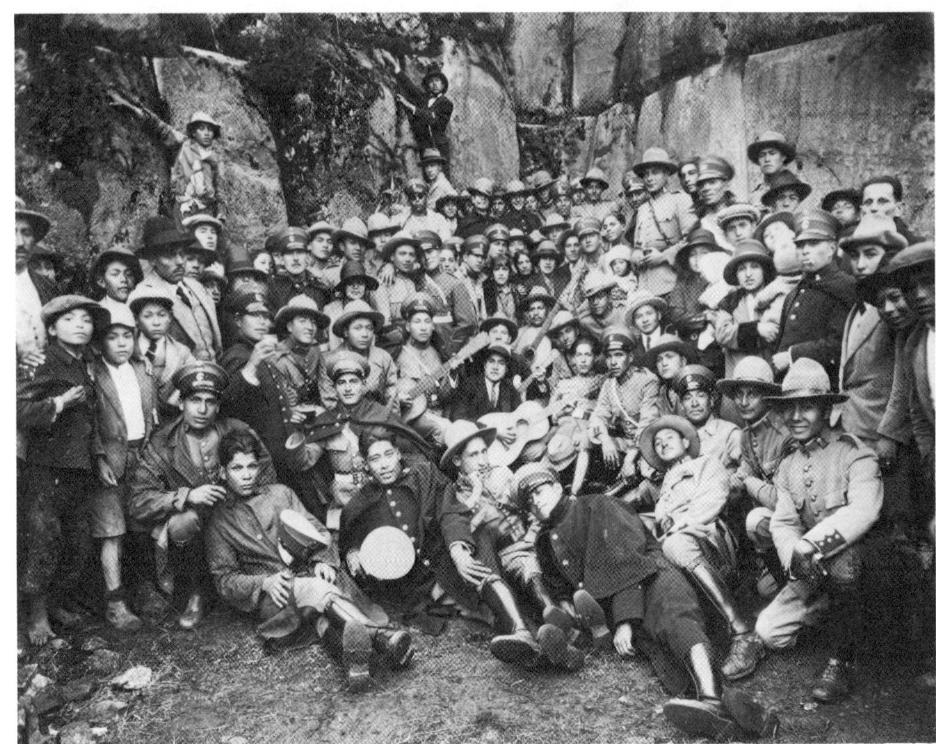

Figure 30. Martín Chambi, *Fiesta of the police, Sacsayhuaman, Cuzco,* c. 1930 (Courtesy Edward Ranney and the Chambi family).

Cerro regime, so that the rhetorics of state and ethnic solidarity, here at least, could coincide.

In the town proper was displayed a more mundane authority which Chambi studied. Large landowners, housed in Cuzco, maintained control over political officials in the district capital of Pisaq and other villages. By these ties they continued to activate a virtually feudal system which demanded free labor and farm goods from the campesinos, as well as the donation of personal services in their town homes. The *hacendados* overlorded marketing of agricultural products, too, and paid far below the set prices offered farmers in communities.[1] Additionally, through a network of vendors, the Indians were obliged to buy from the *hacendados* at inflated levels. If there were inconvenient disturbances about such issues, that same civil guard whom Chambi showed enjoying itself above the town was available to put them down. What is more, peasant leaders had an unlucky habit of meeting with fatal accidents.

With his clear, natural illumination streaming down from a skylight, Chambi shoots six campesinos, cringing under their ponchos as they wait to give testimony in the Cuzco Hall of Justice (Fig. 31). The picture reveals their humiliation, entrapment, and anxiety. Details such as the bare, gnarled feet on the floral carpet are unforgettable. Though separated by only a yard or two, the clerks at the desk belong to another world. For the moment, Chambi himself might have been of this world, a municipal employee.

Often in a more neutral capacity, he fastened on class oppositions. A white-gloved policeman pinches the ear of a small Indian boy, clothed in itchy sacking. The man has the air of an angler showing off his catch. (It's entirely possible that he is symbolizing what policemen are supposed to do, just as drinkers in other Chambi prints make sure they have their bottles with them.) As for the regal bride of the Montes family, she poses in the vestibule of her house, which probably seemed as modest in Cuzco as Garnier's Opera did in Paris. In the shadow to her left sits an old, abject nanny or maid. Far from being accidents or inevitable circumstances, these juxtapositions were made by a comparing mind, and the statement of who's on top and what's on the social bottom is arranged by the photographer with as much blunt deliberation as the innocence with which it is accepted by his subjects.

A similar acceptance crops up in nineteenth-century photographs in which white colonizers stand prominently among Asiatic underlings. Such ingenuous setups were effected by a racist alliance between colo-

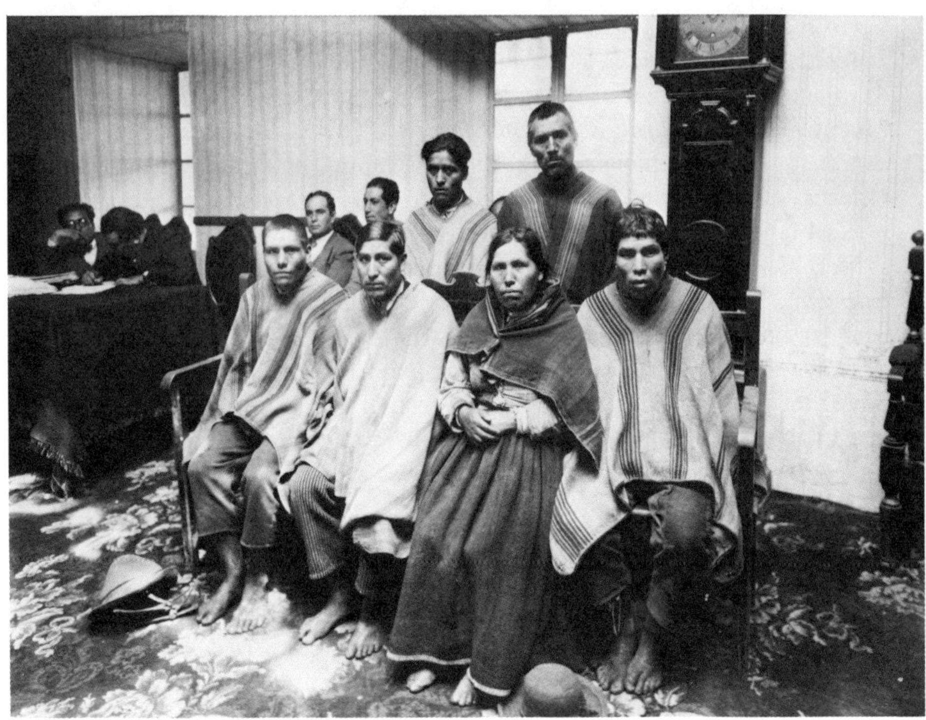

Figure 31. Martín Chambi, *Campesinos testifying, Palace of Justice, Cuzco,* c. 1931 (Courtesy Edward Ranney and the Chambi family).

nists and photographer, and one senses the camera as the coercive extension of European power.

With Chambi, though, the system of dominance (everyone with their appropriate attributes) is examined from the viewpoint of its human cost. He leaves one in no doubt as to its production of victims. Take away the submissive figure in the two frames just described and they would revert from strong indictment to mere genre.

Yet, by genre work itself—group and individual portraits—Chambi earned most of his living. Through this mode alone he presents a social scene undergoing some very curious transitions. The Franciscan monks with their British patron, Mr. Blysdale, project almost the opposite of the power relations I've just mentioned. While Blysdale is placed at the junction of an inverted wedge of figures and echoing cloister, the nearer monks do more than hold their own. Stern of face and assertive in posture, they seem rooted in their verdant garden. Catholic piety really blossoms in many of Chambi's pictures, such as the plunging shot of the festival at Ayaviri, or the flower-drenched mourning that went on at funeral chapels. A riot of Churrigueresque description frets the graphic play of light and dark in these photographs. I don't think it's wrong to imagine that they could only have been made by a profoundly Hispanic temperament, one whose sense of space can be as elaborate as the interior of a Spanish church.

Yet he documented quite simply the first motorcyclist to have gotten over the cordillera and the arrival of the first aviator, too. They had come from the unimaginable distance of modern technology to this place, this nowhere in which Chambi lived. Instead of commemorating the probe of civilization to "another point"—and therefore of having traveled away, as it did when Chambi took it to the mountains—the camera demonstrates just the opposite. The twentieth century is finally shown to have reached "us" . . . here. Whether the monks were as physically solid off-camera as on, or the cyclist more competent than he seems, no one knows. Chambi's work nonetheless makes it clear that in his locale, ancient ritual coexisted with contemporary behavior. Though it passed for current Western manners, this behavior was neither smoothly practiced nor completely naturalized.

One has the feeling that the Cuzco bourgeoisie is half-involved in a charade of which the roles have not yet been adequately learned. (The Gadea wedding is a good case in point.) Bodies and business suits, for instance, get along uneasily with each other, and there's something off in the tailoring. Above the collar the mestizo shopkeeper is often indistinguishable from the menials that surround him; beneath it he

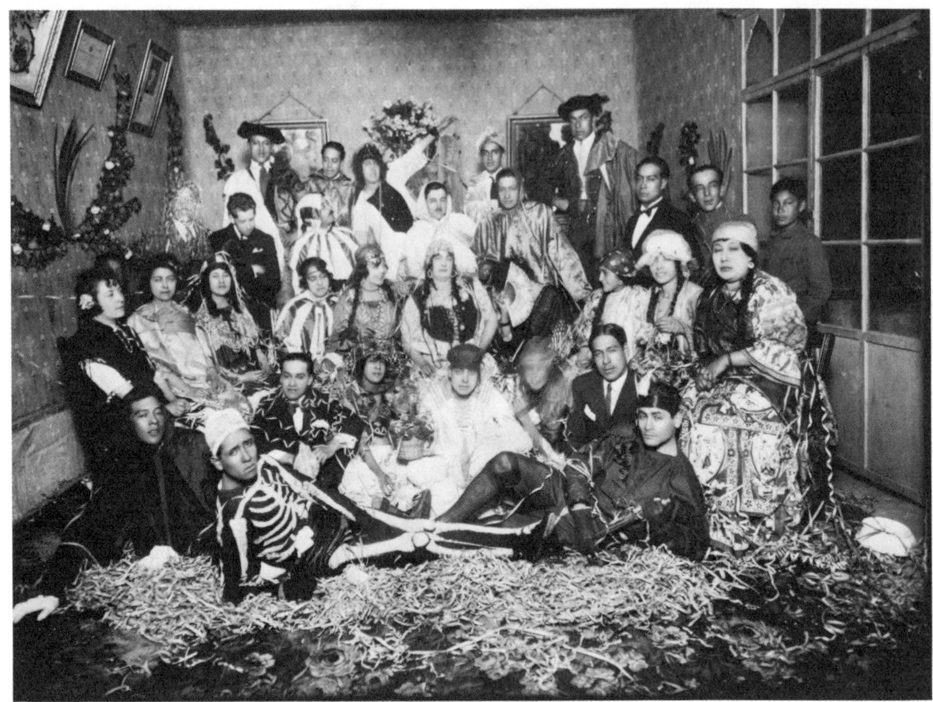

Figure 32. Martín Chambi, *Costume party, Cuzco,* c. 1930 (Courtesy Edward Ranney and the Chambi family).

wears his status. A few pretty mestizas have so powdered their faces that they appear almost as if wearing white masks in Chambi's photographs. The great outside culture, from which some goods have trickled in, though with only hints of its style, both fascinates and menaces these townspeople.

Out of date and slightly awkward, if seen on the coast, such gestures firmed up the needed hierarchy at home. One great rank below the mestizos were the *cholos,* people who had ceased being landless Indians but who still worked essentially as flunkies in town. A still further drop beneath them were the villagers, shepherds, and sharecroppers. If a mestizo spoke to a *cholo* in Quechua, this was meant to be deprecating address. The shock of the new upon the old, and the interweaving of alien with domestic social relations, are implicit in Chambi's unsorted pictorial file.

When they were absorbed in outright impersonation, his subjects only exposed the raw and ill-digested influences that played upon them. Consider a costume party where everyone is decked up as toreadors and gypsies, maitre d's and jesters, with a skeleton and an irrelevant sailor thrown in (Fig. 32). It's a carnival of glitz served on a platter of messy streamers. Possibly close to it in time, another costume party was photographed in Louisville—weirdly enough, constructed along similar lines. The same diminution of the stage-like room and concealed bleachers compress the funny people. It's harder to make out the iconography of the North American scene, apart from its rah-rah, cowboy, dead-end kid and plutocratic references. Even so, the Peruvians show themselves to be more confused in all that tinsel. The norms from which the hammy Kentuckians departed are pretty evident and peep out in a dozen places. In contrast, Chambi's sitters are at a loss to convey their fantasies. They don't seem to have had any agreement about everyday decorum, against which they could play off their one-shot extravagance. The image of one of the revelers has been scratched out in the negative and a certain subtle dejection weighs upon the whole gaudy tableau. Which is precisely what makes it so fascinating.

The last outfit they could have been expected to wear at a Cuzco costume party was that of an Indian, exotic to our eyes but demeaningly vernacular to theirs. One of Chambi's most impressive, even awesome photos shows an Indian from Paruro, all seven feet of him, looming up in the bareness of the studio (Fig. 28). The coarse material swaddling his giant frame has been rent and patched and torn again in a profusion of holes, from which cloth dribbles like strands of llama wool. No one needs to be told that such rags speak of an existence incomparably less comfortable than in town. At the same time they are irrefutably more authentic, since they function not as an "outfit" at all, but as the weathered, shaggy skin of his being.

In 1948 Irving Penn came to Cuzco, rented a studio like Chambi's, and photographed the rural folk against a plain backdrop. The resulting well-known pictures marked the historical occasion when it became cool to appropriate the images of the helpless and undefended poor from Third World countries into the graphic designs of high fashion. Because he was inventing only a new kind of chic, Penn cannot be said to have had enough sensitivity to be accused of moral turpitude. He created exceedingly more stylish pictures than Chambi, but he was never capable of eliciting and then capturing the crazed, indomitable stance of the Paruro Indian. Two years after Penn's visit, Cuzco was ruined by a gigantic earthquake. It shattered a great many of the contemporary buildings and it tumbled in most of the town's colonial churches. The monolithic Inca walls of the old capital remained standing in perfect condition. Chambi is reported to have despaired at the destruction of his town and his work gradually lost its spirit. He died in 1973.

Art in America, *December 1979.*

1. See William Whyte and Giorgio Alberti, *Power, Politics and Progress: Social Change in Peru* (New York, 1976), p. 27.

Meiselas, Mark, and Singh

While it conveys intimate details of a revolution, and therefore of a historical event, Susan Meiselas' *Nicaragua*[1] should not be treated as any kind of historical analysis. The book has been criticized for deciphering less about an event or a situation than a sixty-second television news report, but this is fatuous. Whatever a book of still photos can tell its readers and viewers is clearly not of the same order of experience as a television broadcast. While such a book does not attempt to fill in the gaps between occurrences, it does impart their flavor and mood. If it doesn't furnish corporate and predigested causes and effects, it does offer consultable images—all the more provocative since viewers are challenged to interpret them. More loosely edited and richly various than any spot news account, these books, *as they build up,* establish the social and emotional texture of a locale, which is a form of information in its own right. This knowledge, though miscellaneous, is also more graphic and often more revealing than that found in the pabulum of the nightly update (Plate 6).

Moving through *Nicaragua,* one *feels* engaged, alongside pitifully armed guerillas, in a vicious and confused struggle against a mechanized National Guard. The outcome is by no means clear until the rebel tide subtly begins to rise, about midway through, and the compañeros finally surge forth to their triumphal entry into Managua. Because we've been shown beforehand what their own government had done to brutalize them, in all its chancred ghastliness, the revolution is both subjectively explained and justified. The looks on the faces of these Sandinistas not only register the fact that the battle has turned in their favor, they reflect their moral consciousness as well. They have a gaiety and sweetness, which is what I think the book was planned to visualize. Unless a film documentary realized entirely from their viewpoint has yet to be distributed, I can't imagine a more responsive visual report than this work by a Magnum Agency photographer who did not hesitate to expose herself to gunfire.

Aside from accusing it of being "naggingly incomplete" (because it doesn't show Somoza's casualties!), the *New York Times*'s Andy Grundberg complains that Meiselas's book is the effort of a "glorified tourist." Apparently this is the stigma of all photojournalists, who can "picture with style and preconception" but cannot deliver "essential insights" into a milieu.

Even less charitable judgments stem from the fact that *Nicaragua* is in color. Certain minds can only associate color with playfulness and a charm that deceives. "The sickening," writes John Leonard of *Nicaragua,* "is made slick . . . the grief has too much style." I find this attitude hard to understand. The idea persists that color is misleading and superficial when compared with black-and-white photography—a notion as valid as assuming that we are less serious than we ought to be because we see and live in color. A photographer who acknowledges the full sensory range of our perceptions is somehow considered a tourist to them. We all know revolutions are grim, and therefore they take place in dour black and white—an idea reinforced by the newspaper photos that greet us daily. If a photographer thinks otherwise, she's automatically guilty of flitting about in the cause of chic exhibitionism.

It's difficult, though, to suspect that Meiselas had this aim, consciously or unconsciously, while dodging bullets. Nor do I think that Mary Ellen Mark (who initially endured being pinched, abused, and soused with garbage by the prostitutes of Bombay) should really be called a "tourist," or that Raghubir Singh immersed himself in the windstorms of the Desert of Thar so that he might trivially illustrate the prettiness of Kodachrome. Mark's *Falkland Road* and Singh's *Rajasthan* were published at the same time as Meiselas's *Nicaragua.*[2] Collectively they demonstrate, if this were necessary, that color can enhance involvement with a subject—that color is an inherent and primary factor in the photographic recall of an event, not a distracting irrelevance.

Like flashy and irridescent sardines, the juvenile whores of *Falkland Road* are packed into street-level cages where they're checked out by passing clients. Mark first touches on this public aspect of her locale, then immediately brings us behind its façade to show the girls at work, and sometimes at play. Since their job entails a great deal of makeup—of daubing and powdering the body—and the flaunting of gaudy costume, color display is utterly intrinsic to the subject. Here color performs a role in erotic ritual, as in the mating patterns of natural species, and the fact that the hues are wildly artificial, overpoweringly alien to the flesh, contributes to the sadness of the report. When they appear, the transvestites, with their greasepaint and lipstick above hairy limbs, add to its morbid tone and dismal brilliance. It would not be a world of lower-class prostitution if it did not attempt to cover up, in the most grating way, the difference between the sex that is fantasized and the sex that's there (Plate 7).

Falkland Road, on one level, reads as an obvious exploitation of a vulnerable subject. But the essential pretenses of this scene are driven home by the force of their color, to which these photos accede with a sense of discovery. When the scarlets and cerises of the saris are contrasted with the shiny blue enamel or the green moldiness of the walls and the indescribable chromatics of ooze on the floors, when the mascara blazes up in the light of the flash and the yellows and turquoises of plastic buckets seem almost exasperated, one's sensory perceptions are aroused far ahead of one's social stereotypes. Colors do not harmonize with one another—they offer a series of concussions in an environment of caresses.

It's the reverse in *Nicaragua,* where the foreground violence jolts against the coloristic suavity of backgrounds. Incendiary acts sputter off within the spumoni pastels of tropical villages. Environment and action here are psychically out of joint with each other, casually but inevitably dissonant in their combined impact. You can no more resolve the pleasure afforded the eye with the sorrow and outrage affecting the mind than you can confirm these images in terms of the better-known photographic genres. And this irresolution makes the spectacle increasingly poignant. As these young Nicaraguan guerrillas deck themselves with baseball hats and bandanas over the lower face, or with the weirdly calm masks of an Indian tribe, in conjunction with sweatshirts, plaids, and jeans, they look like amateur desperados—trick-or-treat mobsters escaped from a comic book, except for their very real fright. A shot of Anastasio Somoza with his entourage, all in white suits, has an amazing, bleached yet tender delicacy; a picture of a Somoza informer's van, burning orange against the black smoke and blue sky, or of the phosphorescent greens of a tear-gas assault against demonstrators in the night, is *terribly* beautiful. The contrast between one's moral knowledge of the subject and its sensory effect would have cheapened the photographic witness if it had been made deliberately ironic. Yet it's not that that contrast was knowingly sought, but rather that it was everywhere to be seen, at least by someone with eyes as well as consciousness. In black and white, the visual character of the revolution would have been restricted and schematized. Predictably, the viewer would have been encouraged to deduce a horrific surrounding from the stimulus of its neutral tones. Because this is the opposite of what happens in Meiselas's book, with its broader, wrenching descriptions, the effect is much more irrational and disquieting. The dissonance sinks in, all the more memorably since it serves no rhetorical interest.

Raghubir Singh's book on Rajasthan does have a rhetoric, if a visual affection for the state in which he was reared and here revisits (from Paris, where he lives) deserves that name. His pictures open with a view of the commanding Jodhpur Fort, seen in the raked light of late afternoon, and with this, as in many images like it, color is lifted into a new realm of optical privilege, almost, it seems, as a king ascends his throne. The huge land glows with an awesome opulence, the common possession of its inhabitants high and low. While poor farmers line up for a dilapidated rural bus, a peacock struts in high feather on the damp sand. Having seen his "Villagers . . . [enjoying] iced sweets," one finds hard to forget the orange sting of their ices, simultaneously the hottest color accent in the scene and, by implication, the most refreshingly chilling (Plate 8). If Singh had been attentive only to the thermal extremes of this Indian region, he would have caught one of its basic features, but he is intensely observant of its social range as well. Small artisans, merchants, and peasants, minstrels and erstwhile maharanis, priests and horsetraders, landholders and sheep herders, all figure in the loose structure of his survey, along with the celebrations they enjoy, the work they perform, and the architecture that surrounds them. Singh constantly layers strata of information, so that wall murals, shop signs, movie or circus posters, religious sculpture, graffiti, the body language of ritual, and the repose of prayer interact to form a kind of pictorial regalia. From this material he fashions photographs that are exceptionally dense and complicated when located in the city, though he is equally capable of open and rhapsodic simplicity when out in the fields.

The making of icons, the forms of native decoration, the habits of cooking and ploughing—all are attributes of this culture, or rather, of several related ones. To invoke the grace of these living cultures, in cadences established deep within their long history, is the unified motive of the book. With such a theme imposed throughout, the photographer can allow divergent episodes to compete with or subtly complement each other. As a subject for photographic report, culture has a history of cliché and generally works as a static or inert concept; Singh, however, re-enters the cultures of Rajasthan with an insider's sustained knowledge of their customs, which he respects and continually distinguishes from each other. At the same time, though, he pictures Indian life with a nervous, self-demanding expectancy that sets him off as an artist with the skills of the Western street photographer. Implausible as it may seem, his photographs fuse the soul of a Rajput miniaturist with the outlook of a Henri Cartier-Bresson.

Singh's book, which operates in the appreciative mode, looks more reserved than the images of the Western photographers here, whose work can't be described as positive appraisal. Partly, too, the difference between them and Singh arises from the format of their campaigns, intensive rather than extended. The Nicaraguan revolution, at least in its violent phase, had a temporal frame just as the women of Falkland Road are literally caged, and these perimeters bear a kind of stifling urgency toward the center of the photographer's work and contract it implosively. The rhetoric of these pictures would go quite flat if it failed to establish the strong, primitive illusion that the viewer is physically part of the scene, exposed to all the predatory forces within it. Meiselas's political empathies and Mark's voyeuristic heat demand that the viewer metaphorically close with the subject. That's where color comes in, because it helps to make the sense of participation irremediable and all the more arresting since it is perceived as being, expressively, at odds with the action. With Singh, on the other hand, perception is given over to the phenomenal wealth of shifting chromatic relations, events ever more fine-tuned in a way that does not so much convince that they flatter Rajasthan as that they befit it. One is not urged to empathize with or pry into this world; one is invited to behold it.

Separately and together, these three books perform a familiar social function: to import images of life far outside the ken of their intended audiences. As imagery, they bring us visual gifts no one asked to receive and news that is not always happy. Yet the books do not stand or fall solely on the basis of their pictures, for they contain texts which are in dialogue with those pictures and are meant to illuminate them. Judgment of the photographs can be informed but also tilted by their verbal accompaniment.

Meiselas's is the only book to quote people talking first hand on their own behalf. She herself says merely "NICARAGUA. A year of news, as if nothing had happened before, as if the roots were not there, and the victory was not earned. This book was made so that we remember." The roots are outlined in a historical chronology containing details of the U.S.'s longstanding interventions in Nicaragua and of Washington's prickly alliance with Somoza. How the victory was earned is taken up by the pictures, while the words—a collage of remarks by fully named participants in the revolution—speak of the gradual dawn of the need to resist, the ways resistance was improvised, and the increasing wildfire solidarity among the people. Text and images converge particularly in some shots of funeral demonstrations for rebel martyrs, the interrogation of civilians, jungle bivouacs, and the making of contact bombs. There comes over the viewer, as there came over Nicaragua, the knowledge, at a certain, perhaps indefinable point, that everyone had to be in the struggle together. What's remarkable, then, is how the photographer evidently started with the idea of reporting different communities and found herself swept up in a process whereby a new community was formed—no longer in isolated pockets or scattered groups, but across the country. The ethos of that community as it was patched together, haltingly seen in pictures, is articulated in the statements of Nicaraguans from many walks of life. This is an extremely moving dynamic: the process, we suddenly realize, that the book was made to commemorate. Instead of heroic postures, the camera finds the most heterogeneous sorts of people domestically at ease with each other, bonded in a common emergency (all reminiscent of Robert Capa's Spanish Civil War). Pictures cannot express the determination of the businessman's renegade son who says, "Our generation is doing what past generations should have done." But no words can show precisely the beaten look on the faces of captured guardsmen (who comprised, not a community, but only a force that had dwindled before their eyes). Nor can words, eloquent as they are, convey the unearthly, *delicate* shock of the photo of the woman in the rose-colored dress who sifts through the pink ruins of a house at Masaya. Despite the grievous separation of the text, way in the back, from the pictures, the photographer's art lends the whole package a special and enduring conviction. One of the book's most haunting images is of a howling FSLN crowd, which lifts up above its black-and-red banner an outsized photo-portrait of a girl killed three years before. They're demanding that this one life be remembered, and, mute amidst their shouts, its image is of an incredibly sultry face from another era—in *black and white.*

Though it contains many artful and affecting things, *Falkland Road* is an altogether less humane production than *Nicaragua.* Mary Ellen Mark describes a number of oppressive social relations to which her book inevitably contributes. Her introductory text, which relates some of her, and her subjects', experiences, is an effort to mitigate this defect, not by euphemizing the circumstances of the prostitutes, but by showing how she won their friendship and gained their consent to be photographed. She doesn't explain how she represented the eventual use of her work to them, nor does she even tell us what originally motivated it—beyond an instinctual curiosity, abetted by a voyeuristic dream (of which she says, "I awoke amused and somewhat reassured. Perhaps my dream was a good sign.") As a result, the pathos of brothel life is appropriated for us in the form of glistening visual trophies. In order to rekindle the excitement of the dream that amused her, it was necessary for Mark to photograph subjects with a full enjoyment of their disadvantage. One can't look at these images without being implicated in that enjoyment. Still, it would not have been clear from the photos themselves that the prostitution scene is organized according to the most stringent, ascending bigotries, and survives desperately against pitiless, mercenary rip-offs. At the pinnacle of the hierarchy she describes is the photographer herself, for whom the whole system has an aboriginal glamor, glimpses of which will adorn an art gallery in New York.

Mark writes not only of the adversary tensions inherent in the besieged communities of Falkland Road, but of her acceptance there as a sister. The attention Mark paid the prostitutes seems to have invoked a grateful relaxation and eventual spontaneity beneficial to her work. Instead of acting out their routines, the women, and especially the male inmates, can loll about and mock their own performances. Even during their more professional moments, the camera is quick to pick up distraction, repulsion, or just fatigue—moods that utterly break the soft-core spell. One or the other of the coupled figures is simply not with it, and moist, sorrowful eyes peer out amidst tangled limbs. These are psychologically ambiguous images because the photographer's presence incites an extra dose of feigned behavior that she records, yet wants to undermine Her subjects's self-protective attitudes are worthy objects of study. So, even more, are the expressions that, it seems involuntarily, reflect or wilt away from the pressure of that behavior. In Mark's single portraits one often sees concentrated the stress of all this experience, as in the faces of old and defeated vaudevillians. Whether Mark's continued interest in this kind of pain is to the book's credit or not is a good question, but there can't be any doubt that suffering functions as a plea for photographic credibility. So, too, do all the shots of prostitutes *en famille* crowded around by their children and elders, or doing housework. Despite their exotic (to our eyes) accoutrements, these people, the book tells us, are plain folks. *Falkland Road* resembles what might have happened if Weegee had married Diane Arbus and the two had gone off to do anthropological roadwork . . . in color. The book owes a great deal of its disagreeable power to their tradition, but does strike out on its own. Let me cite one astonishing photograph as an example, a heavy red nursery curtain, decorated with animals and building blocks ("G for giraffe . . . E for elephant"), over a girl pressed on a lumpy bed. From behind the curtain a large male hand reaches out, seemingly about to be bitten by her flashing teeth, while she herself, eyes closed, points to the baby illustrations above. Leaving Bombay, Mark writes that she started to cry. " 'You shouldn't weep,' said Asha. 'You should say goodbye with your head up and proud and then leave.' She walked me out into the street to find a taxi. 'You'd better not forget me,' she said."

Neither a memorializing aim nor intimacies of this sort disturb Singh's *Rajasthan.* His work is concerned with the present as it incorporates the past, and the photographer, therefore, doesn't make any appeal to a nostalgic future. In his opening essay, he says:

> We now have a zinc-smelter, an electronics factory, textile mills and a nuclear power plant. . . . If some of the fruits of the twentieth century have reached the city and the countryside, it does not mean we have substantially absorbed the modern experience. We will do that only when we begin using with ease and grace the products of our century, not merely for our commerce and comfort, but also for our artistic aspirations. . . . In the meantime, our sole democratic arts will be those of the village folk . . . who . . . live in the hardship of shrub and stone.

Singh's amiable introduction couldn't possibly vie with his photography, but it does reveal, in this comment, something of his conceptual stance. Modernity, from which he has profited, has touched his native state only superficially. Because he feels relatively isolated in his possession of a patrician modern consciousness in contemporary India, he compensates by his homage to the indigenous arts. The strength of his feelings for them carries him back to his earliest memories, which possibly accounts for a childlike wonder and freshness in his contact with the scene as it exists now. If one compares his image of folk-theater actors applying greasepaint with Mark's Bombay prostitutes doing their makeup, the contrast is between two Indias kept separate by very different mentalities. Singh associates theater with oral tradition and meaningful legend, while Mark modernistically conjures up an abused charade. He brings no reformist energy to his view of poverty, but he doesn't conceive of being voyeuristic about it either. While *Rajasthan* hardly skimps in describing the conditions of poor people, it announces at the same time that their forms of display spring from the grandeurs of their past, and are therefore precious. When misfortune strikes, as shown in the remarkable drought pictures at the end of the book, it is only nature that has brought people low or displaced them, and not the inequities of their society.

Singh has not always had this vantage. In *Ganga,* his first book, life along the great river is pictured as an alarming 1,500-mile visual fracas; in *Calcutta,* his next, the whole metropolis is represented as a stinking cesspool of filth and degradation. In crucial ways, these books are more activist than many I have seen by Western photo-documentarians in "Third World" countries. Singh's biting color only furthered such an impression. Yet there ran through this earlier work a response to the exorbitant sensuality of India that is continued in this latest effort. Where it had been heavy, tendentious, and starkly contrasted, however, it is now exquisitely modulated. The holy men and screeching ideologues, with their divisive animus, have given way to single figures, meditating at wayside shrines. And the overwhelming, crowded frenzy of urban India has thinned out to small groups whose members act as sentinels of a space that is personal as well as social. Singh's new, elegant inwardness lacks a tragic sweep, yet it enables him, when he wants to, to imply intense feeling with few means. The faces in *Women mourning, Bharatpur* are concealed, but their cradling hands and arpeggiated fingers tell expressively of their grief (as they were culturally intended to). This is indeed an album whose sensitivity reaches out, as if through the tips of fingers. But it never gropes, never approximates what it wants to say. Rajasthan is portrayed as a far more cohesive society than it must actually be; at the same time, its inhabitants are accorded their full idiosyncrasy.

Bathing them all is a light prodigiously more erotic than anything trapped in the steamy, no-exit closets of Falkland Road. It would be ridiculous to claim that Singh overglamorizes his region, just as it would be wrongheaded to say that Mark uglifies the physical Bombay. The real conditions of which still photos form a trace always chaotically exceed any material a camera can supply. What the machine gives us, when handled well, is a visual condensation, structured by knowing reflex and tempered by expressive mood. To his particular mood, Singh brings an acute sense of timing and, above all, of placement—his greatest debt to modernism. The man who flies through the fiery hoop in *Centennial celebrations, Mayo College, Ajmer,* and the girls suspended in mid-air in *Monsoon swings in a village near Jaipur,* will never, to our delight, reach the ground. They mark that same buoyant precision of sighting as Cartier-Bresson's in the famous foot levitated an inch over a puddle near the Gare St. Lazare.

The publishers of *Rajasthan* subtitle it *India's Enchanted Land.* On the flap are notices of companion volumes, *A Portrait of Lost Tibet, Caravans to Tartary,* etc. Could it be that in Singh the right photographer was chosen for laughably wrong reasons—and would anyone finally care?

Artforum, *November 1981.*

1. *Nicaragua,* by Susan Meiselas, edited with Claire Rosenberg (New York: Pantheon Books, 1981).
2. *Falkland Road,* by Mary Ellen Mark (New York: Alfred A. Knopf, 1981).
3. *Rajasthan,* by Raghubir Singh, foreword by Satyajit Ray (London: Thames and Hudson, 1981).

Reflections on Latin American Photography

This essay was originally to have dealt with the subjective experience and multiple readings of photography. You will agree that photos are often ambiguous in effect, so that this amiable topic left me free to say just about anything I wanted. Later, while serving as a juror for the second Colloquio Latino-Americano, it was suggested that I consider the images that had been submitted for the occasion, many of them displayed at the Palacio de Bellas Artes. The dilemmas of Latin American life and the puzzling attributes of photography seemed compatible themes. I planned to limit myself to about eight pictures, looking at them very closely as visual texts that both hindered and furthered an understanding of their subjects. In other words, I would analyze the special possibilities of photography itself, using illustrations from the present show.[1] But now that aim strikes me as too limited and unresponsive.

We are exposed to several hundred works, coming from disparate points in space, if not time. With the naiveté and ignorance, but also the foreshortened perspective of an outsider, I look upon an assemblage of photos that bears witness, frame by frame, to a passionate state of affairs. Each shot is not only weighted by its own cadence, but appears to figure in a larger, off-stage drama, a recurrent tragedy, of which it presents a fragment. The ongoing picture is, of course ramified from country to country and then variegated within each country. While hope, pity, and grief are certainly not monopolized by Latin America, the ways of showing them have a distinct expressive aura. Struck by this phenomenon, I found, then, that my earlier question was reversed: what aspects of Latin-American life have been drawn into and how have they been changed by, these photos?

There exists a close fit between the social consciousness of such photographs and the belief of the Consejo that Latin-American societies are in crisis. It would not have been the first time a sponsor played a role in *generating,* not merely in acknowledging certain forms of communication. Just the same, no single group could account for the flood of images that describe the oppressive power relations of their scene or honor acts of confronting them. Encouraged and displayed, where many would have been censored at home, these ardent works surge forth, as if on a natural tide.

The human face comes to haunt them, as it never would in any comparable sampling of North American work. I am aware of clichés about the Latin search for identity. Here, though, the face is presented not as an apprehensive mask, but as a stage in which sorrowful experience is either remembered or awaited. Because the mobility of the features is a reflex of that experience, the face carries an active principle into this photography. More a source of action than a static portrait, it's like a gauge of outside pressures. Beyond their social class, a particular environment is always implied by these faces, one which elicits the intensity of their gaze. The Panamanian boy in Sandra Eleta's photo doesn't so much stare as drill you with his eyes (Fig. 33). Even at moments of joy or alcoholic release and intimacy, a frantic tone is sensed. As for those scenes of carnival or ritual, when real masks appear, they only serve to emphasize a demonic impulse. The religious celebration and the saturnalia, as seen by photographers throughout Latin America, are but opposite sides of the same grotesque desperation.

The feeling, then, of life being lived at the edge, of the extremity of the human situation being the *norm,* dominates these images. Far from imposing a dismal atmosphere, which might be inferred everywhere by the surroundings, this edginess conveys a harrowing vitality. At funerals, which for us are scenes of piety and reverence, such remorseless vision bites into the social fabric. The effect of the death is established on all faces, yet the loss they have suffered has only lent them an added sting of life. Often, too, photographers, such as the Mexican Pablo Ortiz Monasterio, bring us earlier vignettes of the individual, under the duress of fatigue and sickness, which are in the end compared with the ceremoniously arrayed corpse. Here, at last, is immobility, where the flesh has given out (Fig. 34).

From the psychological point of view, the face in Latin-American photography embodies a paradox. Providing an inexhaustible gallery of expression and temperament, it is studied with frank enjoyment. But it is an enjoyment of character, not a search into the nuances of

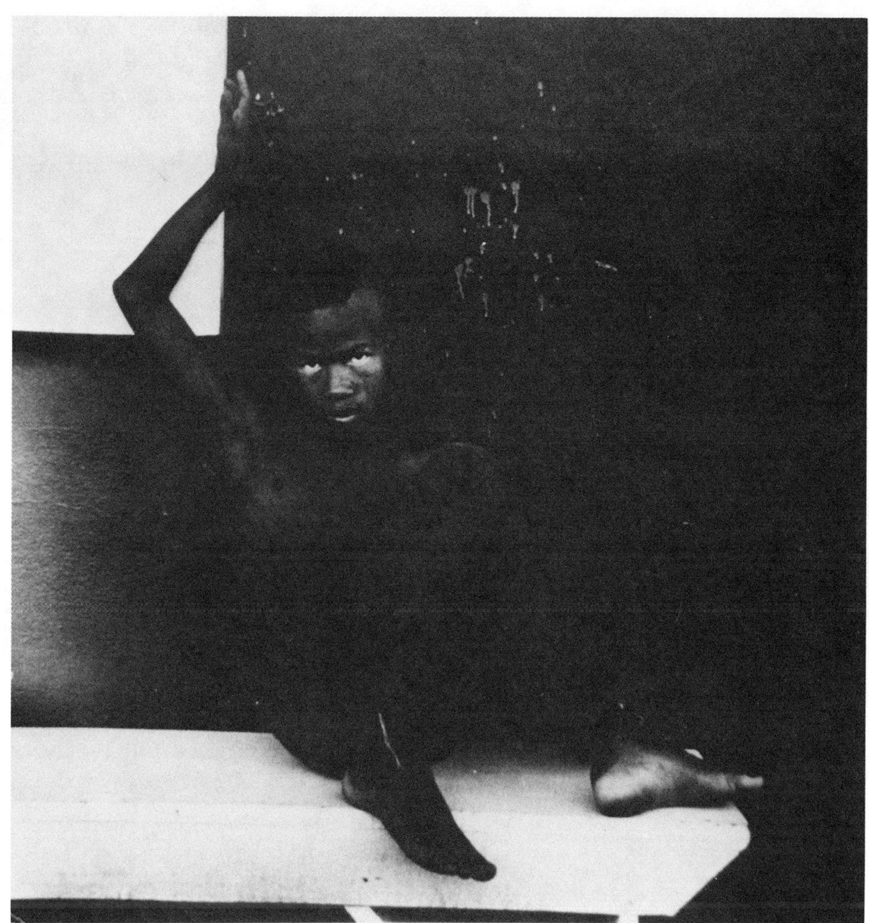

Figure 33. Sandra Eleta, Untitled, n.d.

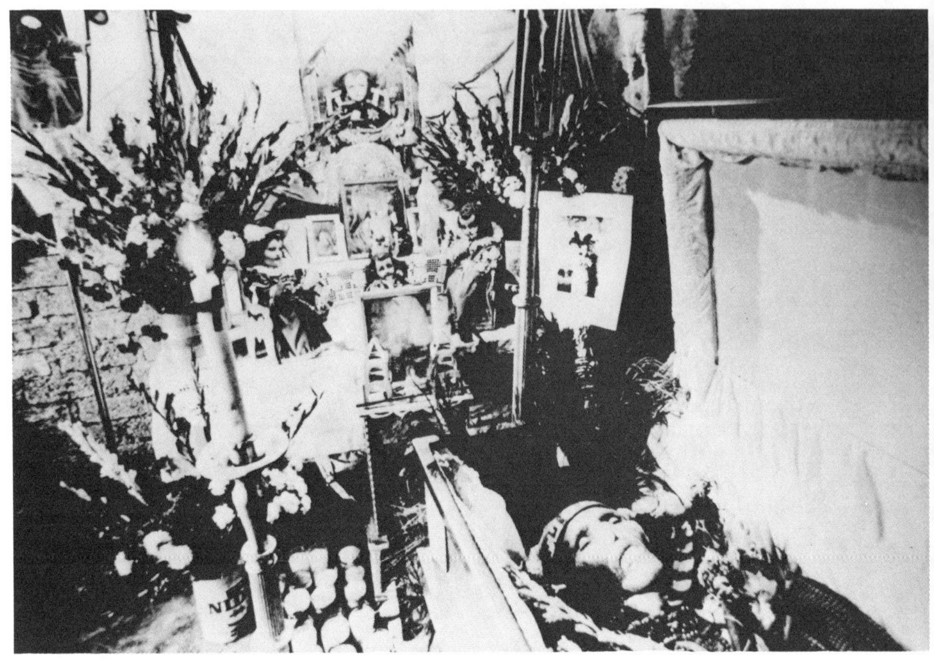

Figure 34. Pabló Ortiz Monasterio, Untitled, n.d.

ego. I don't doubt that faces here are broken down into types, more familiar to local audiences than they are to me. The campesino, the mother, those from the cantina, the old servant, the urchins of the villages, Chicano cliques, and so on. Photography has always been more adept at portraying what people are, rather than who they are. Nevertheless, we do not see any conscious mode or illusion of search into the subject's inner being. Under the circumstances, the kind of emotional knowledge thought to be gained by that inquiry would appear to be a self-indulgence. Each type is stationed in a certain place and intersects with other types, or rather, the forces they represent mingle, either in cooperation or in conflict, with each other. It's therefore no accident that a psychological schematism is paralleled by a social schematism.

One channel in which this schematism is realized is the area of work. To the extent people are made known, it's by their functions in the work activity (a theme comparatively underrepresented in North American photography where individuals are more typically labeled by their life-styles and are therefore shown by what they consume rather than do). That is why the frequent appearance of strike scenes in Latin America indicates a drastic form of social rupture. These shots impart an urgency felt by the strikers to mend the ties that have been broken. In this context, a strike is both an exceptional event, because it uproots a traditionalist people, and a repeated crisis, because labor unrest itself is built into the economic inequities that obviously prevail.

Photographs, however, can clarify far less of the satisfaction or discontent of workers than of the powerful reality of work itself, defined by its particulars. The fact that harvest workers are portrayed as cheerful in Cuba, one of the few Socialist countries in Latin America, impresses one as far more polemical than documentary. Fresher and even startling is Juca Martins's photo series of a prostitute arrested and brutalized by police in Brazil (Fig. 35). I say "startling" because no one in this ugly affair seems to have any consciousness other than of performing their work or of enduring what it requires. In the heat of action, these professionals revert to type and their cool behavior becomes wildly dissonant in a traumatic scene.

Much less illuminating to my Northern eyes are all those scenarios in which subjects have been typecast instead of perceived as emergent from their type. By typecast I mean the rhetorical assignment of moral or sentimental values to the protagonists of the photograph. When we are intended to understand a riot victim as a martyr, a young child as an adorable pet, an armed soldier as an oppressive

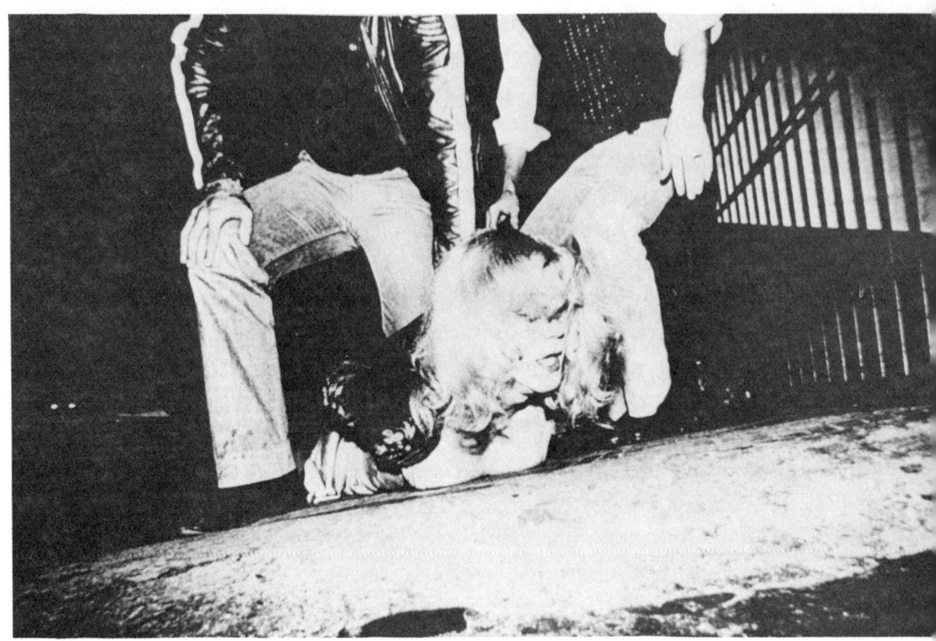

Figure 35. Juca Martins, *Prostitutes being arrested,* n.d.

force, an old man as an incarnation of wisdom, we find ourselves in the one-dimensional world of ready-made judgments. As soon as the photographer *determines* that social types and their expected roles come together, then my ideological tendency is assumed ahead of time, and I can make no emotional or political discovery by means of the photograph. For me, symbolism of that sort works against itself by an effect of closure, lowering my involvement even when a subject might have historical implications.

On the contrary, by imaging the way an environment is programmed by icons, a photograph can awaken political sensibility. The oversized renderings of saints, comic strip or TV characters, and government fixtures reflect institutional and media attempts to control a society. In simply recording, that is, stepping back from such violent presences, the photographer can dissociate us from them. The frame outflanks the message and therefore gives us the psychic room to maneuver with our consciousness. Here, the *photographer* emerges from a role, moving from passive witness or protesting ideologue to productive observer.

The kind of space I just mentioned is peculiar to the photographic medium. A photograph arbitrarily frames a rectangular area in two dimensions, but it also cannot avoid giving the illusion of penetrating into another region, and therefore of pointing to something. This pointedness entails a certain responsibility, a formal responsibility if you will, but I prefer to call it an expressive responsibility to the image. Most of the photographers here apparently stem from photojournalism, an expository mode absorbed with public narrative content. Pictures of this sort must describe the vectors of one or more activities as they come to a head in a unique instant of time. Time itself is a continuum of dynamic, singular, mutating instants, from which the photographer offers newsworthy stoppages.

But in David Cardenas's picture of two men who support heavy sacks on their shoulders, the moment of perception appears stable because the conception of time is fixed (Fig. 36). Past and future fall away before the apparent endlessness of *present* labor. Being a photograph, this picture is still highly descriptive, but it is, of course, no longer reportage. Because the darkness of the picture cavity highlights the weight of the men's burden, we can speak of a symbolist aim. Still, I'm unsure whether the men are actually workers or models, and I don't know as much about the space as I think I should know. Clearly stated facts and dubious circumstances oscillate in my mind, each to undermine the other, and I begin to question what I see.

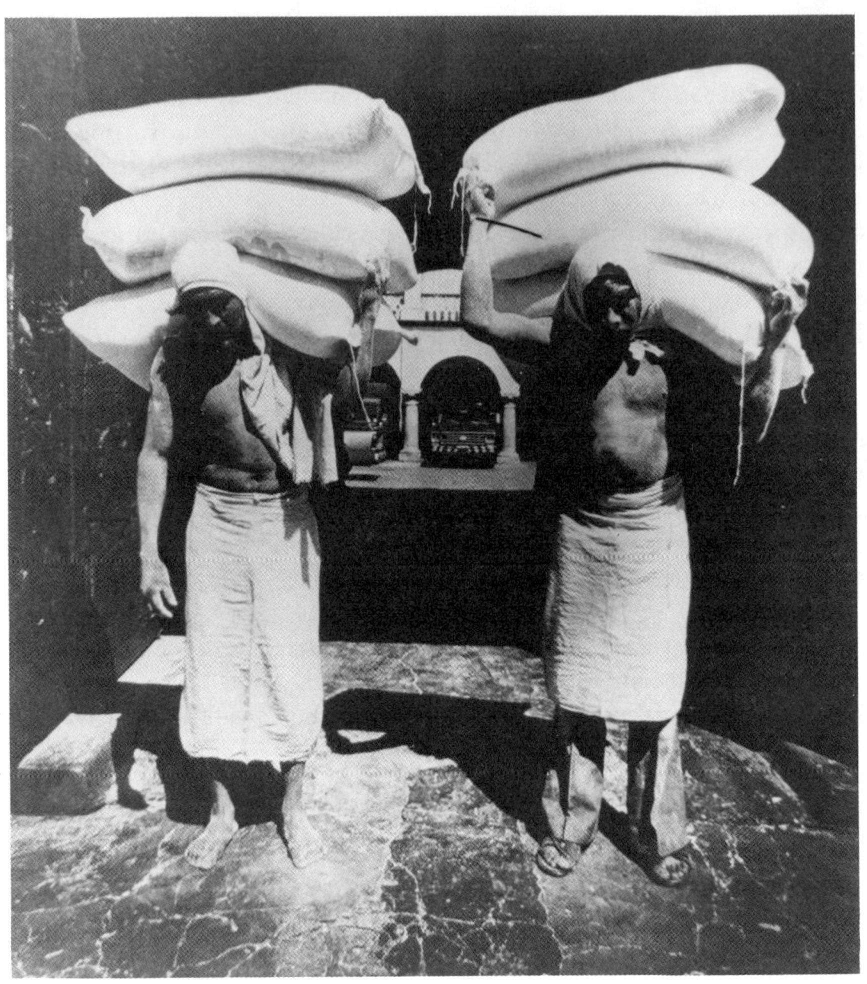

Figure 36. David Cardenas, *Los Cargadores,* n.d.

Or more accurately, I become aware of active thought and imagination that make claim for an order of their own. And they do that through the intervention of light and dark: the sensate stratum of tone which, more consistently in the hands of Latin American photographers than others, alters space and engenders mood. Because of that theatrical sensitivity to tone, objects, figures, and events, which may have suggested one kind of initial meaning, are ultimately perceived to have quite another. The subject is often not merely illuminated but *struck* by light or disjointed or drowned by shadow. You feel the physical force of chiaroscuro as it wrenches apart unexpected zones within the frame. These recreated zones are profoundly disobedient to the natural contours of things, which are now broken down into partial accents or lost in strange depths. Subjects can still be named and described, but they are also disproportionately or inexplicably eaten away by the light, which constantly calls attention to itself. Such an element acts as the counterpart of the face in Latin American photography, a kind of physiognomy of space. Within that space is suggested limitless reserves of loneliness, ecstasy, ominous fears, regrets, and memories of all sorts.

At the same time, I sense that this very extravagance of tonal contrast, with all its attendant tremors, is an everyday affair. It crops up incessantly, and much to the point, in Cuba, Peru, Colombia, Brazil, Venezuela, and so on, evidently because photographers and their audiences are mutually conditioned by it. The boundaries between the more historical space of photojournalism and this timeless fantasy vision are much more fluid than they are in my culture. With us, the interior life is approached through irony, artistic self-consciousness, or narcissicism, and such devices are kept very separate from the modes of objective witness. It is as if the individual exists in a sovereign world, apart from communal existence or public reality. With this show, on the contrary, the easy communication between both spheres is taken for granted. As a result, many Latin American photos, despite their heavy breathing, subtly modulate the known genres of the medium. There comes into view a huge and vaguely defined terrain in which the typical statement is less than a purely personal or introspective construction, and yet portentously more than a detached record.

Take, as an example, Jose Figueroa's Cuban street scene. An apparently casual snap reveals four men, raked by slanting shadows, seated in crate-like booths, as if they were meditating in homemade confessionals (Fig. 37). Next to them, a wall sign of a wind-whipped Cuban flag implies a chance juncture of thought and symbol. The whole of

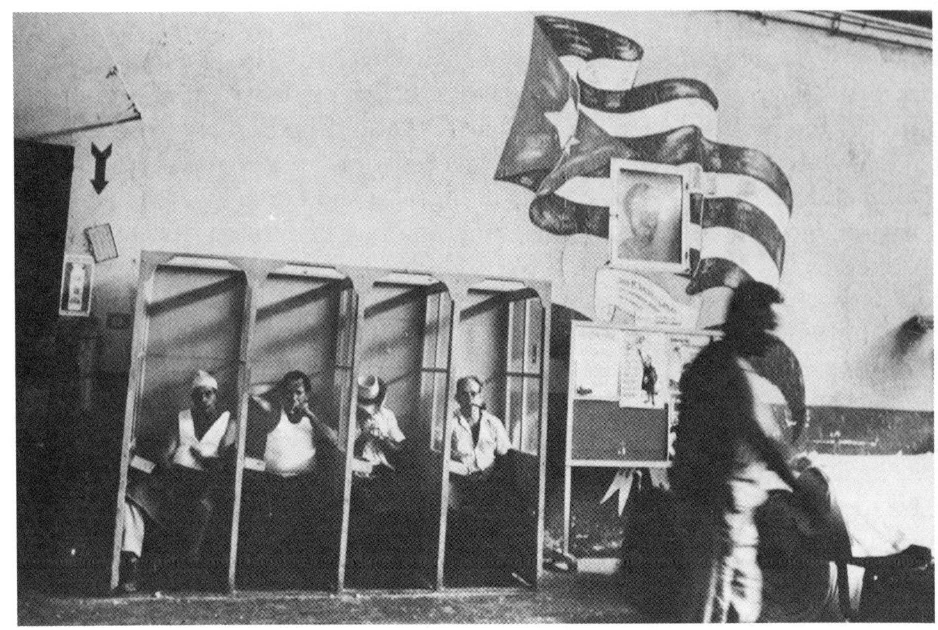

Figure 37. Jose Figueroa, from the series *That Flag, Havana,* 1976.

the possible meaning of this photo—a questioning of a national consciousness—is far larger than the sum of its parts, yet one can't assume the tableau to be other than itself, an ordinary sign available just then to any passerby. In any event, I am less concerned with the accuracy of a conceivable reading than with the temperament that attends to such an image. It tells me about qualities of special alertness, anxiety, and stress that are illuminating in themselves.

Of course, no isolated case proves anything, and this particular photo could have been taken by an outsider. Still less would I argue that Latin American neighborhoods inevitably summon moody responses. Rather, with the blurred but concentrated memory of 2,000 Latin American photographs I *will* say that such neighborhoods can and have been perceived in this fashion. It goes beyond a taste for the incongruous or a delight in mystery, attitudes familiar enough on my home ground. Do we not all notice an instinctive Latin dualism, in which the things of this world can be situated unproblematically in the space of a dream?

When that space erupts, as if from a nightmare, it's likely we're confronting a political testament. But with almost as much frequency, the interior reachs of the photograph draw us toward moments that are without directed purpose or glib schematism, and can only be described as play. I had spoken before of a passionate state of affairs, of which the photographs offered here represent fragments. Faces in themselves, and then in communities, reflected that passion. Work had a dominant role in the proceedings. Just as grave, unified, and consequential, however, is the theme of play, bridging public with private experience through distended time, that marks these photos at their best.

Originally published as "La subjectividad, la fotografia, y sus multiples lecturas," in Hecho en Latino America *2 (Mexico: Instituto Nacional de Bellas Artes, 1982). Subsequently published in* Obscura, *The Journal of the Los Angeles Center for Photographic Studies, December–February 1981–82.*

1. Segundo coloquio Latinoamericano de fotographia, Palacio de Bellas Artes, Ciudad de Mexico, April–May 1981.

Prisoners of Their Class

Portrait photographs conduct their business as a form of delayed social theater. The parties to the portrait exchange—the consenting subjects and the viewers—aren't present to each other when film is exposed, but they're still reciprocally affected by the occasion as if they were. Even though it's known as a short-term hypothesis about the sitter's character, the photograph tends to be read as a lasting statement. No words have yet been found to describe the interaction of those concerned, halfway as it is between indirect address and pseudo-intimacy.

One way of talking about that intimacy is as a kind of class revelation. Dripping with details of expression, dress, body language, and setting, photographs continually point out life-styles and income levels which, in turn, indicate something very concrete about class identity. Indeed, most such images tend to provoke interim judgments on what class roles people play, rather than who they are.

As it happens, the subgroup to which I belong, artists and writers, takes a rather deluded pride in its detachment from class allegiance. It appears to be important for us to feel disaffiliated from bourgeois norms. We cultivate notions of our unhindered movement through ideas, values, and forms, supposedly free from social bias. We can think of ourselves as having local, professional, many kinds of personal interests, but not *class* interests. Maybe that's why the artificial spectacle of social class, given by photographs, intrigues but also nettles us.

Photographic culture works to keep social distinctions very much alive, and it therefore carries a political wallop. By political I mean the sensation of power or powerlessness which a photograph can effortlessly inject into its viewers. A liberal consciousness is unsettled by the spectacle of class barriers firmly drawn across societies at an incommunicable and unreasonable distance from its own. When the liberals are artists, they tend to reflect a well-known liberal guilt in not having closed the distance, not having shared its power. For the artist is a specialist in portraying social life as composed of "others," that is, fellow creatures formed or deformed by values hard to understand or even threatening, because their experience is alien. When otherness looks deprived, it invokes sympathy but also confirms prejudices; when it appears lordly, it stimulates envy but asks to be deflated.

Into this context have recently appeared some post-Arbus photographers, highly focused on class phenomena. Chauncey Hare and Mary Lloyd Estrin deal with the down and out, and with the ultrarich. With an outlook that's persuasive and sometimes bitter, they bring news of social enclaves to the amorphously middle-class audience projected by their books. Hare's *Interior America* and Estrin's *To the Manor Born* introduce but also symbolically insulate their readers from exotic communities. These photographic essays are, at the same time, a little too peculiar—that is, artistic—to be thought of as normal coffee table items. Their aesthetics are imbued with intense ambivalence toward their subjects. With a downbeat, graphic style, they work to discourage any erstwhile notions of human solidarity across class divides.

Quite aside from artistic intent, this discouragement emerges in some inherently loaded conditions and separatist effects of photographic experience. For example, anyone photographed is put into a fix—a time fix. Viewers are recurringly misled by ephemeral circumstances that have been made implausibly durable, in a semirandom process. For better or worse, the subjects hang on in memory as if they were so many two-dimensional statues which have replaced living, warm-blooded creatures. There's a sudden, weird heaviness about them. The framing act has weighted them with a burden that perhaps converts a fleeting gesture into a mood, an individual into a type, or an episode into an event. No matter how unrepeated and singular the data contained in the photograph, or how much it hints of actual contingency, one wants the image to emerge as seductively general and "representative." If only because it works on a summary, one-shot basis, a photograph can't help tacitly simplifying and wondrously congealing a very unstable state of affairs. The experience of photographs bolsters an illusion of viewer control by the contrast of its microspecimen of time, character, and space with one's own real, much more complex, and longer standing experience of them. There's no malice in recognizing this, only an instinctual awareness of what photographs do.

Suppose, for instance, you look at Chauncey Hare's image of a family watching television (Fig. 38). The objects within the living room, such as a ceramic Eiffel Tower or a painting on velvet, speak to me of the most cliché bad, tacky taste. But more significantly, they reinforce a judgment about the leisure activity itself. Who has *not* watched TV—that great American pastime—and yet, who would care to have themselves represented as TV watchers in perpetuity? It's not the evidence the photograph contains that may indict or flatter its subjects so much as the absence of any conflicting or modifying evidence.

If you fancy that a single picture can't characterize you, though it can well incarnate others, it's because photography makes them visible to you as you know you're not to yourself. A photograph can often flatter your "complexity" by handing you a specially reduced extract of someone else's situation. You can't help feeling that their very consciousness is exposed, whereas yours is concealed. Clarified and schematized, the public icon acts as the target for private archery. Estrin and Hare certainly might agree with Proust's remark that "each social class has its own pathology." Yet, to deny them the right to select evidence on this forcible basis, or any other, would be silly.

For the first half of his adult life, Chauncey Hare had been an engineer for Standard Oil of California. In a remarkable autobiographical text, he writes of how his routine for the corporation literally produced nausea, and how, with great trembling and progressive alienation from his domestic scene, he freed himself to become a full-time photographer. His forefathers had worked their way up from blacksmithing and steelworking to factory management. In the course of his job he met other employees, further down the pay scale, who had been bilked of compensation owed them for accidents. "My grandfather," he writes, "lost the use of a leg in a mill. . . . I feel that my camera recalls such experiences when it trains upon modern industrial casualties. . . . It was pure *déjà vu* for me." His book simultaneously resonates with compassion for more exploited victims of corporate callousness, and witnesses the odyssey of a defector who pulls up stakes and searches for a new, autonomous image outside the class to which he had long felt condemned. What finally permits him to take leave of his class origins is his decision to make them an object of study.

Gaining entry into homesteads, in pursuit of his goals, he would wave whatever credentials were at hand—his Guggenheim Fellowship

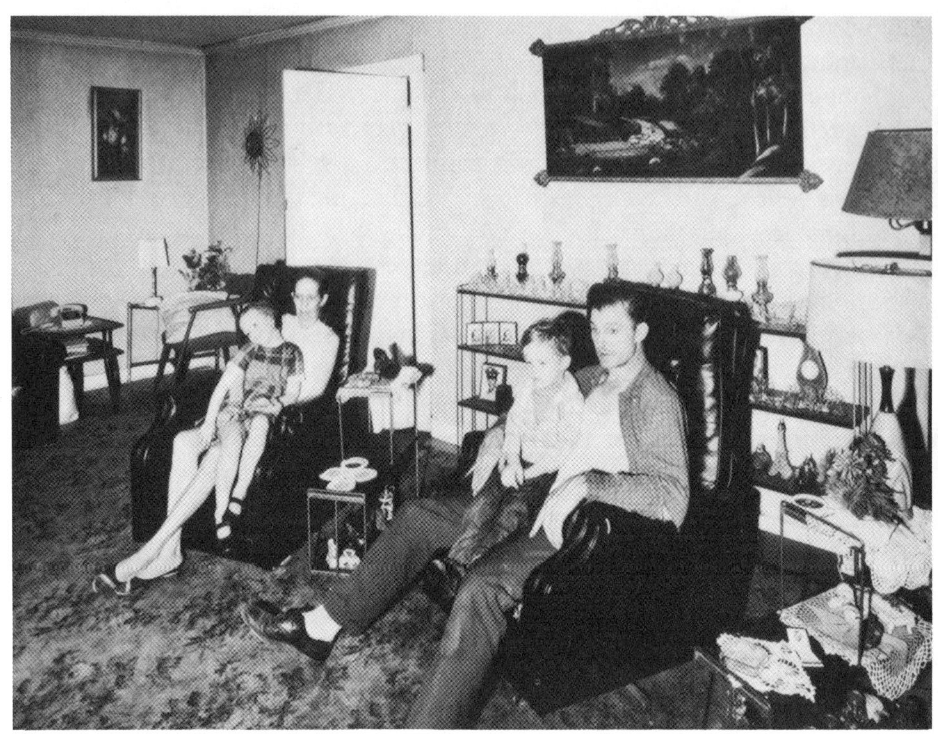

Figure 38. Chauncey Hare, *Wheeling, West Virginia,* 1972.

papers—and he made sure to register with the local police. With his large-format camera and tripod, he wandered through communities with names like Mingo Junction, Weissport, and Steubenville. *Interior America* is, for him, a culture of boarding rooms and row houses, put together with oilcloth and cheap linoleum and naked light bulbs. Its denizens have no place to go and their bodies are sunk, sometimes as if by endless waiting, and often as if by fatigue from work in the factories sensed nearby. Harshly lit by his flash, religious chromos or family heirlooms decorate underscaled rooms. Meanwhile, the wide-angle lens stretches everything as it makes space itself look afflicted by a glandular disturbance.

By contrast, in the grand manors of Estrin's Lake Forest, Illinois, maids have vacuumed, scrubbed, and polished aristocratic furnishings to the peak of sightliness. The decorous, well-coiffed families they serve betray no upward mobility for the good reason that they're already at the top, and have evidently been so for quite a while. Viewed from Mingo Junction, the economic heights of Lake Forest are positively alpine. Just the same, accompanying comments by Robert Coles and Estrin herself speak of the anxiety of some of these socialites.

A few fear the passing of their class and refer to themselves as survivors. They perceive waning respect for the best people—themselves—than there ought to be in this country. Estrin's glimpse into their private lives is, in any event, rare because Lake Forest fully justifies the title "exclusive suburb." Commuting between city and home, this gentry has its separate coach on the Chicago and Northwestern, allowing it to play bridge undisturbed.

Estrin approached her subjects as one who had been raised in the neighborhood, educated in English at Vassar, and now needed their help in completing a photographic thesis. The easy access she gained into this citadel of WASP gentility is reflected in their amiable expressions, which often wins through their haughty poses. Since Estrin's project is superficially about graciousness, and Hare's, desolation, we can see that one photographer needed to be welcomed in order to get her results, and the other to be somewhat resisted.

A number of eccentric and characterful faces in Estrin's book stay in the mind, but hardly any in Hare's. Partly this difference stems from her interest in the formal portrayal of figures within interiors, whereas he's studying interiors with occasional figures. The contrast in psychological focus accounts for the difference in pictorial space. Hare seems to have waited until people were off-guard—not relaxed—before blazing away at them. His subjects remain a little suspicious or awkward, probably unsure of what this stranger expected. "People always apologize for the condition of their homes," he writes, "while at the same time being proud of them." Just as they oscillate between pride and shame, Hare catches them in a null state where they are neither types nor individuals. Estrin, using similar equipment, needed more trust from her subjects, and often deliberately arranged them. For both, the photographic campaign is a return to a personal past. Estrin: "Though I now live in a style quite far removed from that of life in Lake Forest, this was nevertheless my former home and I carry with me much of its heritage." She found people secure enough not to feel threatened by the expectation that they should play their social roles to the hilt. Despite the distanced, cool, and polite tone of her work she is not so respectful as to have collaborated with her sitters. They knew as little about what would be done to them as those in *Interior America.*

They're often framed, for instance, like models for ads—people of "distinction" drinking Dewar's scotch. In other words, they seem to be imitating a commercial hype which got its start by imitating them. Since they're in their own homes, though, and under natural light, the effect can be somewhat deflating, even comical. The leather-bound libraries, china, and dynastic oil portraits are described so matter of factly as to make their owners' possessiveness look foolish. Estrin has two distinct styles that subvert the class imagery of Lake Forest: a deadpan naturalism, and an occasional Expressionist drama or even Surrealist incongruity. Such a clash emphasizes the life-style of her subjects as prolix and orderly to the point of mania.

But there's nothing that Hare relishes more than the askew and irrational clutter of his interiors; he's violently nonhierarchical and disruptive of "good" composition. With him, one feels the presence of a moralist. He draws a comparison between the impersonal vinyl horrors in contemporary interiors, and Victorian woodwork, which expresses an upright and dignified craftsmanship. (His elderly subjects come off much more sympathetically than Estrin's.) Still, he would have those who struggle to make ends meet lead lives even worse than those during the depression—more dejected, wasted, and hopeless. They resemble wax exhibits in a diorama from a museum of natural history. He transmits his "message of rage" with a feeling for corruption of spirit, whose misery is relieved only by the icons of Catholic redemption that crop up in the rooms he invades. (As they did occasionally in Lange's, Evan's, and Russell Lee's—the last an acknowledged influence on Hare.) At first you think you're revisiting the FSA photos of the 1930s, and then you notice that the view is incomparably more

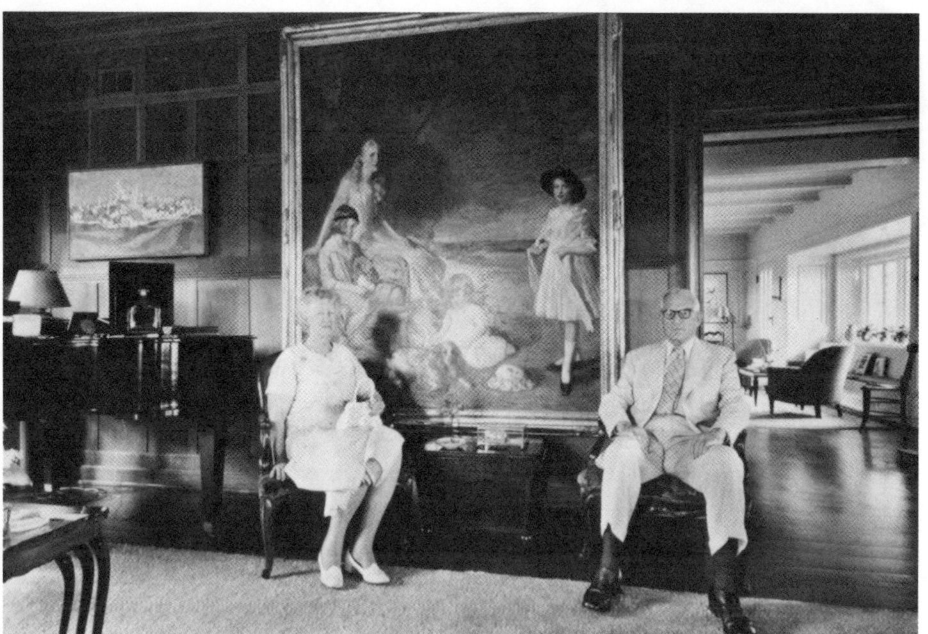

Figure 39. Mary Lloyd Estrin, Untitled, n.d.

grotesque and mannered. Instead of their wholesome yet subtle idealization, he offers a demonic American poverty—which may be either the result or cause of a breakdown of national values. Here is risk-taking of a dissonant kind. The more he insists on this demonology, the more he verges on turning it into an exotic spectacle rather than exciting a corrective anger.

I might want to resolve the conflict between my knowledge that things aren't always the way Hare and Estrin see them, and the emotional grip their imagery has on me. I know that they've richly informed me about the way others live, but at the same time I begin to mistrust Hare's view of brutish deprivation and Estrin's of unearned, smug freedom which have been convincingly put into my head. These photos are little flowers that have sprung from the soil of the new, hardened liberalism. They go Arbus one better by applying her aggressions not to individual psyches but to what is a blurry class structure in this country.

As they determine that structure, we're asked to believe that the ultrapoor and the ultrarich still live in a nasty and mangy past, or according to the rules of an archaic decorum. These photographs grant us more than visitation rights into defective milieus. They suggest that life is a game of *realpolitik* won by those with the steadiest grasp of the present. The stacked message of the photos is dismally clear. What's fuzzy is the degree to which the photographers have fallen beneath their own, good intentions, and the extent that they cause an invidious recoil in their viewers. The conflict, finally, cannot be resolved. One would never imagine holding these works to criteria of truth-telling if they were not photographs, that is, images crystallized with extreme visual credibility. And they would not have been worth appreciating at such length if they were not also art, employing art's privileged fictions and transfiguring mind.

Hare dedicates his book: For Those Who Are Awakening to Their Own Authority. I think he means by "authority" the feeling of power people might have if they take their own lives in hand. If so, the odd, saddening thing about his book is that he realizes his own authority by creating a picture of those who can't or haven't realized theirs.

Village Voice, *December 10, 1979.*

Where Have All the People Gone?

Contemporary American Photography

To a visitor from another country, what does our serious photography have to say about the American environment and the moods in which it's perceived? One question raised immediately by the work is: where have all the people gone? Crowds do not make much of an appearance in these pictures, and one would have to guess at our urban density, which is only glimpsed or implied. Rather, the camera, when it roams at large, emphasizes a certain emptiness and barrenness, blemished by tacky industry or dingbat development. A vaguely despoiled landscape—uneventful horizons and banal closeups—nettles the gaze. Both the city, with its suburban sprawls, and the country wear a slightly deserted air, as if they had nothing better to do, no other purpose, than to sit glumly for their portraits.

The public and private spheres of contemporary life can be precisely described, but they share a common, spiritless identity, and are finally quite interchangeable. Power that has been misapplied and community that has come unraveled: these are the social conditions accepted as if they were a matter of course by some of our serious photographers. The stranger would have to look more closely at this apparently chaotic spectacle in order to understand it in a more fundamental and disquieting guise—as imagery of *raw* phenomena.

Elsewhere, journalistic or heroic traditions in photography are more the rule, as they once *were* here. In these modes, events have meaning as news and appearances are endowed with symbolism. Messages are transmitted along the channels of a known visual rhetoric. Few people in Western industrial nations have trouble with photography as a historical record or as a romantic synthesis of personal feelings. But these are exactly the values that many recent workers have rejected. In their view, "rawness" does not so much suggest lack of form or refinement as it does a more positive condition: *bruteness.* The subjects they frame are not to be recommended for any other virtue than their resistant material character, an incomprehensible, dumb presence, sufficient unto itself. Evidence of a shaping culture and therefore a social intelligence is to be found, of course, everywhere. But the camera does not transcribe it any more fondly than it does weeds or rocks or garbage. Tamed or harnessed nature is no more domesticated than the wildest ranges. They have, in either case, equally brief or enormous stretches of history behind them.

One does not want to call this vision impartial so much as impassive. Though scrupulously attentive in method, it is not scientific in spirit. And while detached in attitude, it is not dissociated in feeling. On the contrary, one feels that the environment needed to be pointless in order to clarify the function of photographic *seeing.* How we are made to see, not the significance of what is seen, becomes the sometimes obsessive rationale of the picture.

Because America is such a large, various country, with conflicting drives, these impressions might sound wide of the mark. American citizens, like those of many other countries, often feel themselves outsiders to each other, habituated only to their own regions, class values, and life-styles. I am a New Yorker, for example, and the ideas I broached above came to mind through examples of western American photography. What would seem to my eyes a focus on enervated and estranging horizontals might have stimulated in those who produce such work a sense of great liberation. If so, however, it's not a liberation from actual facts, which correlate closely with their results.

Anyone who examines the vistas fastened upon by Lewis Baltz, Richard Misrach, Thomas Barrow, and Edward Gohlke recognizes and will not quarrel with the physical account of their motifs. One acknowledges the spatial recessiveness of everything they depict as a just response to actual territory. But, visiting these parts, one is more intent on getting through them than meditating upon their space. The western states often look like an infinitude glued on the wrong end of a telescope. Unless you are a tourist or a camper, travel there distends your sense of destination. It would hardly occur to the visiting mind that this photography has done anything so drastic as *interpret*—though it has certainly selected—its subject. The selection process, however, has been carried out by those who appear to have all the time in the world. They graze upon their turf, finding that which is most visually nourishing in that which is also most typical. So, the "aimless" passage of the photographers I mentioned is not so mysterious. They are fascinated by the nondescript redundancy of the nature that spreads out before them. After a while, the viewer comes to think of it as existing, and above all functioning, only for the photographer.

The landscape, in short, has been rendered useless, which is to impose a very different thought upon it than the sort of thing that occurs to wayfarers or developers. Neither irritating or fetching for any mundane purposes, it has become transformed into an *aesthetic* terrain.

This is a moment of exceeding self-consciousness in the course of American photography. The artistic impulse runs through a great deal of the work we see, at full throttle. On the level in which it defamiliarizes ordinary sensations, the activity of the western photographers is entirely artistic. By isolating and attending to unlikely tableaux, transfixing them with a morbid stare, they perform as artists. If this is so, as I think it is, these men are obliged to behave as *contemporary* artists, which entails the denial of older entries in their tradition, earlier appropriations of their ground.

If one thinks of Edward Weston and Ansel Adams, one easily recalls a rather strutting landscape, concerned always with cutting a figure. Where it had once been anthropomorphized, this landscape is now reduced to base matter. Where photography had once composed an immense natural grandeur with strong, graphic contrasts, it's now seen as rather harshly lit and high-keyed or with an evenness of mid-tones that is anticlimactic in the extreme. But their reaction against an older pictorial mode doesn't really explain the trend of these younger photographers.

Many of them talk with a certain thrill about the unpredictable "information" that the camera itself produces. Fresh sentiments about the Western land are past discovery; strange or inexplicable details, discriminated not by the mind but by the lens—these are the new frontier. In the era of space travel, parts of California and Colorado can seem as totally "other" as Mars. It is an historical moment in which response to the environment can find no release in the idea either of a natural order or of technological progress. The machine, the only presence in the garden, is a camera.

Whether entirely desired or not, there is a dualism in such imagery which is neither affirmative nor demonstrably critical. With the 1950s example of Robert Frank behind him, Lee Friedlander, ranging over the whole nation, initiated this chill curiosity in American chaff. Extremely assertive in the density with which he could stratify incongruous material, Friedlander was also remarkably nonjudgmental. He could observe the furniture of small-town corners, civic monuments, or scraggly bushes and foliage as elements that made up a surprising composition. He has an intimate feeling for dislocation and visual obstruction—things getting in the way of other things—that always stresses the fragmentary quality and limitations of the camera's view. Frank's moral consciousness of the desolation of America was successfully translated by Friedlander into sequences of arresting but unrelated incidents, gaggles of parts in futile search of a whole. There is, in fact, no whole in a Friedlander photograph other than that established by its frame. Friedlander was followed more stolidly in color by Stephen Shore and William Eggleston, and with nervous mannerism by John Gossage. They neither wish to attract nor repell you by the locale, but to show you what it's like. This they're more prone to do by the piling of its features rather than the synthesis of its aspects. In such light, they purvey a numb, selfless, conceptually static art, akin to minimalism, no matter how sporadically busy in effect. There had been too much disappointment and frustration in the national memory to *celebrate* the slovenly loose ends and flagrant excesses of our life, and too little sensibility to indict or want to correct them. The equivocal aspect of this art is that it thins out the possible meanings inherent in the photographic act (let alone its social aims), but holds on to them all the more urgently as imaginative redemption.

A quite separate branch of recent work will not truck with our topography on these puzzling terms, although it is by no means closed to mystery. In the zone in which many figures choose to create, the psychology of the photographer, his or her sensitive ego, is the key resource and, therefore, workers of this type may be regarded as quite recognizable art-makers. Already, among the landscapists, Robert Adams and William Clift have defected from the prevailing minimalism. They have no desire to keep themselves at a psychic distance from their environment, and they begin to revel in the moods of nature, as exalted through light. With them, we're left in no doubt of their frank enjoyment of the scene, or of the importance subject has, a subject that must accord with ideas of beauty that are in the end rather conventional. For those, though, who do not respond to stereotypes of western ruggedness, or who cringe before the American reality because they can see it only as stereotype, the chief strategy has been to burrow within themselves.

I hope I don't digress by stating that introspection, as a dominant mode in American art photography, has an economic base worth talking about. Up to recently, most practitioners had to make their living either in the commercial system (doing their "own" work in their free time for small audiences), or within a university context where they were employed as staff. To be posted as a faculty member in some remote academy meant, and still means, to be in a sort of exile, among visual surroundings that are less than stimulating and rapidly exhausted. The diaristic art fostered in most schools has a lushly involuted character. Among other things, the work is certainly filled with depths and alarms that would seem out of keeping with, and perhaps compensation for, the genteel boredom of its situation. The photographer is engaged in a kind of emotional fathoming only incidentally concerned with the "average" surfaces or sensations of his or her locale. These, in fact, are turned away in favor of nostalgic evocation, narrative fantasies, literary and conceptual conceits, or highly manipulated techniques involving other art media. The protected, nonmarket sponsorship of such imagery has furthered an egocentric flood of photos that offers many striking parallels with the vaunted narcissism of the 1970s. As its status as a legitimate art medium has risen, photography at the colleges seeks to convince as an expression of mind in search of its own possibilities.

Since this is a very open-ended ambition, it encompasses an enormous variety of styles and results. At one end, we see the uncanny icons of Arthur Tress and the sadistic scenarios of Les Krims. At another end, we have the split-screen effects of Robert Heinecken, the drawing or sculptural puzzles of John Pfahl and Robert Cumming, and the narrative sequences of Duane Michals. These names are chossen as prominent but hardly exclusive examples of photographic dynamics that are opposed but also subtly converge with each other. They have in common a strong accent on the artifice of the photographic process, whose fictiveness they emphasize by delirious coincidences of unlike imagery, or by comparing the contents of separate frames with the overall conclusions to which they each only partially allude.

The viewer, in any event, has an intended double-take. Confronting such art, one is asked to judge, but cannot resolve, the conflict between the "transparency" of the photographic record and the way it has been undermined in such a fashion as to stress its object-like character. Tom Barrow, for instance, quite literally points up this tension by marking large "X's" over his western landscapes. There can be no more explicit denial of the claims it may have upon him.

But the stakes are larger than the simple opposition between the perspectival space and the flat surface of the photograph. For, oddly enough, this phantasmal photography depends upon the documentary tradition, from which it obviously but flirtatiously departs. There is just enough credibility in Krims and Michals to make you think the photographer actually witnessed something terrible or miraculous. You oscillate between the idea that you're being conned by an elaborate set-up or illusion and the worry that implausible things do, after all, happen. The photographer Mac Adams goes to considerable pains reconstructing what appears to be the prelude or the setting of a crime and its aftermath, sprinkling odd, fetishistic clues throughout short photo narratives. It would solely be a matter of stagecraft were it not for the highly suggestive and magnifying power that photographic framing itself has upon the anxious imagination.

To the degree such anxiety gets externalized, it comes as no surprise that the main themes with which it's concerned are erotic. One has only to look at the exuberant visions of Joanne Leonard, Karen Truax, and Bea Nettles to become acquainted with the metaphors with which women approach the dream of sex. There was a voyeuristic dimension lodged in photographic culture from its beginning, a current of privileged surveillance which photographs of people taken unaware always insinuated. The aim here, however, is to assume the invasion of one's own privacy in order to incite confessional empathies in one's viewers. When male photographers deal with this theme, theirs are distinctly more violent conjurings of satisfied eros.

It occasionally happens that some diverse impulses come together in the work of artists who quite unwittingly find themselves exceptions to the rule of any one category. The New York photographers I have in mind are recognizably American but straddle the two broad modes I've sketched so far. Ralph Gibson offers parallels with the color work of Jan Groover, particularly in the concept of the found or composed but implicitly libidinal still-life. There is no final way to account for the grip their closely seen objects or textures have upon the viewer's organism except through its unforseen sexual charge. Gibson belongs to the school which prefers an observant posture towards its material. While he insists on modernist flattening of planes—say of someone's clothes or coiffure—the proximity of his lens to the subject invokes an almost carnal possessiveness. It's the vantage of someone who has exceedingly intimate access, conceivably a lover, and a passionate one at that, whose gaze freezes all its objects into an extraordinary immobility. Groover's relationship with kitchenware, vegetables, and nautilus shells is, by comparison, frenzied, but she is even more dogmatically modernist in justifying her "reductions" of content to pure seeing.

With both these artists, the optical ambiguities of design and space are but a reflex, it seems to me, of a regard that is fundamentally animal. Or rather, their probing into minute dislocations sublimates that regard, which can find no overt place in their aesthetics of detachment. (By framing so as to dismember or truncate people caught in the street, and by using a blinding flash, Mark Cohen, in Allentown, Pennsylvania, spells out the underlying aggression of this approach, though he also loses a great deal of its evocative power.)

Regrettably, the convergent aims of giving information about and of showing respect for communal life in America have proved beyond the powers of our better-known photographers. Their visiting camera far more often produces a jaundiced, condescending, or demonic view of social relations than it does a sympathetic one. Chauncey Hare's blue-collar workers and Bill Owen's suburbanites consented to have their pictures taken by strangers. Nothing, though, is clearer than that whatever faith these exploited subjects had in the good will of the photographers was misplaced.

While these two men are unlikely to admit it, we can trace the origins of their negative tradition to the portraits of Diane Arbus and Richard Avedon, dating back fifteen years. It was one of the many unfortunate effects of the New York fashion world to have spawned two brilliant artists who needed to *express* themselves by creating an image of American men and women the psychological reverse of the one they sycophantishly glamorized in their commercial work. In frame after unforgettable frame, with corrosive virtuosity, they etched portraits of malaise and deviance. Though it is intermittently on target and really demystifying, one does not think of their art as a principled social critique. Rather, we have to thank them for teaching us that an *artistic* vision requires itself to be abusive in social portrayal, that it is the mark of the photographic artist that the subject be made a creature essentially vulnerable to the class prejudices of viewers. Arbus and Avedon, of course, have been phenomenally influential. The effectiveness of their vision pivots on the way they both sensationalize and placate liberal guilt.

Once again, however, an exception comes to mind, Larry Clark, the last photographer I want to mention. On the face of it, his book *Tulsa* (published in 1971), appears to be one more gamey installment in the disparaging mode. But Clark was a "family" member of that young clique of junkies, outcasts, and punks, glimpses of whose life he brought together in a narrative that is partly also a *memento mori.* The photographer accepted the fact this life, which he shared, was a form of purgatory. *Tulsa* astonishingly reveals only the values of its protagonists; it assumes nothing because it knows nothing about ours. Clark's pictures convey what it truly feels like to be within a milieu, its shocks and swoons, not some ironic and domineering version by an outsider pandering to our stereotypes.

By any measure, it's a defective milieu and the photographer unflinchingly shows its crushing hurts. Time and again, he describes how sex and its provocations become thoroughly marginal to the escape found in the taking of drugs. But it is a functioning group, of sorts, and the people within it—their soiled humanity upfront—experience real ties with each other. Far from diminishing, Clark's artless style intensifies the candor and immediacy of his report. Still, *Tulsa*'s very credibility has an expressiveness we associate with art, achieved through rather than imposed upon Clark's response to his subject.

When speaking of the western landscape before, I referred to a fascination with "raw" visual phenomena, and with that, a brute quality that intervened across the photographic horizon. Clark espouses, not the bruteness of matter, but a natural brutality of vision. It's a mood that many of the vivid photographers around us emulate, for in itself it symptomizes and defines a very native condition. A recognition of the harshness and lawlessness running underneath an otherwise humdrum social surface is almost a staple of our culture. It's impossible not to be drawn to it, not to recognize its authentic sting, even as it leaves you in the moral lurch. This is not a question of preferring upbeat or reformist compassion to dark and pitiless insights or vice versa. But it is to acknowledge the deep flaws in our psychic environment—our moral quandaries, our feckless alienation—that have hindered photographers from joining heart and mind to make a fuller art. The more they internalize the strains of our historical moment, the more convincingly they reproduce those flaws.

Essay for the catalogue American Photographs: 1970 to 1980 *(Seattle: Washington Art Consortium, 1980).*

Photographers at War

The name Kelso Daly is not one to conjure with in the history of photography. His complete biography amounts only to "American (Dates Unknown)" in *The Indelible Image: Photographs of War—1846 to the Present,* a book accompanying an exhibition of the same title, organized by the Corcoran Gallery of Art. Daly is represented by a picture of a standing middle-aged man in pyjamas with all-over floral whorls, seen from behind as he looks with binoculars across a body of water at a horizon erupting with smoke. Time: Dec. 7, 1941. Place: Pearl Harbor (Fig. 40). In this weirdly calm image, a cozy tidbit of foreground episode contrasts with the enormity of the background event. Global violence has intruded into someone's unprepared domestic moment, and the incongruity makes the picture.

Such an image could easily serve as a curtain raiser for the very bad news that comprises the genre of war photography. For its part, the cover of *The Indelible Image* reproduces another serene picture of looking—a shot of relaxed, goggled observers, seated in Adirondack chairs as they witness an atomic detonation of 1951 (Fig. 41). In both this and the Daly photo, the theme is not the sickening phenomenon off-frame, but the inexpressive spectator. Kelso Daly's photograph was culled from *Life,* while the second, anonymous picture comes from the U.S. Department of Defense. These corporate media and government sources typify the places curators have rummaged for unpublished, obscure or piquant snippets of visual history. Though still vaguely informed by their original use ("human interest" reportage in the first case, documentary in the second), these images are reassigned a new job: to impress a late twentieth-century public with their potential as art experiences. Jane Livingston and Frances Fralin, who worked together on "The Indelible Image," assert that their "aesthetic sense" was

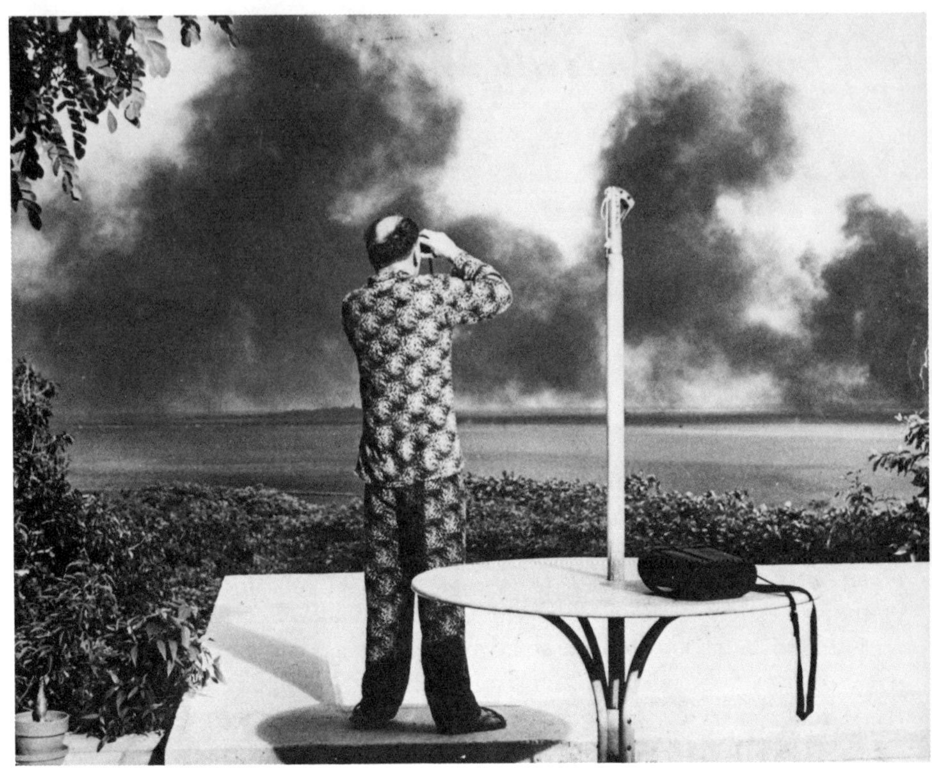

Figure 40. Kelso Daly, *Pearl Harbor Inhabitant Watches Bombing by Japanese,* 1941 (© 1970 Time, Inc.).

"consistently applied to the project at hand," upgrading some otherwise very resistant materials. But the topic of aesthetic distance, like that of physical distance, works here as a consciously protective device, a kind of emotional goggle to keep viewers from being scorched by the malign effusiveness of war.

Certainly a number of the better-known war photographers have thought of themselves as artists, albeit in very hot studios: Felice Beato, Alexander Gardner, Robert Capa, David Duncan, Gene Smith, Don McCullin, Gilles Peress. They exemplify a self-conscious tradition of classicizing formalists in the nineteenth century and expressionist witnesses in the twentieth. But they are overwhelmed in the genre by the unknown workers who have built up the relatively styleless archive of war. When oddments from the archive—and there are amazing ones to be seen—are plucked out for display in an *art* museum, Surrealizing taste tends to influence image presentation. A history of war photography is surely right to include both sorts of pictures. But the retroactive art gambit fails utterly as a means of coming to terms with either of them.

With its need for metaphor and make-believe, art discourse imposes the wrong affective environment upon the *record* of an activity that was literally played for keeps. In war photographs and also those of scenes of crimes—the two are often related—horizontal figures will simply not rise up after the click of the shutter. I remember Lucas Samaras once coming from a Weegee retrospective, quite taken by the shots of dead gangsters but baffled and put off by the fact that Weegee's was "not an art idea." Not even realizing that it seeks to neutralize what it wants to applaud, art talk is too innocent to engage with a vicious image content. What's needed is language that respects and anaylzes that content, but never commits the indecency of appreciating it.

There's a distinction to be made between being excited and being moved by war photographs. Action excites response, but the fatal aftermath of action invokes emotion. With the first, I am caught up in an exhilarating incompletion; with the second, I meditate on something terribly consummated. The moment I am excited I forget everything but present sensation. When I am moved, I am reminded of who I am in relation to others or of what I might be in a broader range of human possibilities. In the one instance, a feeling state is invoked almost as quickened sensory tone; in the other, appearances intimate something about our historical fortune, or I perceive and reflect upon them as such, in grief, astonishment, anger.

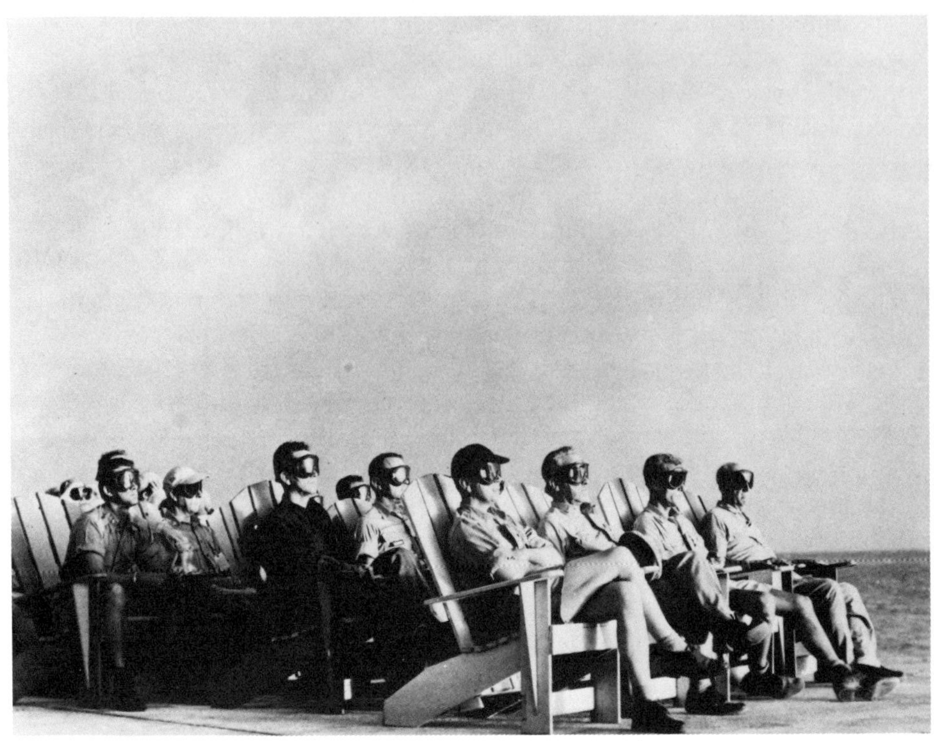

Figure 41. Anonymous, *Observers, Operation Greenhouse* (high-ranking personnel illuminated by atomic detonation), 1951 (U.S. Department of Defense).

For the first half of its history, war photography awkwardly sought to inform, edify, and perhaps to move its spectators; it did not know how to excite them. That task was left to engraved images of combat which continued to appear in newspapers until the First World War, two decades after halftone reproductions of photographs were introduced in the press. If this battle illustration was not supplanted earlier by more efficient, accurate, and cheaper photographic imagery, it may have been because of psychic and cultural factors as well as technical ones. In rendering the excitement of combat as visual theater, artists suggested, through *kinesthetic* emphasis, what it was that attracted men to the wasting of their own kind.

Oddly enough, in far grander prototypes—nineteenth-century military paintings by Détaille and Meissonier—the aim was to sweep up this perception of animal thrill into a *historical* panorama that was combined with a dramatic overview. The bodily sensations of war could thereby be celebrated in the propaganda of the imperialist state, which saw itself in heroic struggle against far weaker societies no less than with its Western competitors.

Early photography was nominally an arm of that same apparatus, though it brought home pictures that showed only the litter of violence—skulls and other moldering things in deserted fields. These vistas certainly did not depict any critical moment: one was given the day before the Afghanis attacked, or a view taken after the mutineers at Lucknow were wiped out. Nor were these spirited pictures: they were, in fact, cautionary, sullen and downbeat. There was no consolation to be taken from them for the sacrifice that had been endured.

Since I want to talk about a distinctive genre rather than just a perennial theme, I have to ask what actually qualifies such Victorian and Lincoln-era scenes as *war* photography. Many of them at first glance look like innocently peopled landscapes. The typical view of a campaign features doll-like troops deployed in distant, ornamental operations, swallowed within a vast, indifferent or alien scheme of nature. Yet the images themselves are hardly pastoral. Fenton in the Crimea and O'Sullivan at Gettysburg were nominally landscapists, but the unsightly and blemished terrain they described skewed the usual landscape readings.

When architectural and surgical photography (then young modes) entered the war zone, their emphases shifted as well, for the stone and the flesh of their subjects had been violated in anger. Each frame provided some piecemeal specialized information, as if that blameless purpose were the sole issue. But an impassive stance led to an unsettling and disproportionate effect. Photographs examined martial themes in an apparently detached spirit, but what really lured the cameramen were signs of aggression and the impact of actual power.

For power is the crux of war—power, that reserve of energy expended to impose the will of one party on another, or to resist that imposition. The activation of power through armed force, war is the ultimate political crisis, and there can be no supposedly detached photographic record of it that is not also imbued with urgent political rhetoric.

In war zones, photographic image-taking is *permitted* by authorities. His mere presence deep in contested territory clearly establishes the cameraman's point of view. Who would mistake which adversary's vantage point is triumphantly represented by the Civil War shot of Columbia, S.C. devastated? Images such as these are always very expensive. They don't need to be theatrical because their effect is based on the viewer's knowledge that overwhelming energy has been exhausted and innumerable lives expended in order for such images of victory to exist. Produced as a first-hand witness in real space, the image verifies the act of conquest.

Photography quite naturally visualizes smaller everyday conquests as well. Even while the image is doing a routine bureaucratic job, the result can be politically expressive. When the rank and file military pose in front of the official camera, they plainly submit to an individual who acts as a representative of institutional constraints. Whether it's a question of examining a recruit's bare sole or of naked black troops lined up for outfitting, as in some U.S. Signal Corps pictures of 1918, there's no doubt of who's in charge. Far from being considered as individuals, these men are looked at merely as bodies to be processed. The photograph unreflectively denigrates them by the act of pictorial description, an act which by itself manifests authoritarian control.

When the camera is focused on those who have been literally reduced to bodies, dead bodies, the photograph's exploitation is shameless. The dead are recommended as subjects because they lack any defense against the camera and because they have top political value. Besides, as war's chief end product, the dead are in abundant supply. (Forget that they were ever thought entitled to their own privacy.) Long after photography had learned to be exciting, or at least quick-footed in the 1914–18 war (the first to be recorded in motion on film), it still insisted on moving its viewers with scenes of corpses.

The dead are cast in all sorts of roles, from faceless offal (long shots), to innocent victims (closer), to heroic martyrs (closest). To the extent that their warmth of body can still somehow be invoked, the image works fully as an icon of remembrance and regret (especially when the deceased's cause accords with the viewer's politics). That was certainly the assumption behind Serguei Strunnikov's picture of the slain partisan *Tania* (1941, Russia), an image which seems to assert that this political homicide is also a sex murder. The persistence of carnage shots in the genre of war photography amounts to an endless record of aftermaths, of final effects of off-frame causes that are briskly assigned to the "them" or "us" of the photograph's historical moment. Local accounts could be said to have been closed with the Juarez forces' picture of the Emperor Maximilian in his coffin, or the Thiers government's photograph of Communards in theirs, apprehended and executed after some of them had been identified from captured group portraits. Often, however, living figures are included in the scene as a kind of chorus—an internal moral comment. When shown in a peaceful or amiable mood, they read as *bystanders*—for example, the British who gathered around a shallow, man-shaped patch impressed in the ground by someone who fell from a dirigible. More frequently seen in extreme lamentation, such figures are identified as *survivors,* often with a score to settle. This is generally the significance of photographic vignettes of currently raging civil wars in Ireland, Lebanon, and El Salvador. Such mortuarial witness is intensely social, speaking of communal bonding that stubbornly increases the more a group experiences the pressures of force.

The near or peak action shots of the modern war photographers are, by contrast, mostly asocial. In them, all consciousness of the past and hope for the future is erased in one instant of oblivion, as flying metal has its killing impact. This may be the key, full-throttle point at which war conducts its business, but it is not the point from which it derives its meaning. Shock only enters into the visual record as a *physical* phenomenon which doesn't even dramatize very well, certainly when compared with the glorious war paintings of old. Since Ethiopia in the 1930s, it has been the goal of the more competitive photographers to be in at the kill. For Soviet photographers in Stalingrad, cameras and tommyguns were interchangeable, and Capa admonished his colleagues by saying that if their pictures weren't good enough, they hadn't been close enough. But the closer the lens's proximity to the heat of combat, when only micro-seconds might separate life from death, the colder in affective tone the photograph becomes. Competitive combat photographers are, I think, mostly looking for the worst kind of event, however ultra-dangerous to be around and hard to foresee. Yet the most notorious images of that quest are inadvertent "luck" photographs, produced out of sheer reflex: Capa's of the dropping Spanish Republican soldier, Eddy Adams's of the plaid-shirted Vietnamese being shot by the flak-jacketed ARVN officer. They are the quintessential kill photographs, the traumatic moment forever suspended. Admonishing, noncathartic, these images endure as icons that chastise excitement itself.

If I accentuate the politics of bodily feelings it's because they feed the moral and ideological passions, which are activated more strongly in war images than in any other photographic genre. On one level, the history of the subject in this medium is the history of how these passions have been played upon. The contemporary political circumstances must always be kept in mind, because they provided the original readings for the pictures.

From his patio, a man looks with binoculars at the start of a war. I wrote earlier that the incongruity of a domestic scene trangressed by global violence "made" Kelso Daly's picture. But this judgment verges perilously close to appreciation. To its public at the time, this scene would have read as a very loaded image. With such photographic "evidence," Americans could say: "Look! We were in our pyjamas! We were totally unprepared, victims not only of a sneak but an *unprovoked* attack." Such an image belongs to a genre that depicts civilians suddenly exposed to cross fire, which naturally drives home the lesson of outraged innocence to other civilian viewers. Wolf Strache's 1943 caped figure with a gas mask pushing a baby carriage along a smoking, shattered Kurfürstendamm was one such image. Jim Nachtwey's shot of terrified campesinos, hurt while airborne forces sweep in, is another. The blurring of lines between war and civilian life is a constant feature of the genre today, as it is of most modern hostilities.

No matter how they may fluctuate, the partisan messages of war photography are based on recurrent traumatic content. It is a content that charges two major categories of the genre: one concerned with images of pride, therefore potency; the other with humiliation. In the first group belong all views of parades, formations, exercises, assaults, as well as shots of individuals who exhibit their weapons or pose with trophies. These tend to be orderly pictures that emphasize social rigidity and hierarchy. The second list would include photographs of enemies captured or dead, interrogations, tortures, hospital scenes, retreats, refugee columns, surrender ceremonies, and executions. In such episodes, the emphasis is on the disarray of the principals, and on a social order severely ruptured or undone.

It's as if war either structures communal life into mechanistic arrangements or unhinges, isolates, and disorients it. The individual is lost in a compulsively ritualized or inchoate mass. When the mass breaks down, it reveals individuals who affirm a nationalist cause, or are exposed to shame in the victor's dock. In fact, effectiveness is weakened if a war photograph does not allude to one or the other of these social extremes—for that is how armed conflict redefines social activity.

But the war photograph often makes us aware of communal status, not as occurring naturally and with free will as in pictures of work, festival, or dance, but as distorted, obsessional experience—a spectacle of pathology. It's sufficient to point out that particularly in images of martial pride, flesh is not depicted in any empathetic relation to the beholder, but rather as something that is dissociated, thingified—truly an other. As it swells up, warlike pride is manifested as a deadening condition, triumphing over the flesh.

Even in a decorative project—or I should say, above all in a decorative project—such as *The Human U.S. Shield,* 1918, that triumph is really stupefying (Fig. 42). It appears to have come naturally to the photographic team, Mole and Thomas, to treat 30,000 men as so many white, gray, and black points. These are not human beings brought together for a group portrait, nor are they a crowd or a mob. They are presented as something far lower, a *pattern* of insensate, deindividuated elements.

But this grandiose conceit merely demotes human beings for the purposes of a stunt. Far worse is a Keystone sterograph called *How Li Hung Chang Deals with the Boxers,* ca. 1900. Depicting a grinning swordsman who displays a bunch of heads as if he were a fisherman and they his catch, this photo is a visual joke that holds human life in contempt. In *Human Shield,* the photographer is dealing with his own people; in the stereograph, a Westerner is portraying an Oriental subject. Though the one merely expresses nationalist progaganda and the other illustrates the pornography of violence, both pictures are deeply inhumane.

When the photographer shows awareness of inhumanity, the moral effect of the image can be, for once, critical. Such is Don McCullin's *Christian militia mock the body of a young Palestinian girl killed in the battle of Karantina, Beirut,* 1976 (Fig. 43). It belongs to the category

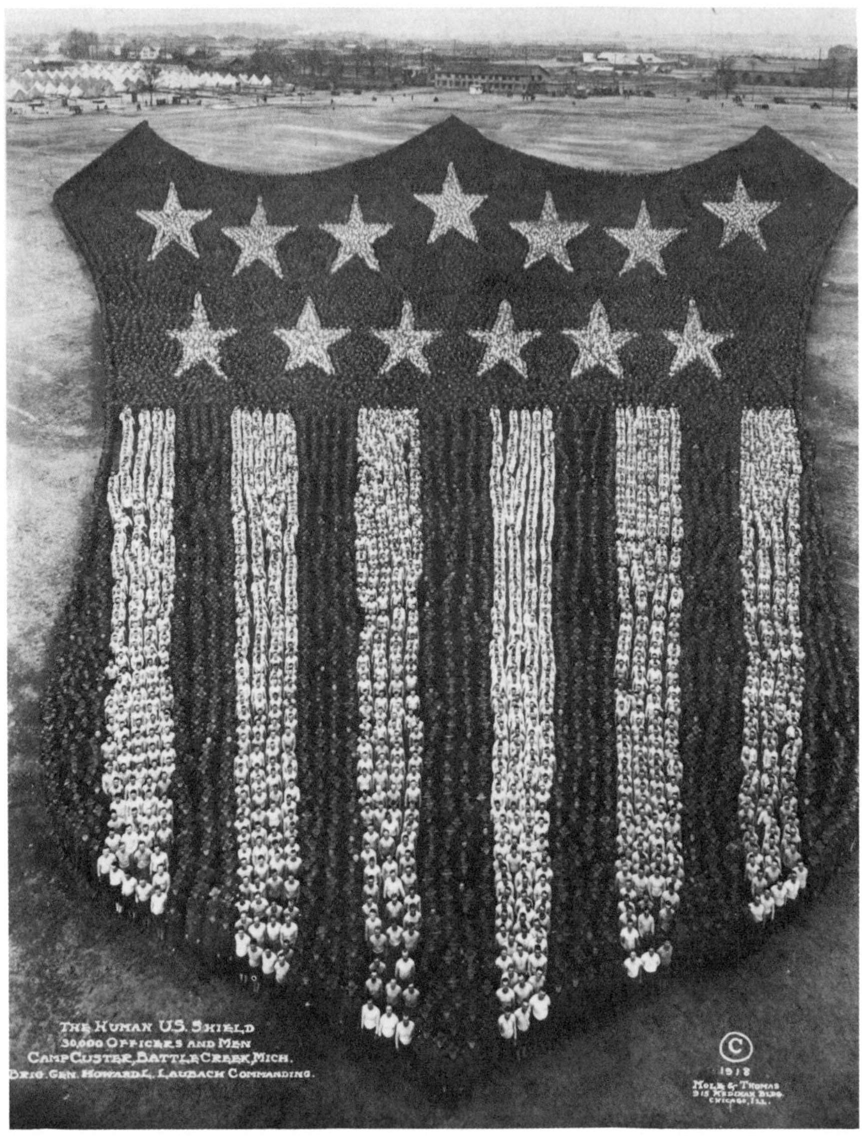

Figure 42. Arthur S. Mole and John D. Thomas, *The Human U.S. Shield,* 1918 (Minneapolis Institute of Arts).

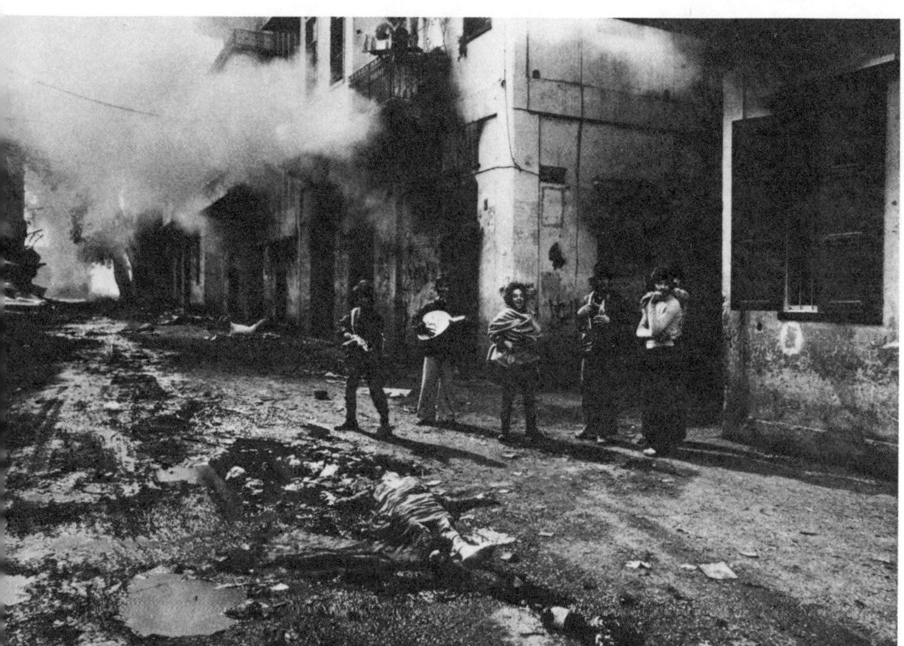

Figure 43. Don McCullin, *Christian militia mock the body of a young Palestinian girl killed in the battle of Karantina, Beirut,* 1976 (Victoria and Albert Museum).

of mortuary witness with chorus, except that here the chorus is a disreputable little chamber group with Ak-47 and lute, neither bystanders nor grief stricken, but celebrants. The contrast between their joyful stance before what they take to be a neutral lens and the repellent effect they create could not be more striking. These smiling and songful faces are made morally hideous by the pleasure they take in the ruin of their own Lebanese community.

As the heat of blood feuds is chilled for us by distance or the causes of wars dimmed by the passage of time, the collusion of photographers with their powerful subjects tends to backfire and become self-indicting. This certainly applies to shots meant to show prisoners as being justly punished. Humiliation is not the most terrible penalty endured by losers, but it can make for some of the most harrowing images of the exercise of power. The Iranian prisoners in Iraq, or the black captive being interrogated in the front-leaning-rest (push-up) position by a Rhodesian white soldier, live in memory as victims whose crimes will never be made clear. I am not arguing whether the judgments imposed upon the defeated are deserved or not. What I am saying is that on these occasions the camera inevitably enters into alliance with the captors.

Nevertheless, to portray someone who had totally lost face, whose abjectness consists in being utterly prostrated before the enemy, is to construct an ambiguous narrative. For the defeated figures, generally the center of regard, must be shown as vulnerable and intensely human in order to register the wounds inflicted by the vengeful power. Set off from the jeering or merely smug audience, they must have their own space, and their bared skin must be all the more tenderly described because it is exposed to so hostile a gaze.

In these humiliation photos, the captured or the accused are crestfallen, benighted, wretched. They slump down, avert their faces if they can. This is what will be remembered from photographs of French women accused of sleeping with the Nazis and whose heads have been shaved in reprisal by their compatriots. Just the same, the anguish of their 1940s disgrace does not prevent them from appearing to us now as martyrs to the guilt of their own countrymen. Such, even then, was the sense of Capa's famous photograph of the woman being rushed through the streets of Chartres. She exemplifies perfectly well, as did so many who became a spectacle of defeat, that the emotional spoils of war produce terrorized loners.

In front of their sixteen-inch guns, the captors in Charles Fenno Jacobs's *Japanese Prisoner Bathing on the U.S.S. New Jersey,* 1944, offer the

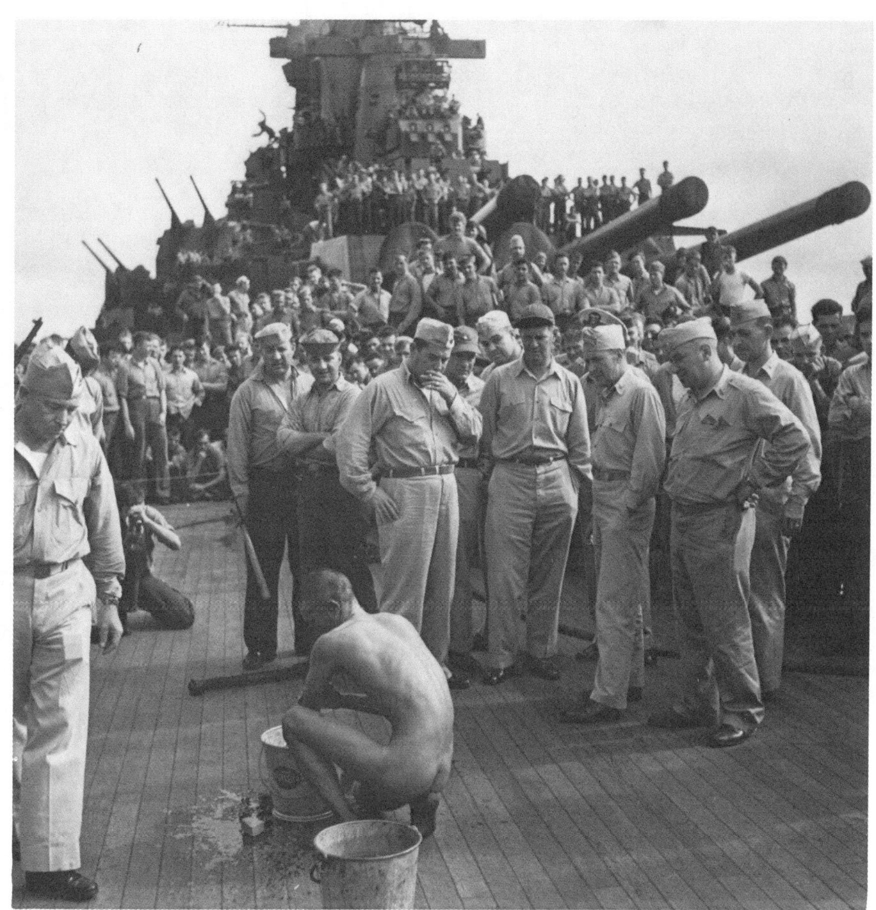

Figure 44. Charles Fenno Jacobs, *Japanese Prisoner Bathing on the U.S.S.* New Jersey, 1944 (National Archives).

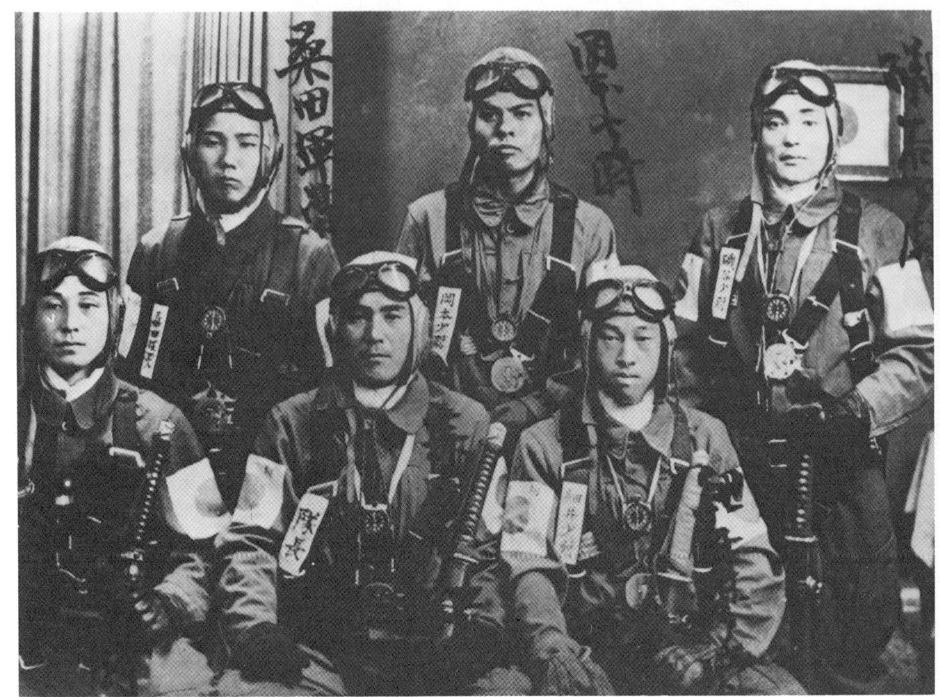

Figure 45. Anonymous, *Kamikaze Pilots Sit for a Memorial Picture,* n.d. (Keystone Press, London).

contrast of their beefy builds with the prisoner's emaciated, bony one, their rumpled clothes with his nakedness (Fig. 44). A member of Steichen's photographic unit attached to the U.S. Pacific fleet, Jacobs can be presumed to express the American point of view here; yet he inadvertently turns the sailors' object of derision into a subject for our pity. Or is this presumption an error? Jacobs's image shows another photographer who crouches farther back behind the officers in order to photograph the POW from *their* perspective. By choosing to shoot from the underdog's space, Jacobs makes that space—and vantage point—ours. The degree to which the polemic of war photographs depends very simply on the vantage point of the camera cannot be overemphasized.

The Jacobs picture could also have been discussed as a photograph of pride. Like Kelso Daly's image of a Hawaiian Sunday, it is concerned with the act of contemplation, but now in the explicit knowledge that contemplation is power. Those who look are secure in the righteousness of their strength. At the end of the war begun long before at Pearl Harbor, somewhere in Japan six young suicide pilots posed in full regalia for their group portrait (Fig. 45). There is something beautiful about their features, their togetherness, their esprit, their dedication. Perhaps it had to do with their unity as kamikazes and the use of the photograph as their last memorial. Here, too, the look expresses a confident knowledge . . . of voluntary and absolutely fatal self-sacrifice. They gaze into their own forthcoming nothingness. The ceremonial swords add an overtly crazy touch. Soon they would be putting on their goggles. I never want to see such faces again.

Art in America, *April 1980.*

IV

Topics in the Theory and History of Photography

Report from the Region of Decayed Smiles

The Voices in Photographic Criticism Symposium
October 1979, New Haven, Connecticut[1]

One reason why the class of familiar objects named photographs excites attention nowadays is that few people know how to talk about them. Photography has socialized us all, variously, but descriptions of the ways it does so continue to be skimpy. The unsettled but picturesque zone of photo writing and photo history invites campers from wide-ranging disciplines, who traipse in with their intellectual baggage. As the baggage grows heavier, the campers increasingly turn into squatters staking out rights to unclaimed ground. Meanwhile, the natives—the photographers themselves—who once roamed freely, are apt to feel squeezed or even colonized, and have hit upon a most ornery form of recoil: unwillingness to contribute to the discourse.

A field for which the terms of inner reference have not been determined enjoys an advantage and suffer from a defect. On the one hand, primary questions, always the most interesting, are pondered from many different angles. What is a photograph, for example, and how should it be treated—as a record of events, or as a more or less fictive construct? We're still early in the process of ordering the varieties, analyzing the uses, and judging the effects of photographs. What a seemingly peppy, up-for-grabs situation this is, provoking the most open, fundamental debates! The folks in the other arts must regard such excitement with envy, for how can the delights of a withered avant-garde compare with the genesis of a new consciousness?

On the other hand, photo theory is afflicted by the energetic and sincere incompatibility of speakers who harp on preliminaries that have been argued over before and never resolved. Lost in the babble of tongues is any conceptual foundation for study. Not so much through lack of will as through lack of common ground, discussion loses range and sputters off without gaining the momentum needed to develop basic inquiries.

I myself can't think of anything intrinsic to the medium that should hinder a development of both detail and depth in photo criticism. Yet, in New Haven, at a conference on the subject, "Voices in Photographic Criticism," sponsored by the Center For Independent Studies, such development was passionately stymied. Talks were delivered by photo historians, philosophers, critics, sociologists and a few photographers, myself included. The affair certainly generated insights into photography, but it also deteriorated into a series of territorial disputes.

Some participants fenced off the ontology of the medium, others cordoned the aesthetics, still others zoned its historical frontage. Instead of consolidating the land of photography, they possessively subdivided it into odd lots, discouraging not only an inclusive survey but even free passage from one turf to the next. It was as if the variables of the medium could only be poached upon, one at a time, and the more poachers the better.

As often happens, however, the really intractable element is the fixed stance, not the condition of the field. If you can think of nothing better than to pile up differing special interests, the eclectic sum will be less than the parts. And no coherent identity will have been imposed upon the research. Unless its form, content, historical value, and poetry are grasped as reciprocal inflections of each other, I do not think the photograph can be understood on its own terms. Like a prism that refracts light according to the incidence at which it's received and the angle from which it's viewed, the photographic image blends, stresses, or separates messages as integral phenomena. The photographic artifact does not require a more or less versatile set of responses than those invoked by the other visual arts. But it does call for a recognition of how those responses are filtered by photography.

Compared, for instance, with cinema, still photography shares many characteristics of painting—its muteness, inanimateness, and spatiality. Likened to painting, however, photography insists on its transcriptual credibility, factored by its cut into time. In other words, we're dealing with a medium as peculiarly temporal as it is evidently spatial, and as implicitly symbolic as it is tacitly narrative. The fuss at New Haven, as in many earlier conferences, revolved around the issue of what these attributes allow us to say about photography—and what they don't.

It was a mark against this discussion that its members spoke like professionals rather than as people, as though being one, you couldn't be the other. If Shaw was right in saying that professions are a conspiracy against the laity, then their family quarrels only disguise an underlying clerical agreement. At New Haven, convergent disclaimers were repeatedly launched from the podium—denials of the factual articulateness of photography, and of the sufficiency of its "evidence." Aspersions were even cast upon its origin in once existent scenes. Joel Snyder admitted that of course Carlyle was there for Mrs. Cameron—where else would he be?—but her metaphors were the only things that counted. The concrete, documentary side of photography, and with it the animation and consequence of the medium as a social instrument, were largely spurned. Anyone present must have been struck by this surreptitiously united front, joined in by speakers who had very different vested interests.

To account for this rapport, I must point to what was manifest in their polemics and latent in their reasoning. The sociologist Erving Goffman outflanked all the other participants, not only in his use of technical language, but in the "hardness" of his criteria for accepting photographic knowledge. With his insistence that science is science and that we all tend to over-read photos, he retroactively stiffened what was already an ungenerous attitude toward image content. When he stated that photos cannot picture social relationships (the visual sampling is too inconclusive), someone in the audience believed he had shown otherwise in his recent book *Gender Advertisements,* a study of the endlessly subordinate roles assigned to women in advertising photography. Goffman countered that he had only been looking at "display expressions," a mimicry of interaction specifically contrived for sales purposes. In his book, he states "Any attempt to produce an appropriate show of involvement in something tends to produce instead an appearance of involvement in the task of affecting such involvement." In other words, he functionally views social life as incessant artifice, a rich interplay of scheduled acts and choreographed gestures that are exclusively self-conscious. Authentic behavior is precluded, but actions can be broken down into broad or detailed types, represented by photos, and monitored. Goffman's is a remarkably denatured, unhistorical and apolitical view of human conduct, but it at least permits a genre analysis of photographs, which are understood as a series of visual forms loading highly differentiated constraints upon subjects and models.

Digressing for a moment, I think of a book by the ethnobiologist

Desmond Morris, *Manwatching,* which uses photographs as highly transparent illustrations of human behavior signaled through body language. The possibility that the photos might have a personal rhetoric of their own is no more examined by Morris than their widely various sources and purposes are acknowledged and explored. In his eyes, the photos work indicriminately as conveyors of expository and even diagrammatic information. Just the same, he has an idea of spontaneous behavior pretty much neglected in Goffman—in fact, his efforts are directed to uncovering that behavior. For Morris, it's forever in the process of being unconsciously disclosed, via candid or unassuming photographs: for Goffman, it is recurrently absorbed and lost into the charades of social activity.

Morris has a heading called "Shortfall signals":

> A shortfall signal is one that fails to reach its usual level of intensity. In some ways it falls short of the expected. The On-Off Smile is an obvious example . . . the performer's true mood is interfering with his social "display." . . . He fails because . . . when he is in the real mood to smile, he never has to calculate . . . the exact relationship between the strength of his smile and the strength of his inner mood. . . . If the human face forces a smile to please a photographer, the false smile soon begins to decay.[2]

But must we judge that the photograph here unmasks a false mood, preferring this idea to the more plausible one that the photographer simply misfired? In this instance it may be the photographer who's too late (or premature); and the medium provides far more examples of "wrong" timing in celebration of social display than it does "right" ones.

Neither author credits the role of timing decisions for the photographic results obtained. Even when posing—holding still—a model is engaged in a process, whereas a photograph takes a momentary appearance out and away from the process, that is, abstracts from it. The experience of a photograph invites a comparison between abstraction and process as no other visual medium does because no other medium pinpoints the difference through frozen time. Whether or not the comparison will prove fruitful depends on the image, but the *invitation* to compare is always open.

The majority of the speakers at the conference, those presumably concerned with the photograph *qua* photograph, had special difficulty with this dual aspect of the medium. Many of them would strip down the perceptual and emotional import of the image with as much empirical zeal as that with which Goffman reduced its social meaning. (It was especailly ironic for Goffman to have called them all "sentimentalists," in view of their own tough-minded reluctance to see any implications beyond the photographic frame.) Yet, in many respects this was a false controversy, its arguing protagonists holding firm—all down the line—to a scepticism about what I have called "process"—the continuum of events that surrounds us.

Unfortunately, the study of that continuum—history itself—was generally implied to be a "soft" discipline. I inferred this attitude by noticing how many speakers emphasized that our grasp of the outer world is purely subjective, composed of a number of *pictures* which are in themselves nothing more than fictional projections of the course of things. The consensus seemed to be that whatever causes us to make an inference about the environment comes to us from a picture we have constructed or inherited, and any picture is testable only by other pictures.

As an instance, Marx Wartofsky, in a paper called "Cameras Can't See," appears to have meant this literally: our mental life is a picturing activity, and in consequence our ideas of physical space, for instance, are determined pictorially. From Byzantine isometrism through Renaissance perspective and so on forward, our dominant spatial images have come from succeeding art styles, until we arrive at Cubism and photography, where multiple, atomized, competing picture visions contribute to the modernist mince of all legible space. The visual aggregate of these pictures, for Wartofsky, far from discrediting the authority of any single model, engenders a fabulous relativism. The only "hard" facts, therefore, turn out to be our inventions.

Now, I certainly think it's reasonable to say that a photograph is a picture that either apes or provides an alternative to a world we can know. But the question remains whether a photograph is the sort of picture a painting is. To this question Joel Snyder ingeniously responded "yes." He started his talk by quarreling with some well-known themes in the literature. Having no patience with John Szarkowski's idea of photographs as pictures "taken" rather than "made" (as are paintings), nor with Susan Sontag's comment that a photo is not only an interpretation of the real, it's also a trace—"something directly stenciled off the real," Snyder warned against the dangerous notion "that in photography, subject matter is given. The primary achievement of any great artist, photographer, painter or writer," he said, "is to *make* subject matter."

Now it would distress me, personally, to learn that George Barnard "made" the ruin of Columbia, S.C., or that Murray Becker engineered the explosion of the Hindenburg. I know that photographers can be a fairly creative lot but certainly catastrophe is beyond them! Snyder, though, was pointing to the "essence" of subject matter, which he defines as the "capacity to think of what we see as being scenic or pictorial."

In support of the primacy of the creative mind over "objective" optical devices, he looked back several hundred years to the camera obscura; this he viewed not as having objectively confirmed realistic picture making, but as having incorporated its rules. In fact, it was only with the advent of quattrocento perspective and Albertian theory that the tool could be improved, because only then could a use be found for it. "The problem for Renaissance painters was *not* how to make pictures that looked like the image produced by the camera, it was how to make a machine that produced an image like the ones they painted." In support of this view, he cited a seventeenth-century Dutch artist who wrote to his camera maker:

> When I use your magic box to make portraits, the distance is all wrong. . . . As everyone knows, the mouth should occupy about one quarter the diameter of the face, but with your pile of junk, it occupies a third. This might do for a humorous rendering of a fishwife, but it will not do for their husbands who wish to be shown as God made them.

That the camera obscura was designed to produce results acceptable to an artist is not actually news, nor is the dominance of certain artistic modes over visual observation at widely dispersed historical points. Snyder could equally well have referred to the triumph of idyllic Barbizon landscape over pictorial photography in the nineteenth century. Then, too, one agrees with his statement that depictive processes are formulated through a systematic notion of vision. Even if one could presuppose the gathering of raw visual data, it would not result in a picture until it had been channeled into a pictorial, that is, an *imaginative* framework. In the end, though, if you want to annex the work of the camera into this fictive realm, all you have to do is deny what the machine accomplished when it produced a photograph.

When we say a photograph "abstracts," we mean that it plucks out an appearance from those that existed, not that it draws forth an idea of an appearance from someone's mind. And the photographic print, or object, distinguishes itself categorically from the projected image in a camera obscura because it exists independently of the light that gave it birth—it is graven light (the meaning of the word *photograph*). When photos were introduced, the camera obscura ceased to have a future, for in the act of being improved, the product irrevocably changed in kind. The photograph reflects a past occasion rather than unfolds synchronously with its stimulus in real time, which is what enables us to attribute historical value to it. Its very capacity for survival is its inherent rationale.

The thinking that went into the development of the photograph—*contra* Snyder—did not produce some late fruition of artistic consciousness by techniques that are identifiable with or even parallel to those of painting. Rather, with the advent of the photograph, we were furnished with a mechanism of visual recall through which artistic intentions (among others) had to be sieved.

It's quite natural, therefore, that we question the photograph as a witness to events we could not have experienced, or only poorly recollect. There's no bypassing this quality of the image as a piecemeal witness, nor of the empathies and frustrations it excites.

Snyder himself alluded to this dynamic by an example he thought proved exactly the opposite: of a well known Robert Frank photo, he said that it shows more than a fuzzy woman walking before a sharply defined crowd. We viewers, he went on, see what those in the crowd can't see: that the out-of-focus blonde has been turned into a metaphor of tinsel and vulgarity. I'm not sure about the metaphor, but he's obviously right about the blurriness of the one female figure, created by a focal length resolved beyond the plane on which she appeared. In other words, we're dealing with a pictorial effect, something undoubtedly *created* by the picturing system in question.

If you were asked to describe a similar effect in a painting, however, you might use phrases like "broken touches" or "open contours." On no account would you *ever* say that you perceive a blurry form that the subjects of the painting cannot see. Of course, it would be strange to think of the images of human beings in a painting—iconic material conjured by the painter—as endowed with independent consciousness. Because they are sealed into the fictive present of the work, they could never have seen or felt anything. One asks, rather, what it was *intended* they represent.

But in photographs, the issue of hindered or averted sight-lines frequently wells up, because these pictures, involved with literal subject, witness real and therefore limited angles of view, relative to those who are framed as well as those looking into the frame. When I spoke of a photo's abstraction, I was indicating something more than phenomena such as Frank's blur; I was thinking of the fact that the abstraction manifests itself by carrying its actual point of reference into our world. You can't have photographic art without that necessarily inequitable reference.

The majority of the papers at New Haven favored the act of conjuring and depreciated the act of witness (although humankind needs them both in order to survive). A photographer, if great (and they're the only ones that matter), was considered to be someone whose performance inspires faith, but whose testimony is base and therefore hard to trust. This, then, was a level of elevated discourse which got along very poorly with its often mundane subject. I was reminded of what Hugh Kenner, the literary critic, said about a poet of Dr. Johnson's time, James Grainger, who

> had the ill luck to epitomize the intractability of Fact, when he commenced a paragraph "Now, Muse, let's sing of *Rats,*" and did not deceive Boswell into supposing that he had effected any improvement when, this apostrophe being greeted with mirth, he later changed "rats" to "the whisker'd vermin race."[3]

I do not think lofty words are inappropriate when alluding to photographic art; but I do believe they come unmoored when they do not acknowledge the texture of that art. Yet, with the extreme aesthetic wing of the conference, represented by Tod Papageorge and Rosalind Krauss, we were led far beyond scepticism about photographic facts to the actual inadmissibility of them.

If Papageorge, a fine photographer, denigrated the historicity of photographs, which are "cripples, fictions that live only by moments and know only the surface of things," it was in order to raise high the idea of the "interesting" photograph, something not accountable to the way the medium is generally "perceived and employed." We can ask questions about the truth value of photographs if we wish, but these questions only confuse photographs with their subject.

Papageorge expounded articulately on the poetic insights of Atget, Brassaï, and Cartier-Bresson, which he epitomized as leak-proof imaginative feats, sealed off from "truth-telling" by their profound self-interestedness. Holding forth on Robert Frank's late 1950s photo of people on a New Orleans streetcar, he called our attention to the truly lovely reflections in the overhead window panels. Someone in the New Haven audience noticed that the black passengers were seated to the right—probably the rear: did this not show Frank's awareness of

American racism? That question was, of course, contemptuously ruled out of order from the platform. When you remember, however, that Frank, as a Swiss, never lived among blacks, that he was now in the heart of Jim Crow territory, and that *The Americans* is, overall, severely judgmental about such matters as our spiritual malaise, the question seems a proper one.

More is involved in this episode than the fact that one professional chooses to talk about reflections, and another person, with a political consciousness, wonders about a picture of social relations. Both situations mingle in the photograph, and I fancy that the bittersweet power of Frank's act of witness—his special capacity to move us—arises from combined dissonant impressions such as these.

Undoubtedly we're highly prone to mistakes when interpreting photographs. But the attitude that prohibits sociocultural interpretations because they are too profane, or because we can never be certain, I find more mistaken still. Instead of giving a few photographic images a privileged artistic status, this attitude alienates and dispossesses them from their nourishing roots in the world. It is possible, also, to resent being told what not to see, what not to ask—an example of what Leo Steinberg, speaking of Greenbergian formalism, called "preventive aesthetics." By contracting the zone of response, these strategies, which were already embarrassing and *vieux jeu* in the art world years ago, seek to intimidate rather than to persuade by reasoning.

Rosalind Krauss's talk began promisingly:

> To come to photography from an intense and often embattled experience of modernism is to feel a peculiar sense of relief. It is like coming in from the cold, like . . . gaining high ground.

Unfortunately, however, the only photographer sighted on that "high ground" was old, overstudied Alfred Stieglitz, attractive to conservative modernists because he talked so much like one. The risky virtue of Stieglitz's *Equivalents,* a series of cloud studies, is that their

> cutting goes beyond simply ripping something out of a larger continuum; it charges the image in such a way that we feel it as something ripped away from us, as no longer the possible extension of our own experience. . . .

In short, Stieglitz is admired for those denials of which photography was said to be the cure. Renouncing the cold of modernism, Krauss sought only to inject its mystifying chill into the discussion of another field.

It's worth pondering why a group of professionals nominally concerned with exploring photography should contrive, in the main, so thoroughly to hedge in its perspectives. The mood of this symposium was a little like the debates on the SALT treaty in the Senate—apparently about disarmament, but in fact propelled by sentiments towards the opposite. Generally, Americans in the late 1970s seemed to feel a diminished power over events and a sense of failed adventure. They grew pessimistic, insecure, and, their confidence at a low ebb, they could become exaggeratedly defensive and mistrustful of other people's motives. It was the region of shortfall signals and of decayed smiles.

Now, photography is all around us, a visual medium that deeply affects our lives, though it has been relatively unstudied. I think it was approached *defensively* at New Haven, which meant with a hard, even wholesale denigration of its worldly witness. How else to explain a desire to turn back the ideological clock, a retrenchment not caring that it belittled photographic culture as long as it preserved and reinforced one category of photographic images as appropriate for hierarchical control?

I am not arguing for a more credulous view of photographic picturing at large. But I am saying we might hold off prematurely managing our image environment until we can understand better how others are doing it for us.

How far or how little other sectors of the photo community share the repressive strictures evident at New Haven, I don't know, but I did hear brief scraps of open-minded comment, and three talks in which common sense took sail. One, by photo critic Ben Lifson, sensitively rounded Atget from biographical, aesthetic, and political vantages. Another, by sociologist Howard Becker, demonstrated that information and expression are inseparable in photographic statements. (If we filter them out, it's because of the needs we want them to requite—so the photograph becomes a reflecting agency that tells us as much about ourselves as it does about the world.) Finally, journalist Vicki Goldberg shifted that self-knowledge back where it really functions, into that area where it must aid us in determining moral choices.

In a paper called "Ethics, The Camera, and Other Problems," she pointed to such obvious dilemmas as the fact that a photograph, when published, can invade privacy or change a life. To notice that a photograph can deeply exploit someone and still be art (cf. Diane Arbus) is to acknowledge some of the real stakes inherent in our commerce with the medium. Actually, by considering the photograph this way, we realize that we live in much greater jeopardy than we may have thought. For the characteristically intrusive photographer, as she argued, reduces our sense of a protected environment—a stripping which may not always be redeemed by an artistic aim.

In the end, I'm convinced that we need to know as much about art's penalties as about its pleasures. Instead of restricting our experience of a class of objects, that knowledge allows us to be more alert in coping with our lives.

Erving Goffman, who was the last speaker on the agenda, disparaged the tendency to rely on what you already know in order to explain a photo situation. If he meant a knowledge that does not include your awareness of your own fallibility and complicity, the point is well taken. But if he intended to discourage your reliance on your own social acumen and sense of humanity, then your contact with photography will be very poverty-stricken indeed.

More and more I have come to feel that the enigmas and illuminations of photography are perceived as much through the resources we have in common with everyone as by the aptitudes and skills we can develop as professionals.

Art in America, *April 1980.*

1. Participants in the conference "Voices in Photographic Criticism" were (in order of appearance): Max Kozloff ("The Photographic Description of Social Class"), Charles Hagen ("Time in Photographs"), Mark Roskill ("Humor in Photography"), Marx Wartofsky ("Cameras Can't See"), Roaslind Krauss ("Case Studies in Criticism: Alfred Stieglitz"), William Parker ("The Object is not the Subject: On Meaning in Contemporary Photographs"), Eugenia Janis ("The Art of Calotype Photography in France"), Joel Snyder ("Photography and the Picturing of Vision"), Howard S. Becker ("Aesthetics and Truth"), Erving Goffman (responding to Becker), Tod Papageorge (responding to Becker, "Aesthetics or Truth"), Vicki Goldberg ("Ethics and the Camera"), Ben Lifson ("Atget's Imagination"), Alan Trachtenberg ("The Languages of Serious Photography").

2. Desmond Morris, *Manwatching: A Field Guide to Human Behavior* (New York: Harry Abrams, 1977), p. 116.

3. Hugh Kenner, *The Counterfeiters: An Historical Comedy* (New York: Anchor Books, 1973), pp. 50–51.

Photography: Straight or on the Rocks?

David T. Hanson and Max Kozloff

DH Polarities have been common in both the history and the writing of photography—the Pictorialists versus the Photo-Secessionists, "art photography" versus the documentary, and, more recently, mirrors versus windows. Allan Sekula and Abigail Solomon-Godeau contend that photographs should function as politics instead of as art. A number of photography critics—Rosalind Krauss and Peter Galassi, for example—are now belatedly applying modernist art criticism to photography, arguing that a photograph should reflect the inherent and unique characteristics of its medium. Much recent criticism seems to be hung up on the nature of photography. What are your thoughts?

MK Imagine this analogy with the world at large: The National Rifle Association says, "Guns don't kill people, people do." We're all familiar with that slogan, right? Transferred to photography, the statement would be, "Cameras don't take pictures, people do!" Cameras are not as lethal as guns, of course, but when you use a machine you can't avoid machine-processed results. Some people claim, though, that it is the conscious effort, the deliberate framing, and the artistic impulse that we appreciate in photographs, and they argue, therefore, that the mechanical nature of the instrument is, while obvious, secondary.

I'm convinced, though, that the "dumbness" of the machine largely accounts for a characteristic photographic sensation with which all viewers have to contend. What point does criticism serve by downgrading this particular sensation? Probably to make the photo picture akin to the painted picture—that is, a willed pictorial creation. Treating them the same is terrifically convenient in language. My own training stems very much from painting; in fact, I'm always at home with it and the critical vocabulary that deals with it. But for that reason I would neither confuse the two modes nor go to the one for what the other specifically delivers.

Photographers can take photographs that are inspired by painting effects, but they can't make photographs by means of painting processes—and that difference is critical. A negative is like a template, or, better, a strainer through which material can be sifted with relatively few options. But a canvas is a ground upon which nothing happens unless, at every instant, a human mind makes intimate decisions and shapes the material. The choices leading up to a particular negative, and later the tempering of it, are essentially reactive. A lighted sense of an outside stimulus blemishes a film. It's hard to think of the image as a photo unless it can be said somehow to be "tethered" to an appearance, whereas a painting is independently added to the stock of objects and bears only a hypothetical relationship to experience.

These points of difference are so obvious and so crucial that I can't figure out why people confuse them all the time. It could be they're so astonished, underneath it all, that something intelligent and coherent could be transmitted by the machine that they imagine the photographer is as literally responsible for the result as a painter is. A photographer can be very serious, executive, and assertive, but, still, it's the lightness of his or her responsibility for the photo product that beguiles—the level on which the world has its way, with or against—or despite—the grain of the photographer's consciousness. There are things in a photo that a photographer may not have liked but couldn't have helped. I am certainly grateful for a photo's deliberateness, when it amounts to something, but I am especially thankful for this helplessness, which makes a photograph unique.

A main distinction between a painting and a photograph is that the painting alludes to its content, whereas the photograph summons it, from wherever and whenever, to us. An indefinite, endless process of surveillance goes on in the world of photographic culture. An imaginative proposal about our environment or a mood might be projected, but mostly it's the overt espionage that sets photography apart. To look at photographs, to get involved with them, is to subpoena something effortlessly that once existed in a fuller, active form. A photograph is an out-take from the work determined by a mechanical or, if you will, a mechanical-chemical action. So *yes,* cameras take pictures, too, as well as people.

DH But isn't it important to realize that, while a photograph is a trace of something that once existed, and though it's sometimes used as evidence in court, it has clearly been modified by the maker through framing, omissions, inclusions, equipment, materials, and length of exposure, among other decisions? The maker and the inherent nature of the camera have both influenced the "slice of life" we are given. For example, anthropologists and social scientists failed to realize for a long time that the photograph was not a simple "transparent" record, but a complex, personally and culturally encoded set of messages.

MK In the medium of photography, just as in any other communicative utterance, a statement cannot be made without filtering it through the interests of the maker. That's why I like to use the word *witness* when referring to a photograph, because it describes a complex role without being tendentious. The word conveys the idea that some conscious party or agency was at a scene and can give an account of events, but it doesn't say anything about the reliability of that account. Those who did not witness an event can learn something about it from those who did. Some witnesses are more competent and privileged than others, but, even so, one wants to verify their statements, if possible. A critic might say—correctly: "It's not usually possible to corroborate evidence in a photo with that furnished by its original subject. All you can do is compare the data in one frame with that in another frame of the same subject, or a part of it." But if the critic concludes from this that the viewer has no right to speak of data, what does he or she call what is seen? I admit a problem exists, but I don't think it can be solved by overlooking that the photo is tethered to appearances.

The continuum in which everyone or everything exists, and existed, is pierced very briefly by what winds up as a photograph, showing surroundings and events as mutable and partial. If this is a lie, photographs would really be fiction, but you can only describe events through the attention you give them, and your attention is always mutable and partial. What's known of an event depends on how it's organized for our perception. A photograph's frame acts as an arbitrary organization. A viewer may feel that the photo excludes far more than it should have. Just the same, an omission is not the equivalent of a lie. I mean in photos we have to make do with a scantiness of pertinent information, but that doesn't imply that the pictorial phenomenon itself is mendacious. In life, we constantly misread and are misled usually because we have not organized ourselves to find out what we want to know.

What does a camera know of our expectation of the truth? It merely processes raw visual material in a surprising correspondence to the way optical particulars are projected through our eyes and understood by our brains. Photographic vision, I believe, has been modeled after human vision, but it's much more innocent, nerveless, and efficient. Come to think of it, that's not so dumb, machine though the camera is. But a work of art—a painting—isn't modeled after anything, necessarily; it's a web of metaphors coded very intricately in freely malleable stuff, designed to elicit feeling states.

If photographs incite feelings, which they certainly do, it's not all clear that they succeed by design. I think they evoke emotion because of our vulnerability to their content as rendered by their particular version of truth. A photographer's narcissism might contribute to this evocation, in which case we're guided to impose metaphors of our own on the image. By itself, a photograph doesn't have the artistic advantage of speaking in metaphors; it's a profane picture, but it often appeals to *our* narcissism—and on a level with which art can't compare.

DH In the past you have expressed interest in the whole of the photographic endeavor, which is enormous, and its impact on our consciousness, rather than just the limiting case of the aesthetic and expressive use of photography for artistic means. This seems to be what we're speaking of here—the understanding of photography in a much broader context, and the nature of the medium and its possibilities for the entire culture.

MK Of course! What work of art, for example, can compare in its impact on human consciousness with the photograph of the whole earth by NASA? This image doesn't imply the slightest imaginative depth on the part of the producer—so it's not a photographer's imagination to which we respond. But it does reflect an extraordinary accomplishment and convey an amazing privilege. Everyone can identify with it, because for a camera to be in space where this picture was taken had been historically unimaginable. The contrast between our helpless isolation and our power to see our solitude so dramatically could only have been effected by a delirious victory over space, over distance, and against spectacular obstacles. As a humble witness, the photograph emits the utmost territorial flattery. It acts as a kind of celebrational image, like Andrew Russell's photograph of the two trains meeting in 1869 at Promontory Point, Utah, which is probably the nineteenth-century equivalent of the NASA photograph. Neither of these shots is unusually interesting as formal space, but each is extraordinary for the way it affects the idea of space in the mind. Another thing: these pictures commemorate history, but their very existence is also history. They are talismans of grand adventures that only huge communities, at climactic moments, could consummate.

Those are examples of momentous occasions, not only in the history of art or photography but in the history of culture and civilization. Yet every photograph, large or small, trivial or somehow significant and heavy, is that kind of witness to an event, of interest theoretically to smaller communities. We prize the photographs, even unconsciously, for that kind of "thereness," that kind of opportunistic impulse, which it excites us into sharing. No ego I know of can resist being transported in this peculiar fashion—in space, but also in time. The photograph gives us a stupefying range.

DH This leads me to Peter Galassi's recent exhibition and essay *Before Photography* and your subsequent criticism of it, in which you argued that the history of photography on one level is the history of a certain kind of regard that did not exist before the invention of the instrument. It's interesting that although the camera was originally devised to confirm classical Renaissance Albertian perspective, which lasted in narrative painting even as late as the nineteenth century, it actually initiated a very different way of seeing. John Szarkowski discussed this in *The Photographer's Eye.* On a more modest level, his recent piece *Atget and the Art of Photography* suggests that the photographer's role is as a pointer.

MK But if you say, "I think he's right," you are saying that the photographer is only drawing attention to something. To that and not to this. Over here and not there. That is a very modest statement. Yet some people, speaking plainly and with apparent calm, have nevertheless made inflated claims about the photographic image, and by so doing have aestheticized the banal. Susan Sontag complained about that problem in *On Photography.* When the photographer points over and over at an obdurate and concrete fact of no evident consequence, you begin to get a little confused. Since the image is deprived of its social context, you have little choice but to think of it as aesthetic. You suddenly begin to wonder about the photographer, who is opaque, instead of about the subject, which would give up its secrets right away, if they weren't delayed by a fantasy about the creative mind. Instead of operating as an incitement to look, the opportunistic impulse is sidetracked into a conceit fabricated by an artist.

Think of how the work of Eve Sonneman and John Gossage, for

example, wants you to worry about that. There's no way of cracking it, no way of getting into it. It's too cool a phenomenon. If I have to guess, literally *guess,* at what someone intended by framing a scene, the matter at hand is either much too self-evident or too obscure—given my ordinary knowledge. A trivial situation is precisely that, notwithstanding the implied mystification of intent. Szarkowski sometimes urges us to be connoisseurs of these things, but I balk. I can see what Ben Lifson is driving at when he talks about the visual acuity of the photographer, which to be sure, may redeem any subject, no matter how sterile. Still, I keep getting distracted by the sensations offered, and what they might tell me about the world is more interesting (and potentially more moving) than what they say about the photographer, even one who mediates extremely well.

DH But this brings us back to the formalist or modernist approach to criticism. When Lifson says that much of contemporary photography is a watered-down imitation of what has already been done in painting, he is arguing that photography is not fulfilling its own unique possibilities.

MK By definition, a photo that looks like a "watered-down" painting, an Aaron Siskind, for example, is unappealing. In general, though, photos have no trouble resembling photos, even when they betray a big crush on painting. Modernist art criticism largely based itself on a theory of form as derived from the ontology of painting. This was intellectually barbarous, quite aside from being determinist and prescriptive. Where Clement Greenberg emphasized flatness, I could talk just as convincingly about the inescapability of illusion and metaphor in the process of applying paint—and this would take criticism far away from an obsession with the picture plane.

But the chief complaint against any formalist doctrine, ontologically based or not, is that it presents content as entirely at the service of form, whereas the opposite is true. To what end is the photographer employing pictorial means, for whom, and why? Without asking these questions, explicitly social questions, philosophical distinctions aren't going to get you very far. I can't think of artistic goals that are philosophically irrelevant or illegitimate. But I can think of artistic results that are not very profitable to a lot of artists and viewers from a social-psychological perspective.

DH In principle I think it's important to be open to as broad a spectrum of photographic activity as possible, and I would hate to see a definition of photography that limited the possibilities of the medium. I have tremendous respect for Frederick Sommer, for example, and the breadth and richness of the work he has done. But in actual practice there do seem to be some problems with the boom in formalist photography that we're seeing now. As Lifson and others have pointed out, a knowledge of the history of modern art makes much current photography seem simplistic and sophomoric, whether it's manipulative photography, collage, conceptual work, formalist or Constructivist photos, cliché verre, the resurgence in nonstandard processes, or the combining of language and images and the influence of semiotics, phenomenology, and epistemology. So often contemporary photography shows undigested influences and a lack of imaginative resources. How do you regard this kind of photographic activity now in vogue?

MK Manipulative photography, or combine photography, where the photographic image is scrawled over or otherwise disturbed or distressed by marks of different sorts, is, I think, a self-defeating activity. In theory, manipulated photography is an unexpected branch of collage, in which art making intervenes in memorabilia from the world, rather than the other way around. In our century, given over to experimentalism and the combination of disparate materials in art, the "unstraights" have done a great deal. We have them to thank for the logic of disjunction. But why would one want to scrawl over or mark a photograph? By putting a mark on the surface of a photographed scene one compares the present activity of marking with the past witness of the imagery. Not only that—one demeans the witness. One obscures it. One shows, if nothing else, a great disrespect for it. How could it be otherwise? The problem is that, while a mark gives some motor potentiality and willfulness, it always covers something. In this case, it covers something of a photograph, and therefore takes out a part, or "wastes," a passage of the photographic witness.

Antiart is certainly familiar in the history of modern art. Manipulative photography could be a mode that demonstrates resentment toward photography, or at least its limitations. The manipulative photographer would argue that the work sets up a kind of dialogue between physical artifice and the mechanistic record of past light. When collage artists included photos, they annexed them into their overwhelmingly fictional fields. When manipulative photographers mark their prints, they're not true imperialists; they hesitate, waffle a bit, and convey the impression of dithering. And no wonder! It's like spreading margarine over butter. Enough of the photograph comes through to betray the puniness of their efforts, but not enough to survive on its own.

DH But in the continuing modernist tradition isn't it possible that some photographers might be using photography to comment on the medium itself, on photography versus collage, photography versus other media, and photography as a "witness" and at the same time a violation of that witness, so that layering of different time frames or new contexts gives the image new meaning? Tom Barrow, for example, has experimented with defacing his work in the "Cancellation Series."

MK Since you mention a specific person, I'll tell you what I think. This man lives out in the West; he has made some photographs of western landscapes, and he calls them the "Cancellation Series." He's made these big crossing marks on them. It's not the first time such a thing has happened in the history of photography. Commercial portrait studios make such literal cancellations of photographs either on the contract or on proofs when the client has not accepted the work. Sometimes the studio has a stamp that says "Cancelled." The artist Larry Rivers has responded to that kind of humble stimulus in a painting loosely based on a Bar Mitzvah photograph with a "Rejected" stamp across it. Looking at a cancelled Bar Mitzvah photograph is to look upon a past phenomenon, into which one can read—although with perfect awareness that it wasn't deliberate—a kind of present symbolism.

With Barrow's photographs, though, the "Cancellation" has to be understood as a perfectly deliberate modernist device. He's affirming the picture plane, or something trivial like that. He isn't making a document of any sort whatsoever; he isn't interested in the photograph his marks spoil. He's interested in the combination of the image and his scrawl. As you look at his photograph, you try to imagine what kind of mind would have done that—since together the marks and the images malfunction.

Whereas, with a cancelled Bar Mitzvah photograph, you want so desperately to look at the crossed-out faces that you begin to wonder why they were somehow deemed unsatisfactory. You understand that the client might have disapproved for reasons that wouldn't be yours. Then you begin to wonder what the others were like, the pictures that *were* accepted.

Most of the time these are fruitless speculations, but by and large photography is the study of fruitless speculations and meager evidence. The problem with Tom Barrow's work, when it comes to such things, is that, while he is no less obscure, he's much more definite, and, while he's just as arbitrary, he's probably more perverse. I feel that in order to appreciate Tom Barrow, I would have to become a little facetious, since he denies what he asks me to look at. I certainly understand that personal sensibility has its rights. But at least in this precious case Barrow's artifice seems far less interesting than the contemplation of a moment of past history, a historical moment of small stature, which has gone through real, though low-level, distress—a minor rejection. For all that, the artist-photographer's self-absorption strikes me as a far poorer stimulus of fantasy than the client's. Tom Barrow, Betty Hahn, Judith Golden, John Wood, and others protest the artistically low status of photography. Van Deren Coke speaks of efforts like theirs as expressions of refreshing vulgarity, as raucous mutinies against the pure. But I think they're not vulgar enough; they haven't gone whole hog! In their curious refinement, or niceness, they're stopped short of granting themselves the complete control signaled by the gesture of violation.

If it's control they want, the optimum kind we associate with art, what are they doing grounding their stuff in photos? When ambiguity or equivocation works, it's fine; but this is temporizing. Instead of accentuating each other, the two media weaken and hedge each other's capacities. They're sacrificed in the mix rather than supplemented. This is not a criticism based on an abstract idea of media purity. It's a complaint of the eye and the mind when dealing with an obtuse convention.

This conversation took place in New York on the morning of November 25, 1981. David Hanson, a 1985 Guggenheim fellow, teaches photography at the Rhode Island School of Design.

Aperture *no. 89, 1982.*

The Amused Consciousness of Roland Barthes

Roland Barthes talks of the banality of the photograph—it's absolutely contingent, "somewhat stupid," crude—an untransformable thing. The figures there "do not *emerge* . . . they are anaesthetized and fastened down." With literary prejudice, he grouses about the photo picture "that cannot *say* what it lets us see." Yet everywhere he confesses to his astonished intrigue with this object. Because of its intractable visibility—"it fills the sight by force"—its meanings escape words. No choice, then, if he's drawn to it, but to drop down into his own depths and regress by self-excavation. Upset by the disorderliness of photographs (who isn't?), skeptical of reductive systems, since they harden discourse, he resolves to disarm himself, to be a primitive without culture, about the last thing one could take him for, since his book disproves it on every page.

With even further risk, his "ontological desire"—to distinguish photography within the range of images—turns out to have a sentimental origin. He had recently lost his mother. *Camera Lucida* pivots around his discovery, in a batch of family photographs, of a shot of her when she was five, the only one that expresses her "truth," and he wonders about it. Remembering that he had nursed her toward the end, he imagines her almost as his own daughter. At the same time, the photo pictured a child he would never have, and a loved being who was irrecoverable. The sense of loss, as usual, twisted about the ego: "Is History not simply that time when we were not born? I could read my nonexistence in the clothes my mother had worn before I can remember her." Barthes's stress on the etymology of certain words may have originated in his curiosity about his own consciousness, which a photograph had set off.

The noun *look,* in French, is written "regard," which is, in turn, an

English verb defined as "to look or think about something with a particular feeling." The feeling startled up in Barthes, which he pursues, even at the expense of synthetic theory, is violent. He senses himself as having been psychically pierced or pricked by a feature of the image. That the stimulus might not appear urgent or extreme is of little import to a man who thinks sugar is violent. The idea of a sweet affliction evokes the pangs he feels before love's object, forever distanced. But of course the object at issue is revealed to be the writer just as much as that to which he knows or suddenly finds himself attached. That is, the photograph acquaints him with the reality of his nothingness in the past, and the imminence of his death in the future.

For good measure, Barthes develops another paradox. The photograph can only excite his desire, kindling his awareness of life, through its resonance of mortality. Though we have no name for it yet, most of us recognize this condition, which acts as an involuntary and helpless wish to extend ourselves— in the tender sense—to the photographic subject. Barthes speaks of it as a hallucination arising out of the temporal peculiarity of photographs. "She is going to die: I shudder . . . *over a catastrophe that has already occurred.*" The time limbo itself is not the cause of his passion, but only the prerequisite for it, the spur of a secret knowledge impossible to transmit.

How this apparently sealed-in intimacy can be used in criticism doesn't seem to concern Barthes, but it does interest me. His book swims with judgments of the broadest sort, but few are based on visual analysis. His formulations, though, are of great value to criticism because he can describe how images are invested with emotional significance. In Lewis Hine's photo of idiot children in New Jersey, 1924, it's not the misshapen heads or the rigid posture of these maimed creatures which disturbs him, but the girl's bandaged finger, a detail that Hine might not have been looking at but couldn't fail to include. This is very delicate and a little perverse. If it is to detonate its affective charge, the detail must be neither expected nor probably even intended. Only because it is gratuitous can the incidental part transcend the dull pathos of the whole. When he is solicited, Barthes recognizes himself to be in a bland situation—the inert world of good intentions, rhetoric, commerce, reportage—in short, the normal gestures of photographic culture. He does not dispute the usefulness of the material given out in these channels, only its warrant on his imagination.

Behind these notions lies an existential influence (the need to choose freely), and a Surrealist pedigree (the thrill of the unforeseen). *Camera*

Lucida fuses the desperate initiatives of the one philosophy with the equally radical passivities of the other and locates their convergence in the photographic experience. The "I" of this book—a tactful way of proposing "we"—is a person for whom photographs introduce an enigma of social deviance. There's a pattern in French films, say by Truffaut, Chabrol, and Bunuel, which studies a comparable theme. The considerate and genteel surface of provincial bourgeois behavior is ruptured by a love affair that has a decidedly selfish infantilism and a marvelous grandeur. These things always end badly, but not before they indict societal restraints, which are a perhaps necessary guide but also a burden on existence. In Barthes's terminology about photos, society is represented by the *studium,* all that which is of no more than general, public, and phlegmatic interest in the frame (the technical and social "blah-blah"); whereas the point of amorous, asocial consummation is called the *punctum.* Barthes writes professorially, and therefore with knowing charm, about his instinctual releases.

This blend of distanced and engaged comment enables him to make humane distinctions, such as one between the pornographic photograph, where the subject is fetishized (the body is shown but not given), and the erotic photo, where appetite is led beyond the frame, as in a naked young man's hand, trailing toward the margin, that has "just the right degree of openness." Nonetheless, while always in favor of "light" rather than "heavy" desire, he ballasts his text with an aesthetics of craziness, linked to the historical perdition of the photograph.

Of history, as intimated in the photo, he says that "in order to look at it, we must be excluded from it." I suppose he could have said that the more he rummaged in old photographs (and even yesterday's are old), the more they lent him their "little touches of solitude." But then he guesses that something similar happened to those who posed. They were looking at nothing and had to contain their angst entirely within themselves. It's as if he perceived that they lacked the power of regard, and it had quite melted him away. Photography is a "bizarre" medium, "chafed by reality," and authenticates no more than "that which has been." "I then realized that there was a sort of link between Photography, madness," and something else which eventuated in Pity. "I entered crazily into the spectacle . . . taking into my arms what is dead . . . as Nietzsche did when . . . he threw himself in tears on the neck of a beaten horse: gone mad for Pity's sake."

Precisely because all this is written from the vantage of self-confession, I can respect and even be moved by it, yet want more. The generosity and denials expressed by this self—brave enough to ask even the most embarrassing question—are the product of its psychic sensitivity, and not of any reasoning about the social and historical placement of its objects. So there is a failure of empathy at the core of a book that stresses empathic perception, and with that, a failure of aesthetic response as well. From Barthes we won't learn how the makers of photographs, our fellow human beings, can project their awareness through images and create persuasive art, let alone how art is inflected by its environment at a particular moment. In magnifying his egotistic regard, he reduces the artistic object, which is not mad enough or rather vulnerable enough to animate his musical pity. Even on his own terms, though, something can be said about the artistic process in photography.

Unlike the mass of viewers, photographers belong to a tiny, self-selected minority. They were the temporary witnesses of temporary events—insiders, therefore, compared to our mob of later outsiders. It occasionally happens that such insiders can have in mind our figurative present as disjunct from their actual one. That is, they're endowed with the gift of viewing their present as history, a whole epoch receding from them despite the fact they were immersed in it. They could anticipate being alienated in time from what was crushingly there, and they could literally see it as a transfigured reality. With nineteenth century work we don't pick up this feature, possibly because our nostalgia is *too* accommodating. Everything then, before living memory, was of the past. But with the twentieth century we begin to recognize this "mythological now," in Atget (for whom Barthes, incredibly, has no use), in Evans during the 1930s, in Klein, Frank, and Brandt. These and other figures are new artistic types, characteristic of our time: the professional strangers whose work deeply signifies because, while they acknowledge our loneliness, they establish our community with what had been.

Though wonderfully suggestive, Barthes's closeup poetics occur too much in isolation and can stifle us. Even still, we sympathize, as when he describes posing for his picture: "What I want to have captured is a delicate moral texture . . . but . . . I don't know how to work upon my skin from within. I decide to 'let drift' . . . a faint smile . . . which . . . might suggest . . . my amused consciousness of the whole photographic ritual." He certainly knew how merciless that ritual was. In speaking of it, Oliver Wendell Holmes wrote: "Men will hunt all curious, beautiful, grand objects . . . for their *skins,* and leave the carcasses as of little worth." What Barthes couldn't have known was his own death by auto, an event as accidental as many a photograph. The on one the flap at the end of the book shows only his "amused consciousness."

Village Voice, *December 16–22, 1981.*

Q. Who do you really believe was present at that Supper?

A. I believe one would find Christ with his Apostles. But if in a picture there is some space to spare I enrich it with figures according to the stories.

from the trial of Paolo Veronese before the Holy Tribunal, Venice, July 18, 1573

The Awning That Flapped in the Breeze and the Bodies That Littered the Field:

"Painting and the Invention of Photography"

One of the ways we recognize a picture as a photograph is by its unimaginable reserves of micro-data, its readiness to provide for unperceived event, its "space to spare." Packing in more discriminated material than is needed for any story, the photograph offers an over-abundance of particulars—images of things or people in the way, irrelevancies of every sort—that might even effectively detract from the story. The medium of photography has been denigrated because it "shows everything and explains nothing," an idea that voices very well the useless grievance that literary people have against the camera.

Examined by the Inquisition in 1573, Paolo Veronese defended his opulent painting *The Feast in the House of Simon,* commissioned by the church of SS. Giovanni and Paolo, against the reasonable charge of secularism. He at first claimed that the clowns he painted were appropriate because Simon was a rich man and could be expected to have had lots of them around. If the aim was to depict "The Last Supper," however, Veronese's "drunkards, Germans, dwarfs and similar vulgarities" must have seemed pretty irrelevant to a clerical audience. Even further, they were thought scurrilous and vituperative. (The Counter-Reformation is speaking.) The artist then immediately dropped his pretext about Simon's worldliness and affirmed his own, that is, the worldliness of the artistic imagination.

He no longer implied that the story was the single controlling factor in the representation, or that all figures in the painting could be held to its account. The action that concerned him resided in the superfluities, for which there could be no alibi other than his will in the matter, sanctioned by the license of other, earlier artists—that is, tradition. In Veronese's picture, the supernumeraries happen to be the protagonists, just as the subject turns out to be "nominal." It finally made little difference to him to retitle the painting *Feast in the House of Levi,* Levi being acceptable, while Simon was not. In the former, less sacred house, it was easier to believe that a man could have a nosebleed than in the latter.

All this sounds remarkably like the conditions under which we see things in photography: the diffusion of subjects, the nonhierarchical principles of the machine, the singular circumstantiality of detail, the manipulation of photographs by captions, the ways content can be patched up or deconstructed by miscellaneous incident, the ways, finally, that meaning is given a primarily material, *secular* weight.

The phrase "space to spare" has a delicious and positively misleading charm. It suggests that after the prime iconic responsibility has been discharged, the painter might still have some unforeseen pictorial obligations, which are satisfied by makeshift arrangements. But the "unforeseen" groups and types for Veronese were, as we know, anticipated from the beginning, and are transparently not what they seem, not expediently ad-libbed, but deliberately scripted. What could not be admitted publicly in so many words, that enrichment is all, was declared visually, in a charade to which literal-minded and pious people could object.

Instead of appealing to a common spiritual consciousness, Veronese addressed himself to individual sense experience. In the mainly decorative invitation to such experience, and in a branch of landscape, it doesn't make any sense to speak of contingent subjects, or extraneous or inconsequential ones, as if we are still thinking from a narrative point of view. If things have a right to be where they are because they afford pleasure or because they seem naturally sited, then symbolism and narrative themselves become contingent.

Such a reversal was achieved earlier in Veronese's century, with great moral pointedness, by Pieter Bruegel the Elder. In his panoramic *Procession to Calvary,* 1564, the centrality of the bearing of the cross, and therefore of Christ's Passion, is overwhelmed within a bewildering throng, a wave of humanity, which clearly could have no center. Bruegel might be said to offer a wide-angle view of the proceedings, as if to encompass a plausible quantity of collateral figures. Rather than treat of their attendance to the tragedy, though, he deals with their pervasive unconcern, magnified by their number. In very high spirits, the crowds gather for the execution, but they don't perceive whose it is.

Once again, a special kind of worldliness is shuffled into an old formula. And in the "hand" now given to the viewer, clues to the narrative are dispersed. The spectacle offered is a radical one, not simply because the religious drama becomes immersed and alienated in several conflicting events, but because a psychological realism insists on a sort of chaos. In asking not what Calvary meant to his audience, or was supposed to mean, but rather what it might have been like, Bruegel revised the story, almost to the point of the unrecognizable. He populates the narrative with creatures whose role is precisely to exhibit their unawareness of having any role. The artist discovers the truth that, close up to it or further away, most people don't share in a critical moment, they're merely there, embroiled in their own diverse pursuits and taking up space. In order to affirm that insight, though, he has to distance himself from what he pretends to be looking at. That is, instead of omnisciently staging behavior, he assumes the mode of detached, even passive observer, so as to let behavior happen. By ceding a closed thematic unity, shattering it into many unequal parts, he gains a startlingly open and credible description.

Still, if I ask what's really credible in this picture, it is certainly not be found in its details of clothing, which are sixteenth-century Flemish, or those of the landscape, drawn from memories of France and Italy instead of Roman Judea. The credibility arises from Bruegel's altitude. It strikes us that he intended to portray his subject as if it were a historical rather than a mystical one. A mystical deed need only appeal to faith; a historical event is experienced or has to be pieced together from evidence. Bruegel's evidence was based on his observation of human nature. As he plays his and our intuition of a historical episode against the unawareness of the actors in it (history is known only after it has occurred), he attains a realism of his own that is also imbued with pathos. For he demonstrates that historical knowledge, unaided by moral consciousness, cannot redeem tragedy.

There was something profoundly liberating about this demonstration even if, in visual imagery, it had to wait until photography to become familiar. In contrast, during a great deal of its history, Western narrative painting assumed that climactic action and spectator point of view were mutually available and well aligned. The spatiotemporal proximity of viewed and viewer, their chronic readiness for each other, was the prerequisite metaphor for visual storytelling. This remarkably convenient system, which made way for intelligibility, had both a practical and an idealistic rationale. Practical because it was the clearest and most economical mode of alluding to the fact that a temporal story was being told within a delimited spatial zone. And idealistic because it suggested a perfection in the beholder's vantage point, exempt from any material hindrance. With this kind of imagery, no one had to scramble to get a good seat.

Going from work to narrative work in a Western museum, one feels conveyed along a track to endless special appointments, an itinerary of conceivable great events offered by art, but not by life. In that sense, even Courbet's *Burial at Ornans,* 1849, though once scourged for its brute, vulgar realism, implies an idealist vision. Obviously, idealist postulates, of which the flattering, preadjusted mode of access is an example, can be embedded in a realist style. Still, such exposition prepares us for dramas and affords us privileges that can be felt as hermetic.

For they seal off the actual misalignment—the largely inopportune character—of the life we know we have to lead. How often does it happen, after all, that we're granted automatic visitation rights to the peak, momentous instant of anything, furnished with a splendid view and exhorted to have a desired response to it? Narrative and symbolic representation, of the classic sort, induce a climate of absolute and therefore complacent expectancy. For they project the assurance that the world is there for us, present for us as we are for it—something, then, to be understood finally as our own creation.

More humble acknowledgments, of our limited field of vision, of the things that intervene within and confuse it, or often our ignorance of material at hand, have been erased from the record. Idealist vision tends to dissociate us from a feeling not only for foreign locales, but for our own, in its historical moment. Art of this sort, if it were to have its way, would dissuade us from realizing that there are aspects of the world not of our own prior making, and therefore yet to be construed. It fell to our evolving scientific culture and historical sense, which are quite meshed with our art, to define that world. To recognize materials in an exploratory spirit was to glimpse activities, with their causes and effects, that could be approached, as it very gradually became clear, only by partial moves, and could be described only from random positions.

Indeterminate and puzzing elements were introduced into the pictorial field, which the picture itself, with its obscure entrances and partial blockages, could not solve, nor did it give any evidence of a desire to solve. Yet that very uncertainty tended to confirm the circumstances under which we do see. The more apparent these circumstances, the more the situation exhibited recalcitrant, unclear, and disorderly elements. It was not as if the painter had denied his will or intelligence but rather that he allowed content to work against some of his normal interests. What made his vision look newly attentive and credible was that it appeared disinterested.

Rigorously untheatrical yet full of dramatic enigma, multiepisodic, yet synthesized from one apparently casual glance, Velasquez's *Las Meninas* brings off this illusion tremendously. It does so precisely by begging the question of point of view, as if it were about the very exigencies of seeing. One cannot, after all, peer into it without eye contact apparently being directed back by represented figures. Most of the sight lines, entering or exiting from the painting, are overtly qualified as a product of the viewer's position, a position temporarily fixed, it would appear, by the act of sitting for a portrait. Velasquez depicts himself as part of the goings-on, ambiguously ranking himself among the dwarfs and servants. He allows us to see the objects of his gaze, the king and queen, implicitly in our space by virtue of their mirror reflection on the far wall, but he conceals his portrayal of them on his averted canvas.

At the same time, his concentration is about to be thrown off by the inopportune arrival of the maids of honor. They are certainly permitted into his studio interior but they do not belong there at that moment. Given the cross purposes at work in this tableau, it's impossible to conceive of anything happening without its being interrupted or stalled, so that distraction itself emerges as the theme of the picture. Velasquez's imminent distraction by the entrance of the outsiders; our distraction due to the gaze of painted eyes upon us. And then it seems that the moment of perception, the viewer's perception as well as that of the figures in the painting, vibrates as does a moment of human life itself, and that it will dissipate as soon as it crystallizes.

Velasquez, servant to the crown, depicts such a moment, in which he is upstaged, a moment that is apparently outside his control, although only his will and imagination could have realized it. It is all very profane and anticlimactic because each episode, and then each nuance within the episode, is psychologically outflanked by something else. Recent studies have emphasized in the program of *Las Meninas* an homage to the perfection of Hapsburg authoritarianism. If, on the contrary, as citizens of late twentieth-century democracies, we ask what moves us in this painting, what distinguishes it from a host of other court paintings that issued from that arch Catholic and monarchic environment, it is not likely to be the expression of values shared with them. Surely, the apprehension of the moment does not fulfill either narrative or hieratic functions, and exists somewhere between, as a perception of instantaneous behavior. Or rather, as gradients of such behavior—from the childishly coquettish through the solicitous, to the entirely unaware or unrehearsed. Even the showing of deference towards rank is viewed as just one event, not the ultimate objective of perception. This doesn't deflate rank, but it does subtly enhance the allusive humanity of the larger situation in which rank finds itself. Being the most encompassing observer, the artist is the true outsider. Yet, by bringing the apparent moment of perception close, as it were, to the moment of pictorial execution, through his rapid, "improvised" brushwork (for example, the demonstrative blur of his hand), he draws the spectator into the scene. The invitational character of the tableau is essential to its expressive mood. And the expressive mood is liberal in the visual sense with which the artist's gaze realizes its objects, accepting them, high and lower, as of equal lightness in phenomenal presence, and equal, too, in an off-hand world of happening for which there is a protocol, but, in this one precious instant, no script.

The real shocks experienced by the narrative tradition were caused by flashes of the instantaneous such as these. Whoever understands their fragmentary, mutating illuminations understands why the camera, with its prodigious twinkle, was slated to be.

Why have I smuggled references to photography into this sketchy talk of old masters? One reason is that, with our advanced twentieth-century vantage point, it's too late to be innocent of the effect photography can have upon ideas of art history. Those ideas were bound to be weighted by the consciousness the camera has imposed upon us. Another reason is the perplexing value of photography as a cognitive record, and one's curiosity about its genesis. The sensations that arrived with photographic culture did not combust spontaneously out of the air; they often evoke memories of other sensations realized by artists.

One can trivialize the relationship between photography and painting by talking about source and derivation. This is the ritual of the academic, who wrongly imagines photo history can be constructed as was orthodox art history, with its great names, prime objects, and coherent outputs. Or one can glorify photography by attempting to show that its insights are *indistinguishable* from some of those of painting, an art form enjoying higher social prestige. This is the strategy of an aesthete, perhaps a trifle embarrassed by the objects of affection. Doubtless, between the two media there flow reciprocating mimetic impulses. But this liaison does not infer that painting could ever extract for itself the magic mechanical facticity of photos; nor could photographers muster an image-constitutive power beyond their means. Practitioners of the two modes might emulate each other through style and structure. But in that event, they provide endless opportunities for only superficial comparisons.

I want to say that a deeper rapport lies between photography and all those paintings whose gesture tended away from principles of integral and sufficient order, regardless of style. Looking back from the perspective of photography, painting reveals, at the onset of such gestures, the first tremblings of appearances, increasingly recognizable as time went on, which do not obey our aims or purposes—phenomena whose intrigues with one another are outside our control, but not our understanding. To explain them, though, we have to rely on sightings that are exceedingly local and discontinuous, much as the eye perceives when it scans. The events visualized were of a world more and more textured by happenstance. And it had a startling new beauty—a beauty indifferent to many prior conventions of the beautiful. Who would say that this world defied our appreciation? It was only that appearances there betrayed no great eagerness to solicit it. One had to explore and investigate this world before one can attach meaning to it.

If there is anything inherent in photographic vision, it might be those of its qualities that lead us to think the camera medium to be the most conclusive denial of idealism we have yet seen in the picture-making arts. It took a device invented in the age of positivism to revoke the charter of the mythic image, that is, the responsive image. Who could have expected that this machine, rationally conceived as any machine must be, was to uncover a very unreasonable spectacle—something not bound or imagined by our desire.

A delightful example of this is contained in a photo called *Triumphal Entry of the Bavarian Army into Munich,* 1871 (Fig. 46). As an image, it has everything called for by its title: banners streaming, crowds cheering, troops marching, and monuments being pompous. But since a striped foreground awning, fluttering in the wind, takes up about one-third of the picture space, and the triumph is reduced to a crowd of mites squeezed off in the distance, everything is not in order. It would have been quite possible to render the awning this way in a painting, and thoroughly inconceivable. Daring as he was, Bruegel would not have imagined it; decorative as he was, Veronese

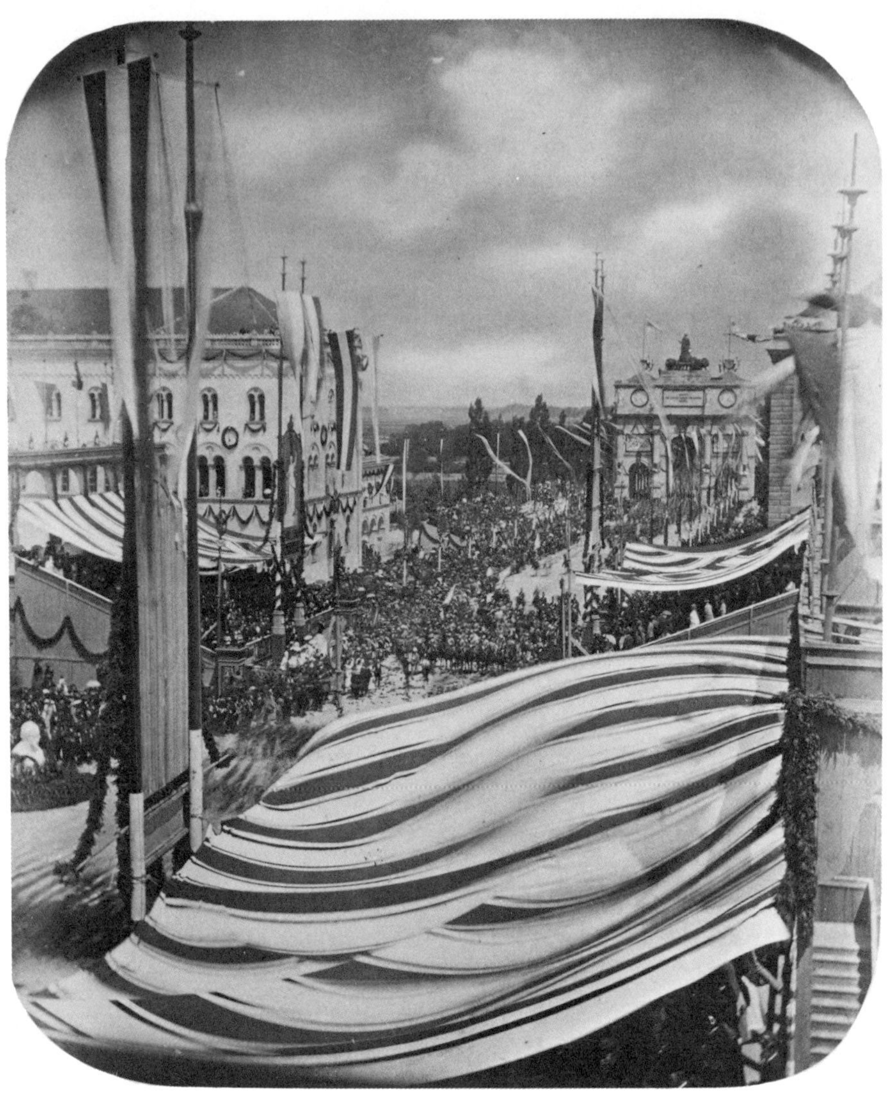

Figure 46. Anonymous, *Triumphal Entry of the Bavarian Army into Munich,* 1871 (Harry Lunn Gallery).

could not have designed it. Their work variously dismantled hierarchy; this one unreflectively reverses it. Absurd, as if it were a picnic cloth spread over human ants, the awning flaps very festively. It's more accurate to use the word "gratuitous" to describe the awning's scale than to call it extraneous. It has a role to play and it contributes to the mood kinaesthetically. We do not know whether such an effect was intended or unavoidable, nor do we know who the photographer was. *The Triumphal Entry* has quite a dubious status, for the issue of whether we determine it to be a failed report or mannerist celebration is left floating, as if in the breeze of its own lovely inconsequence.

This particular picture was included in the interesting exhibition at the Museum of Modern Art in New York, entitled "Before Photography: Painting and the Invention of Photography." Wanting to suggest why photography emerged when it did, in the 1830s, aside from technological reasons and social needs and values, the catalogue essay confines itself to the history of seeing—that is, types of representation. To give his argument even more constancy, curator Peter Galassi then reduces the history of pictorial seeing to only one of its features, the changing concepts of Western space.

"The object here," he writes, "is to show that photography was not a bastard left by science on the doorstep of art, but a legitimate child of the Western pictorial tradition." Some of us had accepted very well the bastardy of the photo, but now it is defensively announced that the foundling, contrary to general belief, had properly married and even noble parents, devoted to the cause of art. Though such discoveries happen more often in fables than in real life, the show does have a historical thesis, designed to persuade us that certain early photographs exhibit a sibling relationship to some contemporary landscape sketches of known lineage.

To trace the genealogy of these offhand and intimate pictures, the catalogue backtracks to Renaissance perspective, "the ultimate origin" of photography. Since we're asked not to bother with the scientific paternity of photos, it's very odd to be confronted with perspective, the chief mathematical contribution to the depictive arts! Of course, as a realist tool—its reason for being introduced—a perspectival system described our optical experience of space, at least urban space, more plausibly than any earlier additive approach or empirical observation. But why would painters have followed up Brunelleschi's invention of the orthogonal scheme imposed by perspective if it could not perform essentially a narrative service?

Imaging a story as the story was now conceived—an account of human energies locked together and coming to a head in synchronized time—painters required rational and predictable space. They needed a frame not only appropriate for the action, but one that could center it for the viewer. So as to prevent them from appearing to run around on the loose, the actors were placed on a stage that appeared as a rectangular inset into the world. Renaissance perspective, therefore, was a containing device that depended on the metaphor of the viewer's fixed position. It was no accident that the earliest camera obscura, with which painters thought to confirm this metaphor, was a not readily portable instrument, whose aperture was immobilized. Perspective enhanced the illusion of interactive figural movement and the recession of things into depth, though, once again, not for their own sakes but as a form of idealist drama. In that sense, of course, perspective, however substantiated by the camera, stands as the *antithesis* of photographic seeing.

A photograph does not assume the existence of pictorial cavity; it sometimes frames a space that looks like one. And while the diagonals in the photo may all obediently rush toward the implied horizon points, its interior perspective doesn't conform to any purpose. The photo furnishes far more accurate information than does a perspectival painting—at the same time as it provides far less a grip on the depicted world. If we happen to be dealing with a narrative painting, its most concrete aim is to deliver its narrative promise according to the artist's will. No such promise exists in a photograph, and from the phenomena it presents we have to eke out narrative bits, according to our will. This is not to say that as a narrative statement a photograph is inherently unreliable or worthless—far from it—but rather that it is inevitably optional.

How quixotic to wonder if a photograph presents a convincing or unconvincing story, as if it had been the photographer's exclusive power to make that a relevant question. If we want to derive meanings from photo occurrences, we have to locate and construct a probable scenario. Despite all that it shows, the photograph remains silent on its own meaning. For there is a gap between what the photographer, in a split-second, seems to or could have meant, and the historical actualities of what is seen (which often fall short of or reach past intent). Viewing a painting, one works on the opposite principle, of the likely convergence between included presences and their import. In contrast, the relatively low or slight mediation of the photographer makes for wide interpretative allowances, though the fact that the photo zone generally slows actual incident reduces the viewer's chance of free association. *In a photograph, what can be known, felt, and seen exists in characteristically unstable and surprising relationships.* On that level, photographs keep us off-balance, a condition which, oddly enough, renews their narrative interest, almost as experience itself charges our personal consciousness.

Perspective had been as successful as it was, possibly because it condensed two powerful drives of science: its synthetic objectives and its investigation of variables. If its early conditions were met, painters could say something grand, that they had presented the general case for appearances. But in the later development of perspective, the one "Before Photography's" catalogue follows with special interest, the investigative impulse becomes dominant. As far as pictorial depth went, Western art would claim to make only particular cases, and yet it's beguiling to see how these particular cases were rapidly installed as norms and just as quickly overturned by new norms. Not only could the frame of vision be theoretically pivoted up and down, or to the left and right, but it could be stopped along any of these vectors at seemingly arbitrary angles to the desired subject. The painter made things interesting by coming in on a slant and accepting the disfigurements, truncations, and obstacles that resulted. In a word, the painter metaphorically carried around his own camera obscura, his eye, which had no choice but to be where he chose to ostensibly locate himself, at the moment of representation.

As time went on, the painter's mobile gaze lost its objective character, for when it caromed from one mass to another, on asymmetric, foreshortened, and overlapped levels, it foresaw a Baroque theater, and when it dwelt within obscure, inaccessible, or "unworthy" locales, it sought out a romantic communion with nature. It doesn't matter that landscape paintings which expressed this communion were sometimes claimed to be "experiments in natural philosophy," as Constable claimed. For him, the freshness of observant discovery was blended into the thoroughly personal, intimate, and subjective energies of the mobile gaze. Much the same applies to innumerable other landscapists of the early nineteenth-century, who found their own distillates of these qualities and perfected them in the sketching genre we see at the Modern. Peter Galassi has brought together work by Christoffer Wilhelm Eckerberg, François-Marius Granet, Thomas Jones, and Friedrich Wasmann, as well as many pictures signed with equally unfamous names. These little paintings study transient effects of atmosphere, insignificant details of wall texture etched by light, crumpled foliage. To the extent such plein-air motifs do not seem to "deserve" the attention that has been meted out to them, the attention itself provides for an undistracted exercise in sensibility. The painter's fragmentary viewpoint, no less than the qualities of his touch, underline that sensibility. In the aggregate, as Galassi argues, these landscape sketches "present a new and fundamentally modern syntax of immediate, synoptic perceptions and discontinuous unexpected forms. . . . It is also the syntax of photography." Whether or not this is a convincing thesis depends upon the usefulness of its terms.

Obviously something deliberate has to be done to nature before it can become what we call a landscape. The outdoors, by itself, does not have a syntax, that is, an ordinance whereby parts are understood to be shaped into intelligible wholes by communicating minds. (What people have constructed on the land is another thing.) The intent to take a photograph and the effect it may have are products of communicating, sentient minds, but *not the activity performed by the camera itself.* And surely here is where we have to talk about the wildness of photographs, that aspect which decisively opposes them to paintings, even those they sometimes closely resemble.

On one level, the difference can be expressed as the desire to represent the unforeseen, contrasted with the inability to make defenses against it. It is not a question of any single ratio of contingent material that distinguishes the photograph; it is the fact that the truly contingent is possible, which crucially alters the way we look upon the photo picture. This state of affairs makes us unsure that individual sensibilities are fully declared in the Modern's photographs of nature, and I, for one, am not convinced that all of them can even be called landscapes or cityscapes.

It's true that in our perceptions of nature, the possible dialogue between painting and photography is at its most deceivingly convergent. What is to be found in our experience of nature, at any one instant, is what is to be found. Our idea of the natural, after all, depends on the givenness of the features with which a scene is made up. We retain that idea through our knowledge that topographies have their indigenous fauna and flora, which varies from terrain to terrain. For all, then, that we can gather of what is normal to the flora of the terrain, and that identifies it, we still can have no determined expectation of how much of it there is in any one instance, the actual spacing between its examples, or their exact scale and placement relative to one another. The bountifulness or the scantiness of these things is not for us to decide, only to observe. Painters, though, are forever tinkering with such spectacles for reasons of their own, even when they want to give the impression that they aren't. They reserve the undeniable right to redistribute the vegetable affairs of the horizon.

In a photograph, though, we're enabled to recollect nature's genuine mayhem. The photo picture restores the minute vagaries of growth, which assure us of the scene's natural roots (regardless of any associations with human symbolism). What price a dozen or several score bushes here, as compared to over there? From a dramatic point of view, all these fixtures are interchangeable understudies, equal in their conditioning role, yet neutral, a kind of collateral roughage. No one among them has star potential, and they are not divisible, except that a limit has to be drawn somewhere in order to obtain a picture. It's precisely when that picture is a photo that we're entitled to speak of the discontinuous because of the photo's massive but interrupted suggestion of the continuous in nature.

What clinches this effect even further is that thc photo's scale of optical differentiation, at maximum depth of field, is effortlessly diligent in its descriptive power. Paintings can register some of the shocking and continuing even-handedness of such power, but only decorously. They came closest around the time photography was invented, but their temporal proximity only made their ontological contrast to photography more evident.

For a camera does only what comes naturally to itself, that is, to a mechanism, whereas a painter defines his or her resources in the act, and therefore we have no concept of what is natural to the painter's eye. Even analogous compositional ideas do not obscure this contrast, of which most people are aware. A photographer who mimics a painter's strategies in this respect is only adjusting a more or less effective frame around an incorrigible surplus of incident (which is to say nothing of the expressive power of the photo, but only something about the matrix through which such power may or may not be transmitted).

We are familiarized with photographic surplus but we never finally come to terms with it, and never, in a deeper sense, get used to it. A photograph can make us uneasy because it suggests that we see as it "sees," and that what is natural to mechanical seeing is natural to us. In proposing this aberrant view, the photograph also offers us dreamlike revelations, with all the abruptness of a dream. I detect that aura in some of the Modern's photos of cities, in Charles Marville's *Place de*

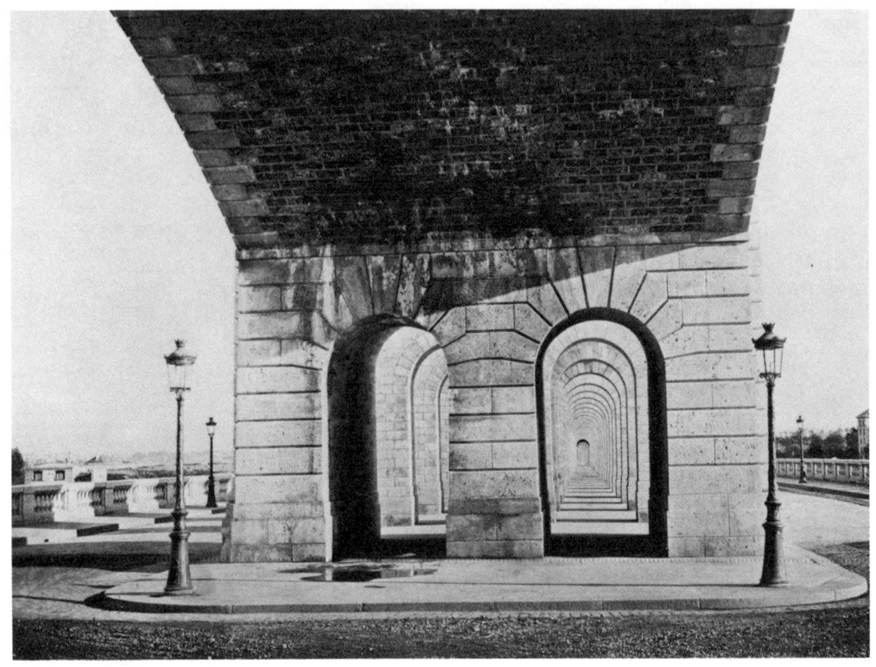

Figure 47. A. Collard, *Bridge,* 1860s (J. Paul Getty Museum).

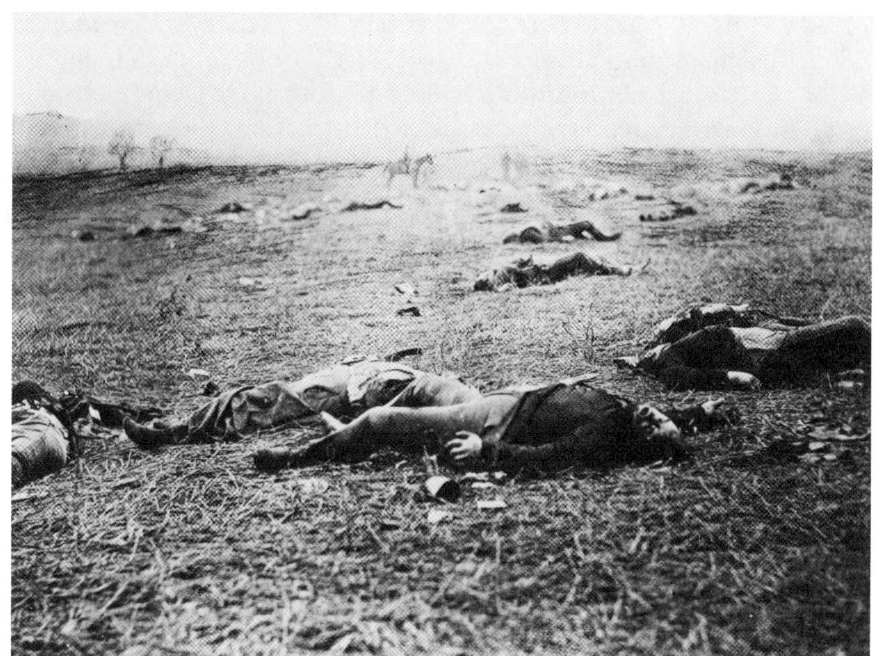

Figure 48. Timothy O'Sullivan, *A Harvest of Death,* 1863 (Grey Art Gallery, New York).

l'Etoile, Paris, 1860s, Robert MacPherson's *The Theater of Marcellus,* 1855, the anonymous shot of what is possibly New York, and, above all, A. Collard's haunting *Bridge,* 1860s (?) (Fig. 47). Despite obvious compositional differences, the status of the structures they show displays an uncanny likeness to that of Timothy H. O'Sullivan's deserts (Fig. 48), or George N. Barnard's and Felice Beato's battlefields. That is, the city, with its empty avenues, has the bearing of their "nature."

In military painting, dead human bodies had been viewed as the heroic aftermath of defeat. There had been no precedent for treating them as the litter of war. Nor had there been any sources in the social townscape tradition for looking at buildings as if they were only forms that took up space. Implications of this sort, which have nothing whatsoever to do with hierarchy, are foreign to painting but are common to photography. We recognize and strive to overcome them, but not before they've lodged their customary strangeness in our minds. It's as if we caught a glimpse of material conditions that were too brusque and dense to assimilate, and it left a residual mark in our perceptions, wounding them. A dream is a riot of images, outside conscious control. If remembered later, the dream, which once had a compelling, visceral reality, is valued for its symbolic resonance or content. Photographs can be very distracting because they often conflict with our symbolic expectations. But they are otherwise like our memories of dreams in their elusive reference to a vanished reality.

There are few images of people at the Museum of Modern Art show. Had there been more, they would have broached problems of social analysis and human psychology to which the schemes of "pictorial syntax" are not suited. Such schemes turn resolutely away from psychology, quite a deficit since the show purports to deal with the psychology of perception. But the trouble is, "pictorial syntax" doesn't work very well with landscape, either. It does not allow the instrumental aspects of landscapes—or of any artistic genre—to have their say. If you can cram painting and photography under the technical, impersonal rubric of their "syntax," you're not likely to allow their internal artifice any stakes in consciousness at large. Rather, you're subscribing to the idealist myth that they are independent structures, modified chiefly by the evolution of their own kind. It's given out that the painting or photograph exists in order to articulate a concept of space, not that its spatial allusions can be seen to further its author's depiction of experience. Ordinary viewers, of course, are not likely to make this mistake, but modernists are especially prone to it.

In the end, but also at the beginning, this show was fashioned along the lines of an old-style modernist argument, with the hope of annexing unincorporated and resistant imagery.

Actually, the only modernists who had a real feeling for photography, because they sensed its recording power as marvelous revelation, were the Surrealists. They had a startled eye for unmediated fact, and the sympathy between Surrealist *poésie* and the documentary mode in photography is an exciting object of study. But Surrealist appreciation lacked any regard for the *uses* of documentary pictures. It was utility, of all sorts, of course, that motivated the inventors of photography. Though that utility can be subverted, one never gets too far away from the influence it has on the image, an influence that determines the meaning and value of the picture as intended or exploited. Even so, a history of those uses can be constructed and not bring us any nearer to the turmoil of photographic experience than the modernist argument can. On one level, the technical work of Louis Jacques Mandé Daguerre, William Henry Fox Talbot, Hippolyte Bayard, and Joseph Nicéphore Nièpce, enhanced by the printing of Louis Désiré Blanquart-Evard, opened up a new communicative channel, as did Bell and Marconi. But in working that channel, images were produced that were as expressive of our cultural and moral dilemmas as they were efficient in transmitting visual data.

In fact, efficiency itself has come to seem desperately problematical to us, as it has more and more usurped the human aspirations that it was reckoned to serve. One can certainly speak of the mindless proliferation of data as a typical drawback of the spirit of efficiency. But as untamed photos have proliferated, they acquaint us with a deflationary view of our environment, which can chasten but also thrill us. I've referred to visions of the natural scene as chaff, of bodies as litter, and of buildings as numb forms. We're made witness to their "otherness," in all its exhilarating authenticity, and come to learn how we are part of it. Compared to that vision, the legacy of Western painting in the main transfomed our world with idealist meanings, exemplary moralism, and fanciful rhetoric, which both inspires and cheats us. We participate in the urgent emotional allusions of painting, knowing full well that they may be about the natural world, but not of it. There can be no question that photography, during this period of the late twentieth century, has become the ascendant visual mode. If it harks back, as it must, to what painting has offered, it makes a subsidiary appeal to the philosophical security we think we are in danger of losing—the conviction, as I say, that the world is there for us. And as painting gradually discovered the contingent, discontinuous, and fragmentry, it anticipated, but could not really foresee, our eventual anxiety.

But then, neither could the Victorians or the citizens or the Juste-Milieu. In realizing that condition, photography, the bastard, came of age.

Artforum, *September 1981.*

Autochromes:

The Bouquet of Lighted Air

Right from its start, photography was expected to bloom one day with hues that resembled those of the natural world. The medium had been born generating far more visual information than that of painting; there was reason to suppose it could be just as chromatic. Before this palette could be obtained, however, difficult optical and chemical problems had to be solved. Was one to proceed best by the mixing of colored lights (filters), or by means of dyes included on the sensitive plate? How was the process to be developed and how was the result to be fixed so that colors wouldn't fade? Further still, what were the mechanical advantages that would make the whole package usable and profitable? Beyond that (and affected by all earlier decisions) what would true color photography look like and how would it feel?

Beginning in 1892, and basing their experiments on a great deal of earlier, theoretical work, two French brothers, the Lumières, who shortly after invented the movie projector, concentrated on making still color photography a reality. Unlike their more mandarin colleagues, these men of the laboratory were as good hearted as they were clever. Stemming from peasant and then petit-bourgeois roots, surrounded by a loving family, they were devoted to public service. They financed innumerable short films, which they distributed themselves. Auguste, the elder, was a biologist who pioneered in chemotherapy and the medical industry. By 1904, the younger, Louis, announced the success of his experimental findings in color to the Académie des Sciences. Three years later, in 1907, he established a factory and was able to market its product, Autochrome glass transparencies. These were the first practical, single-plate renderings of color in photography, and they were hailed throughout the Western world. In fact, this process had no serious competition until after 1930, at which point Lumière had been manufacturing modestly, but steadily, 6,000 plates a day for sixteen years. Considering the accomplishment, what poetry adhered to the name, the Light brothers! And could it have been any less poetic that they were located in a suburb of Lyon called Monplaisir?

The sky and very often the flesh depicted in an Autochrome have an ambiguous cast. As they are generally the lightest areas in the field, they are easily seen to be agitated with myriad color specks or filaments, whereas similar zones in black and white are transparent and serene. Autochrome brought an added, equivocal weight everywhere to the frame, as if there had been some extra density lifted, and spun porously, into the atmosphere. The outdoors dims a little with substance that appears neither precisely tinted in, nor altogether a natural feature of the light. It takes a conscious but by no means strenuous effort to get acclimated to this effect. Perceived as a faint cloud that softens texture but does not blur focus, it transcribes every twig or body of water, field and fold, into a strange, twilight delicacy. It would be easier naming the colors of things if this cloud had not entered into the description and "perfumed" it with a vagrant spray of its own.

Autochrome made commercial sense because, though relatively expensive, it was reliably produced, and regularly developed. The process enjoyed *historical* success because it furthered an illusion of actual color recall. It was felt to be not only pleasing, but also faithful to nature. Yet its illusiveness, for mechanical reasons, called attention to itself. Instead of silkily blending the infinite nuances of color, Autochrome appeared to superimpose the complexion of a scene upon its already modeled contours, creating a vibration from which neither air nor matter could be separated. One does not believe that nature has quite broken out in a rash, but rather that it is busily pigmenting itself as one looks.

So, these pictures can be highly saturated but also tentative, time-released in their coloring. They are suspended between the conviction of impassive finish, given as in the manner of photography, and the artifice of touch and fantasy, familiar in the mode of painting. At times their color seems to exist tremblingly, only to evoke another color, the color of a dream. Technically speaking, Autochromes announce the dawn of modern color journalism in photography. Culturally speaking, they are a manifestation of late Symbolism.

Potatoes, of all things, or more specifically, grains of potato starch, formed the basis of the Autochrome process. Millions of them, dyed green, red, and blue (violet) in equal proportions, were sifted into one powder of no distinguishable color, and pressure-coated on an adhesive-treated glass plate. All microscopic intervals between the grains were stopped by a film of carbon dust. Superimposed upon this mosaic screen was a black-and-white photo emulsion. The plate was inserted in the camera with the screen facing the shutter so that light would be exposed first through the grains, each of them acting as a separate filter, to produce dots the negative equivalent of their colors. Development took place, without fixing, by reverse printing in daylight—a two-stage reduction of silver—which restored the "correct" colors. Originally white in the negative, the black carbon ground was returned to its initial value, reinforcing color intensity. Because the screen and emulsion were bound together in one unit, rather than separately employed, problems of registration in development were eliminated.

For years, the additive (or mixed light) process had been troublesome because of the awkwardness of correlating multiple exposures, filters, or negatives. Now, Lumière had combined them in a workable system, assisted by his own centrifuges and laminators. Though this was of great technical significance, the process created certain physical peculiarities that restricted the Autochrome image. The density of the screen, for one thing, permitted only a very small percentage of light to win through to the emulsion, thereby requiring long exposures. For another, the starch grains tended to aggregate in clumps, some of which were visible to the eye. And, finally, the resulting unique glass transparency, too large to be projected, had to be viewed in a special hand-held device fitted with mirrors.

In standard handbooks, Autochromes are treated with no less, but certainly little more, attention than that meted out to a number of early color systems, emulsions and cameras, at one time enthusiastically introduced and then quickly retired. Joly's screen plates, the Krayn line, Wood's filtered gratings, Ives's Helichromy and Kromskop lantern, Dufay-color, the Jos-Pe process—all these and other arcana are described as if they merited a place equal to that of the Autochrome.

An exhibit at the Library of Congress, "Autochromes: Color Photography Comes of Age" (1980), dismissed this silly equity. Far from being technical curios, the seventy-five prints assembled there (Cibachromes made from the original transparencies by Ilford, Inc.) represent a special world of perception, of great freshness and beauty.

Just as the Daguerrean art had its own perceptual character, calotypes and collodions their particular codes of rendition, so, too, Autochromes, with comparable magnitude, created a way of seeing. Or rather, made it possible—for certain "feeling" tones, symbolic devices and even subject choices were encouraged by the material's airy conditioning of appearances. The fact that a few well-known figures—Steichen, Genthe, De Meyer, Kuhn, Lartigue—sporadically used Autochrome does not, by itself, legitimate the mode. On the contrary, it is the average and continuous imagery of mostly obscure workers that confirms its value. With this mass of pictures, only now beginning to surface, an enchanting and almost lost consciousness arises. Thousands of pallid speculations or memories may now gradually regain their circulation.

Habitually, color is thought to express the present state of affairs, the *immediacy* of sensory encounter. But with Autochromes we sight the chromatic glints of an obviously remote past, a spectrum that traces back into an environment whose actual hues, until now, we could only imagine. The spectacle of Autochrome plunges us into a delicious confusion which destabilizes our sense of time far more than any comparable photography in black and white.

Colors relay sight. If nature were all one color, the eyes would be worn out long before sunset, and in order to recuperate from the effort, man would have to sleep twice as long as he does now. The more colorful the landscape, the more it rests your eyes. Modern eye-fatigue is the result of the unvaried greyness of our cities with their one-crop culture

Malcolm de Chazal,
Sens-Plastique, 1979

The invention of Louis Lumière made it possible to harvest many crops in photography. Yet, multiplicity does not equal credibility.

Around the same time, when Burton Holmes had his black-and-white lantern slides hand-tinted, it was a traditional effort to compensate for the infertile monochrome of his means. (Foreign and exotic places—these were travel pictures—*had* to be "colorful.") A cosmetic ingredient was introduced into the visuals, one that prettified the effect but had no value as record. It was quite otherwise with Autochrome, which actually proposed to give an account of our color experience through a record of its effects. Instead of a gray base with funereal make-up, one had a tissue in which changes of value were expressed through differences of hue. This lively coregistration did not permit fanciful departures from real color, but it did open up the question of what color photography can tell us, what we can certifiably know when we look at a color photograph.

Everyone realizes that a pink photograph of trees is not to be understood as a photograph of pink trees. Because of past encounters with nominally brown and green trees, an allowance is made for the new color in which the photograph renders them. Less clear is the latitude of allowance, abetted by the seduction of photography itself and, in the case of Autochrome, the rhetoric of the color it favors. But then, how "correct" is our requirement for a *natural* color, based as it is on some averaging instinct which may be irrelevant to the particular information reconstituted by the photo? Provided that some hues conform to expectation, anomalous passages are likely to be tolerated, even in photos suspected of serious color imbalance. Such products are held to some criterion of plausibility, but it is a loose one.

This looseness is all the more understandable when we think of color as an outright form of knowledge. Ideas of objects' shape, placement, scale, and boundary are more or less fixed for us in a photograph, relative to the angle at which they're framed. That is, if we can imagine restoring the angle a second time around, we can imagine a photographer being able to line up those same relationships. However, it becomes very hard to consider any duplication of the tonality of the scene, and just plain frustrating to re-image it in the same (or even approximate) boundless, fugitive color. Knowledge of a phenomenon is reassured by the possibility of its recurrence, but the knowledge that comes from bodily infusion is much less readily grasped than the one that comes from spatial measure. The apprehension of color is experience in the round. Beyond general cues, we can be no more certain of what is seen or what is revealed in the glow of dusk as in the flickering of someone's expression. "The rainbow and the human face," Chazal writes, "ask us to consider the same question: where does the picture begin and the frame end?

Think of these mutually affecting variables: time of day and color "direction," season and color temperature, radiance, and induced or local color. When they prevail upon us in the flesh, these mingled aerations obviously have much more guiding value than when seen stilled and muted in a photo. In fact, at a point when photography could at last accommodate color, the medium carried it off, as it did all the other sensations it transcribed, to the usual limbo. With this new endowment, the picture decidedly improved its suggestiveness of lived perception. From now on the frame could almost be said to evoke the breath of a scene and to bring back something of its original flush.

Yet, the effect was pried loose from every influence that acted upon it in time. From this point of view, nothing is more apparent, when you think about it, than the difference between what is deposited on the film and what was chromatically given 'out there." The narrative implications of still photography are best articulated by the unsettled state of moving bodies, but they are mooted in the much more omniscient shift of color. Inevitably, color became a memorial presence, almost a thing in itself, and potentially an aesthetic object.

The first practitioners of Autochrome reacted to their material much as if they had been the Renoirs, Sisleys, and Pissarros of the lens. This reflex was as noticeable to its contemporaries as it is to us today. The great painters were in immediate cultural range and far better known to lay people than were the practitioners of modernism just then waiting in the wings.

It is almost axiomatic that the earliest moves within a new medium refer to an adjacent art for its models. Here Louis Lumière himself instinctively led the way. In the Library of Congress exhibit, his rosy pastorals and ambered interiors (always relaxed, inviting, and light-dappled in their settings) were a clear echo of the Impressionist *promesse de bonheur.* It suited his subjects very well that the Autochrome substance transmitted this particular vision through a haze made up (or broken down, as it seems), of infinitesimal "strokes." Madame Antoine and Andrée Lumière, the little girl in her nursery among dolls, the family on their auto trip south—all appear to inhale the slightly palpitating air, pleasurably, quite as though it were their birthright (Plate 9). Such images perhaps naively recapitulated an older pictorial convention, but one that stressed an easy profusion of hues, the sparkle of motion, and acuteness of glance. Despite the lengthy exposures demanded by the color plate, there was no chance for stiffness or self-consciousness to have risen up in Lumière's unassuming loyalty to the Impressionist mode. And since he was recording, rather than creating the effect of light, his photos do not suffer from—nor even furnish comparison with—the mimetic energy of paint.

For a really retrograde use of Autochrome, one has to turn to those Americans who initially had gotten rather enthusiastic about it: Steichen, Stieglitz and company. The first sampling from France struck them as technically liberating and artistically plebian. In their moody society portraits, a Rembrandtesque luminism takes over, a tonal management of the process, which begrudged or made incidental the presence of color. Actual hues were allowed to seep through from the brown murk only in a few warm highlights. Through chemical means, Steichen even exaggerated the porous effects of the medium and made them gauzy. The lyric mode was evidently too robust for the Americans and in their enervated refinement, typically seen in some studio interiors that verge on duotone, they frittered away the illusory realism that had been offered. I don't say they worked against Autochrome, but they did reject its material witness of the present. Their class self-image demanded a proper metaphor which was found instead in the nostalgic and escapist evocation of a genteel past. In such an atmosphere color could have no place because it was too concrete, too alien to memory. The *Camerawork* crowd didn't take to Autochrome and performed its characteristic activity elsewhere.

Most of the workers in the medium were not, however, so patrician as to underplay their hand. They were full-blooded in their attitude toward a medium which, in retrospect, we view as discreet and low-key. No matter how ethereal, Autochrome was used as a tool to retrieve the natural spectrum of things, not as an artifice to refashion it. Judging by the reproductions known so far, there was repeated in approximately the same order, but with a quicker tempo, the innocent wonderment at a discovered world, that came to us once from forefathers such as Bayard and Fox Talbot. Aside from inevitable scenes of sentiment and genre, landscapes of the most exquisite tenderness have survived, and there was Autochrome tourism, reportage, and documentary. As Autochromes were unique positives, fabricated in an epoch mostly lacking the technology to publish them, it's uncertain how much public consciousness there was of them. Color photography would most likely have been the work of amateurs (in the older rather than newer sense of the word) and of people under special commission.

The Washington show featured some images by a master of the art, Major Jean Tournassoud, who was chief of photographic services for the French army during the First World War. Left to his own devices, this friend of Louis Lumière might have gone on producing color work roughly analogous to that in black and white of Sutcliffe and Martin. His images of the *poilus,* posed woodenly in simple tasks while on field maneuvers, and uniformed in the old blue tunics and red breeches, produce a very different impression. It's impossible to resolve the conflict between the quiet and heraldic sight of these visual reports and our *knowledge* of the war's savagery. These are reassuring, diaristic, and seductive photos, even when the troops are shown butchering a horse. While Steichen, now the consummate realist, was supervising U.S. military photography from the air, Tournassoud found time to sustain loving ties with his own culture, no matter how much it was historically convulsed.

That the possibility existed to show grungy conditions through Autochrome is revealed by a particular hoard of images just now coming to be examined. From 1910 to 1930, seven photographers traveled worldwide for Albert Kahn, a wealthy French philanthropist, on a giant pictorial project, "Archives of the Planet." Its immodest aim, according to André Barret in *Autochromes 1906/1928* (1978), was "to proceed to a sort of photographic inventory of the surface of the globe, occupied and domiciled by humanity such as it presents itself at the beginning of the twentieth-century." An eccentric and idealistic patron, Kahn often dispatched scientists and engineers, along with his cameramen, on what were apparently ethnographic missions and miniature assistance or observational programs. A glimpse of the results, displayed in Barret's recent book, demonstrates the first attempt to establish color as part of a visual document of manners, traditions, and climates.

It's particularly informative—and gratifying—to see how the photographers accepted the palette of the scenes they visited, whether it be Hanoi or Galway, Cairo or Sarajevo. Suddenly, the colors of the medium become miscellaneous and unpredictable—that is to say, localized. They are opportune and descriptive rather than dramatic, picturesque, or celebratory. In Europe and the Near East, everything looks weathered, though nowhere more so than on the somber Mongolian steppes. As the Kahn photographers recorded the movements and routines of large agrarian populations or subproletariats, the medium seems to have picked up dust, increasingly to have delivered various kinds of exhausted chroma. What a jolt to see the weariness and poverty of sixty-five years ago, dun-colored in the main, but pastel by implication. The way Autochrome here hovers just in and out of neutral has an indefinable poignance. There are 72,000 plates in the Kahn collection, most of them yet to be developed.

Still, Autochrome's reserves of indeterminate hue were hardly restricted to the documentary stance. The kinaesthetic attributes of decomposed color, floating in midvalue, were grasped by many a photographer, above all for their expressive potential. One such figure was Antonin Personnaz, a member of the Société Francaise de Photographie from 1896 to 1937, about whom very little is currently known. As if by its moisture, the French countryside in his work releases a bouquet of lighted air, through a mist, downwind to where the photographer takes the "scent." An artist of extreme finesse, Personnaz must certainly have *previsioned* his landscapes through a specific understanding of the Autochrome materials. He achieves a harmony from which gray is never far removed, but it's a gray that activates and includes all the warms and cools, across the granulated surfaces, rather than a tone that tends to rule them out.

In Autochrome, the identities of colors turn out to be much more volatile than their physical presences. By Autochrome's evident *mingling* of hues, it casts doubt on their natural origins and proportions, taking over, in this irresolute fashion, our memory of the real. Considering the more industrial and chancred aspects of twentieth-century experience, Autochrome summons up a palette more appropriate to our feeling for the nineteenth-century, as if the medium were compensating for its late arrival with a retrospective mood. Even so, it's only because time has passed and our sensibility has been honed by Kodachrome (in comparison a much finer grained but also Fauve-like record) that we're able to stress the fictive character of this early color photography.

The chances are, however, that this was by no means so apparent at its inception. Just as we lack the distance with which to judge the treacheries of our contemporary color, so it must have been in the beginning of the century. It's less important that Autochrome is an obsolete technique than that it represents a way the world was perceived—and is, for that reason, precious.

We too, in our historical moment, are becoming more responsive to the mutations of memory, fact, and artifice, as our own color photography begins to explore these issues. I was reminded of the intense, chrome-saturated nocturnes appearing now in some of our photo galleries by a pair of photographs in the Washington show. On the evening of July 19, 1919, a Swiss amateur named Robert Hirsbrunner shot two Autochromes, of the *Grands Magasins du Louvre*—one in early darkness, the other in the night. Ablaze with every conceivable lamp, strung over its facade in celebration of Bastille Day and a great war victory, the store is transformed into a phantasm of brown gaiety against a violet sky. For such fortuitous color to be made deliberate, sixty years had to pass. The festive scene itself justly invokes what they called Paris for so long: *La Ville Lumière.*

Artforum, *October 1980.*

Abandoned and Seductive: Atget's Streets

Here is the desert. In this silence everything speaks to me: and in your noise everything falls silent.
—Joseph Joubert

Among the diverse remnants that survive from a civilization and that contribute a token of it, pictures can be articulate but are also equivocal. Even when those pictures are technical, as are photographs, with high transcriptual accuracy, they're understood as functions of record or media systems whose rules channel and seriously limit the pictorial program. If the system's social or ideological premises are obscured at later points in time, or disregarded, the data it furnished will be blurred. One wouldn't know how to gauge the meaning of individual photographs by the principles that led them to be taken and fabricated and consumed. They could still be said to contain degrees of information, but it would not be information relative to contemporary usage, or even worse, information arrayed in any legible order.

This happens to photographs all the time. If their original purposes were buried or scrambled by later circumstances, they often come to us as visual refugees from unknown texts, fair game to be appropriated into new discourses, such as art hierarchies. Art museums are bequeathed or they scavenge material of this sort. When that occurs, the imagery enters into protective, denaturing storage, awaiting unfamiliar audiences that have been primed by curators to perceive that disutility is an aesthetic virtue. Of course, a photographic image might very well speak past its historical period on grounds unknown to its makers and sponsors, or for reasons counter to their material interests. It might even have subtly diverged from the norms that it publicly served while appealing to smaller constituencies. Cases where visual intent is lost or retrieved against the grain of institutional contexts have a special interest. But it's only by assuming a vantage *outside* the institutions that we can see what was or is historically at stake in claims made for the images. A spectacular and complex instance of this cultural recycling is the Museum of Modern Art's four shows and as many books, "The Work of Atget"—that is, the pictures that have come to the museum from the Abbott-Levy Collection.

Without doubt the photographs of Eugène Atget, admired for good cause because they offer exquisite visual pleasure, are also enigmatic images and uncertain objects. For all that it has given him an artistic notoriety, the literature on this obscure French artisan still stumbles, one way or another, on . . . an Atget problem.

Recent studies have filled in details of the fair amount known of this work's lineage.[1] The nominal place of Atget in various related image genres is clear enough. Originally meant to provide references to familiar cultural artifacts for artists, craftspeople, decorators, archivists, and publishers, this body of pictures evolved (from the 1890s to 1927) into a record of French and most particularly Parisian architectural history. Atget accumulated such a compendious file of multiple building types—business, domestic, and monumental—and of representative neighborhoods that his work has the appearance of an inventory.

Its pedigree stemmed from the *Voyages pittoresques dans l'Ancienne France,* albums of lithographs which appeared from 1820 to 1878; it continued through the topographic imagery of *Excursions Daguerriennes,* and on via photography ordered by the Commission des Monuments historiques, from such pioneers of the medium as Gustave Le Gray, Henri Le Secq, Edouard Baldus, and Hippolyte Bayard. These were visual projects concerned with a national heritage, which, by the Second Empire, included vernacular sections of medieval Paris, as photographed by Charles Marville before they were torn down during Haussmann's modernization of the city.

Because it was an epoch that knew itself to be in the throes of irreversible change, the nineteenth-century developed a historical sensibility, of which such pictorial campaigns were an expression. There needed to be documents of the urban topography that was to be wrecked, which would survive and which were newly produced. Regret for the erasure of certain remnants of the past mingled with a conservationist activism, especially rampant at the turn of the century in the Vieux Paris movement and in a municipal commission to attend to the historic sections of the city. Atget was a small entrepreneur in the business that furnished antiquarian documents, as well as pictorial accounts of the *moeurs,* different classes, and manners of the city. He numbered among his clients the Bibliothèque Nationale and the Bibliothèque Historique de la Ville de Paris. His working methods were rationalized around the commercial requirement to survey and catalogue large sets of generic motifs. He scrutinized door knockers, for example, or confessional booths in churches, and the statuary of the grand gardens and parks, as if they were so many individual items that had to be scrupulously described, every blessed one of them, in order to fill the inventory of their class. To scan his images is evidently to view only what purports to be his stock, his merchandise.

But the viewer of these images falls prey to a loveliness unbound by any consideration of trade. Going through this archive more carefully, one can be enveloped in reserves of poignance, for which the extensively modest function of the imagery and the mechanistic aspects of its coverage do not prepare. In this accumulative experience a sense gradually builds up that the explicit mundane program of the work has been infused into an indefinitely larger and more private vision that nowhere acknowledges itself. The program of Atget is how to talk about that.

There is such a locale as *Atget's* singular Saint Cloud or Versailles, but it does not disclose itself through a handful of frames. In an anthology where they may be surrounded by large amounts of work of their own genre, they're likely to stand out only by virtue of certain distinctive visual qualities of light, mood, viewpoint, and space. One would intuit that a sensitive mind had informed such images. But only on much larger and longer acquaintance with its products would a notion sink in that Atget had depicted and had possessed a world.

The other practitioners in this line of work describe *things,* with as high and as becoming a finish as possible. Atget's pictures belong mostly to a subgroup of that prominent photographic genre that treats buildings. We have the urban topographical or sectional town view, portraits of historical edifices, the imagery of realtors, and photographs taken for the architectural offices themselves. Each of these specialities isolates its chief motif by strategies of technical emphasis. They examine the traits and the structure of their subjects while subordinating other features of the environment for purposes of appropriate exposition. Even when the subject is a general urban prospect, it is understood as an aggregate of things that has a characteristic profile. Commercial tourist imagery is very stereotyped in this regard. For its part, the architectural detail is as idiosyncratic as the larger view, though it permits a clearer, more complex, and more textured statement. A good example of these principles in action, over a long period, is the output of the Alinari Brothers' firm of Florence.

One thing all this architectural imagery engendered in the nineteenth-century has in common is the theme of a building as a hard, permanent material construct, historical in itself but not perceived in any temporal context. In fact, it's contrary to any of these photographic modes that the date of exposure be specific. Another pictorial convention, just as obvious, rules out a survey of people and of any life lived around the building or any community that engages with it. It is as if the building, social as it is, rises above all those features of society that are merely transient and everyday.

The building might have been erected for ritual, commercial, domestic, or civic reasons, but it is most often presented visually *apart* from its functions. Architectural photographs view their subjects rhetorically as an outcome of the effort and symbolic of the values that went into them, but not as working structures. For the job of the image is mainly to *exhibit* stones or other durable materials, composed in an intelligible mass that lies in state for the eye of the beholder. Highly descriptive in its means, this tradition is diagrammatic in concept. It takes insentient matter and portrays it with as much brisk idealism as possible. When that is understood in a Bisson Frères, a Robuchon, or an anonymous, the image acts as a self-sufficient signal. Accordingly, such pictures tend to omit, and Atget's go quite far in omitting, any trace of the inhabitants of the architectural milieu. For the urban space is a de rigueur setting for buildings, exclusively created through the way they're disposed, and is in no sense a backdrop for people.

In many of Atget's pictures, however, one doesn't know the priority of his indications: where to look first, what to regard most. The urban environment isn't defined by distinctions between emphatic and recessive shapes, and as that openness is perceived it alters, even destabilizes, the terms of the viewing experience. While it's obviously normal in other practitioners' work, for instance, the deletion of human traffic in Atget's scenes is spectacular and extremely unreasonable. I would go further: it causes dismay.

Elsewhere, in the architectural genres, there are only empty adjacent spaces; in Atget's tableaux there is a shocking desolation. With the others, one has clean perspectives that lead to the subject; with him, phenomenally deserted streets. Almost everyone who has written on Atget has been struck by this recurring loneliness—the impression

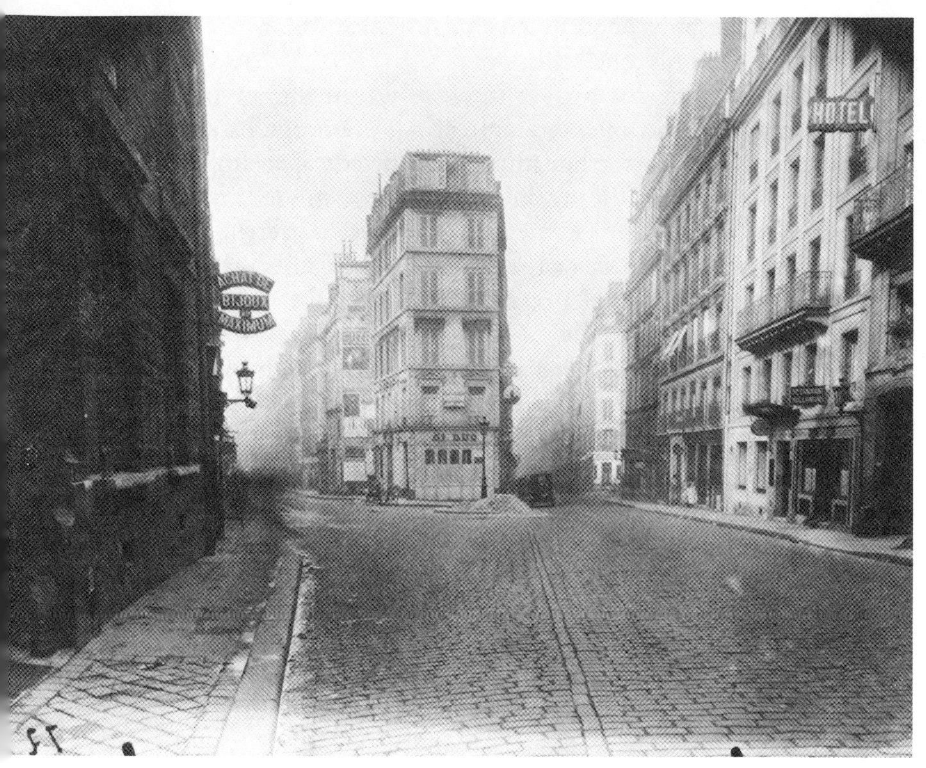

Figure 49. Eugène Atget, *Rue Pigalle, á 6 h. du matin en avril,* 1925 (Museum of Modern Art).

that he was the only one in a city of several million, the only one still to perceive, the only one still *there.*

Without denying them their merit as document, even their possible expressiveness as documents, architectural photographs are never warmhearted enough to transmit any such radical feeling of absence and loss. They do not imply an observant eye guided by any feeling for a subject other than a professional interest in getting down a clarified or picturesque aspect of the thing. Even further, the notion of there being a particular person's eye taking in the vista is foreign to them.

With Atget, on the other hand, the vantage is always one with which a pedestrian could identify. (In orthodox architectural photography, the viewpoint tends to be loftily staged, much more bountiful, and therefore neutral and detached.) Light, in the tradition from which he was moving away, is used to bring out the designed physiognomy of surface or the modelings of volume, never, as he would suggest, to show how the climate capriciously affects a setting. He accepted very well that it had rained and the streetswere still glisteningly wet. He often indicates by his captions the time of day or season of the year. An Atget façade takes tone in the way a shadow comes over someone's face or as an expression is said to darken. Though deliberately composed, the photographic frame is hospitable to unforeseen or random circumstances. Only one of the articles in A. Simon's outdoor shop display, a corset, was ruffled in the breeze. Given all such normalcy—chance moments of perception, states of affairs construed from endless, particular variables—it's outrageous that there should be this one crazy constant—of the city and the suburbs abandoned.

The prodigious care that often had to be taken to ensure this weird, reductive desertedness, as if a neutron bomb had been dropped on Paris, originated in the decorum of architectural photography. To have violated that decorum would have put future sales and the possibility of further clients at some risk in a highly specialized and competitive profession. Even for a mysterious projected album of 1910, *Intérieurs Parisiens; Début du XX Siècle; Artistique, Pittoresque et Bourgeois,* Atget made sure that various bedrooms and salons were devoid of people, again for routine saleability. Whether it was because they were intended only to describe typical living accommodations for future research, portraits of individuals through their effects, or to provide information for illustrators who would people the rooms themselves, the sadness of these pictures is the same. What stays in the mind are

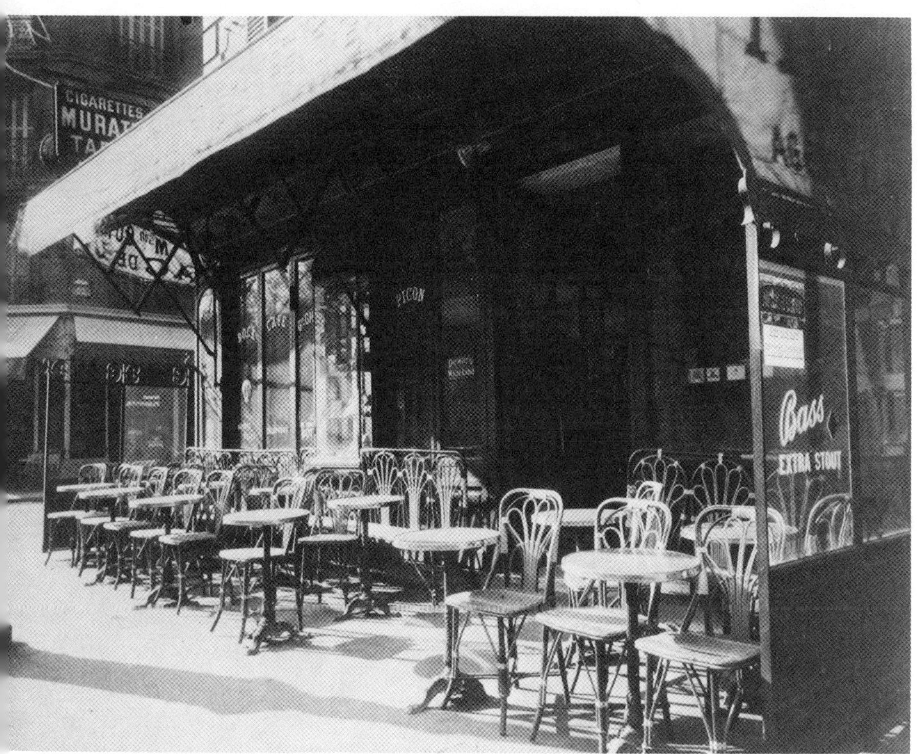

Figure 50. Eugène Atget, *Café, avenue de la Grande Armée,* 1924–25 (Museum of Modern Art).

details such as the lumpiness of the beds, the heaviness of certain draperies, some frayed chairs, a wan light, articles that have taken the imprint of absent bodies. To me, now, these places have the look of disagreeable old hotel rooms that are too personal in their fittings. They may have been intended by Atget to exemplify private life-styles as a function of social class, as has been recently argued by Margaret Nesbit,[2] but no one has said he had in *mind* the pathos of their effect. Man Ray reported that Atget, at the end of his life, allowed his work to be used by the magazine *La Révolution Surréaliste,* provided he was not given credit. Between his conscious purposes and the surrealist sense of wonder, there could be no rapport. But it was the surrealist view that first brought Atget to world attention. His pictures could be said to have been gotten wrong for the right reasons. Later generations, indeed, were to be specially moved by this one element in Atget's output that was *not* officially meant to be indicative.

But was it off the mark to make such a poetic judgment of so evidently an artisan body of work? Born in 1857, Atget intellectually matured a hundred years ago. When he came to visual terms with the twentieth-century, it was through a mode more habitual to the nineteenth-century. His whole career is marked by an heuristic dislocation, not from one country to another, as often happened in the history of photography, but from one time zone to another. Neither the sociology of his business nor his political commitment—he was a radical-syndicalist—would have led him to any enthusiasm for the industrial capitalist dynamic that was transforming the urban street. On those very few occasions when they appear in his work, automobiles look like pitiful emigrés from the zoo. Paris itself, or its outlying districts, was native ground; modernity wasn't. When he documented the twentieth-century world, it could never have been in the euphoric guise of the modernist. The disturbing spirit of the archeologist came more naturally to him (Fig. 51).

When examining the symbols of past power, the gaze of the archaeologist is nonjudgmental. It would have been a gaze familiar enough when trained on the antiquities, say, of Indochina. How reassuring to contemplate the one-time grandeur of exotic civilizations that were now part of the French empire. But it was quite another, more problematic view when the archaeological stance was brought to bear on the neighborhood.

For Atget's photographs could have told people who went to the libraries and saw his efforts in force that the subjects viewed were nonoperational and that their life was definitely over. The ambience of

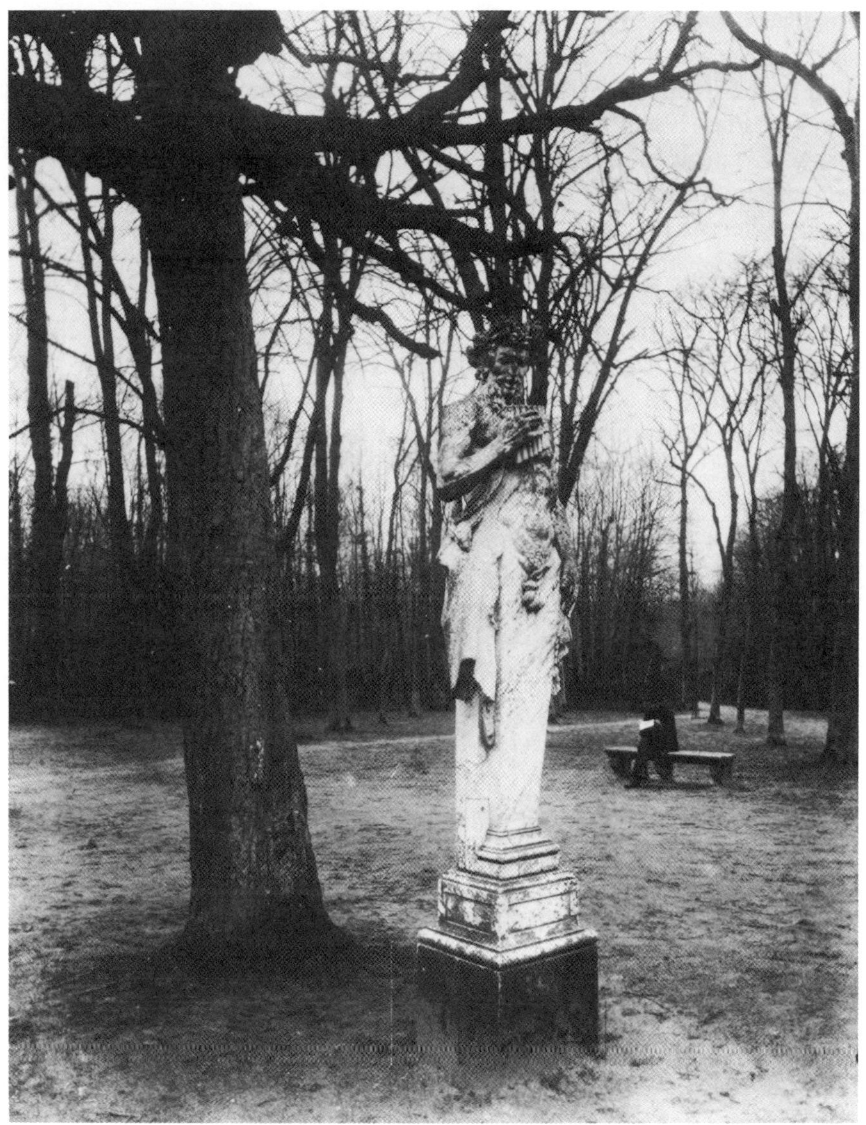

Figure 51. Eugène Atget, *Versailles, parc,* 1906 (Museum of Modern Art).

Paris was composed only of intriguing and complex relics, in varying states of preservation. While this attitude might do to describe St. Sernin or St. Eustache, Atget maddeningly continued it as he photographed Place Pigalle and Rue Mouffetard! He would accession thousands of typical metropolitan appearances, each demonstrating his humane interest in their signs of intelligent purpose, but he denied or was indifferent to something fundamental about them—the worldly and *familiar* sense of them in people's minds. Emerging late from an outdated tradition, with his small artisan's mentality, into a complex media and industrial environment, Atget photographed a ghost city in a time warp. What he saw was certainly there to be seen, but without correspondance to anyone's rational—that is everyday—intercourse with it. The frothing present conceived as a vision of the distant, immobile past: this could only be an hallucination, a long-term dream state. And the Surrealists knew it.

Surely one finds an instinctive energy in these Atget images whose tide sweeps them past a bookish niche, but it won't suffice to explain the phenomenon of his work through the professional constraints he accepted and the requirements of the customers he served. After all, none of his fellow workers in related shops produced such an unrelenting eeriness or struck such a note of contemporary disquiet. He spoke of his views as a collector refers to his acquisitions. For roughly thirty-five years, with an enormous persistence, this man possessed the city, as if it were his territory exclusively. Very few of its inhabitants are ever shown to compete with or share his communion with it. But this notion of a romantic, egocentric temperament doesn't jibe with the psychic distancing of Atget's scenarios, however intimately framed some of them can be. Far from being proprietary, they continually betray estrangement and disorientation, as if to photograph, over and over, using the same tripod method, were a means of affirming the photographer's self-displacement. In such a view, he is attached to the material presence because there is no other object, or objects, no other point of emotional contact. Every frame is a memory rehearsal of a dream—and the city's desolation merely reflects the desolation within, which has to be repeatedly assauged and confirmed by the "objective" and "documentary" record of what is seen. Instead of being a hindrance to his real goals, the conventions of the architectural genre would then act as the ideal cover for an ongoing obsession. But a longer view of the case of Atget doesn't exactly sustain this thesis; rather, it leads it in other directions.

Dealing with figural subjects head on, in characteristic but very isolated sets, Atget achieved muted results. His early series on the small tradespeople of Paris, the *Petits Métiers,* dates from 1899 to 1900. Though these people are made of flesh and blood and are mobile, they have a pronounced woodenness, as if they were thought of only as exhibits or specimens of their class. A concern for them as persons has no relevance to his procedure at all. In fact, there is no more human transaction registered in these pictures than is necessary in order to typecast them as itinerant hawkers, workers, or street concessionaires, festooned with their wares, accoutrements, or tools of their labor. There had been a long literary and graphic tradition that celebrated the contributions of these humble people to the city's style and services, but in Atget's latter-day view they are perceived as already vanishing objects of curiosity. (The same goes for a valedictory series he did on horse-drawn vehicles in 1910.)

Rather than showing them pausing on their rounds, the tradespeople have been inserted stiffly into an artificial space. Partly this is the result of a background so out of focus it seems almost steamed into tone, but it's also the outcome of a deliberately static use of the containing frame. These pavers, window washers, rag pickers, or basket sellers do miscellaneous, low-status jobs, employed by small shops, the city, or often enough themselves, as was Atget himself. Though they came from a different class, they, too, were often in a one-person business, peddling old-fashioned things, a fact that did not seem to evoke any fellow feeling in him.

If, in the body of the urban work he was to do later, Atget depicted the setting without the actors, here, ironically, he gives us actors without any action or mis-en-scène. The style of the Petits Métiers is démodé, in a manner that would have been recognized by John Thomson, author of *Street Life in London* (1877). In a different historical moment, Atget's approach equates human beings with antiquarian objects. Curiously, the feeling that those around us lack our human identity is the inverse of the dream I cited earlier, of being abandoned in the communal place.

At a time when a quick-witted genre of big-city street photography was just gaining international momentum, this related group of Atget pictures seems remarkably out of phase. One thinks of Heinrich Zille in Berlin, Arnold Genthe in San Francisco's Chinatown, Jacob Riis and Robert Bracklow in New York, or Count Guiseppe Primoli in Paris and Rome, to name only some of the more interesting figures in the early street mode. Their observance of the urban mix as it looked in everyday flux (the *instantané,* as the French would call it), included

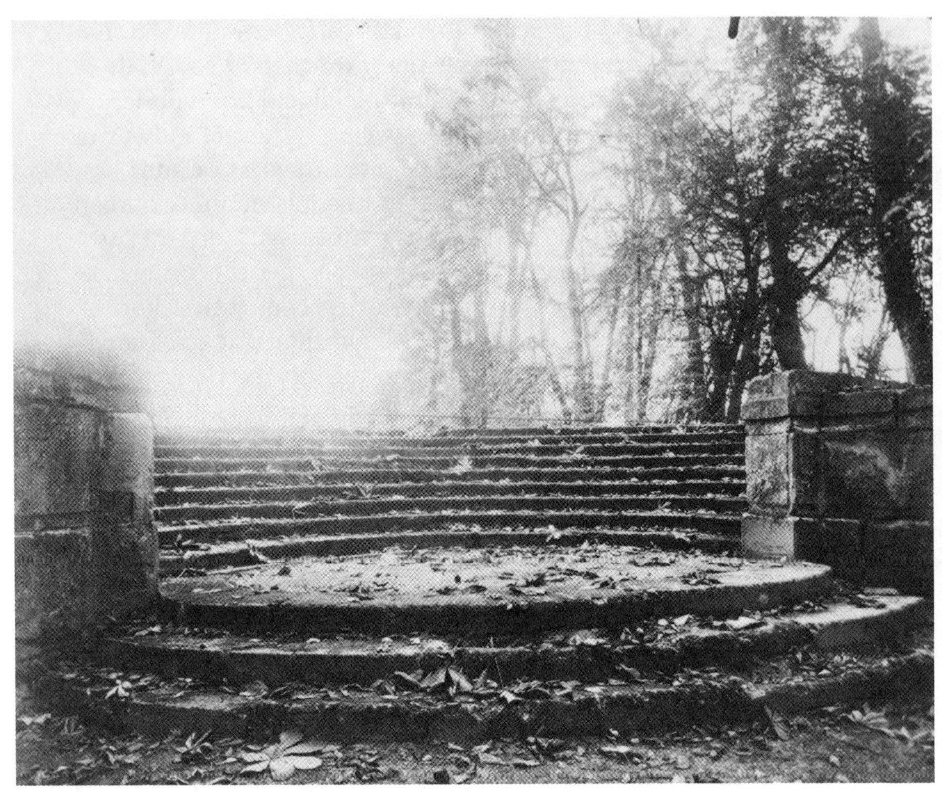

Figure 52. Eugène Atget, *Saint-Cloud,* 1906 (Museum of Modern Art).

casts of all sorts of marginal characters, the proletarian underclass, and ethnic cultures within the city. Though not, on the whole, to be well known or published for several years, this photography is symptomatic of a pre–mass media jumpiness in the history of the camera. Before he found himself, Atget had strangely enough been in the ranks of these amateur forerunners of photojournalism, only to ripen into the impressive quietude of his life work.

In some respects, though he was based in the metropolis, Atget's view of it—and his short inquiry into its denizens—has a rustication that can be associated with a pastoral mode. The country learns of contemporary styles and modern conveniences later than the city and sympathizes with them less. But I was thinking first of the keenness of Atget's response to atmospheric tone, the heft of actual weather, which one notices more with the open skies of the countryside than under the oblique shadows of the metropolis. Not only does one feel more exposed to the climate in Atget's Paris than in the work of other photographers, he was significantly more involved with foliage and trees than they were. Even his urban tradespeople have a rural aspect, and they are sometimes treelike, certainly rooted in their bearing. With great hindsight, though, we know that they were also auditioning for the role of his twenties store-window mannikins and dummies, figures that seem more imbued with organic life than these turn-of-the-century human subjects. A viewer is led to reflect on this photographer's interest in simulacra, statuary, and human effigy. In some deep and perhaps inadvertent continuum, the artifices of mercantile fashion display, along the bargain avenue des Gobelins, were connected through the baroque deities and frozen nymphs of the parks to the imperceptible metamorphoses of biological life. What they all share is an implication distilled in the overview of Atget's world: that there were things whose growth and change, whose capacity to take new form, either through their own processes or in response to the elements, are not discernible to the eye in any single moment of awareness.

One common misperception about Atget's work is that since it is largely depopulated it must be lifeless. On the contrary, he was exquisitely attentive to the vitality of the world, but did not think that it was available on short or casual notice. With him, movement was never so affecting as when it was only a whisper of some imminence. The potentials of it were involved in the long entwined tendrils of a certain cadence, the product of deep complicity between French culture and nature, as cultivated by French minds. Even in their metal guise, floral balustrades could obviously be looked at from a botanical vantage, as variations on a natural theme. It is not surprising to learn that the Musée des Arts Décoratifs had a group of Atget plant studies available for reference by decorators.[3] If there are echoes of similar rhythms throughout these pictures it may be that the forms of vegetal change and decorative style are sensed as long-term applications of each other. Atget's taxonomic impulses figure into this equation, too, for the evident, dense, leveling repetitiousness of motifs is a technique allowing for comparison of different strains and individuals within the same genus. The unique instance is without particular note until its place is marked, relative to others, by the slow vicissitudes of their heritage and use.

At the end of his life, after having abstained virtually for thirty years from pictorial consideration of the human face, Atget came back to it again, in the smile of prostitutes at La Vilette and Versailles (1921). Trivial in number, these few pictures, commissioned by an amateur of erotica, are mordant in effect. For one thing, they bring the previous regard for the commercial attributes of the sitters—these prostitutes were vendors, after all—together with the concrete description of architectural detail, namely the façades of their brothels. The women are shown stationed where they worked, and their come-on expressions were not only meant for the photographer but were performed as a gesture of that work. Engulfed in the silence of Atget's city, the figure is surrounded also by a plethora of surfaces so morbidly eroded and moldy, stained and fermented with age that structure seems close to its inevitable return to the earth. Atget could be counted on to treat the *fille publique,* a provocative subject, in his documentary manner. Prostitution may have been celebrated as the oldest profession in the world, but it remained for him a petit métier, which is precisely what is surprising about this group of pictures.

If I were to speak strictly about the impression they make rather than from knowledge of their use, I would say that Atget's photographs depict a fallen world. The images tell of neglect or disrepair and the mortality of human enterprise that fails, is in the act of dying, or has passed away. But that response is uneasy. Certainly he gives us some explicit portrayals of physical decline, where the subject alone confirms a message about the injurious passage of time. The seventeenth-century figures at the parc de Sceaux are being read the riot act by nature, which chips and fissures and has overgrown them in a tantrum of decay. Industrial wastelands are part of his horizon, too, as at La Bièvre, Gentilly, in 1901, where a little, stagnant stream is fouled by adjoining tanneries. Both these scenes, photographed twenty-five years apart, only emphasize by their motifs the same retrospective aura in which newspaper kiosks are seen or cafés, for instance, and apple trees blossoming in the spring, wretched gypsies in the zone around Paris, village squares, garages, and carved wooden doors . . . as if all these slowly deteriorating things had a comparable significance in the remembering mind, or even that they weighed no differently on any social scale. They are invested with the same indiscriminate seriousness and everywhere studied with an egalitarian melancholy.

Had this been a nostalgic mood, wilfully imposed through a long career, we couldn't account for the frequent unnerving quality of Atget's images. It fell to the photographic avant-gardists of his time, the Pictorialists, like DeMachy or Kühn, to reiterate dreamy states of definition, where the environment is tenderized through gauzy printing. None of their subjects, nor even anything solid, has any existence apart from the worked-up "substance" of the photographic treatment. The Pictorialists were involved with an idealism of perception, transmitted through the monotonous refinement of their effects. Stemming from the same fin-de-siècle conditioning, Atget took in the widest range of idiosyncratic details, transparently, to the end. Given the acuity of his description, even when depicting mists, his view was always rooted in an eternal moist earthiness. Pictorialism implied that states of being and personal affect were indissolubly mixed in a kind of facile, cozy symbolism of reverie, quickly consumed. In Atget's work, contrarily, there's a far less definable blend of appetite and reticence, which yields up its subjects through a languorous inventory of features, held fondly in view for the purpose, it seems, of bidding them good-bye. He takes pains to show that the stamina of matter has its limits, determined on unknown schedules, case by case.

Of course, I have been confusing an aesthetic, or even a moral, with a technical viewing of these pictures. But at this point, we are not sure Atget himself didn't confuse or, better, transpose them, and that, in fact, their particular meaning for us is bound up with this transposition. Certainly his body of work *represents* itself as programmatically detached from its motifs, a warranty of the kind of use it had, while also operating as a stable or unifying factor in an otherwise bewildering catalogue of "documents." Since the historical or archaeological discourse was the only admissible one, it came to the fore. As I've tried to show, however, Atget does not evince detachment so much from the subject as from the ways viewers naturalize it, on the basis of their worldliness. The archaeological mode of address, or an anthropological one when the theme is people, is imposed throughout all the frames, whether the subject is suited to it or not, or whether it even makes sense. Precisely here, the imagery ceases to be a function of its system, since Atget's pictures continue to do their work by raising issues outside their instrumental context, that is, issues of unworldliness and nonsense.

The more efficient a photographic convention in transmitting content on its own track, the more redundant are its data, even though redundancy may be illogical when compared with the vagaries of actual experience, memory, or common sense knowledge of its subject. Atget's photographs subversively invite that comparison without finally declaring themselves to be either on the side of conventional parlance or personal engagement. Their human perspective solicits involvement with the scene; their pictorial rhetoric forbids it. This conflict is fundamental to Atget's vision. It is fixed permanently in the record of what comes to be a transfigured world, a "beyond" pursued by the photographer with an inflexibility that has real grandeur.

If they have consistency in their origins, Atget's photographs are by no means predictable in their effects. The endless milieux he pictured are inflected differently by the principle of human absence because they invoke different ideas of community. An empty plowed field has an indisputable right to be that way. The near vacancy of rue Pigalle is explainable by the caption ". . . at six o'clock in the morning (Fig 49)." These long shots have the serenity of lone contemplation, recorded before work shifts for others. The moment of exposure need not have been one of singular preference, but only of circumstance. As for his visits to the forests or other less-frequented places, the probability of solitude is heightened by obvious remoteness from the workaday ambience of the city. Being by oneself is advantageous for undistracted looking; everything has the aspect of existing only for the one who looks. Yet, in Atget's hands, the pleasure this affords is tinged with sorrow, for the site is unlikely to receive any more regard, or to have any other meaning than the one that is rescued so attentively by Atget's frame. A camera drinks in appearances that are as unsung and as much by themselves as the man who has composed them.

Though only the environs of the city, these sites already have the look of wilderness. When various statues crop up in such surroundings, a viewer comes to closer grips with Atget's pathos. The figures at parc de Sceaux, elements of a defunct decorative scheme, still preserve the intentionality of a dialogue with aristocratic passersby or among themselves. Seen in an oblique or half light, immobile against a sudden fluff caused by a wind on the bushes, they are survivors of a formalized community impossible to recover. All that seems to remain, in the posterity represented by the photograph, is an interchange between organic and brute matter, altering themselves in a drawn-out process. While such images may be placed in the longstanding cult of ruins, which featured the contemplation of human vanity, they switch to a different emphasis. For growth itself, appreciated in its own right, is the main subject. Once again, the sense of landscape here is like that of an empty room, a meticulously described decor serving future narrative ends. And yet, how meager is this likely text compared with the plenitude of Atget's vigil. As he shows, culture subsides or has lapsed into nature, to partake of a spectacle that clearly thrives where people and their memories have moved on. The statues punctuate but also serve to amplify the vehemence of the energy that surrounds them. Like the prostitutes, Daphne is only doing her job, posted where she has to be. Still, the indifferent but musical disorder of the foliage only enhances the stony charades and petrified sex that were more decorous in their own historical time.

As it shifts from natural to fabricated densities, always keeping aloof from human beings, Atget's regard begins to weigh heavily in the viewing act. For the lonely glance must now seem far more of an artifice and self-reflexive in the crowded city than in the country. Paris emerges as an anthology of still lifes, of still points. The camera pastures among these arrested settings, generating an unheard-of willfulness and inwardness of vision, based on metaphors of objectivity. Of course, my literal reading makes these metaphors strange. That is, I take from these pictures what is repeatedly shown in them, not what is represented. Time and again, Atget indicates signs or articles of communal life—advertisements, magazines, carafes, windows, clothes, price tags, suitcases, furniture, kitchenware, bistros, benches, and so on—insisting that they are understandable in terms of their history, whereas they actively promote a deep anxiety about their future. Often, to be sure, the viewpoint is neutral: the wavy wooden frames of the pebbled-glass windows at 14 rue Mazet being no more than a nice picture of façade arrangements. Such things are designed to be looked at; others, however, need to be bought to realize their purpose. They have meaning as liquid supply to be replenished. If Paris were to be understood as a network of economic transactions, as a market of

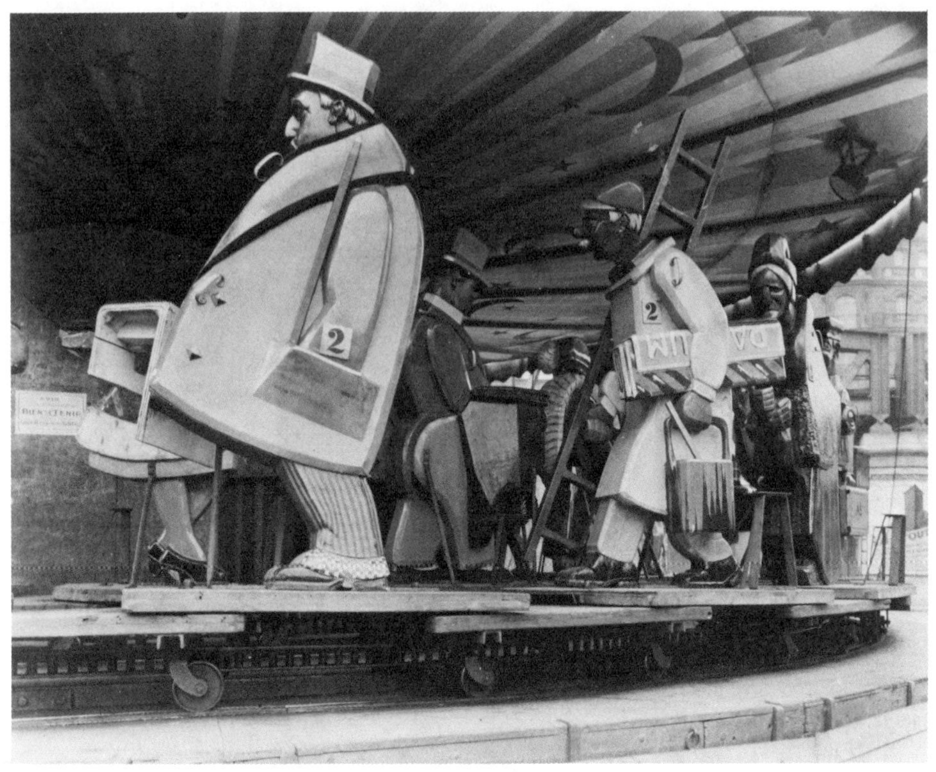

Figure 53. Eugène Atget, *Fête de Vaugirard,* 1926 (Museum of Modern Art).

produce, services, and diversions activated through the flow of cash, one could only conclude from Atget that it had dried up. Given his proclivities, he described a scene in which there is a universal but uncalled-for readiness and in which displays are forlorn of audience. Unintentionally, he portrayed salesmanship in a limbo, all prospects of business seemingly vanished.

No one is going to crack the hard-boiled eggs on the wine merchant's bar nor try on one of the crumpled top hats at a boutique, Marché aux Halles. The odd thing is that tableaux devoid of people were meant to clarify a certain spatial and tactile order, yet they wind up introducing a kind of psychic disorder. Everywhere it is suggested that productivity can manifest itself limitlessly, but to no avail. Endless hours of labor, transport, planning, and craft—but, above all, the ordinary hopefulness behind them—amount only to avenues of surfeit or waste. That thought alone is touching enough. But it is really heartbreaking when Atget visits the kiddy parks around town, the saucy carousels at Vaugirard, la Vilette, and the Fête du Trône. No children there, of course, no laughter, just merry-go-rounds that circle in a void.

But it would be seriously mistaken to imply that these pictures gain their allure only through the undertow of their negations. They are more mysterious than that. To our eyes, they are informative because they end by being more improbable than they started out to be. Just the same, this would be to value these works on the basis of what has been excluded by them. To enter again into the quiet territory of Atget's world is to realize how precious are its appearances as signs, outcomes, or creations of a remarkable culture, vernacular as well as dynastic. It's that spectacle, of course, rather than any of its creatures to which the photographer was paying his modest tribute.

In the course of his enterprise, he depicted the traces of culture but sought to invest them with an unauthorized life that was nominally banished from his program. Its rendering of vivacious substance distinguishes Atget's work from idealism, while his fancifulness set him apart from the closures of materialism. I would rather say that the power of these photographs lies in their *animism,* the implicitness of change in his motifs, and the creaturely potentials of the forms which he treated. Old French culture obligingly supplied him with the icons for this great transforming sweep, in illimitable echoes of human gesture and behavior. Here was a swarm of extra presences, to compensate for the one prevailing absence of human beings in society. Since his mission was a historical one, he was concerned with the aspirations that had been bred into objects, often made more expressive by the passage of time. It was a happy fate that his sensitivity to nature became the vehicle for transmitting the effects of physical change and that this, in turn, dramatized a historical process.

Atget's pictures tend to superimpose the memory of the pastoral upon the urban scene. Though still familiar in its contours, Paris seems to be holding its breath as a new disorienting mood settles upon it. It appears now, as I look, that the viewing time of the present is suspended and reversed into the past—the past, not of 1926 compared to my 1986—but of another kind of era, which recedes into the imagination. The typical ploy of architectural photography had been to suggest that the moment of perception was disembodied—no one's or everyone's, at an undetermined point in time. Atget, on the other hand, particularizes the moment and subverts it, as if he were actually looking at appearances from a *temporal* distance.

Of all the works he surveyed, it should be remarkable that he left out those of the nineteenth-century. I suspect they were omitted because they belonged to his mental present, the one he had grown into and that stayed with him as an image of the contemporary. He denied the monuments of that period, but not its photographic style. How else am I to regard the color of these photographs—those sepia lavenders—than as a palette that had once been in favor sixty years before his last work? Full-blooded color proposes transparent immediacy of contact with the subject; black and white, a more obvious abstraction, neither denies nor encourages that immediacy. Atget's demi-chroma, for its part, acts like a filter and would have been associated with an earlier vision, of the world bodied forth at some remove from the current moment. Just as graphic was his acceptance of top vignetting, a mechancial intervention of a long-lens barrel. The effect this gave, of looking through a tunnel, must have been congenial since it was repeated. Such deliberate techniques of an author-editor, as he called himself, accentuate a feeling of displacement in time at odds with solid locations in space. So the consciousness that most often informs the work of Atget is unbelievable. It would delude us to think that an eye can look *back* on its own era, as things occur. If nothing evident occurs in these pictures, that itself is a requirement of "pastness," as well as an assurance of solitude.

It is the long-celebrated work of this formidable conservative that the Museum of Modern Art has now (1981–85) elevated to the head of its small canon of exemplary modern photographers. The role is no doubt very grand, but I wonder if Atget is the right actor for the part the museum has cut out for him. John Szarkowski, MOMA's director of Photography, says that "Atget's pictures are informed . . . by the *clarté* that is the highest virtue of the classic French tradition. This quality was achieved . . . by discovering precisely what one meant to say, and saying neither more nor less."[4] He writes further that he knows "of no other photographer who responded with Atget's boldness and imaginative intelligence to the new perception of range and flexibility that first came to photography around the turn of the century."[5] Enthusing in shorthand over this simultaneously "classic" and progressive artist, Szarkowski's essays use words such as *talent, grace, simplicity,* and *experience* to help install Atget on his throne. Behind these schematic appreciations there is certainly a genuine response to the imagery, but what do they actually tell of the response?

Millions, after all, have been spent, a series of four gorgeous books has been published (more than the museum has devoted to any artist of our time), scholarship has been labored at, and complex shows have been mounted. What justification could any of this enormous effort have had unless its subject moved the doers at MOMA, and moved them a great deal? Why should anyone try to figure out the old man's treacherous filing system, as historian Maria Morris Hambourg has, if not to contribute a better understanding of his gift to our imaginative life? Any conviction about that first had to be a critical one, for research is not motivated until it is spurred, in the long or the short term, by criticism—that is, by values activated in texts. And criticism will not be activated (it will only assert rather than argue) unless it faces the question of how the work, and knowledge gained about it, give rise to the feeling instilled in the experience of the critic. Reciprocally, the more historical awareness is aroused by critical interest, the more, I would say, criticism itself is bound to be altered.

Approaching Atget historically, the museum had a critical problem on its hands. The most staggering detective work by Hambourg has revealed marvels about city lore and a rich lode of data about Atget's commercial practices, but hardly a smidgen of an artistic credo, no more than one phrase that would reveal what we call an artistic consciousness. On the contrary, Atget avowed only that he would *serve* artists. In order to reverse that lowly self-estimate, the museum had to construct an artistic identity for him, no matter how ill it fitted with the biographical and social facts uncovered and brought out to support his institutional status. Szarkowski struggles with that identity more than once. He believes, for instance, that "the idea of artistic service to an artistically extraneous cause does have much to recommend it."[6] (Luckily for us, for if it didn't there wouldn't be a history of art.) But Atget's work gives him trouble because it would have been "more reasonable" were there two photographers who had produced it, a talented one ("with the sure intuitions of a great lyric poet"), and a pedestrian partner whose output is filled with more or less representative images "of that time and place."[7]

"For us, perhaps 20 percent of Atget's work attains the formal surprise or original grace by which we identify a successful work of modern art."[8] The operative word here is *we*—we, that is, at the Museum of Modern Art. With a display of apparently severe connoisseurship, this institution finds that 20 percent of Atget's pictures (around 2,000) live up to its highest artistic standards. The standards themselves are never explained and are, in any event, external to anyone's experience of a work of art, insofar as they wouldn't have any usefulness as tags unless their weight could be rhetorically *imposed* by the institution. So, the talented Atget is made out to be an artist intent on realizing an abstract quality called "formal surprise."

More peculiar still, MOMA inadvertently demeans the work it sets out to eulogize by denying significant artistic content to any Atget photograph that is held to be deficient in a visual quality of "grace." On the contrary, if it were endowed with all the grace in the world, but bereft of Atget's special time-haunted sense of the world, we would not recognize or care that the image is his. It would truly be soft in content, regardless of how well masses are arranged within the frame. Misconceptions about the role of form, favored over perceptions about the much more determining element of time in photographic discourse, are typical of modernist apologias of the medium. Since Atget so clearly transgressed the humble utilitarian functions of his job, he must be an artist, despite himself. The model for ascribing value to art at MOMA is still derived from an idealist thesis about the autonomy of abstract painting and sculpture, roughly inspired by Clement Greenberg in the 1960s. Happily, Atget cannot be squeezed into that bigoted frame of reference.

If, in fact, formal analysis appears very perfunctorily in MOMA's treatment of Atget, it's because the word *description* rightfully usurps it in the interpretative task. In 1964, Berenice Abbott wrote, "For Atget, the subject was the important thing. The structure . . . was dictated by the subject. The subject creates its own design and the 'style' of the photographer . . . is principally faithfulness to it."[9] Szarkowski knows that "in Atget the idea itself seems provisional and open . . . in the process of taking form from the facts of the image before us,"[10] but he tends to compromise that notion by hankering after the meaning of individual images, which express not the final order of stasis but "a vital order of equilibrium."[11] This is indeed a tension that skewers any attempt to place Atget in the roll call of previous modernist heroes. For if Atget's admired fluidity of particulars displaces the "fixed Platonic verity" of a Stieglitz, it is that verity that epitomizes the historical moment of modernism in photography, whereas Atget's example, while expressively of an earlier moment, speaks more provocatively to the consciousness of today.

Long in the making, MOMA's canonization of Atget has an air of redress about it, giving honor to a figure who lacked any sort of power base and support system while he lived. Just the same, the validating strategy calls upon testimonial by Berenice Abbott, Walker Evans, Edward Weston (where it is diluted), and Ansel Adams (where it is completely irrelevant). These last two artists were, however, particularly central to the museum's mid-century view of progressive American photography, a fact that has more importance than the unrelatedness of their aesthetic to Atget's. His example was refracted most corrosively, charged with the deepest intimation of urban loneliness, the surrogate animism of objects, and the politics of class contrast, is in the art of Bill Brandt. (If one wanted to trace Atget's influence on *American* photography one might do well to examine Brandt's effect on Robert Frank—especially the sense of alienation—and then of Frank's viral transmission of it to most everyone in recent times.) I wondered why Brandt was barely mentioned in MOMA's Atget books. And I questioned why those photographers who drew variously but nourishingly from Atget into French tradition—the early Henri Cartier-
Bresson, Brassaï in the whorehouses, and Robert Doisneau, with his amorous statues and working-class quarters were not even touched on. Finally could there be any more bewitching chateau or woods of the sort that Atget saw than in Jean Cocteau's *Beauty and the Beast*?

These points are interesting not so much in themselves as in the way they suggest positions that could be followed in a debate about the impact of Atget in the present. For reasons internal to its own history, MOMA presents the case for a scrupulously honest, forward-looking, sweetly affirmative artist, endowed with a poetic sensibility. This promotion strikes me as wildly unengaged and worse, as undialectic. It can do no justice to the subversiveness of Atget's practice within his tradition, nor does it see that there is a fundamental denial in the oeuvre of one who avidly embraces the widest range of social and historical culture but generally does not accord the human beings who inherit and continue culture the right to be depicted within it. If the interplay between absence and presence, nature and culture, and past and present is basic to Atget's vision, there is something darker and more critical to be learned from it, that shades into the pleasure to be taken from its grace.

To some extent, understanding this is a historical problem issuing from the erupted rationale of his procedures, but it is more crucially a psychological challenge, stemming from our experience of the American inner cities today. Here, people do not have to be cleared away in order for documentation to take place; they have already gone, or their numbers are drastically thinned and their chances have withered. When such Gothams are rebuilt, they only rise up in a familiar corporate sterility that is inhumane and daunting. No wonder our photographers retreat from this defeated public culture, though only to make vacuous celebration of the landscape or minimalist records of outlying developments.

How dispiriting this is when put next to Atget's teaching that while time does not count for nature, it matters very dearly for us. "Through memory," wrote Joseph Joubert, "we travel against time, through forgetfulness we follow its course."[12] Atget's remembrance will not allow for a sanitized view of history, for it patiently witnesses not only the ravages of time, but compares the inequities of power that continue into the present. In the guise of selfless documentarian, he exhibits a resistant temper.[13]

I want to acknowledge the invaluable study of Margaret Nesbit, mentioned previously, which has refreshed the entire problem of Atget. She views his work as the product of a dissident political consciousness, inseminated within practical constraints and traditional idiom, from which there arose innumerable ambiguities. For instance, the difficulty of figuring out Atget's subject categories is compounded, not only because he kept on adding to them, but because he frequently and intentionally multiplied the functional possibilities of individual frames. Though it was accepted by his clientele, this made the commercial forms strange, debouching in "many different streams, which have a tendency to run off separately."[14]

Meanwhile, this nineteenth-century craftsman desperately wanted to span the normal outlet of his work for files into book production with halftone plates, though he never reached this wider audience. Instead, visitors to libraries would become acquainted through his pictures with a concept of style "as a function of class" that needed to be preserved "before novelty intervenes and deflects the class differences into unfamiliar fields."[15] Nesbit thinks that this is politicized looking, depending on a contrast between the partial information contained in each frame and an appeal to the viewer's general knowledge. One had "to know to compare the old costume shop of the Rue Cordier with the unseen splendor of the Bon Marché."[16] Some subtle ideas proceed from this notion, as, for instance, a note about recurrent coverage of motifs: "The picture is repeated each time but it not allowed to repeat itself. . . ."[17] Or this thought: "Space in the decor signifies absence with presence kept deliberately outside as both suspect and ghost."[18] Though the emptiness of Atget's pictures, the "infernal emptiness" she calls it, was planned as a service feature, it may be that Atget saw how an expressive principle was invoked by "taking human relations out just at the point where one expects to find them."[19] The moeurs photographs, as a result, are turned into what must be *conscious* paradoxes. (It's more intriguing not to be decided about this.) I don't know if the bourgeois viewer was therefore put "into an alien position" or that Atget's paradox actually declared that he was no longer "the lackey of antiquarians." Certainly it looks that way to us now, schooled as we are by the surrealists to value the effect of delirium in Atget's vision. But the surrealists did not care for civic community, and so they missed his sadness. We are probably closer now to one of Margaret Nesbit's summarizing comments: "Once one sees photography as a social form of production, it is difficult to see a photograph signifying all at once, even an Atget photograph. . . . One can still see its profundity but it resides in its inflected, fragmented, rebellious, melancholy and moral sense of history."[20]

Afterimage, *April 1986.*

1. These include James Borcoman, *Eugene Atget* (Ottawa: National Gallery of Art, 1984); Margaret Nesbit, "Atget's Seven Albums," Ph.D. dissertation, Yale University, 1983; and John Szarkowski and Maria Hambourg, *The Work of Atget,* 4 vols. (New York: Museum of Modern Art, 1981–85).
2. Nesbit, p. 98.
3. *Ibid.,* p. 19.
4. Szarkowski and Hambourg, vol. 1, *Old France,* p. 17.
5. Szarkowski and Hambourg, vol. 4, *Modern Times,* p. 28.
6. Szarkowski and Hambourg, vol. 1, p. 19.
7. *Ibid.,* p. 18.
8. *Ibid.*

9. Berenice Abbott, *The World of Atget* (New York: Horizon Press, 1964), p. 25.
10. Szarkowski and Hambourg, vol. 1, p. 25.
11. *Ibid.*
12. Paul Auster, ed., *The Notebooks of Joseph Joubert* (Berkeley: Northpoint Press, 1983), p. 14.
13. See end of text.
14. Nesbit, p. 191.
15. *Ibid.*, p. 109.
16. *Ibid.*, p. 185.
17. *Ibid.*, p. 31.
18. *Ibid.*, p. 12.
19. *Ibid.*, p. 122.
20. *Ibid.*, p. 191.

Illustrations

Figures

Plates